Immigration Outside the Law

Immigration Outside the Law

HIROSHI MOTOMURA

OXFORD
UNIVERSITY PRESS

OXFORD
UNIVERSITY PRESS

Oxford University Press is a department of the University of Oxford.
It furthers the University's objective of excellence in research, scholarship,
and education by publishing worldwide.

Oxford   New York

Auckland   Cape Town   Dar es Salaam   Hong Kong   Karachi
Kuala Lumpur   Madrid   Melbourne   Mexico City   Nairobi
New Delhi   Shanghai   Taipei   Toronto

With offices in

Argentina   Austria   Brazil   Chile   Czech Republic   France   Greece
Guatemala   Hungary   Italy   Japan   Poland   Portugal   Singapore
South Korea   Switzerland   Thailand   Turkey   Ukraine   Vietnam

Oxford is a registered trademark of Oxford University Press
in the UK and certain other countries.

Published in the United States of America by
Oxford University Press
198 Madison Avenue, New York, NY 10016

Library of Congress Cataloging-in-Publication Data
Motomura, Hiroshi, 1953- author.
Immigration outside the law / Hiroshi Motomura.
pages cm
Includes bibliographical references and index.
ISBN 978-0-19-976843-1 (hardback)
1. Illegal aliens—United States.   2. Emigration and immigration
law—United States.   I. Title.
KF4800.M68 2014
364.1'370973—dc23
2013048514

5 7 9 8 6 4
Printed in the United States of America
on acid-free paper

For Linda and Amy

Contents

Preface and Acknowledgments

A FEW YEARS back, I wrote a book, *Americans in Waiting: The Lost Story of Immigration and Citizenship in the United States*. It explored a question of great public significance: the treatment of immigrants in the United States in the past, present, and future. That book had two main goals.

One was to suggest a three-part framework for thinking about the treatment of immigrants throughout the history of US immigration and citizenship law. I explained how some laws and policies might reflect a view of immigration as contract or, in other words, the idea that newcomers enter into a sort of agreement when they come to America. They can be held to the conditions of admission, and both sides should have their expectations protected. Other laws and policies can be thought of as a matter of immigration as affiliation, or the idea that a newcomer develops ties or a stake in the United States that should be protected by law. The third view of immigration is immigration as a transition to citizenship or, in other words, the idea that immigrants should be treated with the expectation that they would become citizens—as Americans in waiting.

The second major goal of *Americans in Waiting* was to show how the idea of immigration as transition faded over much of the twentieth century. No longer are immigrants treated with the same expectation of future citizenship that prevailed in the nineteenth century, at least for white European immigrants. Immigration to the United States became more open in the twentieth century, but America's welcome of immigrants became more hesitant, and the idea of immigration as transition faded. *Americans in Waiting* explained why it is important to recover this fundamental aspect of the treatment of immigrants in US history.

At least on the surface, *Americans in Waiting* was about immigrants who are lawfully in the United States, and how they make the transition from immigrants to citizens. But I have often been asked: Why focus on lawful immigrants? After all, the hot topic today is noncitizens who are here *unlawfully*.

The treatment of immigrants who are admitted under US immigration laws generates much discussion, but it does not incite the heated, often angry debate about "illegals" or "undocumented immigrants." When it comes to unauthorized migration—what I call "immigration outside the law" in this book—even the words that are used are vehemently contested. By paying close attention to lawful immigrants, *Americans in Waiting* did not directly address some tough questions: Why do many immigrants come to the United States outside the system of lawful immigrant admissions? What should be done about immigration outside the law? These questions are at the heart of this book.

I wrote *Americans in Waiting* first, because it is impossible to assess immigration outside the law without understanding what makes immigration decisions fair and just. In turn, a coherent sense of fairness and justice in immigration requires carefully considering how *lawful* immigrants are treated. The reason is that the boundary between lawful immigrants and US citizens is a line of both intimacy and contrast between outsiders and insiders. Though lawful immigrants and citizens are often treated alike, the line between them still matters. How that line is drawn says much about what it means to be a nation of immigrants. By exploring these questions, *Americans in Waiting* developed a conceptual framework for understanding immigration law and policy as a whole.

I now tackle immigration outside the law. This book tries to help anyone with opinions on the topic to understand what separates their own views from those held by others, and how those differences might rest on different assumptions, preferences, or views of history, human nature, and the capacity of governments. That reciprocal understanding is essential for any constructive dialogue on one of the most contentious yet crucial issues of our time. I also hope to show how to find durable, politically viable responses to immigration outside the law. Toward that end, I offer specific recommendations. Some would reshape immigration law, but the most promising and important recommendations address immigration-related problems in more fundamental ways, by affecting other areas of economic and social policy that generate international migration and the responses to it.

I HAVE BEEN working for many years on the ideas that appear in these pages. My prior publications allowed me to develop, test, and refine some of my thinking, but this book goes far beyond a recombination of earlier work and reflects a new synthesis and some evolution of my earlier views.

Some of the core conceptual building blocks first appeared in *Immigration Outside the Law*, 108 Columbia Law Review 2037 (2008). I addressed some aspects of the tolerance of unauthorized migration in *Choosing Immigrants, Making Citizens*, 59 Stanford Law Review 857 (2007), the related topic of legalization in *What Is "Comprehensive Immigration Reform"?: Taking the Long View*, 62 Arkansas Law Review 225 (2010), and related thoughts on the rule of law in *The Rule of Law in Immigration Law*, 15 Tulsa Journal of Comparative and International Law 139 (2008). Some of my analysis of the legal rights of unauthorized migrants was published in *The Rights of Others: Legal Claims and Immigration Outside the Law*, 59 Duke Law Journal 1723 (2010). Part of my exploration of enforcement discretion and state and local law enforcement appeared in *The Discretion That Matters: Federal Immigration Enforcement, State and Local Arrests, and the Civil-Criminal Line*, 58 UCLA Law Review 1819 (2011), and later in more concise form in *Prosecutorial Discretion in Context: How Discretion Is Exercised Throughout Our Immigration System* (Immigration Policy Center Special Report March 2012). I evaluated unauthorized migrants' claims to legal status in *Who Belongs?: Immigration Outside the Law and the Idea of Americans in Waiting*, 2 U.C. Irvine Law Review 359 (2012), and in *Making Legal: The DREAM Act, Birthright Citizenship, and Broad-Scale Legalization*, 17 Lewis & Clark Law Review 1127 (2013). An earlier, differently focused version of my analysis of temporary worker programs appeared in *Designing Temporary Worker Programs*, 80 University of Chicago Law Review 263 (2013). Some passages scattered throughout this book first appeared in short pieces in the *Room for Debate* feature of the *New York Times* opinion page. Also included here is some material that I drafted for the casebook, *Immigration and Citizenship: Process and Policy* (7th ed. West 2012), which I have had the privilege to co-author over multiple editions with Alex Aleinikoff, David Martin, and Maryellen Fullerton. I draw on some discussions in *Americans in Waiting* when they provide useful analysis in this new volume.

AS WITH EVERYTHING that I have ever written, this book reflects the generosity of many friends and colleagues who took the time to share their thinking and their wisdom in many ways large and small, and who inspired me to press onward (often without knowing that their involvement mattered as much as it did).

For many helpful, perceptive, and often challenging and provocative comments and suggestions, I owe thanks to David Abraham, Tendayi Achiume, Muneer Ahmad, Laurel Anderson, Kif Augustine-Adams, Asli Bâli, Lenni Benson, Fred Bloom, Linda Bosniak, Kitty Calavita, Devon Carbado, Jack Chin, Eileen Cheng-Yin Chow, Elizabeth Cohen, Wayne Cornelius, Adam

Cox, John Coyle, Scott Cummings, Keith Cunningham-Parmeter, Nestor Davidson, Annie Decker, Ingrid Eagly, Kevin Escudero, Tia Katrina Canlas, Nicholas Espíritu, Jill Family, Adam Feibelman, David Franklin, Maryellen Fullerton, William Funk, Lauren Gilbert, Hannah Gill, Roberto Gonzales, Adam Goodman, Jennifer Gordon, Abner Greene, Ariela Gross, Deep Gulasekaram, Lucas Guttentag, Kay Hailbronner, Cheryl Harris, Janet Hoeffel, Mary Hoopes, Margaret Hu, Clare Huntington, Melissa Jacoby, Michael Jones-Correa, Jerry Kang, Aliza Kaplan, Ken Karst, Jennifer Koh, Sarah Morando Lakhani, Joseph Landau, Stephen Lee, Stephen Legomsky, Hans Linnartz, Jerry López, Stephen Manning, Peter Margulies, Helen Marrow, Bill Marshall, David Martin, Marc Miller, Claudia Moatti, Nancy Morawetz, Stephen Munzer, Lise Nelson, Gene Nichol, Carolina Nuñez, Michael Olivas, John Parry, Caitlin Patler, Huyen Pham, Noah Pickus, Cristina Rodríguez, Carlos Rojas, Victor Romero, David Rubenstein, Margo Schlanger, Hilary Schor, Peter Schuck, Suzanne Shanahan, John Skrentny, Sarah Song, Niklaus Steiner, Katherine Stone, Nomi Stolzenberg, Alex Street, Juliet Stumpf, Rick Su, Margaret Taylor, Chantal Thomas, Daniel Tichenor, Laurie Trautman, Sabine Tsuruda, Joanne Villanueva, Leti Volpp, Shoba Sivaprasad Wadhia, Roger Waldinger, Michele Waslin, Deborah Weissman, Adam Winkler, Michael Wishnie, Stephen Yale-Loehr, Elliott Young, and Noah Zatz.

This project also benefited greatly from insightful comments and engaging discussion at workshops, symposia, and lectures at the law schools at Brigham Young University, the University of California, Berkeley, the University of California, Irvine, the University of California, Los Angeles (UCLA), the University of Chicago, the University of Colorado at Boulder, Cornell University, the University of Denver, DePaul University, Duke University, Fordham University, the University of Florida, Lewis and Clark Law School, Loyola Law School–Los Angeles, the University of Miami, the University of Nevada at Las Vegas, the University of North Carolina–Chapel Hill, the University of Oregon, the University of Santa Clara, the University of South Carolina, St. Thomas University (Miami), Southern Methodist University, Stetson University, the University of Tulsa, Washington University (St. Louis), and Yale University, as well as at the 2013 Annual Meeting of the Association of American Law Schools, the 2010 and 2012 biennial Immigration Law Teachers Workshops, and the 2013 Conference of Asian Pacific American Law Faculty (CAPALF) at the University of California Hastings College of the Law.

My thinking was enriched by opportunities to discuss the ideas in this book with colleagues in other academic disciplines at the 2010 and 2012

Annual Conferences of the Law and Society Association; Arizona State University; the Changing Face of America Institute at the Graduate School of Journalism at the University of California, Berkeley; the Population, Society and Inequality Colloquium Series at the University of California, Irvine; the School of Public Affairs at the University of California, Los Angeles; the Program on International Migration at the University of California, Los Angeles; the Center for Comparative Immigration Studies at the University of California, San Diego; the Mario Einaudi Center for European Studies at Cornell University; the Kenan Institute for Ethics at Duke University; the Institute for the Study of the Americas at the University of North Carolina–Chapel Hill; Pomona College; the Center for Law, History, and Culture at the University of Southern California; Stonehill College; the Transatlantic Exchange for Academics in Migration Studies (TEAMS) meetings at the University of Virginia and in San Diego, California; and the Fairhaven College of Interdisciplinary Studies at Western Washington University.

Much of this book also reflects the influence of my friends at the Puget Sound Guitar Workshop, where musical immersion each of the past 15 summers has taught me many lessons, not just about music but also about both teaching and writing and about the connections between them, all of which I have taken to heart.

I am grateful for generous research funding from the UCLA School of Law, the UCLA Academic Senate, the Japanese American Remembrance Fund Endowment, and the UCLA Asian American Studies Center. My research assistants—Megan Brewer, Ryan Chin, Denis Griffin, Laura Hernandez, Nhu-Y Ngo, Alexandra Pauley, Amanda Pourebrahim, Kate Raven, Salvador Reynozo, Brittney Stanley, and Brian Tanada—not only provided excellent research and editorial assistance, but also asked many probing questions that sharpened and clarified the analysis in many parts of this book. Kasse Reyes of the Faculty Support Group of the UCLA School of Law helped in countless ways to move this project to completion.

I owe a great debt to my editor at Oxford University Press, David McBride, for his superb guidance and his faith in this project from the beginning.

Most of all, for love and support from Linda, Amy, and Remy, I am grateful beyond words.

I have been blessed with a lot of help. But of course, all remaining errors are mine.

Immigration Outside the Law

Introduction

The Children

Here between the hither and the farther shore
While time is withdrawn, consider the future
And the past with an equal mind.
—T. S. ELIOT[1]

TURN BACK THE clock several decades, to a time when immigration was much less in the national eye. In the early 1970s, long before the issue became familiar throughout the United States, unauthorized migration was already a prominent and controversial issue in the Lone Star State. Many Texans and their legislators, mayors, and school superintendents were asking themselves—what can be done about the flood of migrants streaming across the Mexican border? Many of these newcomers were bringing along children who, like their parents, were in the country in violation of federal immigration law—and taking up precious seats in public school classrooms. They spoke no English and needed all sorts of extra help from teachers and teachers' aides. Why should they be allowed to attend schools funded by hard-earned taxpayer dollars, especially in hardscrabble border areas where all but a rich few struggled to make ends meet?[2]

Of the proposals driven by these sentiments, the one that would make history was a law adopted in 1975. The Texas legislature passed it by voice vote, without formal debate, hearings, or committee reports. The idea seems to have come from school superintendents in districts near the Mexican border. Its title was unwieldy—Education Code section 21.031—but its impact was dramatic. The law denied local school districts any state education money for children who were not "legally admitted" to the United States. The law also allowed districts to bar such children from public schools, or to charge them tuition. Some districts did neither, but others moved to bar them outright. Still others planned to charge tuition, knowing that these children's families could not afford to pay.[3]

In northeast Texas, about halfway between Dallas and the Louisiana state line and nearly 500 miles from the Mexican border, the Tyler Independent

School District continued at first to enroll children who were in the United States unlawfully. At most, an estimated 60 such children attended Tyler schools out of a total enrollment of 16,000. But the district decided in July 1977 to charge any child without lawful immigration status an annual tuition of $1,000. Other districts throughout Texas implemented the new law in various ways that led to the same result—shutting public schoolhouse doors to unauthorized migrant children.[4]

THE 1970S WAS a pivotal decade in the civil rights struggle in the United States. African American advocacy organizations in the preceding decades had focused many of their efforts on access to education. Their struggle had been rewarded in the US Supreme Court's 1954 decision in *Brown v. Board of Education*.[5] But the racial integration of public schools stalled in the two decades that followed, and education remained a battleground for civil rights activists. Raising parallel concerns on behalf of Latinos, organizations like the Mexican American Legal Defense and Educational Fund (MALDEF) pressed claims to educational access as key to fighting what it saw as a battle against the social and political exclusion of Mexican Americans.

Part of MALDEF's strategy was challenging the stark imbalance in public school funding. Some districts in Texas—especially those with predominantly white, Anglo student populations—enjoyed property tax funding at many times the levels of poorer districts, where the majority of students often traced their ancestry to the other side of the Rio Grande. The US Supreme Court upheld this sort of unbalanced funding as a matter of federal constitutional law in 1973, though some similar challenges were successful under various state constitutions.[6]

MALDEF also targeted Texas Education Code section 21.031 and its practical exclusion of unauthorized migrant children from public schools. MALDEF's efforts were animated by the prospect that this challenge could become the Mexican American *Brown v. Board of Education*, as legal scholar Michael Olivas later put it. The two MALDEF advocates who shaped much of the strategy were the organization's young president, Vilma Martínez, who had been a civil rights attorney with the NAACP Legal Defense Fund, and Peter Roos, the MALDEF staff attorney who became its lead attorney in challenging the Texas statute. Martínez and Roos filed their case on behalf of several children whom the new Texas law would bar from the Tyler public schools. They sued the Tyler Independent School District and its superintendent, James Plyler, arguing that the state statute violated the US Constitution. And so began the case that became known as *Plyler v. Doe*.[7]

The children's parents were José and Rosario Robles, José and Lidia Lopez, Felix Hernandez, and Humberto and Jackeline Alvarez. They were concerned about the threat of deportation for any family members in the United States unlawfully. President Jimmy Carter's administration decided that it would not arrest or deport any of the plaintiffs or members of their families, but in order to minimize the risk of enforcement, federal district judge William Wayne Justice let the children sue anonymously, using the pseudonyms Doe, Roe, Boe, and Loe. The Carter administration also sided with the children on the core legal question, arguing that Texas could not block their access to public schools.[8]

Similar lawsuits—17 in all—soon challenged other public school districts throughout Texas that had implemented the statute. Of these other suits, the one involving the most children was brought by Peter Schey, a Los Angeles-based civil rights lawyer, against the Houston Independent School District. As in Tyler, Houston charged $1,000 annual tuition for children without lawful immigration status. All of the lawsuits except the one in Tyler were combined with the Houston case.

As the two parallel cases moved through the courts, Roos and Schey guarded their own strategic prerogatives. Roos was intent on pursuing the litigation in Tyler and not folding it into the consolidated lawsuit in Houston. He believed that he could minimize adverse press coverage by keeping the case in a rural area. Roos also thought the school district lawyer in Tyler was a less skilled adversary than the big-city lawyers defending the statute in Houston. And he felt fortunate to have his case assigned to Judge Justice, whose track record of ordering schools to desegregate and prisons to correct inhumane conditions suggested that he would be receptive to the children's legal challenge. Indeed, Judge Justice ruled on September 14, 1978, that the Texas statute was unconstitutional.[9]

The case in Houston proceeded more slowly. After a 24-day trial, federal district judge Woodrow Seals decided in July 1980 that the Texas statute was unconstitutional.[10] The two parallel lawsuits, in common cause but with separate teams of lawyers, went independently to the federal court of appeals for the Fifth Circuit. The cases were combined only when granted review by the US Supreme Court, which issued its landmark decision on June 15, 1982.

I HAVE OPENED this book with *Plyler* because it is a landmark case that offers an especially illuminating window on immigration outside the law. But before saying more about the decision, let me identify this book's two main aims. The first is to provide a framework for understanding why this is an area of law and policy marked by ambivalence and disagreement. At the extremes, the disagreements run deep, with voices vehement and shrill, fighting over the very words deployed. One side rails against "illegals," while the other speaks of "undocumented immigrants" with tolerance or perhaps approval. I intentionally use "unauthorized migrants," "unauthorized migration," and "immigration outside the law" to adopt terms that try to avoid prejudgments, and to minimize the baggage that burdens more commonly used phrases.[11]

The phrase "immigration outside the law" deserves further explanation. I recognize, of course, that the law itself is what makes some migration unauthorized. The law matters, and most of this book analyzes how the law addresses migration. Though I concede that law is relevant in this way, "immigration outside the law" is an accurate term for unauthorized migration in two important ways. I have mentioned one—the phrase refers accurately to migrants who are outside the zone of permission in US law, while moving away from politically charged wording.[12]

The phrase also reflects a less obvious yet crucial sense of being outside the law. As Chapter 1 explains more fully, unauthorized migration is outside the law, but so too is much of government regulation of immigration to the United States. Immigration law in practice differs drastically from immigration law in theory. This gap between law on the books and law in action is filled by countless government decisions that reflect the exercise of discretion, which responds to political and economic pressures that fluctuate over time and across locales. In this second sense, immigration law itself can operate outside the rule of law.

The very debate over the words deployed underscores how unauthorized migration can quickly incite angry exercises in point and counterpoint. At the same time, it is not uncommon to hear fundamental ambivalence and uncertainty about the most desirable or effective responses. For example, some find it harsh to deport noncitizens who came to the United States to work hard and provide a better life for their children, but also find it disturbing that their very presence is against the law. My first aim, then, is to offer ways to understand current debates.

This book's second aim is closely related to the first. It is to evaluate and suggest responses to unauthorized migration. Above all, it is important to avoid the quick fixes that many lawmakers have found to be an irresistible temptation. More Border Patrol agents or razor wire on one side of the debate—or a one-time legalization or amnesty on the other side—may do little more than mask today's problems and defer reckoning. To preview one of my conclusions, it is important to give unauthorized migrants access to lawful immigration status, but legalization or amnesty is just a short-term response. Sound policy requires both foresight beyond immediate political election cycles and the courage to work toward what will matter several generations from now.

This approach requires thinking beyond the issues of enforcement and legalization, and instead reworking admission schemes for both immigrants and temporary workers. This approach also demands considering how migration patterns reflect areas of law and policy outside immigration itself, especially domestic economic policy, domestic education policy, and international economic development. Without understanding immigration outside the law within these broader analytical frameworks, no responses will be effective in the long run, the gap between immigration law on the books and immigration law in action will remain wide, and an immigration system that is opaque, deceptive, and lawless will persist.

Working toward this book's two goals requires delving deeper than various conventional wisdoms. An accurate conceptual roadmap is essential. Drawing this roadmap starts with a close look at *Plyler v. Doe*.

The Court's Decision

In *Plyler v. Doe*, the US Supreme Court struck down the Texas school statute. Justice William Brennan wrote for a bare majority of five justices. As a matter of constitutional law, *Plyler* held that no state can limit a child's access to K–12 public education based on his or her immigration status. The federal government might deport any noncitizen in the United States who lacks lawful immigration status, but all children have the constitutional right, free of state restrictions based on immigration status, to attend public elementary and secondary schools where they live. But there is much more to *Plyler*.[13]

Both sides in *Plyler* sought the support of the president of the United States. In September 1977, at an early stage in the case, President Carter's Justice Department joined with the children, but Ronald Reagan defeated Carter in the November 1980 general election. The Reagan administration shifted course in September 1981, little more than one month before the Court heard oral arguments. Department of Justice lawyers filed a friend-of-the-court brief, expressing only limited support for the children. Though the brief endorsed the general idea that the Constitution can protect unauthorized migrants, it took no position on whether the Texas law violated the children's constitutional rights.[14]

The Supreme Court reached its decision by a razor-thin margin. Justice Lewis Powell was ultimately the swing vote, as he was in many other significant cases of that era. How did he come to join Justice Brennan's opinion for the Court? The archived papers of these two justices show that Powell was especially concerned about the fate of the children. From the very start of the Court's deliberations, Powell was firmly committed to striking down the Texas statute. But he wanted a rationale consistent with his views on other important constitutional issues.[15]

Justice Brennan drafted and redrafted his opinion to win Powell's support, so that the Court could issue not just a judgment striking down the statute, but also a majority opinion with a clear if narrow rationale. Brennan stressed the value of education and the innocence of children brought to the United States by their parents. He avoided broader reasoning that might give Powell pause because of its uncertain implications for future cases involving other unauthorized migrants or involving issues besides education. By limiting his draft's scope, Brennan managed to craft an analysis that reflected the common ground between them. Joined by Justices Blackmun, Stevens, and Marshall, the opinion for the Court had its majority of five.

That Powell's views would be pivotal was not lost on the litigants. As journalist Barbara Belejack recounted many years later: "The day the opinion was issued, a little-known Department of Justice lawyer co-wrote a memo chastising the US Solicitor General for not filing a brief taking Texas' side. Had such a brief been filed, future Supreme Court Chief Justice John Roberts wrote, Powell might have voted differently."[16]

WHAT WOULD BE the lasting impact of *Plyler*? The day after the decision, a *New York Times* editorial cautioned that "the 5–4 vote was too close and the legal rule too narrow to make the case one of liberty's landmarks." This caveat echoed a prediction in Chief Justice Burger's dissent: "[T]he Court's opinion rests on such a unique confluence of theories and rationales that it will likely stand for little beyond the results in these particular cases." For many of its critics, *Plyler* was an analytically flawed decision driven less by faithful adherence to constitutional law precedents than by a desire to make sure that the children won.[17]

But *Plyler*'s place in today's legal culture and public imagination goes well beyond its significance as a constitutional law decision. As often seems true in the United States, the law—especially constitutional law—says much about our society's values and attitudes in concrete terms. *Plyler* did much more than announce the Court's answer to a constitutional question. The decision's influence has been enduring and profound. Coming early among a few modern Supreme Court cases involving unauthorized migration, *Plyler* crystallized the issues that have framed thought and rhetoric on both sides in subsequent decades. In turn, *Plyler* offers a listener's guide to the debate and a framework for assessing options, whether one agrees with the decision or not. This becomes clear from looking closely at what the Court decided, and how.

In challenging the Texas statute, the *Plyler* children made two main arguments. One was that the statute was unconstitutional because it conflicted with federal immigration law and was therefore preempted. "Preemption" is based on the idea that under the Supremacy Clause of the US Constitution, federal law overrides any inconsistent state or local law. A state or local law that is displaced by federal law is said to be preempted. But the Court sidestepped this issue with a footnote that said clearly that it was not addressing preemption.[18]

Instead, the Court agreed with the children's second argument—that the Texas statute unlawfully discriminated against them. In constitutional law terms, they claimed that the statute violated their right to equal protection of the laws under the Fourteenth Amendment to the US Constitution. This is one of the Reconstruction Amendments, added to reflect the nation's new beginning after the end of the Civil War in 1865. The Thirteenth Amendment abolished slavery. The Fifteenth Amendment guaranteed the right to vote regardless of "race, or previous condition of servitude." The Fourteenth Amendment defined US citizenship, prohibited states from depriving persons of life, liberty, or property without due process of law, and guaranteed equal protection of the laws to all persons.

ALL NINE JUSTICES in *Plyler* agreed that the Constitution in some way applies to unauthorized migrants. In other words, constitutional protections come, at least initially, with physical presence in the United States, whether or not that presence is lawful. But applying this abstract idea to the facts of the case divided the majority from the four dissenters. What explains the gulf between them? The answer starts with a basic idea in constitutional law: The government does not violate the Constitution just because it treats two groups of people differently. Whether such line drawing is lawful depends on how deferentially or skeptically the courts examine it. The pivotal question is how much courts will defer to a federal, state, or local government decision to distinguish between two groups.[19]

Courts generally decide whether a difference in treatment is constitutional by applying a "rational basis" test. As the name implies, the government must only offer a rational basis for the difference. This test is very deferential to the government and only infrequently leads to invalidating the statute. In contrast, a statute that treats two groups of people differently is most likely to be struck down when a court applies a "strict scrutiny" test to assess the statute's constitutionality. The government must then carry a very heavy burden. It must show that the difference in treatment is necessary to serve a compelling government interest. Strict scrutiny applies to any difference in treatment based on a "suspect classification," such as race. Strict scrutiny also applies to any law that infringes on a "fundamental right," such as a law that curtails the right to vote. Legal scholar Gerald Gunther wrote that strict scrutiny, though strict in theory, is fatal in fact. Modern decisions suggest that this statement was too pat, but strict scrutiny is no doubt a tough test for the government to pass.[20]

In *Plyler*, the Court first addressed whether the Texas statute could be considered rational. This opening hinted that the Court might defer to the Texas legislature under the rational basis test. But the Court's reasoning probed further: "the discrimination contained in section 21.031 can hardly be considered rational unless it furthers some substantial goal of the State."[21] By asking for a substantial goal, the Court signaled that its analysis might be closer to what is called "intermediate scrutiny"—more than a rational basis but less than strict scrutiny. The Court did not so label its analysis, but it seemed to require that Texas show something more than a rational basis. This part of the Court's decision emphasized, consistent with Justice Powell's views, that the case involved innocent children who should not suffer for their parents' decisions.[22]

The Court held that Texas violated the children's constitutional right of access to public elementary and secondary schools by making educational access depend on immigration status. The state of Texas offered three justifications; the Court rejected all three. One was "to protect itself from an influx of illegal immigrants" that would strain the educational budget. The Court responded by doubting the economic burdens on the state, and by noting that these migrants went to Texas to work, not to get their children a free education. Texas also argued that illegal immigrant children imposed "special burdens...on the State's ability to provide high-quality public education." But in the Court's view, Texas lacked proof that excluding unlawfully present children—as opposed to simply reducing the total number of children—would improve public schools. The Court also rejected the third justification: that these children were "less likely than other children to remain within the boundaries of the State, and to put their education to productive social or political use within the State." It is uncertain, said the Court, whether any child, regardless of immigration or citizenship status, would stay in Texas or leave.[23]

Chief Justice Burger dissented, reasoning that the statute was constitutional, even if profoundly unwise. Joined by three justices, he saw the choice as between strict scrutiny and a rational basis test. He observed that strict scrutiny was inappropriate because illegal aliens are not a suspect classification and education is not a fundamental right. Since established law calls for courts to apply strict scrutiny only when a suspect classification or a fundamental right is involved, Burger argued that the statute was constitutional because it had a rational basis.[24]

THE REASONING IN *Plyler* was tied closely to the facts of the case. The Court's focus on children's educational access largely explains why the decision as a constitutional holding has remained cabined. *Plyler* has not led courts to invalidate other laws that disadvantage unauthorized migrants. For example, courts are unlikely to sustain claims that denying admission to a public college or university violates their right to equal protection. *Plyler* remains a high-water mark for the constitutional protection of unauthorized migrants against laws that treat them differently because they lack lawful immigration status.[25]

Though its constitutional holding was narrow, the broader significance of *Plyler* in framing debates about immigration outside the law has been fundamental, profound, and enduring. The same *New York Times* editorial that doubted that the decision would be one of "liberty's landmarks" in constitutional law also presaged its broader impact when it ventured this policy appraisal: "any other result would have been a national disgrace. It was intolerable that a state so wealthy and so willing to wink at undocumented workers should evade the duty—and ignore the need—to educate all its children."[26]

Years after the Supreme Court upheld his decision to strike down the Texas law, Judge Justice, the trial judge in the case against the Tyler school district, said, "As a result of that decision, I think probably several million children got an education. And that's the case I'm most proud of." After the judge died in 2009, a reflection on his passing told a story related by his wife, Sue Justice. Soon after her husband issued his decision, a small bouquet of flowers arrived at their home in Tyler. On the note was a card, signed with one illegible name and two X's. To find out who had sent the flowers, Mrs. Justice called the florist, who told her that three Mexican laborers had come in and paid with two dollar bills and some change—all the money they had with them—and asked him to send the bouquet to Mrs. Justice.[27]

But it is fair to speculate that many Texans might not have viewed this story about the flowers as sympathetically as Judge Justice's biographer seemed to. If their reaction was different, why? The answer to this question starts with a closer look at the core themes in *Plyler* as viewed by the Court majority and dissenters.

Three Themes in Plyler

The reasoning and outcome in *Plyler* depended on a combination of three themes that have remained pivotal for more than a generation in public debates about unauthorized migration. Throughout this book, I will refer to these *Plyler* themes. But it is important to remember that *Plyler* merely provides the most prominent example of a case in which all three themes were pivotal and explain the wide gap between majority and dissent. Even if the case had come out the other way, these are the three themes that still would be central to today's debates.

The first essential theme is the significance of unlawful presence. What does it mean to be in the United States without legal permission? Are unauthorized migrants "illegals," or are they "undocumented immigrants"? Though all nine Justices agreed that the children were not entirely outside the protections of the US Constitution, Chief Justice Burger's dissent emphasized that the children's illegal presence fatally weakened their constitutional claims. Likewise, many who urge strict responses to unauthorized migration today start—and sometimes end—their arguments by emphasizing that the offenders are illegal aliens. As *New York Times* editorial writer Lawrence Downes put it (both ironically and satirically): "[W]hat part of 'illegal' don't you understand?"[28]

For the majority of the Supreme Court, however, the fact that the children were in the United States unlawfully was just the start of the analysis. Even children without lawful status still have some concrete constitutional rights because they live in the United States, even if their presence violates federal immigration law. The Court reasoned that the US government has tolerated a sizable unauthorized population, so "there is no assurance that a child subject to deportation will ever be deported." Today, those who are sympathetic toward unauthorized migration likewise maintain that history complicates what it means to be in the United States unlawfully. What matters is not lawful or "illegal" presence as a formal matter, but rather the ties that unauthorized migrants forge in this country and the contributions that they make—with the government's acquiescence.[29]

THE SECOND THEME that was essential in *Plyler*—just as it remains essential today—is the role of states and localities, including cities, counties, school districts, and other local government entities. Do states and localities have the same power as the federal government to decide how to treat unauthorized migrants? The clear answer in *Plyler* was no. The federal government may put unauthorized migrants in a worse position than citizens or noncitizens who are lawfully present, but a state or local government that does so may violate the US Constitution. Texas crossed the line in *Plyler* by denying public elementary and secondary education.[30]

In the generation since *Plyler*, the state and local role in immigration has remained a hotbed of controversy that produced two major Supreme Court decisions in 2011 and 2012, both involving the state of Arizona. Many advocates of stronger immigration enforcement call for greater state and local power to counter unauthorized migration and to minimize its harms. Echoing Texas's efforts in *Plyler*, a number of states and localities adopted measures to block access to work, housing, driver's licenses, and higher education. They tried to deter new unauthorized migrants and to force those already present to "self-deport." Other measures authorized state and local police to enforce immigration law directly by checking immigration status when they make stops or arrests. A related approach has been to impose state criminal penalties for federal immigration violations.[31]

Skeptics of state or local enforcement respond that both the Constitution and sound policy require nationwide uniformity in immigration law. They argue that although the federal government has the authority to draw lines based on immigration status and to enforce federal immigration law, any state or local role in direct immigration enforcement is unconstitutional without express federal authorization. These skeptics argue that state and local enforcement is also bad policy because state and local officials involved in enforcement are prone to misapplying federal immigration law or discriminating by race and ethnicity. State and local enforcement may also undermine community trust in police. This point of view raises a related question: Should any limits on state and local enforcement apply just as strongly to laws and policies that *insulate* unauthorized migrants from federal immigration enforcement?[32]

THE THIRD ESSENTIAL *Plyler* theme is the integration of unauthorized migrants. Quoting *Brown v. Board of Education*, the Supreme Court emphasized that without education, the children would be disadvantaged for their entire lives. The Court also underscored that the emergence of a permanent subcaste is intolerable within a national constitutional culture based on equality. This strong endorsement of the need to integrate unauthorized migrants— at least when they are children—was essential to overturning the Texas statute.[33]

This theme, like the first two, remains highly prominent today. One side often argues that unauthorized migrants are "Americans in waiting" who already are a part of American society. It should be national policy, the argument continues, to acknowledge or foster the integration of unau-thorized migrants through access to work, housing, education, and identity documents. Moreover, unauthorized migrants should be offered lawful status through legalization that includes a path to citizenship. In contrast, the *Plyler* dissenters viewed any need to integrate unauthorized migrants as a topic for legislatures, not courts. And as a policy matter today, those who oppose the integration of unauthorized migrants characterize them as unworthy of any recognition through amnesty, let alone a path to citizenship. The argument on this side is that unauthorized migration imposes tremendous costs on taxpayers and on US society generally, especially on the most disadvantaged Americans. From this viewpoint, the rule of law demands stern measures to block the arrival of unauthorized migrants and to compel the departure of those who are already in the United States.[34]

COMBINING THE COURT'S approaches to these three essential themes, the *Plyler* decision reflects a certain ethos—a way of thinking not just about children who are in the United States unlawfully, but also about unauthor-ized migration in general, and even more broadly about immigration to the United States and US citizenship itself. This book explains why the ethos of the *Plyler* decision supplies the foundation of the most effective and durable responses to immigration outside the law. Much of my reasoning is based on close examination of the *Plyler* Court's approach to these three themes, but let me first offer some general observations.

The *Plyler* ethos reflects a sense of fairness that is informed by pragma-tism, realism, and an appreciation of the complexities of human migration. Relatedly, the *Plyler* ethos values the lessons of history in two ways. One is that the most vexing questions of public policy must be addressed with an acute awareness that they have a complex past that took generations to evolve, and that it may require time to find and adopt effective solutions. The *Plyler* ethos also respects essential challenges of the American narrative, such as racial discrimination, economic upheavals, and national security threats. As a way of taking history's sobering lessons to heart, the *Plyler* ethos remains open to second-best solutions, while remaining skeptical of quick fixes and of blind reliance on formal labels and categories.

These aspects of the decision amply justify legal scholar Peter Schuck's view that *Plyler* broke fundamentally away from an earlier conceptual framework that assumed the power of government to dictate the terms of immigration and belonging. The *Plyler* ethos reflects a keen awareness of practical limits on the capacity of any government to persuade or coerce individuals in ways that will alter or control migration, given limited resources and competing public values such as liberty and privacy, and given the sheer power of social and economic forces that shape migration patterns throughout the world.[35]

Building on *Plyler*

When the US Supreme Court decided *Plyler* more than a generation ago in 1982, about 3.3 million unauthorized migrants lived in the United States, or 1.4 percent of the total population of about 231 million. Today, that number is between 11 and 12 million, or around 3.5 percent of the total US population of about 315 million. Of the foreign-born US population of more than 40 million, about 28 percent is unauthorized. Many of the unauthorized are established as residents of the United States. As of 2011, about 86 percent of unauthorized adults arrived in 2004 or earlier, and 57 percent in 1999 or earlier.[36]

Beyond the broadly shared belief that something must be done, there is little consensus. Serious proposals span a breathtaking range, from broad-scale legalization with expanded lawful admissions to zero-tolerance enforcement with criminal prosecution of immigration law violators. Many of today's debates over immigration outside the law seem to pit endorsement of the *Plyler* ethos against those who would reject it. In short, discussion of unauthorized migration has involved some combination of the three essential themes evident in *Plyler*. Analyzing each of them separately is the task for this book's first three chapters.

Chapter 1 analyzes the meaning of unlawful presence. It shows how being present in the United States without lawful immigration status is inconclusive in several distinct but related ways. It can be hard to tell if someone is in the United States unlawfully. Or even if unlawful presence is clear at any given moment, noncitizens can acquire lawful status through channels that are well-established in current law. Even if unlawful presence is clear and not easily changed, the consequences of unlawful presence are highly variable, depending on the exercise of enforcement discretion. These aspects of unlawful presence have roots in the historical development of US immigration law and policy. All of this adds up to a system of highly selective admissions, a large unauthorized population, and highly selective enforcement. Immigration law on the books creates a large number of immigration violators who may or may not be deported in practice, depending on vast government discretion, exercised against the backdrop of political and economic pressures. In this system, unpredictable and sometimes discriminatory discretion have replaced the predictability and uniformity that is usually associated with the rule of law.

Chapter 2 looks at the state and local role in matters relating to immigration and immigrants. It traces the evolution of state and local involvement from early in the Republic through the American Civil War, and then to the give and take among federal, state, and local governments in the modern era. Chapter 2 provides a framework in two dimensions for analyzing the vast array of state and local activity. One dimension is a spectrum that runs from enforcing immigration law to insulating unauthorized migrants from enforcement. The other dimension runs from directly enforcing or resisting federal immigration law—such as by arresting and detaining immigration violators or refusing to do so—to indirect enforcement or resistance, such as by limiting or allowing access to public colleges and universities.

Chapter 3 examines the integration of unauthorized migrants into American society. It starts by analyzing the tension between the very idea of national borders and the commitment to equality that is part of American political and constitutional culture. Chapter 3 then explains why the integration of immigrants is essential for reconciling the tension between borders and equality. These reasons to integrate immigrants apply in substantial measure to unauthorized migrants. The view that many unauthorized migrants are Americans in waiting with valid claims to membership in American society can be based on some combination of two ideas. One is that the immigration system is one of discretionary tolerance, and that unauthorized migrants have effectively accepted an invitation to work in the United States, forming a type of contract that has benefited both themselves and the United States. A related basis for claims to be Americans in waiting is the idea that unauthorized migrants have built up a stake in the United States and have made contributions that justify recognizing and fostering their integration.

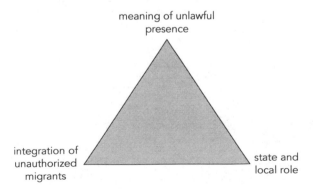

FIGURE I.I

Figure I.1 shows how these first three chapters are related, and it guides later discussion of key concepts in relation to each other. Of course, these three themes are not the only crucial ideas in thinking about immigration outside the law. Major factors and concepts include the global economy, race, language, gender, national security, enforcement, and guilt and innocence, to name just a few of the most prominent. But the basic relevance of these elements is so vigorously contested—even if they are pervasive—that they offer little help as a framework for organizing analysis and understanding debates. Some observers would emphasize the central role played by race, while others would downplay race. In contrast, there is little doubt that the meaning of unlawful presence, the role of states and cities, and the integration of unauthorized migrants are zones of vigorous debate.

The three *Plyler* themes offer an essential roadmap because they help unpack whether and how the global economy, race, gender, and national security matter. For example, perceptions of race—in its many possible meanings—have strongly influenced debates over immigration outside the law, but those effects have varied from one *Plyler* theme to another. Chapter 1 explains how race-related considerations have shaped the meaning of unlawful presence and have contributed to the highly discretionary system that exists today. As Chapter 2 makes clear, race has been historically pivotal in justifying limits on state and local authority to regulate immigration and citizenship. Chapter 3 analyzes how race has influenced the integration of unauthorized migrants. In these ways, the three themes help unpack the different roles of race in each area, and then in immigration law and policy overall.

CHAPTERS 4, 5, AND 6 explore the deeper implications of the meaning of unlawful presence, the state and local role, and the integration of unauthorized migrants. These chapters show that assessing each theme in isolation is too narrow an approach. They are intertwined in underappreciated ways that produce complex tectonics.

Chapter 4 shows how the meaning of unlawful presence and the role of state and local governments combine to influence the basic question of enforcement authority. The connection is that the proper state and local role in immigration enforcement depends on what unlawful presence means. If unlawful presence and its consequences are clear based on immigration law on the books, then expanded state and local enforcement becomes more sensible. But suppose that unlawful presence is inconclusive, that assigning consequences requires considerable expertise, and that immigration law in action depends heavily on case-by-case discretionary decisions that are unpredictable, inconsistent, and perhaps discriminatory. If these things are true, then it may be unwise or even unconstitutional to expand the circle of government officials with the power to enforce.

Chapter 5 connects another pair of themes—the state and local role and the integration of unauthorized migrants—by discussing how small-scale communities might include or not include unauthorized migrants. Opponents of such integration argue that only citizens and lawfully present noncitizens are legitimate members. But others counter that states and localities should foster the integration of unauthorized migrants into everyday community life by allowing access to education, work, public benefits, and identification documents, and by insulating them from immigration enforcement. Chapter 5 explores this debate, including the question of whether any restrictions on state or local enforcement apply equally to limit state and local efforts to integrate unauthorized migrants.

Chapter 6 links the last pair of themes—the meaning of unlawful presence and the integration of unauthorized migrants—in order to examine the acquisition of lawful immigration status and citizenship by unauthorized migrants. Some believe that unlawful presence is straightforward no matter what history suggests. Illegal means illegal, so past enforcement lapses should not govern the future, and the illegal population should be denied lawful status and barred from mainstream society. If, however, unlawful presence is inconclusive and immigration law in action is highly unpredictable, arbitrary, and discretionary, then unauthorized migrants who have lived in and have contributed to American society should be offered lawful immigration status,

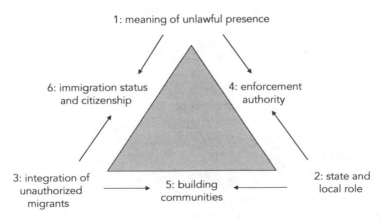

FIGURE I.2

including a path to citizenship. In short, Chapter 6 considers whether claims that have arisen in the past should be recognized by granting lawful immigration and citizenship status to unauthorized migrants, especially whether such recognition is consistent with the rule of law. Figure I.2 maps how the three themes in *Plyler* connect to each other, chapter by chapter.

Chapter 7, the last chapter, combines lessons from the first six chapters to assess the approaches that policymakers should take in responding to immigration outside the law. It starts by asking: What about temporary workers? Because this topic can provoke sharp debate—even among those who generally agree on immigration issues—temporary worker programs offer a vantage point for understanding responses to unauthorized migration. The close connection between temporary workers and unauthorized migrants highlights the importance of three larger perspectives on immigration outside the law. First, unauthorized migration is a fundamental force within the US domestic economy. Second, unauthorized migration is an essential aspect of international economic development. A third perspective considers how fundamental questions of US citizenship and integration should inform the treatment of unauthorized migrants. All three perspectives combine to lay the foundation for durable, effective responses to immigration outside the law.

THE HOLDING IN *Plyler v. Doe* was narrow as a matter of constitutional law, and its ethos remains deeply contested. One can reasonably ask if the US Supreme Court would reach the same result today. But this uncertainty shows precisely why *Plyler* endures as an essential lens. The gap between arguments and counterarguments on many aspects of unauthorized migration reflects how much each side accepts or rejects the *Plyler* ethos.

Both *Plyler v. Doe* and *Brown v. Board of Education* stand for broad notions of equality in educational access. But *Brown* became iconic, first to establish a principle of racial integration and equality that is well-established in the abstract, and then to serve as the starting point for eliminating racial segregation in many concrete settings. The basic principle in *Plyler*—forbidding different treatment of unauthorized migrants because of their immigration law status—remains contested, and as a matter of law it seems limited to the context in which it arose. And yet, *Plyler* and *Brown* are alike in one striking way. Just as the lessons from *Brown* for racial equality remain a compass, *Plyler* continues to define the central issues in debates about unauthorized migration.[37]

The *Plyler* ethos addresses immigration and US citizenship in ways that are consistent with some of the noblest impulses and highest values in American history. This historical grounding is essential because immigration debates today are a modern version of this nation's most fundamental and formative challenges—to decide who belongs, and who does not. It is no accident that immigration issues have emerged repeatedly as pivotal, most recently after the reelection of President Barack Obama in 2012. With support among Latino and Asian voters crucial to his margin of victory, the presidential campaign highlighted the importance of immigration as a national issue and spurred renewed congressional attention.

Periods of intense political activity will come and go, but the challenge is constant. The nation has fought mightily but with mixed success to overcome the exclusions of slavery and its vestiges, and to struggle with the many forms of inequality that persist today. Much of American history has reflected the efforts of excluded immigrant groups to secure their place in this country, including the acquisition of US citizenship itself. With our best national future at stake, the subtleties of immigration outside the law demand conscientious thought—and courageous decisions—to answer this most essential of questions: Who are *we*?

I

Undocumented or Illegal?

ON DECEMBER 1, 1981, a crisp day in Washington, D.C., the lawyers in *Plyler v. Doe* went to the US Supreme Court to make their arguments to the justices, 45 minutes for each side. John Hardy was the attorney for the state of Texas. As he spoke, Justice Thurgood Marshall interrupted to ask if Texas could deny fire protection to illegal aliens. Apparently nonplussed, Hardy bought a little time: "Deny them fire protection?" Marshall persisted: "Yes, sir. F–I–R–E. Could Texas pass a law and say they cannot be protected?" When Hardy said that he did not think it could, Marshall responded pointedly: "Why not?...Somebody's house is more important than his child?"[1]

Justice Marshall's question was one way of asking about what it means to be in the United States unlawfully. How does the law treat someone who is in the United States without lawful immigration status? Even if she can be arrested and deported, does this mean that local firefighters will not protect her home? Can she get married? Use public roads? Can an unauthorized migrant fight in court for child custody or sue for personal injuries? The answers to these questions have profound practical meaning for the lives of unauthorized migrants, shaping their days and nights and reflecting how much they are part of American society—or are excluded from it.

Another true story raises questions about the consequences of unlawful immigration status in the workplace. In May 1988, a man going by the name of José Castro applied for a job at Hoffman Plastic Compounds factory in Paramount, California. Then as now, it made polyvinylchloride (PVC) pellets for sale to companies that formed the PVC into pipe, insulation, fabric, and other products. Castro presented three documents with his application: a Social Security card, a California state identification card, and a birth certificate showing that he was born in El Paso, Texas. Hoffman Plastic hired him to operate machines that extruded PVC pellets before they were bagged and shipped to customers. While working there, Castro lived at his niece's home, where he slept on the living room couch.

Around Christmas 1988, when Castro had been on the job about six months, a union—the United Rubber, Cork, Linoleum and Plastic Workers of America, AFL-CIO—started to organize the plant workers, enlisting the help of some, including Castro. The next month, the plant management heard about the organizing and questioned Castro about his involvement. Soon afterwards, the plant laid off nine workers, including José Castro. The company's owner, Ron Hoffman, would later insist that declining business prompted the layoffs. One of the discharged employees filed a claim with the National Labor Relations Board (NLRB), which ruled about 18 months later that the layoffs were an anti-union tactic that violated federal labor law.

In federal labor law, the normal remedy for this type of employer violation is back pay. A wrongfully fired employee gets the money that he would have earned if he had stayed on the job. But as the NLRB looked into the case, it came out that José Castro was in the United States unlawfully. He had used a borrowed birth certificate, and in all likelihood the name José Castro was an alias. The question emerged: If an unauthorized worker is laid off in violation of federal labor law, is he eligible for back pay?

No, said the US Supreme Court in its 2002 decision in *Hoffman Plastic Compounds, Inc. v. NLRB*. The Court explained that federal immigration law barred José Castro from working, so he should not get the money he would have earned. As in *Plyler*, a 5–4 vote of the justices decided *Hoffman Plastic*. The decision seemed like it might severely limit workplace protections for unauthorized workers. And yet, courts and agencies in other cases since *Hoffman Plastic* have distinguished back pay from other workers' remedies. Unauthorized workers can receive unpaid wages for work performed, damages for employment discrimination, and remedies for other employer violations of workers' rights. These workplace cases, like Justice Marshall's question about fire protection, probed when and why the law protects unauthorized migrants.[2]

ASKING ABOUT THE practical consequences of unlawful status is just one of four ways to ask what it means to be in the United States in violation of immigration law. The *Plyler* Court was considering the consequences of unlawful status when it observed that "there is no assurance that a child subject to deportation will ever be deported." In *Plyler*, it seemed beyond doubt that the children who challenged the Texas statute were in the United States unlawfully, and the Court referred to the children as illegal aliens, but it is not always clear if someone's presence is unlawful. A third way to think about unlawful presence is to ask if someone, even if clearly violating immigration law, can acquire lawful status in the future. On this issue, the *Plyler* Court observed that Congress might adopt a legalization or amnesty program, but this routinely happens (without a broad-scale program) through many narrow avenues in current immigration law, making unlawful presence changeable.[3]

A fourth aspect of unlawful presence is its meaning in moral or social terms. Does it carry the sort of deep stigma that might follow a conviction for a violent crime, or is being in the United States illegally more like littering in a public park or driving faster than the speed limit? *Plyler* addressed this question indirectly by seeming to absolve both the children and their parents from guilt. The Court observed that "[s]heer incapability or lax enforcement of the laws barring entry into this country" had led to a sizable unauthorized population, and that unauthorized migrants were "encouraged by some to remain here as a source of cheap labor." This moral or social meaning of unlawful presence may be the aspect that most directly affects whether migrants who lack lawful status have a claim to take part in American society.[4]

These four aspects of unlawful presence overlap, and it can be natural to consider them together. The *Plyler* Court addressed both the practical consequences of unlawful presence and its social meaning in this passage: "the confluence of Government policies has resulted in 'the existence of a large number of employed illegal aliens...whose presence is tolerated, whose employment is perhaps even welcomed.'"[5] The Court's opinion as a whole seemed to adopt the view that unlawful presence is inconclusive in several key respects, and that immigration status is just the start of deciding how unauthorized migrants should be treated.

One central goal of this chapter is to examine each of these four aspects of unlawful presence, especially by explaining the complexities of federal immigration law related to each. The history of immigration to the United States combines with the present contours of immigration law to show that immigration status often is hard to ascertain or is changeable. And even when a violation is clear, its consequences are not. Moreover, the history of immigration law suggests strong reasons not to treat unlawful presence as deeply immoral or to assign serious stigma to unauthorized migrants, and not to treat being undocumented—literally, without papers, *sin papeles*—as diminishing claims to participate in American society.[6]

This chapter's other central goal is to explain how these four aspects of unlawful presence are related to each other. Unlawful presence is inconclusive in four ways, but more significantly, it is inconclusive by design. My argument goes beyond saying that unlawful presence is too indeterminate to allow comfort in neat divisions between *legal* and *illegal* and between *us* and *them*, and that immigration status can only be the start of a conversation and never its end. I go further to explain that the vagueness of the legal/illegal line is part of an immigration system in which both lawful admission and enforcement are highly selective. Immigration law on the books creates a large number of violators; immigration law in action has historically tolerated them. Whether they are ultimately deported depends on countless decisions by government officials who exercise discretion, always aware of political and economic pressures, and often in ways that can be inconsistent, unpredictable, and sometimes discriminatory. Unauthorized migrants are often accused of breaking the law, but the real threat to the rule of law comes from the system as a whole.

Of Paths to Lawful Status and Gray Areas

Even when a noncitizen's presence in the United States clearly violates immigration law, that status may change. Many unauthorized migrants can be very close to having lawful immigration status. Some meet all requirements to qualify for lawful status but must file applications and await processing. Others have successfully qualified in an admission category, for example as the spouse of a citizen, but must wait in one of the several lines for admission to the United States because of an annual limit on immigrant visas. Others are in one of the lines but they are disqualified for some reason, such as unlawful presence in the United States, and need to restore eligibility through a waiver.

In fact, many noncitizens who become lawful permanent residents have been in the United States unlawfully at some earlier time. According to a study led by sociologist Guillermina Jasso, about 19 percent of new permanent residents originally crossed the border without inspection at a port of entry. Another 12 percent were lawfully admitted but then overstayed.[7] This does not mean that 31 percent of unauthorized migrants have a path to permanent resident status. Many noncitizens who cross the border without inspection or overstay after admission as a nonimmigrant have no way to acquire lawful permanent residents. But it is striking that so many of those who become lawful permanent residents were unauthorized migrants at one time.

Explaining further how someone who is in the United States unlawfully can qualify for lawful immigration status requires a quick tour of the main federal statute, the Immigration and Nationality Act (INA). Among the complexities of this intricate body of law are the many narrow paths from unlawful to lawful status under current law.

IMAGINE THE CASE of Mariano, who came from Mexico to the United States four years ago. He had temporary worker status as a computer programmer at a software company in Boulder, Colorado. He traveled from his hometown, a place not far from Guanajuato, to Denver International Airport, where he was admitted as a "nonimmigrant." This term refers to noncitizens who are admitted for a specific purpose and a limited time. United States immigration law has many nonimmigrant categories, including business visitors, tourists, and students. Mariano was admitted as an H-1B temporary worker for a period of three years.[8]

Mariano decided that the job was not for him and quit one year after his arrival. An accomplished musician, he now makes a living as a guitarist in several bands and as a guitar teacher at a local music store, H. B. Woodsong's. Mariano also works the early morning shift as a barista at Vic's Espresso. Having quit his job and overstayed his three-year admission, Mariano is in the United States unlawfully. He could be deported—or "removed," in the language of the statute. But Mariano recently married Rachel, a US citizen, who can file a petition for Mariano as her "immediate relative." Though unlawfully present in the United States, Mariano now qualifies to become a lawful permanent resident without a waiting period. Through a procedure called "adjustment of status," Mariano can become a permanent resident without leaving the country.[9]

Lawful permanent residents are noncitizens who have been admitted for an indefinite period. They get what are often called "green cards" due to the card's traditional hue. After five years—or just three years for spouses of citizens—permanent residents can become citizens through a process called "naturalization." A total of almost 7 million permanent residents naturalized in the decade from 2002 through 2011. Permanent residents may lose their status if they leave the country for a long period—generally one year or longer. But unless they become deportable, for example because of certain types of criminal convictions, they may live in the United States indefinitely as permanent residents. No law requires them to naturalize as a condition of staying.[10]

NOW FOR SOME complications: Suppose that Mariano had not come through Denver International Airport as a nonimmigrant, but instead had crossed the border by avoiding an official port of entry. His marriage to Rachel still qualifies him as an immediate relative who is eligible to become a lawful permanent resident, but his clandestine entry disqualifies him from getting a green card through the adjustment of status procedure inside the United States. Mariano can still go back to Mexico for his immigrant visa, but then he would face another problem.

Federal immigration law restricts the admission of noncitizens who leave the country after at least 180 days of unlawful presence. For unlawful presence between 180 days and one year, they generally must leave for three years before they may return. Noncitizens like Mariano who have over one year of unlawful presence face a longer penalty period of 10 years.[11] This rule applies only to noncitizens who leave the country, so Mariano could avoid it through adjustment of status. But noncitizens who enter without inspection generally are ineligible to adjust their status inside the United States. Mariano would have to leave the United States to get his green card. The only way to avoid a 10-year wait is to ask the government for a waiver, which requires showing that barring Mariano from admission as a permanent resident would cause extreme hardship to Rachel, a US citizen. This waiver is discretionary and a decision can take time, but approval rates are high.[12] In this scenario, too, Mariano would be in the United States unlawfully, but it is also true that he qualifies for permanent residence.

Even if unauthorized migrants fit no admission category, they may become permanent residents on a case-by-case basis. Ever since 1917, federal law has allowed immigration officials to grant permanent resident status to noncitizens. The current version of this scheme, called "cancellation of removal," was set up in 1996. Each year it allows up to 4,000 noncitizens who are in the United States unlawfully to become permanent residents. The applicant must have been physically present in the United States for 10 years and must show that his removal would result in exceptional and extremely unusual hardship for a US citizen or permanent resident spouse, minor child, or parent. Criminal convictions can be disqualifying. If the applicant meets these threshold eligibility requirements, immigration judges have the discretion to grant cancellation.[13] The current eligibility rules for cancellation of removal are much stricter than they were before 1996, when Congress substituted the exceptional and extremely unusual hardship standard for the "extreme" hardship required by earlier law. But even under the new, more demanding standard, it remains true, as the *Plyler* Court noted, that an "illegal entrant might be granted federal permission to continue to reside in this country, or even to become a citizen."[14]

Overall, then, unlawful presence is more nuanced than it seems, first in that current law allows immigration status to change. An estimated 4.4 million noncitizens are waiting in line with approved immigrant visa petitions. Of this group, it is safe to assume that many are currently in the United States without lawful immigration status, though the exact number is unknown.[15] For these noncitizens who meet the basic green card requirements but must wait, or who can get green cards through cancellation of removal, "illegal" does not mean "absolutely illegal." It seems especially cavalier to dismiss a non-citizen's presence as illegal if she only needs to file paperwork or wait in a line for which she has qualified, or if she lacks the money to pay filing fees and for the help of a lawyer to navigate the complexities of federal immigration law.

WHAT ABOUT THE millions of unauthorized migrants who do not have approved immigrant visa petitions or strong claims for cancellation of removal? For many in this group, unlawful presence is inconclusive in a different way. They are in a gray area between lawful and unlawful status. Well over one million have some form of federal government permission to stay in the country in a twilight status, as legal scholar David Martin put it.[16]

For example, "temporary protected status" (TPS) shields noncitizens who are in the United States from removal to countries that are beset by disturbed conditions, such as political strife in Liberia, Somalia, Sudan, and South Sudan. The government also granted TPS after volcanic activity in 1995 on the Caribbean island of Montserrat, after Hurricane Mitch in Honduras and Nicaragua in 1998, and after earthquakes in 2001 in El Salvador and in 2010 in Haiti. The federal executive branch designates countries for TPS and can extend such designations. TPS designation typically ends when home country conditions improve, but the duration of TPS can be long, even lasting for years. To keep TPS from attracting new arrivals, applicants usually must be in the United States when the country is designated. TPS holders are not permanent residents, but they are allowed to work.[17]

Another twilight status is "parole," which is a form of limited government approval for noncitizens to be in the United States, even if they do not qualify immediately for lawful admission. Parole has served as a form of refugee protection when the circumstances were compelling but existing laws provided no options for formal admission. In 1956, when the Soviet Union sent tanks to put down unrest in Hungary, the annual cap on immigration from Hungary had been reached. No refugee category was available, but the Eisenhower administration paroled about 30,000 Hungarians into the United States. In more recent decades, the federal government has granted parole to hundreds of thousands of persons from a variety of countries including Cuba, as well as countries in Asia and elsewhere in the world. Parole is also used on a case-by-case humanitarian basis to let noncitizens into the United States for medical care for themselves or family members, sometimes for long stays, even if they have no basis for admission.[18]

Though these examples show how the federal government uses parole as a substitute for formal admission, it has also granted parole as a bridge toward permanent residence for noncitizens who are in the United States unlawfully. In 2010, for example, the Obama administration started to grant parole to Haitian orphans who were in the process of being adopted by US citizens and to unlawfully present spouses, parents, and children of citizens serving in the US military. Parole allowed these unauthorized migrants to become permanent residents through adjustment of status without leaving the United States, thus avoiding the three-year or ten-year bars to admission for noncitizens who have been unlawfully present.[19]

Discretion and Legalization

The number of unauthorized migrants who may acquire lawful permanent residence or who may be in a twilight status still falls well short of the total US unauthorized population of over 11 million. For the majority of unauthorized migrants, unlawful presence is also inconclusive in a third, more fundamental way that affects the entire unauthorized population and gets closer to the essence of the immigration law system as a whole.

The practical reality of immigration law enforcement is that the federal government tries to remove only a small fraction of the unauthorized migrants in the United States. The statement by the *Plyler* Court in 1982 that "there is no assurance that a child subject to deportation will ever be deported" is just as true today. The arrest and deportation of any particular unauthorized adult or child has been predictably improbable for at least a century. The reason has been that the administrative capacity and political will to apprehend and remove immigration law violators have been limited. The letter of the law creates a large removable population, but whether an individual is actually targeted for removal has long depended on government discretion and bad luck.[20]

To be sure, there are signs that this situation is changing, especially with the infusion of ever more resources into enforcement. I will look closely at these developments, but my focus for now is the long-standing system that has led to the current state of affairs. Even if some consensus were to emerge that future immigration enforcement must be more effective, wise responses to the current unauthorized population of over 11 million must be grounded in a sound understanding of historical patterns, starting with the outsized role of discretion in immigration law.

It is useful to distinguish between two types of discretion in immigration law. Both are exercised outside any statutory provision, so they are unlike the immigration judge discretion specifically authorized as part of the cancellation of removal statute. Instead, both types of discretion come from the inherent authority of any federal agency to make a broad range of choices about how it administers and enforces any body of law.

One type might be called *macro* discretion, which agencies and officials exercise when they set enforcement priorities, such as border enforcement or anti-terrorism efforts, and support them with funds and other resources. The available statistics are rough, but they make clear that an unauthorized migrant's chances of arrest have historically been very low, even quite recently. In 2009, the Border Patrol and the Bureau of Immigration and Customs Enforcement (ICE) arrested only about 600,000, or under 6 percent of the estimated unauthorized population of 11.2 million.[21] I cite arrest figures for 2009 because that was the last full federal fiscal year before a new federal enforcement initiative called Secure Communities allowed routine state and local arrests to bring unauthorized migrants to the attention of federal enforcement agencies. This shift represents the start of a major increase in enforcement activity, but my immediate concern is historical enforcement patterns and practices.

Other federal agencies such as US Citizenship and Immigration Services (USCIS) can initiate removal proceedings against unauthorized migrants. In this respect, the 600,000 arrests in 2009 by the Border Patrol and ICE are an undercount that omits some enforcement activity against unauthorized migrants. On the other hand, the Border Patrol makes most of its arrests at or near the border, so the 600,000 number exaggerates the chances of a federal arrest *inside* the United States. Overall, vast macro discretion that results in incomplete enforcement has been an important aspect of immigration law in the United States, at least until late in the first decade of the 2000s.

Another type of discretion might be called *micro* discretion—whether or not to pursue the removal of someone after she has been individually identified as unlawfully present or otherwise removable. If the federal government opts for removal, it typically starts a civil removal proceeding. It might also press criminal charges based on the immigration violation.[22] Or federal officials might exercise discretion to not seek removal. The term "prosecutorial discretion" usually refers to this type of micro discretion.

PROSECUTORIAL DISCRETION OF this individualized sort has long been commonplace in immigration enforcement, but it first became highly visible in a case involving the Beatle, John Lennon. In 1971, Lennon was admitted to the United States as a visitor while he and his wife, Yoko Ono, tried to assume custody of Ono's daughter from a prior marriage. But the father had taken the daughter into hiding, and they could not be found. While Lennon and Ono searched for the child, Lennon overstayed his admission and thus became deportable. The Immigration and Naturalization Service (INS) placed him in deportation proceedings and denied his request for nonpriority status, a form of prosecutorial discretion. Lennon's lawyer, Leon Wildes, succeeded through a Freedom of Information Act request in discovering the reason for denial, which apparently was his British conviction for marijuana possession. Lennon was later granted permanent resident status in the United States as a noncitizen involved in a profession or the arts, but his efforts to see his INS files opened up public access to the nonpriority status guidelines.[23]

Two decades later, during the Clinton administration in the 1990s, the INS started to issue public memos outlining the factors that would govern prosecutorial discretion. A milestone was 1996, when amendments to the Immigration and Nationality Act narrowed the availability of cancellation of removal and similar forms of relief in the federal immigration statute. Previously, a much larger group of unauthorized migrants and lawfully present noncitizens who had become deportable could ask an immigration judge for discretionary relief, for example under the precursor to cancellation of removal. But under new, much tighter eligibility rules, many could no longer apply to immigration judges for such relief and instead had to ask the INS for a more informal exercise of prosecutorial discretion.[24]

Congress dissolved the INS in 2003 and reorganized the federal agencies responsible for immigration, absorbing INS functions into various parts of the new Department of Homeland Security (DHS). Since then, the Bureau of Immigration and Customs Enforcement (ICE) has been the DHS agency charged with immigration enforcement inside the United States, including removals. In June 2010, John Morton, the director of ICE, issued a public memo estimating the practical capacity of the federal government at 400,000 removals per year—under 4 percent of the unauthorized population. Citing this number, Morton explained the need to exercise prosecutorial discretion in light of enforcement priorities and listed factors to guide federal officials in deciding to seek or not to seek a particular noncitizen's removal. Criminal convictions, for example, would make noncitizens a priority for removal. In contrast, low priorities for removal included US military veterans, pregnant and nursing women, and victims of domestic violence, trafficking, or other serious crimes.[25]

DHS later issued several more memos to guide prosecutorial discretion. It sometimes designates a noncitizen's case as a low priority for removal or closes the noncitizen's immigration case file, but nevertheless leaves her in practical limbo in the United States without permission to work. In other cases, DHS acts more formally by granting "deferred action" status. This means that although a noncitizen is unlawfully present, the government will not seek her removal and thus will allow her to stay as a practical matter, with eligibility for work permission based on economic necessity. However, deferred action is usually granted only for limited periods of time and does not provide a path to lawful permanent resident status or citizenship.[26]

Several Obama administration programs granted deferred action on an individualized basis to persons who meet certain criteria. Starting in June 2009, DHS granted deferred action to noncitizen widows and widowers of US citizens living in the United States, as well as to the widows' and widowers' unmarried children under 21 years of age. At that time, the federal statute required two years of marriage before it would make them eligible to become permanent residents. This deferred action policy was intended to let these noncitizens live and work in the United States while Congress considered legislation, ultimately enacted, that conferred permanent resident status without a minimum period of marriage.[27]

In June 2012, President Obama announced DHS guidelines for two-year grants of deferred action for individuals without lawful status who had been brought to the United States as children. Under this program—Deferred Action for Childhood Arrivals (DACA)—applicants had to be under the age of 31 in June 2012 and in the United States for the previous five years. They must have arrived before turning 16 and have no disqualifying criminal convictions. DACA shows yet again that limited federal enforcement capacity and the need for prosecutorial discretion can allow unauthorized migrants to acquire formal permission to stay and work in the United States. Permanent residence and citizenship may follow only if the noncitizen qualifies on some other basis.[28]

PLYLER ACKNOWLEDGED THAT unlawful presence was inconclusive in another way when it observed that Congress might adopt a legalization or amnesty program. This aspect of unlawful presence can be considered an example of changing immigration law status, or of discretion exercised on a very broad scale. Either way, legalization is exactly what Congress approved as part of the Immigration Reform and Control Act (IRCA) of 1986. Four years after the Supreme Court's decision in *Plyler*, IRCA offered permanent residence to noncitizens who had been in the United States unlawfully since January 1, 1982. They also had to show knowledge of English and civics, and have a clean criminal record. IRCA also included a legalization program with less demanding requirements for unauthorized agricultural workers. If they had worked at least 90 days in seasonal agriculture between May 1985 and May 1986, they could become permanent residents by working three more years in the fields.[29]

About 1.6 million unauthorized migrants became permanent residents through IRCA's general legalization program, plus another 1.1 million through the agricultural program. When IRCA became law, the estimated unauthorized population of the United States was about 3.2 million. Many were ineligible because they had arrived in the United States after January 1, 1982, but if they had close relatives who did qualify, they were allowed to stay and work in a type of twilight status. Many later became permanent residents by qualifying in the standard family admission categories.[30]

The *Plyler* Court's recognition that Congress might enact legalization was borne out not only by IRCA, but also by the life stories of the children who were the plaintiffs in *Plyler*. In the 1990s, a *Los Angeles Times* reporter traced 13 of them. All had become lawful permanent residents of the United States. Ten finished high school in Tyler, Texas, and many went to college, though none graduated from a four-year institution. In 2007, another journalist interviewed three of the plaintiff children and found that two had become US citizens.[31] Though these are individual stories, they are typical of the opportunities that IRCA and other features of immigration law made possible.

Congress has not enacted broad-scale legalization since IRCA, but as Chapter 6 will explore, other pieces of federal legislation have conferred lawful immigration status on smaller groups of unauthorized migrants.[32] Since the year 2000, several broad-scale legalization proposals on the congressional agenda seemed to come close to congressional approval, though all fell short of enactment.

IN SUM, UNLAWFUL presence under current US immigration law is inconclusive in related but distinct ways. Immigration status can change, even if it is clear. Or status may be in a gray area between lawful and unlawful. And a great many noncitizens whose presence clearly violates immigration law have historically not been apprehended and deported. Moreover, Congress adopted a broad-scale legalization or amnesty program in 1986 and has seriously considered similar proposals.

A skeptical reader might view these possibilities as loopholes and unauthorized migrants as lawbreakers, even if deportation is improbable, and even if some of them may acquire lawful status some day.[33] From this perspective, nothing about the changeability, ambiguity, or uncertain consequences of unlawful presence should keep the government from insisting on broader compliance with the law to correct past enforcement failures. To test whether this view is justified, it is essential to ask more closely what it means in a moral or social sense to violate immigration law. The answer depends on a further question: Do the changeability, ambiguity, and uncertain consequences of unlawful presence reflect a failure to implement and enforce immigration policy, or are they a consequence of immigration policy that makes unlawful presence inconclusive by design? The answers to this question emerge from the history of unauthorized migration to the United States.

We Asked for Workers

History shows that the US economy has long had a nearly insatiable desire for a flexible, pliable, and inexpensive labor force supplied by immigration, including unauthorized migrants. As I will explain, early immigration patterns and the growth of the American nation created a persistent demand for workers that was satisfied with immigrants from Asia in the late 1800s, and then from Mexico starting in the early 1900s.

From these beginnings, the immigration system that became entrenched in the 1960s was marked by selective admissions combined with selective underenforcement. This history is a tale of labor, race, and discretion, and of policies that led to a large unauthorized population. And since the late 1960s, what has mattered has not been the line between the legal and the illegal, but rather the exercise of enforcement discretion. It can often turn harsh, but it can also be lenient. This history shows that the changeability, ambiguity, and uncertain consequences of unlawful presence are essential features of US immigration law. The corollaries to these aspects of unlawful presence are unpredictability and inconsistency in immigration enforcement that undermine the rule of law.

The origins of this immigration system go back to the early 1800s. In an ebb and flow that continued through the entire nineteenth century, the dominant attitudes in the making of US policy favored a sustained flow of migrants from northern and western Europe. The reasons were largely economic. The expansion of railroads made it possible to reach and settle previously inaccessible lands, where immigrant labor was badly needed: first to farm the new land, then to mine it, and later to work the factories and mills as industrialization spread.

By the mid-nineteenth century, American public opinion began to harden as new and different groups of immigrants came to the United States. Until about 1830, most newcomers had been Protestants from Great Britain or elsewhere in western Europe, but over the next two decades, immigrants started to come from a broader array of lands. Most prominent among the new source countries were Ireland and Germany. For the first time, sizeable groups of Catholic immigrants came to America.[34]

The sheer number of immigrants also grew dramatically, reflecting rapid population growth in Europe as well as major upheavals that included the revolutions of 1848 and the Great Irish Famine of 1845–1849. The tendency of immigrants to cluster in a few American cities made them more conspicuous. From the 1860 census through the 1920 census, around 13 percent of the total US population was foreign-born. In contrast, more than 40 percent of the population in New York, Chicago, San Francisco, and six other cities was foreign-born in 1870.[35]

Popular reaction against the new immigrants soon fueled organized nativism, centered around the American Party, also called the Know-Nothings because its members were sworn to secrecy. But business interests generally favored unrestricted immigration to maintain a continuous source of cheap labor, and the nativism of the 1850s receded with the Civil War. The practical urgencies of war drew a diverse array of newcomers into common cause, especially on the Union side of the conflict, leading to greater immigrant integration and acceptance. Almost a quarter of Union soldiers were foreign-born, including large numbers of Irish and German immigrants who had encountered a skeptical or hostile reception just a few years earlier.[36]

THE EVOLVING RECEPTION of European immigrants was just one part of the story of immigration to the United States in the nineteenth century. During the same period, and more directly relevant to unauthorized migration today, the nation expanded westward across the continent. As settlers pushed the national frontier west to the Pacific, one prevailing vision was immigration as settlement, with enlightened Europeans fulfilling their destiny by civilizing the land enough to make it worthy of statehood. Even after nativism declined as an organized political force that resisted waves of unfamiliar Europeans, it lived on as an ideology of conquest and settlement of new territory in the American West.[37]

In 1821, Mexico granted land to Texas pioneer Stephen Austin in what was then the Mexican state of Coahuila y Tejas, and American settlers followed. Even earlier, tensions had emerged between the newcomers from the north and the Spanish-speaking and native populations that were already there. In 1829, the Mexican government abolished slavery, a move directed against US citizens in this territory, now called Texas. Mexico also announced the end of legal immigration into the territory, repealed the property tax exemption for immigrants, and increased duties on US goods. But the American influx continued, and by 1834 an estimated 30,000 US citizens lived in Texas, compared to 7,800 citizens of Mexico.[38]

General Antonio López de Santa Anna then suspended the Mexican Constitution in 1835, limiting the rights that Texans enjoyed inside Mexico. In March 1836, Texas declared its independence from Mexico, continuing what historian Amy Greenberg called a state of intermittent warfare between Texas and Mexico. The annexation of Texas by the United States, once considered a remote possibility, occurred in February 1845, and the Mexican-American War followed. On February 2, 1848, the Treaty of Guadalupe-Hidalgo between Mexico and the United States officially ended the conflict. For a sum of $15 million paid by the United States, Mexico ceded over half of its pre-war territory. This land became the states of California, Nevada, Texas, Utah, and parts of Arizona, Colorado, Kansas, New Mexico, and Oklahoma. The treaty turned the estimated 100,000 Mexican Americans who lived in the vast ceded area into strangers in their own land. Almost all of them later automatically acquired federal citizenship in the United States, though not the state citizenship that was the main source of political rights at the time. Only about 5,000 left the region or exercised their right to stay while retaining Mexican citizenship.[39]

The aftermath of the Treaty of Guadalupe-Hidalgo saw the gradual loss of the economic, social, and political position that Mexicans had enjoyed in these lands before 1848. In California, the Spanish-speaking settler families—known as the Californios—who traced their ancestry back to Spain or Mexico had dominated political and economic life up to the mid-1800s, but they lost their influence in just one generation's time. More generally, the treaty brought into the United States large populations whose race and ethnicity left them outside prevailing concepts of what it meant to be American. In these southwestern borderlands, vanquished Mexicans and Indians were cast as inferiors, even though the expansion of the frontier gave the formal status of US citizenship to many of the Mexicans who lived there.[40]

The legacy of conquest would be even more profound for noncitizens who found themselves on the Mexican side of the new border, because as noncitizens of the United States they were even more susceptible in the decades that followed to the discretionary management of immigrant labor by employers and the US government. Even if the territorial expansion of the United States and the treatment of Mexican workers were distinct phenomena, they were related. Vanquishing Mexico made it easier for the United States later to treat Mexican migrants from south of the new border with less respect than would have emerged from a stable Mexico-US relationship as independent neighboring countries of equal stature.

THE ORIGINS OF the current unauthorized population of the United States also lie in the fact that questions of belonging and exclusion well into the twentieth century did not necessarily depend on the tight control of a physical border. Though it served as the symbol of national aspirations in an era of expansion and conquest, the boundary often defied precise demarcation, let alone enforcement in the modern sense of immigration control. More important was defining who was a citizen settler and who was not. In turn, citizenship depended heavily on race, as it had from the earliest years of American history.[41]

The first naturalization statute, enacted in 1790, allowed only "free white persons" to become US citizens. Though prevailing understandings of race into the early twentieth century cast many new and unfamiliar European immigrants—especially the Irish—as racially different from the dominant Anglo-Saxon stock of the US population, they were considered white for this purpose. And linking race and citizenship even more fundamentally, the American Civil War was fought over the power of the states to decide if African Americans could be citizens or property.[42]

The example of slavery makes painfully clear that labor and race were closely intertwined. And as the country continued to push west, an essential part of settler society was a hierarchy of work and workers. Many European immigrants found their place in the expanding nation as independent yeoman farmers and entrepreneurs, or as workers in factories. Their treatment under a variety of US laws reflected the assumption that they would become Americans. Even before becoming citizens, European immigrants were allowed to homestead, and in many states and territories to vote. They only had to file a declaration of intent to naturalize—an opportunity limited to white immigrants as the only ones eligible to naturalize. Though newcomers, they were Americans in waiting.[43]

Many states and territories enticed European immigrants with advertisements both overseas and at ports of entry. But much of what had to be done in fields and factories was dirty or degrading manual labor. Who would do the dangerous and backbreaking work to build the transcontinental railroad? The western states' enormous needs for cheap and ample labor led the federal government to negotiate the Burlingame Treaty with China in 1868. It declared the "inherent and inalienable right of man to change his home and allegiance, and also the mutual advantage of free migration and emigration of [American and Chinese] citizens…for purposes of curiosity, of trade or as permanent residents." Chinese immigrants came in great numbers, making up 90 percent of the crews that laid the Central Pacific tracks east from California to Promontory Point, Utah Territory. Leland Stanford, as president of the Central Pacific Railroad, hefted the silver maul that drove home the golden spike on May 10, 1869, but eight Chinese workers laid the last rail.[44]

When the completion of the transcontinental railroad put some 10,000 Chinese laborers out of work, they spread out into new occupations. They drew blame for taking jobs from Americans and depressing wages throughout the West. A deep recession from 1873 to 1878 further fueled anti-Chinese hostility in California and neighboring regions. Calls to limit Chinese immigration grew louder, first in California, and soon pushed Congress toward a national policy of Chinese exclusion.[45]

In 1875, Congress passed the Page Act, sponsored chiefly by California congressman Horace F. Page, from Placerville in the heart of the gold country. It was phrased to keep convicted criminals and prostitutes out of the United States, but Congress intended the law to bar Chinese women, reflecting the widely held view that the majority of Chinese women coming to America were prostitutes or second wives in polygamous marriages. In intent and effect, the Page Act was the first of many Chinese exclusion laws. In 1877, a special joint congressional committee urged that Chinese immigration be curtailed by modifying the Burlingame Treaty. Two years later, Congress approved a law that drastically cut the number of Chinese passengers allowed to arrive by ship, but President Rutherford B. Hayes vetoed it. Some states decided to act on their own, rather than wait for federal action. One provision, in the 1879 California Constitution, allowed incorporated towns and cities to expel Chinese.[46]

In the 1880 presidential election, both Democratic and Republican party platforms called for restrictions on Chinese immigration. That year, a new treaty with China allowed the United States to "regulate, limit or suspend" the immigration of Chinese laborers. In 1882, Congress adopted a 10-year ban, based on a congressional declaration that "the coming of Chinese laborers to this country endangers the good order of certain localities." With President Chester A. Arthur's signature, this became the 1882 Chinese Exclusion Act. Congress renewed it several times over the next two decades and then extended it indefinitely in 1904. Chinese exclusion was the law of the land until 1943.[47]

LIKE MANY ANTI-IMMIGRANT movements in US history, Chinese exclusion was born of hostility driven by an economic recession and by the fear that strange and unassimilable newcomers would not only flood the labor market but also undermine American society more generally. But as the national economy rebounded near the end of the nineteenth century, it needed workers. Chinese exclusion forced employers to find cheap labor elsewhere, but where? The next answer—and the next milestone on the road to over 11 million unauthorized migrants today—was Japan.

Until the 1880s, the Japanese government severely limited emigration, but starting in 1884 it allowed laborers to go to the Hawaiian Islands to work on sugar plantations. The next year, Japan let emigrants go directly to the continental United States. In the 1890s, total Japanese immigration to the United States was ten times what it had been in the previous decade. And when the United States annexed the Territory of Hawaii in 1898, the many Japanese there gained lawful access to the US mainland.[48]

As the number of Japanese immigrants grew, so did hostility toward them. In 1905, the San Francisco School Board required Japanese immigrant children to attend a segregated school that it operated in Chinatown for Chinese children. The Japanese government protested with the argument, among others, that the local requirement violated a treaty between the United States and Japan. Recognizing Japan's growing stature on the world stage, President Theodore Roosevelt's administration sued to block the school board's order, but then it pressured the Japanese government to curtail emigration. In 1907, a presidential order barred Japanese and Korean immigration from Hawaii to the US mainland. Later that year, the two governments adopted the so-called Gentlemen's Agreement, which called for the Japanese government to limit emigration by no longer issuing passports that would allow Japanese laborers to travel to the US mainland. In return, the US government allowed new Japanese immigrants to join their parents, spouses, or children already in the United States. Many of these immigrants were picture brides—so called because their husbands relied on photographs to choose them from across the ocean.[49]

THESE RESTRICTIONS ON Chinese and Japanese immigration might have opened the door for labor migration from elsewhere in Asia, but new federal legislation in 1917 imposed further limits on Asian immigration. Except for the Philippines and other US possessions, immigration was forbidden from a so-called Asiatic barred zone that swept eastward from Saudi Arabia to Southeast Asia, and north from Sri Lanka, India, and Indonesia up through Afghanistan and what would soon become the Soviet Union. The

1917 law also barred immigrants who traced their ancestry to these countries. The barred zone did not include Japan, but only because the Gentlemen's Agreement made outright exclusion seem unnecessary.

Then, in 1921, Congress passed the first of several laws that limited immigration in ways that were expressly intended to preserve the ethnic composition of the United States. The 1921 law capped immigration from regions other than Asia and the Western Hemisphere at 3 percent of "the number of foreign-born persons of such nationality" residing in the United States as of 1910. Because most immigrants from southern and eastern Europe had arrived after 1910, this scheme drastically reduced the numbers of migrants from those regions. The 1921 law was intended as a temporary measure, but Congress soon replaced it in 1924 with like-minded legislation, the National Origins Act.[50]

These laws, adopting what became known as the national origins system, were the first comprehensive federal statutes regulating the number of immigrants admitted to the United States. Prior federal laws had excluded various undesirable groups without imposing numerical limits. The formula for capping immigration from each country changed in 1924 and again in 1929, but the system kept immigration to the United States almost entirely white and largely western and northern European for over 40 years, from 1921 to 1965.

The national origins system made Asian exclusion nearly complete. The 1917 Act had already cut off immigration from independent nations in Asia except Japan. The 1924 National Origins Act ended what little Japanese immigration survived the 1907 Gentlemen's Agreement. The National Origins Act also barred the Asian spouses and children of US citizens and admitted only the white inhabitants of countries in Asia. After 1924, only the Philippines, a US possession since the Spanish-American War of 1898, sent large numbers to the United States. Filipino workers could travel freely to the United States as noncitizen US nationals—a status between citizen and alien—making them the most significant Asian labor source. Immigration from the Philippines increased rapidly, from about 27,000 in 1920 to 108,000 in 1930, but Congress intervened with the Tydings-McDuffie Act in 1934. This law provided for Philippine independence in 1946, but it applied the national origins system immediately to the Philippines as if it were already a foreign country, subject to a limit of 50 immigrant visas per year.[51]

Six Hundred Miles to That Mexico Border

So far, the saga that leads to over 11 million unauthorized migrants in the United States has been a story of the shrinking supply of Asian immigrant workers. It is also a story of the persistent tension between the economy's thirst for workers and some Americans' fears that too many of the wrong kind of newcomers would arrive. With a growing US economy in the early twentieth century, the question was unavoidable: Where would factories and fields find cheap labor? The answer was plain: with each new restriction on Asian immigration, the demand for Mexican workers intensified.[52]

Mexican labor migration to the United States began in earnest with the emergence of large-scale agriculture in the American Southwest in the early 1900s. In a period when the Gentlemen's Agreement of 1907 and federal legislation in 1917 and 1924 radically restricted Asian immigration, irrigation opened up vast croplands, and the invention of the refrigerated boxcar made distant markets reachable. These factories in the fields needed armies of workers to plant, tend, harvest, and load the crops.[53]

The first decade of the twentieth century was a period of great dislocation in Mexico. A depressed economy and the Mexican Revolution of 1910 spurred northward emigration. Meanwhile, the US government did little to control its land borders. Immigration enforcement focused on coastal ports of entry like New York, with inspection stations at Castle Garden and later on Ellis Island, and on Angel Island in San Francisco Bay. In 1906, only 75 immigration inspectors on horseback patrolled the 1,900-mile border with Mexico. Their core mission was not to stop Mexicans, but to keep Chinese from evading the Chinese exclusion laws by traveling through Mexico to reach the United States.[54]

The southern boundary remained porous, even after the Border Patrol was established in 1924.[55] Lack of enforcement was consistent with the substance of immigration law at that time. In contrast to strict limits on Asian immigrants, US law did not limit the number of Mexicans entering the United States. In the debates that led to the 1924 National Origins Act, some legislators pressed for a numerical cap on Western Hemisphere immigration, but their efforts failed. Instead, federal immigration statutes restricted entry from Mexico primarily by requiring proof of financial means. But at the behest of Southwestern growers, ranchers, mining companies, and railroads, some of these requirements were not applied to Mexicans, were applied to them selectively, or were phased in only gradually.[56]

Immigration law framed Mexican labor migration to the United States during this period, but the story has two other essential parts—race and discretion. Racial perceptions cast Mexicans as a subordinate labor force. This was the role imposed earlier on Chinese and other Asian workers, but geography led to different attitudes toward Mexican workers. They were expected to work when they were needed, but when they were not, they could be sent home more easily than Asian workers. In contrast to formal exclusion of Asian immigrants by law, Mexican workers could be managed with flexible or informal forms of immigration control. In 1911, the 42-volume final report of the Dillingham Commission, established by Congress in 1907 to "make full inquiry, examination, and investigation... into the subject of immigration," observed:

> Because of their strong attachment to their native land... and the possibility of their residence here being discontinued, few become citizens of the United States. The Mexican migrants are providing a fairly adequate supply of labor.... While they are not easily assimilated, this is of no very great importance as long as most of them return to their native land. In the case of the Mexican, he is less desirable as a citizen than as a laborer.[57]

Recruitment of Mexican workers both within and outside the law became commonplace. Southwestern farmers began to rely heavily on Mexican laborers, but as more came, they spread throughout the United States, helping to meet the needs of employers far from the border and in a variety of industries.[58]

To understand this formative period in the history of unauthorized migration, it is crucial to appreciate that the lines between various categories of lawful admissions and between legal and illegal immigration had not acquired the meaning that they sometimes carry in today's immigration debates. When "permanent resident" entered the legal vocabulary in the 1920s as a synonym for immigrant, the immigration statutes reflected a pervasive, entrenched view that European immigrants were Americans in waiting, and other newcomers were not. And regardless of whether immigrants from Asia or Latin America had formal permanent resident status, what mattered more was what they were expected to do in the United States. No matter if they came as permanent residents or as temporary workers, or came outside the law, the more basic fact was that they were needed as workers.

An emerging pattern brought Mexicans as migrant workers or commuters, though many eventually stayed indefinitely. Many employers preferred temporary workers over Mexican Americans who had become lawful permanent residents or US citizens. A temporary worker's permission to be in the United States depended on his job, and this dependence on an employer kept them more subservient while working for low wages in harsh conditions. The most prominent lawful path for workers was the Bracero program, which operated from 1942 until it formally ended in 1964 and finally was phased out in 1967. The program institutionalized the expectation that the vast majority of Mexicans who came to the United States did so temporarily to work.[59]

Equally essential to understanding this formative period's legacy is that crossing the border to work largely disregarded the line between the lawful and unlawful. Many employers of that era—like many today—also understood that unauthorized workers were easier to control and exploit than lawful temporary workers or permanent residents.[60] Many Mexicans came without papers and readily found work in the United States. A vast border and minimal available resources limited what the US government could do to control crossings, but it could choose to tolerate unauthorized migration or sometimes move vigorously to control it, depending on what economic conditions and politics dictated. Enforcement was highly discretionary, and its intensity ebbed and flowed. Many of today's debates over unauthorized migration have their roots in the perceptions formed in this era among employers, and among migrant workers and their families.

IN JANUARY 1948, an airplane—a Douglas DC-3 known as a Skytrain—caught fire over Los Gatos Canyon, in western Fresno County, California. It was headed for the Imperial County Airport and then to the INS Deportation Center in El Centro, California. But it crashed, killing all 32 people on board. Iconic folksinger Woody Guthrie was outraged that news accounts named the pilot, copilot, stewardess (who was the pilot's wife), and federal government guard, but referred to the other passengers as "twenty-eight Mexican deportees." In protest, Guthrie penned a poem about the tragedy, giving the deportees symbolic names. The chorus begins, "Good-bye to my Juan, good-bye Rosalita, adios mis amigos, Jesus y Maria...." A schoolteacher, Martin Hoffman, later set the poem to music, and Pete Seeger popularized it as the song *Deportee (Plane Wreck at Los Gatos).*[61]

As Guthrie's lyrics tell their story, some of the deportees on that plane were in the United States illegally, while others had worked legally until their work contracts ran out.[62] The distinction may not have mattered much for work in the fields. In practical terms, Braceros were as firmly in the grip of employers and the government's deportation power as workers who came outside the law. But that power was a matter of discretion.

Historian Kelly Hernández has shown how decisions to arrest and deport suspected unauthorized migrants on the US-Mexico border from the 1920s until modern times depended primarily on decisions by local Border Patrol officials and individual officers on the line. Officers operated with considerable independence, able to decide day-to-day when to enforce immigration laws—or when not to. In periods of vigorous enforcement, the targets were not only Mexicans, but also US citizens of Mexican ancestry, most infamously during the Great Depression of the 1930s. Federal immigration officials and local police went door to door in predominantly Mexican and Mexican-American neighborhoods in Southern California, asking residents for proof of lawful immigration status, arresting those who failed to show any, with deportation often the ultimate outcome. When the State of California offered a formal apology in 2005, the legislative history estimated that about two million people, including over one million US citizens of Mexican ancestry, had been forced to leave the United States as a result of these raids.[63]

Part of the explanation for today's unauthorized population of over 11 million is that US immigration policy has treated some groups—Asian immigrants in the late nineteenth century, then Mexicans in the twentieth—as workers, not as Americans in waiting. Of course, these groups differed, as did their treatment under immigration law. Asian immigrants were potential settlers who had to be excluded when they were not wanted. Mexican immigrants were expected to come to work and to go home of their own accord when the work was done. A related major difference was that as Mexican workers took over for Asian workers, the law came to matter less. Some Mexicans workers came legally, and others did not. Though formal legal barriers to immigration and citizenship defined Asian exclusion, the hallmark of US policy toward unauthorized migration from Mexico became discretion that fluctuated from acquiescence to raids, arrests, and other visible and harsh enforcement.

Today, about 70 percent of unauthorized migrants in the United States are Mexican. Even if significant numbers of unauthorized migrants come from other regions of the world, the dominant image is one of unauthorized migrants from Mexico or elsewhere in Latin America. This image strongly influences public perceptions and de facto US policies toward unauthorized migration by signaling what unauthorized migration means in numbers, types of immigrants, and possible countermeasures. In this way, the story of the US-Mexico borderlands broadened into a national story of an immigration system marked more by discretion than by uniformity, consistency, or predictability.[64]

Selective Admissions

Selective enforcement of immigration law against a large unauthorized population is now a core feature of current US immigration policy. Discretion exercised by government agencies, especially in the federal executive branch, matters far more than the letter of the law.[65] But this would not be true with a more open system of admissions. It is the highly selective nature of the modern immigration system that helps to create a large unauthorized population, which in turn has made discretion in enforcement inevitable.

Unauthorized migration often prompts this skeptical question: Why not just get in line and come legally, like my grandparents did? The answer is that many would-be immigrants are not allowed to come legally. There is no line for them. This contrasts sharply with previous eras, when immigration was less restricted. Or, to be more precise, it was less restricted for European immigrants who came to America before 1965, when US immigration law favored them explicitly and flatly barred other immigrants by race and nationality. As one study of unauthorized migration quipped: "Saying, 'Let them get in line' is like saying, 'Let them eat cake.'"[66]

For immigration from Mexico to the United States, the current mix of lawful and unauthorized migration began to evolve in the 1960s, with drastic changes to the legal framework that had shaped Mexican migration up to that time. The Bracero program had operated for a generation as the major legal path for Mexican temporary workers, with about 500,000 coming and going each year. The program ended in 1964, largely because of conspicuous employer exploitation and abuse of the migrant workers that seemed intolerable in a political climate that would soon produce significant domestic civil rights legislation. Since the end of the Bracero program, the US government has gradually revived and expanded various admission schemes for temporary workers, but without the same scale or reach, and without a focus on workers from Mexico or any other specific countries.[67]

As for immigrant admissions, the McCarran-Walter Act of 1952 reorganized federal immigration laws into the Immigration and Nationality Act, which retained the national origins system from the 1920s. Though President Harry Truman vetoed the bill, Congress voted to override, and the discriminatory limits remained in effect. But as legal historian Mary Dudziak later documented, the Cold War intensified the pressure to shed the nation's history of racial discrimination, and the 1960s brought renewed calls to abandon criteria that explicitly discriminated by nationality.[68]

In 1960, John F. Kennedy was elected the first Catholic president of the United States. Some congressional power brokers—among them Peter Rodino and Dan Rostenkowski—belonged to nationality groups that had suffered under the national origins system. After President Kennedy was assassinated, his brother, Senator Ted Kennedy, took up the cause of immigration reform. Major amendments adopted by Congress in 1965 replaced the national origins system with a new scheme that abandoned the effort to preserve the nation's ethnic mix. When President Lyndon Johnson signed the 1965 amendments into law at the base of the Statue of Liberty, he declared that the legislation would "repair a very deep and painful flaw in the fabric of American justice.... The days of unlimited immigration are past. But those who do come will come because of what they are, not because of the land from which they sprung."[69]

The coalitions that won repeal of the national origins system also secured other important civil rights legislation, most prominently the Civil Rights Act of 1964 and the Voting Rights Act of 1965. For Latin America, however, the repeal of the national origins system came at significant cost, by introducing numerical limits. Previously, the national origins system had set a numerical limit for overall immigration from the Eastern Hemisphere. The number of immigrants from the Western Hemisphere was not capped, even if individuals could be barred if they fell within certain exclusion grounds, such as those for immigrants without sufficient financial means.[70]

The 1965 amendments changed this. Some legislators pressed for a cap on immigration from Latin America, expressing concerns that it would otherwise increase dramatically. Reform-minded legislators could not fend off the argument that ending the national origins system, with its discriminatory caps, meant that all countries and regions should be treated equally. Congress decided to limit Western Hemisphere immigration to 120,000 per year starting in 1968. Similar pressures led in 1976 to a new annual limit of 20,000 per year on immigration from any single country. These per-country limits exempted spouses and unmarried minor children of all US citizens and the parents of adult US citizens, but they applied to all other categories, including other relatives and all immigrants in employment categories. Further amendments folded the Western Hemisphere cap into an annual worldwide cap of 270,000 immigrants. Long lines soon formed for populous countries where the desire to go to the United States was strong due to geographical, historical, or economic ties.[71]

THE POST-1965 per-country and overall caps on the number of immigrants only partly explain the growth of the unauthorized population to over 11 million today. Another crucial contributing factor has been that the qualifying categories for admission as a lawful immigrant have been defined narrowly and limited in number.[72] The admissions system forces many qualifying immigrants to wait years or even decades. The system completely shuts out many other immigrants who have neither qualifying family ties nor a high level of formal education. Explaining why this is true requires an overview of the admission system.

The most favored immigrants are the immediate relatives of US citizens. This group consists of spouses and unmarried minor children, as well as parents of citizens who are at least 21 years of age. An unlimited number of immediate relatives can become permanent residents. But the other family-based categories—children and spouses of permanent residents and adult children and siblings of US citizens—face annual limits and long waiting periods. As of February 2014, unmarried adult children of US citizens could immigrate only if they applied before January 2007. Siblings of US citizens could immigrate only if they applied before late October 2001.[73]

The annual per-country cap makes the lines longer for many immigrants born in Mexico, the Philippines, India, and China. The longest waits are for Philippine-born brothers and sisters of US citizens, who reached the front of their line in February 2014 only if they applied over 23 years earlier, before August 1990.[74] Federal immigration law makes some close relatives of US citizens and lawful permanent residents eligible for admission, but it then forces many of them to wait for years.

A snapshot shows that over one million new permanent residents were admitted annually in the period from 2005 through 2012. The family categories account for about 700,000, around 65 percent. Roughly 15 percent are refugees who applied for admission from outside the country or for asylum at a port of entry or inside the United States. About 4 percent won an annual lottery open to noncitizens from countries that have sent low numbers of immigrants in recent years. About 1 percent of permanent residents are unauthorized migrants who were granted cancellation of removal or another type of discretionary relief.[75]

As compared to other admission categories, employment-based immigration is more limited. There are only 140,000 slots annually—16 percent of the total—for all employment categories workers and their families combined. At least as striking is the almost complete exclusion of workers without four-year college degrees—even if the workers are skilled or soon acquire skills, and are sought by US employers. All but 10,000 of these employment-based immigrant visas require at least the equivalent of a four-year US college degree, and these applicants face very long lines. The employment categories with shorter lines require more education or experience. As in the family categories, the per-country limits force immigrants from Mexico, China, India, and the Philippines to wait longer than equally qualified individuals from other countries.[76]

The current scheme admits temporary workers, most of whom would not qualify for the employment categories for immigrants. A rough average of about 165,000 workers were admitted annually from 2008 to 2012 in the H-2A category for agricultural work. Annual admissions in the H-2B category for nonagricultural temporary workers averaged around 78,000 in the same period. But the use of these programs remains limited, largely because various procedures, requirements, and a cap on H-2B admissions curb their appeal for employers. These programs are also unattractive for workers, tying them like indentured servants to one employer and exposing them to exploitation in wages and working conditions. All in all, current programs do little to satisfy the economy's apparent need for workers. The number of lawful temporary workers is tiny compared to an unauthorized US workforce estimated at 8 million as of March 2010.[77]

THE END OF the Bracero program in 1964 blocked the broadest lawful official employer access to cheap, flexible, temporary labor from Latin America. Soon afterward, three new features of the admission scheme—the new Western Hemisphere cap, per-country limits, and restrictive employment-based immigration categories—combined to make it very hard for workers from Mexico to come as permanent residents.[78]

But it would have been naïve to expect the number of Mexican migrants to drop. Migration continued, even after US immigration law made it harder. As sociologists Douglas Massey, Luin Goldring, and Jorge Durand have shown, migration networks and patterns are self-perpetuating and durable once they are established. Migration transforms sending and receiving communities in ways that sustain more migration, largely oblivious to what the law may or may not allow. Over generations, migration patterns, both lawful and unlawful, came to be normalized as the expectations of sending communities, US employers, and the migrants themselves.[79]

Even after the Bracero program ended and new restrictions were in place, migrants were able to come illegally with relative ease. A migration industry emerged to help them cross the border and reach locations in the US interior for work and housing. Employers continued to depend on a steady supply of inexpensive labor. Stagnation in the Mexican economy made northward emigration attractive to many Mexicans, no matter what US immigration law said. The Mexican government's policy of developing its northern border cities as part of its Border Industrialization Program drew workers up from other regions of Mexico, and many kept going to the United States.[80] Around the same time, Central America was destabilized by coups, civil wars, and other political upheavals in El Salvador, Honduras, Guatemala, and Nicaragua, accompanied by economic instability—all powerful forces that pushed people to emigrate. With admissions highly restricted but economic conditions at home deteriorating and US employers willing to hire, it is no wonder that many migrants came from Mexico and Central America to the United States outside the law.

Selective Enforcement

A combination of historical migration patterns, strong transnational networks, and robust demand for foreign workers has sustained patterns of immigration to the United States, much of it unauthorized, and all in spite of restrictions on lawful immigration. With the unauthorized population far exceeding federal enforcement capacity, enforcement must also be selective, both in the interior and at the border.

To be sure, enforcement is better funded than it was in the early 1990s. Congress has directed more resources to the US-Mexico border. Removals of unauthorized migrants consistently increased during the Obama administration, largely by enlisting state and local law enforcement to assist in identifying and detaining unauthorized migrants. This emphasis on enforcement is open to a range of reasonable interpretations.[81]

One might say that, in spite of everything that increased enforcement has appeared to accomplish, it has not fundamentally changed the reality of unauthorized migration to the United States or the overall tolerance of a sizable unauthorized population within a highly discretionary enforcement regime. Or one might say that repeated infusions of money and other resources into immigration enforcement, combined with changes in immigration law that started with the Illegal Immigration Reform and Immigrant Responsibility Act (IIRIRA)[82] of 1996, represent a fundamental shift. In June 2013, the US Senate approved comprehensive immigration legislation that would have directed massive resources toward enforcement, especially on the US-Mexico border. Such moves suggest a continuing shift away from the traditional tolerance or acquiescence that prevailed over much of the twentieth century.

Accurately assessing the significance of enforcement requires first identifying the aspects of enforcement that suggest a policy of acquiescence or tolerance. This is essential because these features of the traditional immigration system have led to a large population of unauthorized migrants and are the source of their claims and expectations. Whether or not the upsurge in enforcement reflects a fundamental shift away from a discretionary system of highly selective admissions and highly selective enforcement, these claims and expectations need to be assessed by understanding the context in which they arose. Government policies can change, and sometimes they should change, but justice requires dealing fairly with the consequences of prior policies.[83]

A KEY AREA of traditional acquiescence in significant unauthorized migration has been the treatment of employers who hire unauthorized workers. Before the Immigration Reform and Control Act (IRCA) of 1986, 12 states had some sort of ban on the hiring of unauthorized workers, but there was no such federal law. In 1952, Congress made it a felony to harbor an alien unlawfully in the United States. But at the insistence of Southwestern growers and other agricultural interests, Congress added the so-called Texas Proviso, which defined harboring *not* to include employing an unauthorized worker.[84]

IRCA's federal employer sanctions scheme did not broaden the definition of harboring, but it was a major shift, at least on the surface. The federal scheme relies on employers, who face penalties if they fail to meet either of two basic obligations. They must fill out and keep paperwork designed to deter and expose unauthorized employment. And they may not knowingly hire or continue to hire unauthorized workers. Congress debated but rejected criminal penalties for the unauthorized workers themselves, though they may face criminal charges for using a false Social Security number or similar offenses.[85]

Employers comply with differing degrees of diligence and punctiliousness. Even when they do what the employer sanctions statute demands, they need only complete the required forms and check an employee's identity or work authorization document to see if it "reasonably appears to be genuine." Congress declined to require a closer look out of concern that a stricter system will lead employers to discriminate against some workers. In fact, Congress authorized discrimination claims against employers who probe a document's authenticity. Congress also required a US government study of discriminatory effects, which later showed that employer sanctions led employers to discriminate against workers with a "foreign" appearance or accent.[86]

Because employers may not look closely at employees' documents, fake green cards and other documents that are good enough to get work are readily available and are frequently used. This is true in many occupations and industries, but employer sanctions are especially ineffective in informal economies like house cleaning, child care, and landscaping, where wages are often in cash, with little paperwork of any sort. Congress's reluctance to burden employers with paperwork and other requirements also limits the effectiveness of employer sanctions. If employers minimally check documents and fill out forms, the risk of penalty is minimal, but so is the scheme's value in immigration enforcement. Because employer sanctions need to strike a balance between enforcement and other concerns such as cost and discrimination, their effectiveness in stopping unauthorized work is predictably limited.[87]

Instead, immigration law enforcement against unauthorized work depends heavily on direct action by federal agencies. Worksite enforcement by Immigration and Customs Enforcement (ICE) agents who appear without warning to check documents and arrest unauthorized workers has waxed and waned as an aspect of enforcement strategy. Under President George W. Bush, ICE conducted relatively little worksite enforcement until the winter of 2006–2007, when it started to emphasize raids for the remainder of his administration. Arrests typically led to removal proceedings for immigration violators, but the federal government sometimes also brought criminal charges.[88]

The combined use of immigration and criminal law reached its apex in May 2008, when federal agents raided the Agriprocessors meat-packing plant in Postville, Iowa. The raid was harsh, dramatic, and controversial, with about 300 arrestees confined in livestock rings at the National Cattle Congress fairgrounds. The government put unauthorized workers in removal proceedings in immigration court, but it also brought criminal charges against them in federal district court for using false identity documents and Social Security numbers. Instead of relying principally on immigration removal proceedings, the government pressured the unauthorized workers to plead guilty to immigration-related criminal charges and to accept removal as part of criminal sentencing. There were other workplace raids during the final year of the Bush administration, but not with the same large-scale, coordinated criminal and immigration prosecution as in Postville.[89]

After President Obama took office in January 2009, federal workplace enforcement patterns shifted. Rather than emphasizing high-profile worksite raids and sending agents to make arrests, ICE devoted more resources to checking electronic databases for employees' work authorization and sending the results to employers, who predictably responded by firing the workers. The federal government also relied more heavily on E-Verify, the federal employment verification database. E-Verify became mandatory in 2009 for federal contractors and subcontractors, and the federal government has encouraged its expansion in the private sector. But E-Verify is still plagued by significant error rates that pose major practical and political obstacles to replacing the paperwork now required. E-Verify also does nothing to prevent unauthorized employment by someone who assumes the identity of someone who has permission to work. And there is deep resistance to a more regulated labor market with more intrusive monitoring—such as a national identity card—that would burden citizens and noncitizens alike. In fact, much of the opposition to making E-Verify mandatory has come from conservative, libertarian groups.[90]

THE REAL SIGNIFICANCE of these flaws and fluctuations in enforcement against unauthorized work becomes clearer from the big picture. Despite recent upswings in workplace enforcement, the current unauthorized workforce of over 8 million is a significant part of the overall workforce, accounting for about 5 percent of all workers in the United States, and far more in some occupations and industries. Current immigration law makes it very difficult or impossible for employers to sponsor and hire temporary workers or for immigrants with little formal education to come to the United States lawfully. Responding to this mismatch between the immigration law system and their workforce needs, employers have the political and economic clout to inhibit raids, to resist stronger employer sanctions, and to eliminate jobs if they fail to secure a suitable workforce. Congress can enact no more than a system that looks good on paper but is designed to acquiesce in significant levels of noncompliance.

Naturally, enforcement inside the United States intensifies from time to time in response to political pressure, just as is true on the border. The upsurge in interior enforcement—at worksites and in other settings—may target unauthorized migrants viewed as especially undesirable, such as national security threats or noncitizens with criminal convictions, or it might sweep more broadly. But when any priority emerges to focus limited resources, it reduces the intensity of enforcement against the unauthorized population as a whole. Another complication is that immigration enforcement competes with the other missions of federal agencies. The Department of Labor and the Department of Health and Human Services, for example, often deal with unauthorized migrants in ways that put low priority on immigration enforcement or block it altogether.[91]

More generally, enforcement has typically been more vigorous in hard economic times, or whenever the balance of political imperatives favors getting tough on migrant-intruders. The Obama administration has deported more noncitizens than any other administration. Much of this effort has been exerted in the belief that establishing government control over unauthorized migration—especially enforcement credibility through high removal numbers—will win political support for legalization and related measures.[92] If history is any guide, enforcement inside the United States will rise and fall with its value as political currency.

BORDER ENFORCEMENT HAS displayed patterns that resemble interior enforcement, but with some significant differences. In the 1990s, the Clinton administration reshaped enforcement on the US-Mexico border, especially near population centers like San Diego and El Paso. Rather than try to catch border crossers as they walked, ran, or swam from Mexico, the Border Patrol shifted strategy to deter entry with more imposing fences, high-tech surveillance, and many more Border Patrol agents on the line. The number of agents on the southern border more than doubled from about 3,400 in 1993 to about 8,200 in 1999. Congress almost tripled the INS budget from $1.5 billion in 1993 to $4.2 billion in 1999. The trend continued through the decade of the 2000s, with the combined budgets of the INS's successor agencies exceeding $20 billion by the fiscal year 2010. That was also the year that President Obama reached beyond the Department of Homeland Security for federal enforcement resources, ordering National Guard units to the border.[93]

The federal government has also adopted stricter policies toward border crossers who are apprehended. It is a federal misdemeanor crime to enter or attempt to enter the United States other than at an official port of entry. But the federal government has not always systematically filed criminal charges for simple illegal crossings—as opposed to repeated crossings, illegal reentry after deportation, or smuggling others. For simple crossings, the Border Patrol typically sent the offenders back across the border, often without a formal order of removal. Under this policy, sometimes called "catch and release," the migrants could, as Woody Guthrie's lyrics tell, "pay all their money and wade back again."[94]

Starting around 2005, criminal prosecutions to penalize and deter illegal crossings became much more common. In Arizona, New Mexico, and Texas, a federal initiative known as Operation Streamline calls for the criminal prosecution of anyone caught crossing the border illegally. The number of criminal prosecutions for border crossings rose dramatically to account for about half of *all* federal criminal prosecutions as of mid-2013.[95]

A higher, smarter border fence backed by the weight of criminal law seems like a natural response to unauthorized migration. The next logical question is whether intensified border enforcement has reduced the number of clandestine crossings. Some effect seems reasonable to assume, but any actual decrease depends on how much harder the crossing becomes in a given location and what new strategies border crossers adopt. Many now avoid the fortifications between Tijuana and San Ysidro, California, once the scene of nightly crossings by large groups of migrants.[96]

Their journey takes migrants further east to try their luck, where the fences are lower and fewer Border Patrol agents are on watch. This typically means crossing the harshest terrain on the US-Mexico border, trudging for days across the intense Sonoran mountains and desert into Arizona, New Mexico, and Texas. A growing number cross in another way—aboard panga boats that speed to landing spots up the California coastline. The migrants increasingly rely on smugglers—called *coyotes*—whose services have become more indispensable and more costly, not only to cross the border but also to evade checkpoints on the northbound route to destination cities. Over 4,000 travelers have died of heat and thirst, and yet they persist in their journey to jobs, willing to brave burning deserts and suffocating truck trailers.[97]

A related but different question is whether intensified border enforcement reduces the unauthorized population—as opposed to reducing the number of illegal crossings. Border enforcement does nothing about the 25 to 40 percent of unauthorized migrants who were admitted lawfully and then violated the terms of their admission. The unauthorized population also fluctuates depending on how many leave, either permanently or in seasonal or circular patterns. As for unauthorized migrants who cross the border, stricter border enforcement has seemed to increase their number, paradoxically yet predictably. In earlier decades, they might have traveled back and forth, but the increased risk and cost of each crossing means that they stay longer once inside the United States, and that their close family members are more likely to join them.[98]

A more fundamental puzzle is how demographic and economic factors influence the effectiveness of devoting more resources to border enforcement. The unauthorized population of the United States decreased from a little over 12 million in 2009 to over 11 million in 2012. Economic stagnation in the Mexican economy might have been expected to increase the number of Mexicans who sought work in the United States, but the United States also had a substantial unemployment rate. In the same time period, the growth rate of the Mexican population slowed significantly, and new employment and educational opportunities may have kept people in Mexico who might have gone to the United States in earlier periods. In these ways, which tend to elude measurement, the consequences of border enforcement depend not only on its intensity, but on the larger economic and demographic context in which enforcement operates.[99]

Regardless of the actual effectiveness of enforcement resources, voting for fences—like voting for employer sanctions—can be smart pragmatic politics. The idea has become entrenched that robust border enforcement is an essential part of any rational immigration system. But as with employer sanctions, intensified border enforcement runs up against heavy counterweights that diminish real effects. These include the economic imperative to ease border crossings for trade and tourism, the reluctance to impose restrictive monitoring on US citizens, and the sheer cost of border infrastructure and Border Patrol salaries. Fiscal estimates for border fencing vary from $3 million to $21 million per mile. Although border-related spending can be more politically attractive than interior enforcement and makes a powerful symbolic statement that the government takes immigration enforcement seriously, high-tech border fortifications are in place only for a fraction of the 1900 miles from Imperial Beach near San Ysidro, California, to the mouth of the Rio Grande near Brownsville, Texas.[100]

The Meaning of Unlawful Presence

This chapter has explained why saying that a noncitizen is in the United States unlawfully can be a logical start to analysis but should never be its end. Unlawful presence can be inconclusive in several ways. It can change, it can occupy a gray area between lawful and unlawful, and its consequences are highly uncertain. These insights were essential to the US Supreme Court's understanding of unlawful presence in *Plyler v. Doe*. But a more basic truth—crucial to understanding the social and moral significance of unlawful presence—is that unlawful presence is inconclusive by design. A highly restrictive admissions system predictably produces a large unauthorized population, to which the response is selective enforcement, which various government actors administer with broad discretion that can be unpredictable, inconsistent, and sometimes discriminatory. If unauthorized migrants are violating immigration law by their very presence in the United States, they are here within a system that also disregards the rule of law in its own ways.

A crucial question is whether selective, discretionary enforcement in immigration law is unique or instead resembles enforcement in other areas of law. An answer might start with the likelihood that an individual violator will be detected and penalized. The unauthorized population of the United States is over 11 million, and the current enforcement system can remove only 400,000 noncitizens per year, including permanent residents and other lawfully present noncitizens who have become deportable. So an unauthorized migrant's risk of removal is low. And yet, rates of detection and enforcement may be similarly low with regulatory offenses such as traffic and alcohol violations.

Two key features distinguish selective discretion in immigration enforcement from enforcement in other areas of law. First, detection and enforcement lead to a very severe penalty—removal from the United States, often preceded by a period of detention that can be prolonged. This contrasts sharply with the typical penalty for violations with similarly low detection and enforcement rates.[101] Second, the uncertainty that selective discretion creates for unauthorized migrants is an essential part of the system itself.

The best way to analyze why immigration law operates as it does is to consider what it would take to transform it. There are signs that the commitment to immigration enforcement is changing. Since around the year 2009, the deputization of state and local police to identify noncitizens who may be removable from the United States has significantly increased the chances that any given unauthorized migrant will be apprehended, detained, and deported. A bill approved in 2013 by the US Senate (but not the House of Representatives) would have combined a broad-scale legalization program and an expansion of lawful admissions with both a massive infusion of funds into US-Mexico border enforcement and a requirement that all US employers use E-Verify.[102] Yet it remains to be seen whether these developments will move away fundamentally from the discretionary system that prevailed for much of the twentieth century.

Any fundamental change of this sort cannot be durable unless two things both happen, and if that is improbable, then it is fair to consider the current state of affairs to be a system that operates by design. First, the system for admitting new immigrants and temporary workers lawfully needs to expand dramatically. Or, enforcement could intensify to a level that would seriously reduce unauthorized migration. Several factors suggest strongly that the second option is not politically sustainable.

The wages, working conditions, and even the jobs of citizens and lawful permanent residents throughout the US economy can depend on the availability of unauthorized coworkers to fill out an employer's workforce. Domestic economic growth in many sectors depends on the availability of workers to fill informal, temporary, low-wage jobs. This is not just a matter of employer preferences. The demands originate throughout the population of the United States. Consumers want lower prices, which depend on minimizing labor costs, even if they seldom stop to consider what keeps prices low. The result is broad, if controversial, acquiescence in unauthorized migration.[103] Though they are in the United States without lawful permission, they are tolerated as workers at first, though over time they make lives, families, and communities. As the Swiss writer Max Frisch wrote about the northern European experience: "we asked for workers, but people came."[104]

Acquiescence in a flexible unauthorized workforce also reflects deeper rationales. The pragmatic reality is that good workers are essential to the economy but are hard to identify in advance. The US immigration system seems to reflect the temptation—messy and cruel—to let them come and work unlawfully, and then later to grant lawful status to some who can show strong histories of work, integration, and other contributions to US society. In the meantime, they serve what amounts to a probationary period when they are paid less, are laid off more easily, work with fewer protections than US citizens or permanent residents, and suffer other indignities. Compared to pre-selecting the best workers, this sort of screening after some time in the United States may more accurately find the best contributors. It may also be more sensitive to the economy's needs than legislation or other categorical approaches to choosing immigrants in advance.[105]

Unauthorized migration also gives the US government a flexible option for addressing international economic development issues. Unauthorized workers send substantial amounts of money to their home countries. These remittances are an essential part of those economies, especially in developing countries with substantial numbers of expatriates in the United States. Preserving these streams is an essential part of US international economic policy. If immigration enforcement constricts remittances, the US government may need to foster development more directly in migrants' home countries, or to safeguard political stability there by other means. Such initiatives might be inflexible, unfeasible, or less politically attractive than allowing remittances from unauthorized workers to continue.[106]

Similarly, unauthorized migration functions as a safety valve for political and economic pressures in sending countries, including the consequences of US government actions that generate migration to the United States. For example, the North American Free Trade Agreement (NAFTA) transformed the Mexican economy in ways that have disrupted the livelihoods of many small-scale farmers. Prices for some crops have tumbled to levels that make farming unsustainable. Feeling that they have no choice, many of these farmers become migrants. Some go elsewhere in Mexico, while others come to the United States, many of them unlawfully. If immigration enforcement were to become much stricter and cut off the option to leave Mexico for the United States, NAFTA's political consequences for the Mexican government, and in turn for the US government, would be much more serious and hard to contain.[107]

Later chapters will return to the design of a workable immigration system in which enforcement is not only feasible and effective, but which also respects the rule of law by being predictable, consistent, and non-discriminatory. My goal in this chapter has been more limited—to explain how it is a predictable consequence of US immigration policy that 11 million live in the United States without lawful permission, and how these aspects of the past and present immigration system complicate the seemingly simple question of whether someone is present in violation of law. Even if future policies and practices are different from what prevails today, this history is essential in deciding how to treat unauthorized migrants already living and working in this country.

IN *PLYLER V. DOE*, the US Supreme Court refused to let unlawful presence extinguish the rights of children or undermine their future. But the meaning of unlawful presence was just one of the three essential themes in *Plyler*. In assessing the Texas statute, the Court had to decide whether responses to unauthorized migration should come from the federal government, or in some measure from states and localities. This second *Plyler* theme—the role of state and local governments—has assumed great urgency in recent years and is the focus of the next chapter.

What State and Local Role?

IN FEBRUARY 2009, Joe Arpaio—the sheriff of Maricopa County, Arizona, in the greater Phoenix area—announced that he would expand his Tent City jail, known as the "Alcatraz of Arizona." Arpaio built Tent City in 1993, soon after he was first elected to office, using surplus military tents from the federal government. The outdoor jail can hold about 2,500 inmates. No matter how full it gets, a neon "Vacancy" sign posted on the guard tower stays lit, visible for miles. Temperatures in the tents can reach 135 degrees in the Arizona summer. Inmates are required to wear pink underwear and retro-style black-and-white striped prison suits, for what Arpaio seems to see as the humiliation factor. They work in chain gangs to pick up trash and to dig graves at the county cemetery.[1]

In his announcement, Sheriff Arpaio said that he was making room for illegal immigrants, who would be segregated from the rest of the prisoners by an electric fence. Though his Tent City had come under withering criticism from a wide variety of political quarters for degrading, unsanitary, and inhumane conditions, Arpaio defended this expansion as necessary to curb jail overcrowding. He added that it was a "financially responsible alternative to taxpayers already overburdened by the economic drain imposed by a growing number of illegal aliens on social services like education and health care." In a public spectacle, 200 detainees held for immigration violations were shackled and forced to wear prison stripes for the march from the jails where they had been housed to Tent City, where they would ostensibly remain until they could be deported.[2]

Joe's Law, the 2008 book that lists Arpaio as co-author, called him "America's Toughest Sheriff," but his overall law enforcement record has come under serious, consistent fire in recent years. Numerous lawsuits against his office—over 1,800 of them—have cost Maricopa County taxpayers over $50 million, according to one estimate. In 2011, a three-year US Department of Justice investigation concluded that Arpaio had violated the constitutional rights of Latinos by habitually targeting them for discriminatory arrest and detention for immigration violations and other charges. Federal investigators also looked into Arpaio's apparent practice of retaliating against critics. He came under similar but inconclusive scrutiny by the US House Judiciary Committee and a federal grand jury.[3]

After negotiations with Sheriff Arpaio to address the Justice Department's findings went nowhere, the federal government revoked the agreement that had authorized the department to enforce federal immigration law in some situations and then, in May 2012, filed a civil lawsuit against Arpaio and his department. Several individuals sued separately, alleging racial discrimination and unlawful detention in violation of the Fourth Amendment's protection against unreasonable searches and seizures. In May 2013, federal district judge Murray Snow ruled in the private lawsuit that Arpaio and his deputies had engaged in racial discrimination and related wrongdoing.[4]

None of this scrutiny seems to deter Arpaio. If anything, the criticism seems to invigorate him. Arpaio heads only one local law enforcement agency among tens of thousands around the country, but he has broad influence. Maricopa County is one of the most populous counties in the entire United States and home to over 4 million people, over 60 percent of Arizona's total population. Arpaio has become a popular, if highly polarizing, politician among Maricopa County voters, who returned him to office in 2012 for a sixth four-year term.[5]

From this political base, Arpaio's image as a bold crusader against illegal immigration has brought him a national constituency. He is a folk hero among advocates of stronger immigration enforcement, who shower him with praise for his defiance in devoting local law enforcement resources to cracking down on illegal immigrants. For Arpaio and his supporters, making a public example of marching immigration violators in prison stripes sent a powerful warning.[6]

JOE ARPAIO REPRESENTS an attitude toward unauthorized migration that is more popular than some of his adversaries might want to admit. But if Arpaio seems to be an extreme example, he is also part of a long history of state and local responses to immigration. Understanding where he draws his popularity and why his policies find support in locales around the United States is an essential step in understanding the role of state and local governments. This is the second theme at the core of the US Supreme Court's decision in *Plyler* and one of the central topics in immigration debates today.

This chapter presents a conceptual framework that makes sense of the vast array of state and local engagement with immigration and immigrants. This framework is essential for assessing whether such state and local activity is lawful and wise. The most accurate and helpful way to think about the state and local role is to apply several cross-cutting distinctions. In one dimension, state and local activity can fall on a spectrum from what I describe as direct involvement with immigration law to involvement that is more indirect.

At its core, direct involvement in immigration law refers to government decisions to admit noncitizens to the United States or to exclude them, and to deport noncitizens who are in the country or to let them stay. These issues are the focus of federal statutes enacted and occasionally amended by Congress. Federal agencies administer and enforce these statutes, and they create gap-filling policies. In the enforcement setting, direct involvement with immigration law means some type of state and local role in detection, arrest, detention, fines, imprisonment, or removal based on a federal immigration violation. For example, when the Maricopa County Sheriff's Office arrests someone suspected of unlawful presence in the United States, it is directly involved in immigration enforcement. As another example of direct enforcement, in 2010 the State of Arizona enacted a law, SB 1070, that sets out state criminal penalties for some violations of federal immigration law.

State and local involvement in immigration enforcement can also be indirect. Rather than arrest and jail unwanted unauthorized migrants, a state or local government can make life hard for them. State and local laws can make it difficult or impossible for unauthorized migrants to rent housing, find work, or go to school. The Texas statute struck down in *Plyler* was largely an effort to enforce immigration law indirectly by persuading or inducing unauthorized migrants to leave the state. Such laws that indirectly regulate immigration are typically what legal scholars call "alienage laws," so called because they determine the consequences of being a certain type of alien or noncitizen, as opposed to being a citizen.

Of course, not all states and localities try, in one way or another, to enforce federal immigration law. Some adopt the opposite position, trying to avoid any actions that support immigration enforcement, and sometimes going further by trying to protect unauthorized migrants from the reach of federal immigration authorities. One way to characterize this sort of state and local activity is to call them anti-enforcement measures. However, it is more accurate to discuss these activities by identifying their purposes rather than what they oppose. The ultimate purpose of measures that try to remain neutral or try to neutralize immigration law enforcement is to integrate unauthorized migrants into local communities, regardless of their immigration status. The term "sanctuary" is often applied to such laws and policies, but this label covers an array of measures so vast that the label supplies more of a political characterization than any precise analysis of laws and policies.

The direct versus indirect spectrum also applies to state and local efforts to neutralize or to remain neutral regarding federal immigration enforcement, just as the spectrum helps in analyzing state and local pro-enforcement efforts. Examples of indirect state or local involvement that tries to protect or integrate unauthorized migrants include making them eligible for driver's licenses, or for resident tuition and financial aid at public colleges and universities. As another example of indirect involvement, a city might issue identification cards to allow unauthorized migrants to open bank accounts and conduct other transactions in the mainstream economy. As for direct involvement, suppose that local police arrest and book a noncitizen on an ordinary, nonimmigration criminal charge, but the charge is later dismissed. If database checks suggest that she is violating federal immigration law, a state or local government might involve itself directly in immigration enforcement by refusing to detain her until federal immigration officials can take her into custody.

This framework is indispensable for understanding current policy debates on a wide array of recent immigration-related developments at the state and local level. History shows that state and local activity has ebbed and flowed in a close relationship with federal immigration law and policy. Moreover, these patterns of immigration-related activity, at all levels of government, have deep roots in American history that reach back to the American Civil War and even further into the past.

Arizona and Beyond

By the time of his Tent City march in 2009, Arpaio was already a major player in a powerful group of Arizona politicians who pressed the state legislature for several laws targeting unauthorized migrants. One of them is the Legal Arizona Workers Act (LAWA), which took effect on January 1, 2008. It requires all employers in Arizona to use E-Verify. The federal government makes this database available so that employers can check if their employees are working legally, but its use is not required by federal law.[7]

Though LAWA imposes no direct penalties on employers who do not use E-Verify, anyone may file a complaint with the state attorney general against any such employer who hires an unauthorized employee. A first violation puts the employer on probation and requires it to terminate all unauthorized workers, imposes reporting requirements for all new hires, and allows for temporary suspension of the employer's Arizona business license. A second violation leads to permanent revocation of the license. Lawsuits asserted that federal law preempted LAWA, but the US Supreme Court rejected those challenges in 2011 in *Chamber of Commerce v. Whiting*.[8]

In April 2010, Arizona adopted the Support Our Law Enforcement and Safe Neighborhoods Act. More commonly known as SB 1070, it was the first of a new wave of state and local laws targeting unauthorized migrants. Section 1 of SB 1070 states: "The legislature declares that the intent of this act is to make attrition through enforcement the public policy of all state and local government agencies in Arizona." Section 2(H) allows anyone to sue any state or local official or agency that fails to enforce federal immigration law to the full extent permitted by federal law.[9]

In 2012, the US Supreme Court considered four core provisions of SB 1070 and struck down three of them. For now, my focus is how Arizona's efforts fit into an analytical framework for understanding the state and local role. Unlike LAWA, which addressed unauthorized migration indirectly by restricting access to jobs, SB 1070 took direct action against federal immigration violations in several ways. Most prominently, it targeted federal immigration violations directly through status checks. Section 2(B), allowed to take effect, applies if a state or local law enforcement officer stops, detains, or arrests someone and reasonably suspects that she lacks lawful immigration status. If she cannot prove that she is in the United States lawfully, the officer must detain her while verifying her status with the federal government.[10]

Under section 3, a noncitizen's failure to comply with certain federal registration requirements for noncitizens would have been a new state crime, punishable by up to a $100 fine and 30 days in jail. Under federal law, merely being in the United States unlawfully is only a civil violation. Section 5 would have made it a new state crime, with a maximum $2,500 fine and six-month sentence, for unauthorized migrants to apply for work, solicit work in a public place, or work as an employee or independent contractor. Working without federal permission is not a federal crime. The analogous federal laws penalize employers, not employees. Section 6 would have authorized police to make arrests without a warrant, if the officer has probable cause to believe that the arrestee has committed an offense making him removable from the United States. SB 1070 also makes it a new state crime to encourage a noncitizen to enter Arizona illegally, or to transport, harbor, or conceal unauthorized migrants while otherwise engaged in unlawful activity.[11]

SB 1070's lead sponsor in the Arizona legislature was State Senator Russell Pearce. The law's principal drafter and legal mastermind was Kris Kobach, then a law professor at the University of Missouri–Kansas City, later elected Kansas Secretary of State in November 2010. Kobach first immersed himself in immigration law in 2001, when Attorney General John Ashcroft chose Kobach as his chief advisor on immigration law and border security. In this role at the Department of Justice, Kobach was the architect of many of the Bush administration's post-September 11 anti-terrorism immigration law initiatives. A prominent example was the National Security Entry-Exit Registration System (NSEERS), which imposed special reporting requirements on certain groups of noncitizens from predominantly Arab or Muslim countries. After leaving the federal government, Kobach became active in efforts throughout the country to enact state and local laws addressing unauthorized migration and to defend them against legal challenges. These laws included LAWA and SB 1070.[12]

In 2006 and 2008, the Arizona legislature passed measures that resembled parts of what became SB 1070, but Governor Janet Napolitano, a Democrat, vetoed both. In January 2009, Napolitano became President Obama's Secretary of Homeland Security. By state law, Janice Brewer, the Arizona Secretary of State and a Republican, became governor. The Arizona legislature approved SB 1070 in April 2010, and Brewer signed it into law. Feelings on both sides of the SB 1070 debate were intense before enactment and grew even more vehement after it became law. Opponents organized protests and boycotts of travel to Arizona. Among the state's voters, SB 1070 consolidated core political support for Arpaio, Brewer, Pearce, and politicians with similar views, most of them Republicans. After a reelection campaign in which immigration eclipsed all other issues, Governor Brewer won a full term in November 2010 with 54 percent of the vote.[13]

THE SECOND ESSENTIAL theme in *Plyler*—the state and local role—was a key ingredient in the Supreme Court's conclusion back in 1982 that Texas could not keep children who did not have lawful immigration status from attending public schools. Arizona's LAWA and SB 1070 likewise belong to a long history of state and local laws relating to immigration and immigrants. To examine this aspect of US immigration law, a logical first question is why states and localities might adopt their own measures on immigration and immigrants. The goal might be to vary from federal laws and policies or to fill in perceived gaps. Such state and local inclinations may be natural in any system of government that allows regional or local decision-making. Residents of a community may view state and local officials as more receptive and more able to respond effectively to problems.[14]

Unauthorized migration might not elicit much interest in some states and localities, but it can be a wedge issue in others. The unauthorized population has grown steadily since around 1970, after the Bracero program ended and new legislation limited the number of immigrants from Mexico and other Latin American countries. This trend has varied among different parts of the United States.

Unauthorized migrants are highly concentrated in some states and regions. Out of an estimated total of 11.7 million unauthorized migrants in the United States in 2012, California was home to about one in five, or over 2.4 million. Over half are in just four states—California, Texas, Florida, and New York. The unauthorized share of a state's population also shapes perceptions and politics. Unauthorized migrants were 3.7 percent of the total US population in 2010, but over 7 percent of the state population in Nevada and at least 6 percent in California, Texas, New Jersey, and Arizona. Unauthorized migrants were less than 1 percent of the population in Alaska, Maine, Montana, North Dakota, South Dakota, Vermont, and West Virginia. Assessing the workforce shows more striking variations. In 2010, 10 percent of all workers in Nevada, 9.7 percent in California, and 9 percent in Texas were unauthorized.[15]

The concentration of unauthorized migrants in some states and regions matters for a variety of reasons. A revenue imbalance may arise because the federal government typically receives more in taxes and Social Security contributions than it spends on unauthorized migrants, while states and localities collect less than they pay out. Beyond fiscal issues, the answers to other questions may influence regional and local immigration politics. Does the ethnic mix of the unauthorized population set it apart from the voting citizen population? Are unauthorized migrants recent arrivals or long-time residents? Can state and local politicians use immigration as an issue to win positive attention and party primaries, and to build political constituencies and careers? If a voting bloc in any state or locality sees unauthorized migrants as politically powerless recent arrivals who are different in ethnicity or language, then the political context may produce harsh state and local responses.[16]

As of 2011, 42 percent of unauthorized migrants in the United States had arrived after 1999. Some never had lawful status, while others were admitted and violated the terms of admission. But even if unauthorized migrants have been in the United States long enough to build lives here, perhaps even with little memory of their countries of origin, many may be viewed as newcomers. As of 2011, almost 60 percent of unauthorized migrants were from Mexico, and about 75 percent from Latin America as a whole. Many unauthorized migrants live in states where the Latino population (including citizens and permanent residents) and the unauthorized population were small until recently but have grown rapidly. In 1990, 4 percent of the US unauthorized population lived in Arizona, Georgia, and North Carolina combined. In 2009, it was 10 percent and growing. In 1990, North Carolina had about 8,000 Mexican-born residents, including US citizens, permanent residents, lawfully admitted nonimmigrants, and unauthorized migrants. In 2000, this number was 172,000—almost a 22-fold increase.[17]

Changes of this sort can lead to an easy assumption in some regions that unauthorized migration is dramatically swelling a Latino, Spanish-speaking population. In turn, state and local politicians and personalities have sometimes cast the unfamiliar influx as foreign, criminal, and dangerous. As a telling example, the brief filed by the State of Arizona in the US Supreme Court to defend SB 1070 against constitutional challenge included this description of Arizona's problem: "This flood of unlawful cross-border traffic, and the accompanying influx of illegal drugs, dangerous criminals and highly vulnerable persons, have resulted in massive problems for Arizona's citizens and government.... Unlawfully entering aliens include criminals evading prosecution in their home countries and members of Mexican drug cartels...."[18]

Partisan politics also seems to be a crucial contributor to state and local enforcement-oriented measures. Studies by political scientists Karthick Ramakrishnan and Tom Wong and legal scholar Pratheepan Gulasekaram have shown that even when regional or local demography suggests that unauthorized migration may be a hot issue, government decision-making may be more receptive to state and local enforcement where the Republican Party dominates local or state politics and winning the Republican primary is the key to winning office.[19]

Given what seems to influence regional and local immigration politics, it is unsurprising that Arizona generated the first of the wave of state laws adopted after 2000 that targeted unauthorized migrants. The federal government intensified stricter border enforcement in the 1990s in the areas near San Diego, California, and El Paso, Texas. Many migrants tried to cross elsewhere, and Arizona was a natural choice, even with its deadly terrain. After crossing into Arizona, they were more conspicuous than they might have been in San Diego or El Paso, where they could blend into a large US-citizen Latino population. To many new Arizona residents, especially to recent transplants from regions with small Latino populations, the state's new demographics may have been unfamiliar, bewildering, or even threatening. The Republican Party was strong enough to make the only path to some offices go through its primary elections, which rewarded tough attitudes on unauthorized migration. These factors, coupled with the low percentage of Arizona's Latino population that was eligible or expected to vote, paved the way for state laws like the Legal Arizona Workers Act and SB 1070.[20]

OTHER STATES FOLLOWED Arizona with laws that directly addressed unauthorized migration with some combination of detention, apprehension, or penalties for unlawful status. In the 18 months after SB 1070, more than half of all state legislatures considered similar bills. Though most were defeated, Alabama, Georgia, Indiana, South Carolina, and Utah enacted laws that included some of SB 1070's core features, with variations. As with SB 1070, courts have invalidated most of the provisions in these laws, for reasons that Chapter 4 will assess. For now, these laws fill out the framework that this chapter proposes for analyzing state and local immigration activity.

Alabama HB 56, enacted in June 2011, would require public schools to check the immigration status of new students, for the stated purpose of measuring how unauthorized students affect school budgets and the quality of education for citizen children. The same law would also make many contracts involving unauthorized migrants unenforceable, and would make it a felony for an "alien not lawfully present in the United States" to conduct a business transaction with the state of Alabama or any of its political subdivisions. One provision unique to Utah's law is a state guest worker program contingent on federal government approval, but Utah's law otherwise resembles the others. Like SB 1070, it would require detention and an immigration status check of anyone arrested or stopped who is suspected of being in the United States without lawful immigration status.[21]

After SB 1070 and similar state proposals became law, some of their initial popularity abated. Nationwide boycotts of Arizona severely hurt the state's convention and tourism industry, a major sector of the state's economy. In a recall election in November 2011, Russell Pearce lost his Arizona Senate seat to a moderate Republican supported by the business community, which had become concerned about the fiercely negative reaction to SB 1070. Jay Reed, the president of the Associated Builders and Contractors of Alabama, wrote in an industry publication that construction, agriculture, and poultry industries were unable to fill jobs vacated by immigrants after HB 56 took effect. Karen Bremer, the executive director of the Georgia Restaurant Association, cited a 500-restaurant survey to object that the departure of unauthorized migrants in response to the new state law created a labor shortage. Even with a high state unemployment rate, Bremer explained, most restaurants could not fill the vacated positions. According to Charles Hall, head of the Georgia Fruit and Vegetable Growers Association, over 11,000 jobs were unfilled at peak harvest season.[22]

Numerous other groups opposed SB 1070 and similar state laws from the time they were first proposed. After the proposals were enacted, these groups tried to mitigate their practical effects and block their implementation. The groups sued in court, making two types of arguments. One was that the state laws violated the rights of affected individuals. The other was that these laws were preempted by federal law. In constitutional law, the balance between federal and state or local authority is often called federalism, so the term "immigration federalism" is sometimes used in analyzing state and local activity affecting immigration or immigrants. The general notion that the federal government has the exclusive power to regulate immigration goes back to the late 1800s, but this principle defies easy application. To answer the questions about state and local authority posed by SB 1070 and similar laws, and to fill out this chapter's conceptual framework for state and local activity, some historical perspective is essential. The dominant and sometimes exclusive federal role in immigration-related matters has a foundation in the bedrock of American history, especially in the idea of national citizenship that emerged from the Civil War.

State and Local Laws in Historical Perspective

Today it is easy to overlook what legal scholar Gerald Neuman called the lost century of US immigration law, when states and localities were practically the *only* source of immigration regulation until the 1870s. For most of the nineteenth century, states routinely regulated immigration as part of their general governmental authority—often called the police power. States withstood court challenges to such regulation as long as those laws did not conflict with federal regulation of commerce or foreign affairs. The 1837 US Supreme Court decision in *City of New York v. Miln* helped to establish this principle by upholding a New York state law that required masters of all ships arriving in the port of New York from outside the state to report on all passengers or pay a $75 penalty per passenger.[23]

Before the end of the Civil War in 1865, very few federal laws addressed migration. An 1803 federal law barred the entry of free blacks and slaves in violation of state laws. An 1819 federal law limited the number of passengers on any ship arriving from a foreign port. It also required shipmasters to record information on passengers and to provide them with basic necessities, including "at least sixty gallons of water, one hundred pounds of salted provisions, one gallon of vinegar, and one hundred pounds of wholesome ship bread for each and every passenger on board." The 1862 federal Coolie Trade Law prohibited the transportation of "the inhabitants or subjects of China, known as 'coolies,'... for any term of years or for any time whatever, as servants or apprentices, or to be held to service or labor."[24]

Other federal laws through the mid-1800s regulated immigration in a broader sense by shaping the settlement of newly acquired lands to the west and southwest. So viewed, federal immigration laws included the 1862 Homestead Act, which made land available to settlers and thus shaped a favored population of newcomers who pushed the frontier west to the Pacific. The Act allowed and encouraged settlement not only by US citizens, but also by immigrants who, as "free white persons" eligible to naturalize under federal law, filed declarations of intent to become citizens.[25]

Alongside these few federal laws on arrivals and settlement, state and local laws were the primary vehicles for regulating or encouraging the movement of people in the half-century before the Civil War. Some of these laws, directed at US citizens and foreigners alike, kept out criminals or quarantined anyone with a contagious disease. Some states and localities required shipmasters to post money bonds or pay into a welfare fund in case their passengers became indigent. Other state and local laws restricted the movement of free blacks.[26]

Some reasons for state and local predominance in shaping the population were practical. The vastness of the expanding nation and the rudimentary nature of communication and transportation precluded comprehensive immigration control. The national border was more an aspiration and a symbol than a defined physical reality. It mattered more who counted as a citizen or future citizen, and who would settle. Many states and territories attracted new immigrants with incentives, prominently featuring access to property ownership. The Homestead Act was a federal umbrella, but settler society was shaped regionally and locally by recruiting the desirable and by keeping out the unwanted.[27]

Race was pivotal, not only in settlement and in labor migration, but in fostering communities in racial terms. Legal scholar Kerry Abrams has shown, for example, that local governments in the Washington Territory encouraged white women in New England to emigrate west to Washington. They were expected to find white husbands—who might otherwise marry Native women—and put down settler roots. In this role, state and territorial governments effectively created a body of immigration law by shaping migration and settlement.[28]

Slavery was an even more fundamental reason that state and local laws defined belonging and settlement. As long as states in the Southern tier had slavery, intractable questions about the movement of slaves and free blacks prevented the federal government from addressing the migration of people. After all, it was unclear who counted as people. The divide over whether African Americans were property, rather than persons, left the nation unable to speak in one voice on who counted as Americans and when they could move to new work and new homes.[29]

In the first half of the nineteenth century, Northern states recognized free blacks born in the United States as citizens, but Southern states did not. This changed in 1857, when the US Supreme Court held in its infamous *Dred Scott v. Sandford* decision that blacks born in the United States were not citizens. This question of citizenship—or slavery—for African Americans was a major catalyst for the American Civil War. Only after the war did the 1866 Civil Rights Act and the Fourteenth Amendment to the US Constitution, ratified in 1868, effectively overrule *Dred Scott*.[30]

The Fourteenth Amendment includes this sentence: "All persons born or naturalized in the United States, and subject to the jurisdiction thereof, are citizens of the United States and of the State wherein they reside." These words established the formal citizenship of African Americans for the first time in US history. They also made clear that children born on US soil—except the children of diplomats—are citizens, even if their parents are in the United States unlawfully. Moreover, citizenship under the US Constitution became indisputably national citizenship. These three ideas, central to the Civil War's legacy, continue to shape debates over state and local laws on immigration and immigrants, by laying the foundation for federal immigration law and for the idea that only the federal government, not states or localities, has the authority to regulate immigration. Arizona's LAWA and SB 1070 show the intensity of state resistance to federal exclusivity, but history explains the depth of today's controversies.[31]

IN 1875, A decade after Appomattox, Congress adopted the first federal laws that directly regulated immigration by saying who may enter and stay in the United States. The first was the Page Act, which barred convicted criminals and prostitutes from admission to the United States. The historical record shows that the ban on prostitutes was intended to restrict immigration by Chinese women. More generally, the same 1875 statute also barred persons with convictions for non-political offenses from the United States. Congress later filled out this list of undesirables with provisions excluding "lunatics," "insane persons," "idiots," contract laborers, persons with a "loathsome or a dangerous contagious disease," and polygamists (with this last clause targeting Mormons). These and similar federal immigration laws of this era defined who would be excluded rather than who would be admitted, and they did not regulate the number of immigrants to be admitted. Only in 1921 did Congress first impose an annual cap on the number of immigrants.[32]

In 1876, the Supreme Court issued the first landmark decisions that continue to define the limits on state and local immigration authority today. The Court had addressed the topic but left lingering uncertainties in 1849, when it decided the *Passenger Cases*. By striking down Massachusetts and New York laws that required shipmasters to pay taxes or post bonds for passengers, the *Passenger Cases* endorsed the general idea that the authority to regulate immigration is exclusively federal. But a majority rationale was hard to discern, and the decision seemed to leave states with some undefined authority to regulate arrivals at ports of entry.[33]

The Court acted more definitively in 1876, when it struck down two state laws because they encroached on exclusive federal authority over immigration. The first was a New York statute that required arriving shipmasters to report all immigrant passengers. Shipmasters then had to pay a $1.50 tax for each, or post a $300 bond to indemnify states and localities if any arriving immigrant sought public assistance within four years. In *Henderson v. Mayor of the City of New York*, the Court ruled that this statute (and a similar one in Louisiana) infringed upon federal power to "regulate commerce with foreign nations." Citing the contributions of immigrants, the Court held that New York had infringed on the federal policy of recognizing that "immigrants...come among us to find a welcome and a home." These newcomers "bring...the labor which we need to till our soil, build our railroads and develop the latent resources of the country in its minerals, its manufactures and its agriculture."[34]

On the same day as *Henderson*, the Court decided *Chy Lung v. Freeman*, which struck down one of several California laws limiting Chinese immigration. This one gave state inspectors the discretion to deny admission to new arrivals unless the shipmaster or shipowner posted a $500 bond or paid a sum set by the state inspector. Expanding its *Henderson* rationale, the Court held that the California law, by regulating immigration, interfered with exclusive federal authority over foreign affairs.[35]

Even after *Henderson* and *Chy Lung*, states had a role in regulating immigration and citizenship into the early twentieth century. States continued to impose quarantines and other public health measures into the 1920s. Until

1906, states also had a significant role in naturalization based on the 1790 federal naturalization statute, which authorized "any common law court of record in any one of the States" to confer US citizenship. Federal law set the requirements for naturalization, but this provision let state courts follow their own procedures in naturalizing new citizens.[36]

If federal immigration laws had not expanded in number and coverage starting in 1875, states might have kept more power to regulate immigration. Over time, however, the cascade of federal immigration statutes, combined with the emphasis in *Henderson* and *Chy Lung* on preserving federal prerogatives, left virtually no room for states to address immigration without conflicting impermissibly with federal immigration authority. Over time, state immigration regulation faded. In 1906, a federal statute centralized the naturalization process in the Bureau of Immigration and Naturalization within the US Department of Commerce and Labor, ending the states' role in citizenship decisions. To make their case for restrictive immigration laws, local and regional advocates understood early in this period that they had to direct political pressure toward Washington, DC. One prominent sign of their successful shift to federal lobbying was the Chinese Exclusion Act of 1882.[37]

Indirect Enforcement from Plyler to LAWA

Today, it is now a distant part of American history that immigration laws were once primarily state and local laws, and that a bloody Civil War established the primacy of national citizenship and allowed immigration regulation to become exclusively federal. Over the past century and a half, the abstract principle that only the federal government can regulate immigration and citizenship has become deeply ingrained in the public culture and law of the United States. At its core, exclusive federal immigration authority means that state and local governments cannot have their own admission categories and border stations to control who enters their territory.

Because the definition of immigration regulation is elusive, this principle of exclusive federal immigration authority defies precise application. It remains uncertain how the US Constitution allows states and localities to address immigration and immigrants in other ways. And even if state and local activity is constitutional, it may be unwise for other reasons. These issues continued to arise all throughout the first half of the twentieth century, as state and local governments enacted laws that imposed various restrictions or requirements on noncitizens. But they arose with renewed and sustained intensity as the unauthorized population of the United States grew after the 1960s, when Congress ended the Bracero program and imposed new restrictions on immigration from Latin America.

The 1975 Texas school statute in *Plyler* is an early modern example of indirect state and local immigration enforcement. The Texas statute did not directly penalize unlawful presence. Given the accepted principle that only the federal government may regulate immigration directly, this indirect approach reduced the statute's exposure to a federal preemption challenge. In the end, however, *Plyler* did not address the preemption issue in that case. The Court instead based the outcome on finding that Texas discriminated against schoolchildren in a way that violated equal protection of the laws.

To be sure, *Plyler* made clear that it matters for both preemption and equal protection whether the government decision being challenged is federal or state. The Court's equal protection analysis relied on the idea that because states and localities have only a limited role in immigration, they have fewer legitimate reasons to treat people differently based on immigration status. So the second essential theme in *Plyler*—the state and local role—implicates both equal protection and preemption. But by deciding on equal protection grounds, *Plyler* left it for the next wave of court decisions to decide when federal law preempts state and local immigration-related measures.[38]

A DECADE AFTER *Plyler*, California was feeling the pain of an economic recession. The causes were complex, but a major factor was the decline in defense spending in the early 1990s after the breakup of the Soviet Union and the end of the Cold War. Southern California, home to most of the state's population, was hit especially hard by the downturn in aerospace manufacturing and related industries. There were 337,000 aerospace jobs in 1990, but by 1994 that number dropped to 191,000. From 1990 through 1994, personal income in California grew at only half the nationwide rate. The number of new residential building permits in California fell from 300,000 in 1986 to just 85,000 in 1993. In 1990, the unemployment rate was about 5 percent both in California and nationwide, but by 1993 it rose in California to almost 10 percent.[39]

These economic conditions, combined with a growing unauthorized population, were fertile ground for Proposition 187, dubbed by supporters as the Save Our State (SOS) ballot initiative. California voters approved it in November 1994 by a margin of 59 to 41 percent. Though most of its provisions never took effect, it would have barred unauthorized migrants from most state public benefits, including non-emergency health care. Directly challenging *Plyler*, Proposition 187 would have kept children out of public elementary and secondary schools if they were in the United States unlawfully. Other sections required certain state and local government employees to verify the immigration status of persons they encountered in their duties, and to report suspected unauthorized migrants to federal immigration officials. Proposition 187 also introduced state criminal penalties for manufacturing, selling, and using false documents to conceal an individual's "true citizenship or resident alien status."[40]

Like the Texas statute in *Plyler*, Proposition 187 did not try to regulate admission directly, but the measure's supporters argued that it would deter the arrival of new unauthorized migrants and would lead to the departure of those already in California. It "would effectively lead people to 'self-deport,' " in the memorable words of Governor Pete Wilson, the most prominent politician to throw his weight behind the initiative. He rode its popular support to his own reelection in 1994, though many observers later came to believe that Wilson's alienation of Latino voters in campaigning for Proposition 187 was a major reason for the decline of the Republican Party in California starting in the mid-1990s.[41]

The Mexican American Legal Defense and Educational Fund (MALDEF), the American Civil Liberties Union (ACLU), the League of United Latin American Citizens (LULAC), and other organizations and individuals sued to block Proposition 187. In 1995, federal district judge Marina Pfaelzer ruled, to no one's surprise, that denying access to public elementary and secondary schools was unconstitutional under *Plyler*, but she allowed the new criminal penalties for false documents to take effect. Judge Pfaelzer also ruled that federal law preempted the provisions that required state agencies and employees to report suspected immigration violators to the federal government. The reason was that the requirement did not rely on federal immigration law categories, but instead used state rules that might penalize individuals who were in the United States lawfully. Pfaelzer deferred a decision on the provisions that denied state public benefits, giving California time to adopt regulations that would be consistent with federal immigration law. Overall, the ruling was a partial victory for Proposition 187's opponents, but there is much more to the story.[42]

ONE IMPORTANT LESSON from Proposition 187 concerns the political relationship between state and federal decision-making. Indirect enforcement at the state level—especially if those efforts fall short—can influence the federal government, which might then intensify direct or indirect enforcement.

Proposition 187 was a state measure, but much of its impact was national. Ever since federal regulation displaced state and local immigration authority after the Civil War, much of the real influence of state and local politics has been in national debates on immigration and citizenship. For example, the US Supreme Court's *Chy Lung* decision in 1876 invalidated an attempt by California to restrict Chinese immigration, but it led to the first Chinese Exclusion Act in 1882.

Proposition 187 was likewise part of a national effort. A year before it won at the state ballot box, Governor Wilson published an open letter to President Clinton demanding stricter federal immigration enforcement. Around the same time, California and several other states sued the federal government to recover costs that they attributed to unauthorized migrants. One of their arguments was that the federal government had failed to prevent what the states called an "invasion." These suits uniformly failed in court, but they attracted considerable public attention.[43]

After Judge Pfaelzer blocked most of Proposition 187 on preemption grounds, much of the political pressure that led to its ballot box victory shifted to Congress and the federal executive branch. This is the context in which the Clinton administration stiffened enforcement on the US-Mexico border starting in the mid-1990s, emphasizing deterrence over apprehension of border crossers and dramatically increasing Border Patrol funding. In 1996, three new pieces of federal legislation achieved two of the general goals of Proposition 187's supporters, approved with strong bipartisan support in a Republican-controlled Congress and signed into law by President Clinton, a Democrat. Two of them intensified direct enforcement of federal immigration law. The third restricted access to public benefits for noncitizens.[44]

On the immigration law side, the Anti-Terrorism and Effective Death Penalty Act (AEDPA) and the Illegal Immigration Reform and Immigrant Responsibility Act (IIRIRA) combined to make enforcement of federal immigration law much stricter in a number of ways. For example, these federal enactments expanded deportation grounds and made it much harder for noncitizens to get discretionary relief from removal. They categorically barred many noncitizens from release from detention while immigration courts heard their removal cases. They also expanded the use of streamlined procedures to remove noncitizens more quickly. And they sharply curtailed the jurisdiction of federal courts to hear noncitizens' appeals in removal cases.[45]

A third 1996 law—the Personal Responsibility and Work Opportunity Reconciliation Act (PRWORA), sometimes called the Welfare Reform Act—fundamentally changed the federal benefits scheme for all recipients.

For noncitizens, its primary effect was to cut off federal food stamps and Supplemental Security Income (SSI), even for lawful permanent residents who were already receiving these benefits. Previously, permanent residents had generally been treated like citizens for public benefit eligibility. Unauthorized migrants were already ineligible for most federal public benefits, but the Welfare Reform Act made it harder for state and local governments to provide benefits for unauthorized migrants.[46]

Its close link to the Welfare Reform Act shaped Proposition 187's ultimate fate. In 1997, Judge Pfaelzer ruled that the Welfare Reform Act preempted the parts of Proposition 187 that she had not already found invalid—the provisions that denied state benefits. The reason was that federal law now addressed noncitizen eligibility for both state and federal public benefits. The State of California appealed, but Governor Wilson was term-limited and did not run for reelection. In November 1998, Gray Davis, a Democrat, was elected governor. In his first year in office, Governor Davis dropped the appeal, effectively taking Proposition 187 off life support. Though the result was complete federal preemption of the public benefits restrictions in Proposition 187, its supporters succeeded in a broader sense. In combination, the three federal laws enacted in 1996 achieved similar federal restrictions on noncitizen eligibility for public benefits, and they enhanced federal immigration enforcement.[47]

STATE AND LOCAL activity reemerged with intensity in the first decade of the 2000s. The focus stayed on indirect enforcement of federal immigration law. Regional and local growth in the unauthorized population raised awareness and created political openings. As an early sign of immigration's return to the front burner of state and local politics, Proposition 200 in Arizona—the Protect Our State ballot initiative with provisions resembling parts of Proposition 187—won approval in 2004 with 56 percent of the vote. Proposition 200 limited unauthorized migrants' access to public benefits and required proof of citizenship for voting. It also required state employees to report to authorities any unauthorized migrants who applied for public benefits.[48]

As activists began to press state and local governments, especially influential was a proposal in San Bernardino, a city of about 200,000, located about 60 miles east of downtown Los Angeles. Proposed in 2006, the Illegal Immigrant Relief Act would have denied city funds and permits to any business that employed unauthorized workers. It also would have allowed police to seize vehicles used by employers to pick up day laborers. Another law would also have banned housing rentals to unauthorized migrants and made

English the exclusive language for official city business. The proposal was never adopted, but it became a nationwide model.[49]

A cadre of enforcement advocates coordinated nationwide efforts to draft and enact state and local laws based on the San Bernardino model. In 2006, two such ordinances became law in Hazleton, Pennsylvania, a small city about 100 miles northwest of Philadelphia. Hazleton had undergone dramatic demographic change, with its Latino population rapidly growing from 5 percent to roughly one-third of the city's residents. Mayor Lou Barletta—who later became the area's congressman—and the city council blamed unauthorized migrants for rising crime and declining public services. Though Barletta said later that he had "no idea how many illegal immigrants live in his city," one of the ordinances declared in its preamble that the influx diminished the "overall quality of life" and imposed "debilitating effects on [the] economic and social well being" of Hazleton's lawful residents.[50]

One Hazleton ordinance targeted unauthorized work, making any employer who hired unauthorized workers liable in money damages to any lawful employee that it had discharged. The ordinance also required repeat violators of federal employer sanctions to use federal E-Verify, foreshadowing the 2008 Legal Arizona Workers Act's E-Verify requirement. The second Hazleton ordinance required anyone living in rental housing to have an occupancy permit, which in turn required proof of US citizenship or lawful status under federal immigration law.[51]

Indirect immigration enforcement, by taking aim at housing and employment, became typical of state and local proposals scattered throughout the United States. The rhetoric of "self-deportation" and the strategy of reducing the unauthorized population by attrition echoed Proposition 187's support a decade earlier. A 2006 ordinance in Escondido, California, required city officials to check any renter's immigration status with the federal government if any resident, business, or city official complained in writing that the renter was in the United States unlawfully. The same ordinance penalized landlords for "harbor[ing] an illegal alien in the dwelling unit, knowing or in reckless disregard of the fact that an alien has come to, entered, or remains in the United States in violation of law." Valley Park, Missouri, adopted ordinances in 2006 and 2007 that made it unlawful to provide housing or employment to unauthorized migrants. In Farmers Branch, Texas, a series of city ordinances starting in 2006 required landlords to have "evidence of citizenship or eligible immigration status for each tenant family." Other localities enacted laws targeting day laborers, or they used existing trespassing, anti-solicitation, and similar ordinances to keep day laborers from gathering or seeking work.[52]

Several states moved to restrict unauthorized employment. Some required all employers to verify work authorization beyond what federal law requires. Other states adopted such requirements for public contractors and other employers who receive public funds, and some other states imposed additional penalties beyond federal law on employing unauthorized workers. The Legal Arizona Workers Act was one of the most comprehensive statutes in this wave of pre–SB 1070 state efforts to enforce federal immigration law indirectly through employment restrictions. Oklahoma required the use of E-Verify for employers who contracted with public entities and made it unlawful to discharge a US citizen or lawful permanent resident while employing an unauthorized worker. Comprehensive measures targeting unauthorized work became law in Colorado, Georgia, Mississippi, and South Carolina, and then in Alabama and Utah.[53]

On another front for indirect immigration law enforcement, several states moved to keep unauthorized migrants out of public colleges and universities. Statutes or regulations in Alabama, Georgia, and South Carolina banned admission. Arizona, Colorado, Georgia, Indiana, Ohio, and North Carolina admitted unauthorized migrants but charged tuition at much higher non-resident rates. Almost all states deny public state-supported financial aid to unauthorized migrants, who are already ineligible for federal financial aid.[54]

Access to driver's licenses and other identification documents can be another area for indirect enforcement against unauthorized migrants. For many years, most states issued driver's licenses only to US citizens and lawfully present noncitizens, but some states did not require lawful immigration status. A few more states restricted driver's license eligibility after it came out that several of the September 11 hijackers had multiple driver's licenses that may have helped them plan and carry out the attacks. The 9/11 Commission's 2004 report characterized travel documents "as important as weapons" for terrorists and urged national standards for driver's licenses and other identification. In 2005, Congress responded with the federal REAL ID Act. It provides that after a long phase-in period, states may issue driver's licenses valid for boarding commercial airline flights only to US citizens and lawfully present noncitizens.[55]

Although some state and local measures—the Texas statute in *Plyler*, Proposition 187, the Hazleton ordinances, and the Legal Arizona Workers Act—attracted the most attention, they were only the most prominent of numerous efforts to enforce federal immigration law indirectly by restricting unauthorized migrants' access to work, housing, education, and identification documents. Chapter 4 will explain how lawsuits challenged all of these measures on constitutional grounds, typically arguing that federal law pre-empted them and that they violated the constitutional rights of individuals. For now, my chief concern is filling out this chapter's framework for under-standing the state and local role. The next step is to explore state and local laws that enforce immigration law directly. This part of the story ultimately comes back to Arizona's SB 1070, but like the evolution of indirect enforce-ment, it starts much earlier.

Direct Enforcement: Before SB 1070

Arizona's SB 1070 and similar laws in Alabama, Georgia, South Carolina, and Utah go beyond indirect enforcement by directly involving states in enforc-ing federal immigration law. Analysis of direct state and local enforcement starts with two points on which courts and legal scholars seem to agree. First, state and local police may enforce the criminal provisions of federal immigra-tion law and may ask federal authorities to take noncitizens into custody for removal proceedings or criminal prosecution. Some federal immigration vio-lations, including unlawful entry, are crimes, while others, including unlawful presence, are only civil violations. The second area of consensus is that the federal government can delegate to states and localities part of its authority to enforce both criminal and civil provisions of federal immigration laws. Combining these points, state and local police have inherent power, even without federal delegation, to enforce criminal provisions of federal immigra-tion law. With federal delegation, they can enforce all provisions.[56]

The first point—inherent state and local power to enforce criminal provi-sions of federal immigration law—is the basic lesson from *Gonzales v. City of Peoria*, a decision issued in 1983 by the federal court of appeals for the Ninth Circuit. Peoria happens to lie mainly in Maricopa County, Arizona. In 2010, its population was over 150,000, but Peoria was much smaller in 1983, with just over 12,000 inhabitants. The 11 plaintiffs in *Gonzales* were of Mexican ancestry. Guadalupe Junior Sanchez was a US citizen. Raul Gonzales, José Manuel Quintanilla, and Magdaleno Chavez-Diosdado were Mexican citi-zens living in the United States as permanent residents. The court identified the seven others—Reinaldo Arbiso, Pedro Ramirez, Socorro Guerra, Pablo Trejo, Bernarbe Garay, Aurelio Gonzales, and Gustavo Gonzales—as "citi-zens and permanent residents of Mexico who migrate to Maricopa County, Arizona to harvest citrus crops."[57]

The plaintiffs alleged that from 1977 to 1981, Peoria police officers, follow-ing city policies, "engaged in the practice of stopping and arresting persons of

Mexican descent without reasonable suspicion or probable cause and based only on their race and appearance." The lawsuit detailed how the officers detained and questioned the plaintiffs after stopping them in the parking lots of supermarkets, the US Post Office, and a shopping center. The official reasons were that the plaintiffs fit "the profile of an illegal alien" and engaged in "suspicious behavior." The plaintiffs alleged violations of their rights under civil rights statutes and the US Constitution.[58]

The plaintiffs argued that federal immigration power was exclusive, leaving state and local police with no authority to make arrests for immigration violations. The appeals court rejected this argument, noting that the Peoria police sought to make arrests only for federal immigration crimes, and that entering or attempting to enter the United States other than at an official port of entry is a misdemeanor punishable by up to six months of imprisonment. The criminal provisions in the Immigration and Nationality Act were "few in number and relatively simple in their terms" and left room for state and local enforcement, the court explained. The court cited nonimmigration decisions establishing that state and local police may make arrests for federal crimes in general. In contrast, state and local police lacked civil immigration arrest powers, because "the civil provisions . . . regulating authorized entry, length of stay, residence status, and deportation, constitute . . . a pervasive regulatory scheme, as would be consistent with the exclusive federal power over immigration."[59]

What does it mean in practice that state and local immigration arrest power is limited to federal immigration crimes? Of over 11 million unauthorized migrants in the United States in 2010, an estimated 43 to 70 percent—between 4.7 and 7.7 million—committed the federal misdemeanor of entry without inspection. The rest were admitted lawfully and then overstayed or violated another condition of admission. They may be deported, but they have committed no federal crime by falling out of lawful immigration status.[60]

The US Constitution and most state laws require that every arrest be based on facts that satisfy the legal definition of "probable cause." A brief investigatory stop, short of an arrest, requires less, but still must be based on "reasonable suspicion" of unlawful activity. Even assuming that officers have reasonable suspicion or probable cause that someone is in the United States unlawfully, it is not clear away from the immediate border area how they would also have reasonable suspicion or probable cause that the individual's unlawful presence followed an illegal crossing. In short, the inherent state and local authority to make arrests for federal immigration crimes may seem broad, but it does not allow state and local police to arrest someone merely for being in the United States unlawfully.[61]

Because state and local arrest authority for federal immigration crimes stops far short of arresting individuals for mere unlawful presence, the key question is whether state and local police have the inherent authority, without federal delegation, to make arrests for civil violations of federal immigration law. In 1996, a legal opinion by the Clinton administration's Department of Justice explained that state and local police lack authority to make civil immigration arrests unless expressly authorized by the federal government to do so. In 2002, however, the George W. Bush Department of Justice rescinded the earlier opinion and took the opposite position: state and local police do have inherent arrest authority for civil immigration violations. This debate over state and local direct enforcement lingers, but other developments have largely superseded it.[62]

THE DEPARTMENT OF Homeland Security (DHS) has expressly delegated various aspects of immigration enforcement to state and local governments, mooting the issue of their inherent authority. This trend to delegate is decades old, but it shifted into high gear around 2002. Within a decade, DHS had 13 programs authorizing some state and local role in enforcement, all under an administrative umbrella known as ICE ACCESS—Agreements of Cooperation in Communities to Enhance Safety and Security. These federal agency programs, like enhanced border enforcement and enforcement-minded federal legislation in the 1990s, have been an important outlet for some of the state and local political pressures that led to Proposition 187, the Hazleton ordinances, the Legal Arizona Workers Act, and eventually to Arizona's SB 1070 and similar state laws.[63]

The oldest ICE ACCESS program is the Criminal Alien Program (CAP), which has existed in some form since 1986. Under CAP, local jails give access to ICE officers to screen arrestees—either in-person or remotely—to identify and detain noncitizens who may be removable. CAP also operates in state and federal prisons, where an immigration judge may conduct removal proceedings while the prisoner is still incarcerated under the terms of a criminal sentence.[64]

Another major program implements section 287(g) of the Immigration and Nationality Act. Enacted in 1996 and first implemented in 2002, this provision allows DHS to enter into agreements that let state and local officials carry out specified immigration enforcement functions with federal supervision and training, usually at state or local expense. Agreements follow two basic models. The jail model resembles CAP. State or local officers interview detainees in local jails, check federal databases for immigration status, and sometimes transfer detainees to ICE custody. The task force model makes immigration status checks part of state or local police work in the field. At the program's height, DHS had a small but significant number of agreements— about 80 state and local entities in 24 states. Jail model agreements accounted for the overwhelming majority of immigration detainee transfers from state or local authorities to federal custody. Since then, the 287(g) program has been reduced. In December 2012, DHS announced that it would not renew its agreements adopting the task force model, explaining that other programs, especially Secure Communities, use enforcement resources more efficiently.[65]

Secure Communities is the third major program. It started in 2007 and emerged as a centerpiece of immigration enforcement in the Obama administration. It calls for the fingerprints of anyone arrested and booked by state or local law enforcement to be checked for criminal history and immigration violations using IDENT, the DHS biometrics-based immigration database. If an immigration violation shows up, DHS can issue a "detainer," which is a request to state or local police to hold the individual for transfer to federal custody. With much broader coverage than section 287(g), Secure Communities included 97 percent of all jurisdictions in the United States by August 2012 and is approaching nationwide implementation, with a stated priority of removing noncitizens with criminal convictions, especially for serious crimes.[66]

A fourth vehicle for explicit federal recognition of a state or local immigration enforcement role is a federal statute: section 1373(a) of title 8 of the United States Code. This provision originated in the 1990s, when New York City prohibited municipal employees from communicating with federal authorities about an individual's immigration status. Congress responded in 1996 by enacting this statute, which prohibits any such state or local restrictions on providing such information to the federal government. A related provision, section 1373(c), requires the federal government to respond to federal, state, or local government inquiries about any individual's citizenship or immigration status. The statute says nothing about the use of such information. The DHS Law Enforcement Support Center responded to 1.3 million requests for information in the federal fiscal year 2012.[67]

Express federal authorization has significantly expanded the state and local role in direct enforcement of federal immigration law. This trend has helped to satisfy state and local pressures to get tough on unauthorized migration by getting directly involved in immigration enforcement, even if the vehicles for a state or local role are limited and seem to leave federal authorities in the driver's seat. In contrast, work and housing restrictions like the Hazleton ordinances and the Legal Arizona Workers Act allow state and local governments to act independently to target unauthorized migrants, but such measures enforce immigration law only indirectly. From a perspective that seeks to intensify state and local efforts, both indirect enforcement and direct enforcement under federal supervision have serious limitations. It is unsurprising, then, that a few states adopted comprehensive laws that assert a direct, independent role in immigration enforcement.

BEFORE ARIZONA'S SB 1070 and similar laws in the 2010s tried to enforce federal immigration laws directly, some states criminalized certain behavior by unauthorized migrants. Some state laws made certain activities illegal for unauthorized migrants, even if the activities are lawful for citizens and lawfully present noncitizens. Other activities are unlawful in general, but unauthorized migrants face stiffer penalties. In 2002, Louisiana made it a felony, with a maximum penalty of a $1,000 fine and one year of imprisonment, to drive without proof of lawful immigration status. In 2008, South Carolina made it a felony, punishable by up to a $10,000 fine and ten years of imprisonment, for "an alien unlawfully present in the United States to possess, purchase, offer to purchase, sell, lease, rent, barter, exchange, or transport into this State a firearm."[68]

This story of the evolution of the state and local role in immigration enforcement now loops back to the start of this chapter. Arizona's SB 1070 and the laws that soon followed in Alabama, Georgia, South Carolina, and Utah try to involve state and local police directly in the enforcement of federal immigration law by checking the immigration status of individuals encountered in routine police work and by detaining suspected immigration law violators. They impose various state law criminal penalties for federal immigration violations. And they expand the power of state and local police to make arrests based on an individual's suspected immigration status.[69]

Viewing these laws in historical context makes their emergence unsurprising. They illustrate the relationship between federal and state or local immigration enforcement. After several decades of indirect enforcement through measures like the Texas school statute in *Plyler*, Proposition 187, and the Hazleton ordinances, states and localities have tried to carve out a direct enforcement role. State and local pressure prompted the federal government to delegate some of its power to enforce immigration law directly. But some state and local governments wanted their role in immigration enforcement to be larger and more independent than the federal government would allow, leading to SB 1070 and similar statutes.

A number of lawsuits tried to keep SB 1070 and its counterparts in Alabama, Georgia, South Carolina, and Utah from going into effect. The plaintiffs raised a variety of constitutional challenges, alleging federal preemption and violations of constitutional rights. In a highly unusual development, the federal government filed its own parallel suit against several of these statutes, though its constitutional challenges were limited to federal preemption. The most visible and important of the resulting decisions came from the US Supreme Court in *Arizona v. United States*, which struck down much but not all of SB 1070. As a group, these lawsuits were largely successful. Numerous court decisions invalidated most of the state provisions, including precursors like the Louisiana felony for driving while unauthorized.

State and Local Insulation from Enforcement

So far, this chapter has examined state and local efforts to enhance immigration enforcement, but many states and localities have adopted a quite different attitude toward immigration enforcement. Some measures directly address immigration enforcement by shielding unauthorized migrants from federal immigration agencies through various degrees of noncooperation. Other state and local measures address immigration enforcement more indirectly, not by trying to blunt or neutralize enforcement directly, but instead by fostering the integration of unauthorized migrants even if their presence may violate federal immigration law. According to one estimate using 2000 Census data, about 27 percent of the foreign-born population of the United States lives in a locality that limits enforcement cooperation with the federal government.[70]

An early example is Special Order 40, adopted by the Los Angeles Police Department in 1979. It states that "officers shall not initiate police action with the objective of discovering the alien status of a person." In 1985, the City and County of San Francisco adopted a resolution that declared itself a "City and County of Refuge for Salvadoran and Guatemalan refugees" and instructed its agencies and employees to "not jeopardize the safety and welfare of law-abiding refugees by acting in a way that may cause their deportation." This evolved into a San Francisco ordinance prohibiting municipal agencies and employees from obtaining information about an individual's immigration law status or communicating information about unauthorized status to the federal government.[71]

These early policies remain in effect, but they now operate within the constraints established by section 1373(a) of title 8 of the United States Code,
enacted in 1996. Though it bars any state or local restrictions on the flow of
information about an individual's immigration status to the federal government, it does not require or otherwise address the collection of such information. Heeding the limits set by section 1373(a), other cities have joined Los
Angeles and San Francisco in restricting the collection of information on
immigration status, and thus limiting their role in enforcement. For example,
Seattle adopted a policy in 2003 barring city workers from "inquir[ing] into
the immigration status of any person, or engag[ing] in activities designed
to ascertain the immigration status of any person." Several states, including
Alaska and Oregon, have more broadly phrased prohibitions on the use of
state resources for immigration enforcement.[72]

The typical rationale for these protective policies is to let unauthorized
migrants seek help from police and other city employees without worrying
about immigration enforcement. When Los Angeles police chief Charlie
Beck pledged in late 2009 to adhere to Special Order 40, he explained: "It is
extremely important to build relationships with all the communities of Los
Angeles. That cannot be done when people are afraid to have legitimate contact
with police because of their status." In adopting its policy, the City of Seattle
explained that the September 11 attacks "left immigrant communities of color
afraid to access benefits to which they are entitled, for fear of being reported."
The assumption is that even citizens or noncitizens with lawful immigration
status may hesitate to call the police if doing so would expose their relatives
or neighbors to questioning and arrest for immigration violations. Similar
concerns may explain why only about 80 state and local law enforcement
agencies—out of many thousands nationwide—ever entered into 287(g)
agreements to assist the federal government with immigration enforcement.[73]

These state and local measures limiting cooperation with federal authorities do not necessarily apply when a specific immigration enforcement action
is a priority. For example, local law enforcement might transfer into federal
immigration custody a noncitizen who is arrested for a crime that makes him
deportable, especially if the crime is serious. Even so, local laws that inhibit
immigration enforcement have generated countermeasures. Some states have
adopted laws that prohibit local governments from shielding unauthorized
migrants from federal immigration enforcement. When the State of Illinois
tried to limit the use of federal E-Verify to check employment authorization,
the federal government sued, and a federal district court held that federal law
preempted the Illinois statute.[74]

These debates about state and local authorities gathering immigration status information could be rendered moot by the nationwide coverage of the Secure Communities program. Because it turns every state or local booking into an automatic check for federal immigration status, the program exposes unauthorized migrants with no criminal record or only minor convictions to deportation. Reflecting the same views that have led local governments to limit police inquiries into immigration status, critics of Secure Communities have objected that this merger of local police activity and federal immigration enforcement undermines the relationship between police and immigrant communities. Related concerns are that the program mistakenly flags noncitizens (and even US citizens) as deportable, and that it invites racial and ethnic profiling by police officers who may want to trigger immigration enforcement selectively.[75]

Persuaded by these arguments, some state and local governments have moved to curb implementation of Secure Communities. The federal government made it clear that participation is mandatory in that any background check in federal databases will alert federal authorities to immigration status violations. But requiring states and localities to hold detainees for transfer to federal custody probably "commandeers"—forces state and local government to enforce federal law—in a way that violates the Tenth Amendment to the US Constitution. The State of California and a number of local governments have tried to limit the practical impact of Secure Communities by enacting laws that allow state and local law enforcement agencies to hold detainees for federal authorities only under limited circumstances.[76]

OTHER STATE AND local measures that try to neutralize or remain neutral on federal immigration enforcement do not address enforcement directly. Instead, they try to offset or blunt enforcement indirectly by recognizing or fostering the integration of unauthorized migrants. One significant area is public colleges and universities. Though some states have restricted access, a significant number—including Texas, California, Utah, New York, Washington, Oklahoma, Illinois, Kansas, New Mexico, Nebraska, Maryland, Connecticut, Rhode Island, Oregon, Minnesota, Hawaii, and Colorado—now allow unauthorized migrants with connections to the state to pay tuition at resident rates that are significantly lower than nonresident rates. For example, in 2001 California adopted AB 540, which offers resident rates regardless of immigration status to students who graduate from a California high school that they attended for three years. Financial aid eligibility is more exceptional, but California adopted legislation in 2012 that makes some state financial aid available to students without lawful immigration status.[77]

Identification documents give states and localities another way to recognize or promote the integration of unauthorized residents. One document widely used by unauthorized migrants from Mexico is the *matrícula consular*, an identity card issued by the Mexican government. The *matrícula* dates back to 1871, but its popularity among unauthorized migrants grew as driver's licenses became harder to get in the early 2000s. The Mexican government made the *matrícula* easier to get and added new security features. The *matrícula* won recognition by some state and local governments and private companies, especially banks, but the FBI took the position that it would allow criminals to enter the United States with false identities. The perception lingers that only unauthorized migrants use the *matrícula*, but because hundreds of local government agencies and banks still recognize it as adequate identification, it allows a significant number of unauthorized migrants to participate in the economy and broader society.[78]

The use of driver's licenses as an identification document for unauthorized migrants remains even after the federal REAL ID Act of 2005 accelerated the trend to limit eligibility to US citizens and lawfully present noncitizens. The Act left room for state driver's licenses that would not require lawful immigration status, though they could not be used to board commercial airline flights. In 2007, New York took initial steps toward a dual license system but abandoned the proposal. By the end of 2013, however, at least eleven states—California, Colorado, Connecticut, Illinois, Maryland, Nevada, New Mexico, Oregon, Utah, Vermont, and Washington, plus the District of Columbia and Puerto Rico—had legislation allowing driver's licenses to be issued without proof of lawful status under federal immigration law.[79]

Starting before the recent expansion of driver's license eligibility, some state and local governments issued identification documents that would make it easier for unauthorized migrants to enter into ordinary financial transactions, especially those involving rental housing, bank accounts, and car insurance. In practical terms, documents allow a person to take part in modern society outside the home. An early proposal, though never implemented, came in 2002 from California's Little Hoover Commission, a state agency charged with making recommendations to improve state government. It proposed a Golden State Residency Program with identification cards based on California residence. The Commission explained that widespread participation in civic affairs by all California residents regardless of immigration status would lead to a more effective and responsive government.[80]

The City of New Haven, Connecticut, started issuing municipal identification cards in 2007 to help all residents regardless of immigration status "become active participants in the community." San Francisco adopted a similar program in 2008, as did Oakland in 2009, though lack of funds kept Oakland from issuing the cards until 2013. In New Jersey, the cities of Trenton, Princeton, and Asbury Park have endorsed private identification cards rather than issue their own. Other localities, the City of Los Angeles being the largest, are actively considering similar programs. Just as non-enforcement laws and policies seek to counter federal immigration enforcement directly, these identification card programs counter federal immigration enforcement indirectly by helping to integrate unauthorized migrants locally.[81]

———————

THE SECOND THEME that was essential both in *Plyler* and in immigration law and policy debates in subsequent decades is the role of state and local governments in addressing unauthorized migration. The Supreme Court held that the State of Texas went too far when it kept schoolchildren out of public schools based on immigration law status. This chapter has proposed a conceptual framework for understanding the two main dimensions of the state and local role. One is the spectrum from enhancing enforcement of federal immigration law to remaining neutral or neutralizing federal enforcement and integrating unauthorized migrants. Another dimension is a spectrum from direct to indirect engagement with federal immigration enforcement.

These two dimensions provide a crucial way of understanding the wide range of state and local activity, but full analysis requires putting this framework in historical context. A major part of this history is the give and take that puts state and local activity in tension with federal activity. At various times, states and localities have adopted their own initiatives, reflecting localized politics and demography. They have often made a difference on the national scene, even when their efforts were thwarted in the courts because the measures exceeded state and local authority.

Now, more than a generation after *Plyler*, the state and local role has become an area of pivotal uncertainty. In 2012, state legislatures considered nearly 1,000 bills, enacted 156 laws, and adopted 111 resolutions on topics relating to immigrants and immigration. This was a decline from 2011, but the 2012 numbers were still over three times the 2005 levels. In the five-year period from 2008 through 2012, almost 7000 bills and resolutions were introduced and over 1,400 were adopted.[82] Courts continue to consider close questions of whether states and localities have overstepped their constitutional authority by encroaching on federal immigration power. In addition to the constitutional uncertainties, persuasive policy assessments of state and local involvement remain elusive.

3

Americans in Waiting?

MY FAMILY CAME to America when I was three years old. Some of my earliest memories of our first years in this country take me back to the Fourth of July fireworks at the Marina Green in San Francisco. For the several years that we lived in an apartment on Bush Street, my father would take me up the hill to Alta Plaza Park to see the show. I do not know exactly what my father thought about on those evenings, but I am pretty sure that he considered the Fourth to be a special day—for complicated reasons that many immigrant families share and probably always will.

The Fourth of July was my father's way of marking some sense of belonging to a new land, and of sharing that feeling with his firstborn child. So it was a day of appreciation and celebration. But I also know that the Fourth of July must have been a day of unease and doubt for him. Being an immigrant in America and starting a new life here meant everything to him, and yet his Independence Day was always tempered by his doubts of ever truly belonging. Like many immigrants throughout American history, he must have taken some comfort in hoping that his children would. We were, in ways that mattered profoundly to both of my parents, "Americans in waiting."

THE IDEA OF Americans in waiting is an expectation, held by both a newcomer and those already here, that the newcomer will belong someday. In considering how this idea may apply to unauthorized migrants, it is illuminating to see how Pablo Alvarado, the national coordinator of the National Day Labor Organizing Network (NDLON), has used the phrase, which I introduced and examined in another book, *Americans in Waiting*. NDLON is a collaboration of several dozen local worker centers and community-based groups that organize and campaign on behalf of day laborers in the United States.[1]

The ties between day laborers, many of whom are unauthorized migrants, and traditional labor unions tell a complex tale. Starting in the late 1990s, the American Federation of Labor and Congress of Industrial Organizations (AFL-CIO) moved to undo decades of union distrust and even hostility toward new immigrant workers, especially unauthorized migrants. In February 2000, the AFL-CIO called publicly on Congress to grant lawful immigration status to unauthorized migrants in the United States—then estimated at 6 million—and to repeal penalties on employers who hired them. For the AFL-CIO and other labor organizations that had lobbied successfully in 1986 for the federal employer sanctions in the Immigration Reform and Control Act, this was a dramatic shift.[2]

The AFL-CIO took another big step toward uniting its interests with those of unauthorized workers in August 2006, when it signed a formal partnership agreement with NDLON. The two organizations pledged to join forces in national lobbying on workplace and immigration issues. The agreement gave the AFL-CIO organizing access to local worker centers. In exchange, the agreement allowed worker centers to send nonvoting representatives to central labor council boards across the United States, even if the immigrant workers did not become dues-paying union members.[3]

In September 2009, Alvarado made an impassioned speech to the AFL-CIO annual convention in Pittsburgh. Reaffirming NDLON's partnership with the AFL-CIO, he urged Congress to pass legislation to give lawful immigration status to unauthorized migrants in the United States. Alvarado framed his call for legalization this way: "The very people being called 'illegal'—who I prefer to call Americans In Waiting—they, like me, will one day be citizens of this country." Six months later, in a statement urging opposition to Arizona's SB 1070, Alvarado declared with emphasis, "Undocumented immigrants are *Americans in Waiting*."[4]

Other advocates for unauthorized migrants have adopted this rhetoric. Jorge Maria Cabrera, speaking for the Coalition for Humane Immigrant Rights of Los Angeles (CHIRLA), wrote in *The Huffington Post* about marchers in the 2010 May Day rally for immigrants' rights, calling them Americans in waiting. Cabrera continued: "[W]e were all here, 250,000 of us, united by a sea of white t-shirts, American flags that seemed to float on their own atop the crowd, and the dream that one day 'America' will truly mean home for our families." Psychologist William Perez concluded his book on unauthorized students with this plea: "It is time to reform immigration laws and give dignity to the millions of hardworking Americans-in-waiting and their children, recognizing that they are, in many respects, already good citizens of the United States."[5]

SHOULD IMMIGRANTS WHO are in the United States unlawfully be considered future members of American society? Many of them may already feel very American, having spent much or most of their lives in the United States.

But should American society as a whole and US law treat them like Americans in waiting, or is it fair and more justified to view them as outsiders who have broken the law and have no claim to a full role in America's future? These questions go to the heart of the third theme that was essential in *Plyler*: the integration of unauthorized migrants.

Plyler treated the Texas schoolchildren as future members of US society, even though they were in the country illegally. Part of Justice Brennan's opinion for the Court viewed unlawful presence as inconclusive, but he also linked the meaning of unlawful presence with a concern for the integration of the children: "Sheer incapability or lax enforcement of the laws barring entry into this country, coupled with the failure to establish an effective bar to the employment of undocumented aliens, has resulted in the creation of a substantial 'shadow population' of illegal migrants—numbering in the millions—within our borders." Brennan continued: "This situation raises the specter of a permanent caste of undocumented resident aliens, encouraged by some to remain here as a source of cheap labor, but nevertheless denied the benefits that our society makes available to citizens and lawful residents. The existence of such an underclass presents most difficult problems for a Nation that prides itself on adherence to principles of equality under law." The Court saw a peril of constitutional dimensions: "The Equal Protection Clause was intended to work nothing less than the abolition of all caste-based and invidious class-based legislation." These passages, linking the meaning of unlawful presence to grave concerns about a permanent underclass, show how the Court saw the children's unlawful presence as just the start of an inquiry into their integration.[6]

In addressing how the children would participate in society as they came of age, the Court emphasized the importance of access to education. Quoting *Brown v. Board of Education* and calling education "the very foundation of good citizenship," it explained: "[I]t is doubtful that any child may reasonably be expected to succeed in life if he is denied the opportunity of an education." It went on: "By denying these children a basic education, we deny them the ability to live within the structure of our civic institutions, and foreclose any realistic possibility that they will contribute in even the smallest way to the progress of our Nation."[7]

In these ways, *Plyler* affirmed that the children, though lacking lawful immigration status, were likely in the United States to stay, and at least in that sense were Americans in waiting. But these were children whose parents had brought them to the United States. The issues become more complex when the discussion broadens from children to adults whose presence in the United

States is unlawful. One crucial question is whether the need to integrate unauthorized migrants applies more broadly than just to children. Historical documents show that Justice Powell cast the pivotal fifth vote for the Court's opinion only because its reasoning was limited to the education of children and avoided broader pronouncements about constitutional rights.[8]

This chapter explains why the fundamental reasons and justifications for integrating unauthorized migrants are not limited to children. My analysis starts with the role of integration in immigration and citizenship generally. Integration is essential to reconciling an inherent tension in immigration law—between the basic idea of national borders, which inherently discriminate between insiders and outsiders—with a sense of justice that embraces a commitment to equality. I can provide only an overview of issues that are the focus of voluminous attention by philosophers and political scientists, but I will lay a foundation for my analysis of the integration of unauthorized migrants.

Next, I will explain how US law historically treated some immigrants— generally only those of European descent—as Americans in waiting whose integration should be fostered, while others from elsewhere in the world were viewed less inclusively, and typically as a flexible labor force. To square this history of borders and immigration law with a professed national commitment to equality, the integration of many unauthorized migrants is just as important as the integration of immigrants who are in the United States lawfully. This chapter concludes by exploring two different types of claims that unauthorized migrants can make to be treated as Americans in waiting.

Borders, Equality, and Integration

In simple terms, the most basic dilemma of immigration and citizenship law in American political culture—or in any liberal democratic society organized as a nation—is a fundamental tension between two ideas that are widely and deeply held. The first idea is that there are good reasons for some regulation of immigration and citizenship, and in turn for some kind of national borders. The second idea is individual dignity based on equality. National borders impair that dignity and equality, because borders limit the freedom of movement of noncitizens, who are not the equal of citizens for this purpose. This means that the idea of equality counts only among a finite group of citizens; it does not apply as between citizens and noncitizens. Borders thus constrain noncitizens' decisions about where and how to lead their lives and thus may infringe on the personal dignity that can come from those aspects of individual liberty and choice. There are, however, conceptually and morally convincing ways to reconcile borders with equality, and not all exclusions are unacceptable insults to individual dignity. This chapter's first aim is to explain how this can be so.[9]

The history of US immigration law is highly relevant to understanding the tension between borders and equality in the United States, but first I should set out a general framework that illuminates that history. I begin with the general idea that the law expresses and reflects the existence of borders when it creates a body of immigration and citizenship law. As a matter of logic, citizenship law comes first, by deciding who is a citizen and who is not.

In theory, citizens belong to society as full and formal members. Though reality often falls short of this ideal, it is within this group of citizens that the concept of equality is taken seriously. Noncitizens, on the other hand, are outsiders in numerous meaningful ways. Immigration law comes into play here. Its basic functions are to keep some noncitizens out of the United States and to admit others, and to decide that some who were admitted are later to be removed. By directly regulating noncitizens but not citizens, immigration and citizenship laws necessarily discriminate on the basis of citizenship.[10]

This discrimination between citizens and noncitizens conflicts directly with the robust view of equality that is central to American notions of individual dignity and liberty based on an equal opportunity to pursue happiness, as the founders put it. In American constitutional law, this idea of equality underlies the constitutional guarantee of equal protection, which supplied the rationale for the US Supreme Court to strike down the Texas school statute in *Plyler*. Extending well beyond constitutional doctrine and the legal system, a rhetorical commitment to equality has become central to the self-image of the United States.

Given the tension between values of equality and immigration and citizenship laws, why should the United States have such laws and borders in the first place? Put differently, I have identified dilemmas generated by borders, but what are the dilemmas connected with not having borders? My answer starts by acknowledging that human beings have a basic urge to group themselves and to find comfort and protection in such solidarity. Sometimes this happens in very small groups, like the family. Sometimes it happens at the national level, which immigration and citizenship laws typically reflect.

As a matter of political reality, even those who advocate for open borders typically recognize that some sense of national belonging and some immigration control at the national border are unavoidable. The world is made up of nation-states, whose sovereignty and independence are broadly believed to include the right to decide who is a citizen and who is not, and to decide who should be admitted and who should not. Prevailing thought about public resources persistently frames questions in national terms, asking, for example, if immigrants will help *our* American economy. Will they undermine or enhance *our* national security? With basic policy debates so framed, any candidate for national or statewide public office in the United States would commit political suicide by adopting the rhetoric of open borders.

But political realities, even if sufficient to explain the persistence of national borders and immigration law in some form, do not provide convincing or satisfying answers to moral dilemmas. Political realities also do little to answer complex questions about the *types* of borders that might exist. The fundamental choice is not simply one between borders and no borders. Even the rhetoric of open borders versus closed borders masks a more complex reality. Those who argue for closed borders generally acknowledge that some noncitizens should be allowed to enter, even if the number is tiny or the circumstances very narrowly defined. And those who argue for open borders generally acknowledge that the exclusion of some individuals may be justified. In short, borders come in many varieties. There are many ways to write, administer, and enforce immigration and citizenship laws. The choices made in making the rules, in designing the institutions, and in exercising administrative and enforcement discretion combine to determine how well or how poorly the tension between borders and equality will be reconciled in practice.

MY NEXT STEP is to explain what I consider the most persuasive justification for immigration and citizenship laws: that national borders can create bounded societies in which meaningful versions of equality can flourish. Of course, equality can have various meanings. The equality compatible with national borders is not that every human being is treated exactly the same at any given moment in time. It is, rather, an equality grounded in providing human beings with two forms of equal opportunity.

One is access to equality, even if equality is not immediate. The other is meaningful choice, so that differences reflect individual preferences rather than coercion or constraints. This may seem like a very diluted form of equality, and perhaps it is. But the question is not whether this form of equality is as robust as fully equal outcomes; the answer to this question is clearly no. Rather, the key inquiry is whether the capacity of national borders to foster access to equality and meaningful choice is sufficient to justify those borders.

I believe that national borders have this capacity, and that they are superior in this pragmatic regard to a world without national borders.[11]

Borders can foster access to equality and meaningful choice if they reinforce civic solidarity. I use "civic solidarity" as a rough shorthand for some sense of being involved in a joint enterprise for a common purpose. It is one way of understanding the human inclination to group together for comfort and protection. If this idea is typically taken for granted in families, it may be less intuitive or natural in larger groups unless something like civic solidarity emerges to make the group meaningful to its members.

As political scientist Sarah Song has explained, civic solidarity is important for several reasons. One core feature of civic solidarity is the mutual trust that is necessary before members of a society will participate in strengthening it. In turn, mutual trust requires a belief that others are like oneself in some meaningful sense. Being involved in a joint enterprise for a common purpose can lay the foundation for that trust. Also at the core of civic solidarity is a concern for the common good. This concern is a pre-condition for members of a society to participate fully in collective decision-making through social and political processes that foster the sharing of opportunities, assets, and responsibilities. Especially important in these processes are protective mechanisms like a robust system of rights, responsibilities, and remedies. These protective mechanisms are the foundation for both access to equality and meaningful choice.[12]

The next question is why civic solidarity should be a matter of *national* borders and a *national* framework for equality. The most persuasive answer is a pragmatic one: national civic solidarity is more inclusive and egalitarian than the alternatives. If national civic solidarity matters less, individuals and groups will likely adopt alternatives to national citizenship. Religion, race, class, localism, and other exclusionary and undemocratic groupings would inevitably matter more. The result might be a world without national walls, but also a world of a "thousand petty fortresses," as political philosopher Michael Walzer observed.[13]

The crucial thought is that national borders and citizenship include protective structures, like constitutional law, that have nothing analogous in these other groupings. This means that erasing national borders would dilute or eliminate the equality that can be achieved within the protective mechanisms that have emerged in the framework of national borders. Or erasing national borders would at least require starting all over. In other words, the most compelling reason to maintain national borders is to maintain national commitments to enhancing such protections. Though unbounded egalitarian societies may be ideal, bounded egalitarian societies are surely preferable to abandoning equality altogether. Erasing national borders would dilute equality where it flourishes, and would keep equality from flourishing where it might do so.

THREE INTUITIVE CONCERNS deserve attention. One is that I am citing an idealized version of American history and constitutional culture, and that the protective mechanisms that would justify national borders have been notoriously weak. A second, closely related concern is that I am underestimating the potential of international human rights and other frameworks to protect equality and individual dignity without insisting on national boundaries. The next section of this chapter will address the relevance of the many troubling episodes that have exposed the deep flaws in the aspects of American culture that strive for equality. But first it is important to explain that reliance on human rights give me less confidence as a vehicle for equality than domestic law protections and a domestic public culture that generally takes rights seriously.

The fundamental shortcoming of human rights protections is their inherent minimalism in practice. For persons who are in the United States and strive for inclusion, constitutional law and other national frameworks for individual rights are more robust in practice than any other schemes. Though the language that is the source of constitutional rights may seem cautious and vague, these rights have become rich and nuanced through judicial and legislative interpretation. The claims of immigrants—including unauthorized migrants—to recognition and integration into American society are based on much more than their human rights. Their claims are based, even more persuasively, on their significant role in this particular national society regardless of their immigration status. Human rights concepts and rhetoric can usefully influence the content of domestic protections as a matter of both law and policy, but the protections of national citizenship are fuller than what is available under a human rights scheme that is untethered to any national system of rights.[14]

A third concern is that by emphasizing national borders, I am overlooking the real possibility that the best solutions to problems associated with national immigration and citizenship laws need to reach well beyond national borders to engage international economic development and other profound influences on global migration. But the search for answers in broader international spheres is consistent with maintaining national borders. Nothing about globalization and the growing interconnectedness among nation-states necessarily replaces or supersedes the protective potential of national societies. The challenge is how to maintain the nation-state's protective potential while taking the forces that drive global migration into account.[15]

NATIONAL BORDERS CAN reflect a commitment to meaningful equality, depending on how immigration and citizenship laws operate. What matters is that national borders and those who make, administer, and enforce them must respect six essential ideas. The first two ideas strive to fulfill the potential of the protective measures of national citizenship, especially a prohibition on discrimination. The next three refine the idea of immigrant integration. The sixth idea addresses inequality among nations.

The first essential idea is that immigration and citizenship laws must not discriminate against noncitizens on any basis other than citizenship itself. Though immigration and citizenship laws inherently discriminate between citizens and noncitizens, any such law loses its most persuasive justification if it discriminates not only by citizenship, but also by race, religion, language, or gender. An immigration or citizenship law that discriminates on grounds other than citizenship would be no more justified than the petty fortresses that national citizenship has the potential to avoid. It is impossible to reconcile borders with equality if, for example, the law governing citizenship makes it less accessible for people of some races than for those of other races.[16]

The second essential idea is that immigration and citizenship laws must treat all citizens equally. For example, sponsoring a parent to come to America as a new immigrant must not be harder for Asian American citizens than it is for European American citizens. Phrased more generally, immigration laws cannot discriminate among citizens on any basis that would be unconstitutional in domestic law contexts.[17]

The third idea is that the line between being an immigrant and a citizen must be permeable. Immigration and citizenship laws necessarily treat citizens and noncitizens unequally, but nothing about immigration and citizenship laws says that this inequality must be permanent. Such laws do not need to keep noncitizens, once lawfully admitted, from equal treatment over time. Nor do such laws need to bar those outside the national boundary from any possibility of admission. In fact, both permanent inequality for those admitted and denial of any hope of admission would make it impossible to reconcile national borders with equality and individual dignity. This is why the crucial idea is access to equality, which in turn depends on the integration of immigrants. In turn, integration is fostered most effectively by assuming that new immigrants are Americans in waiting—that they will eventually become US citizens. This reflects the idea of immigration as a transition to citizenship. My main point is that at least for some groups of noncitizens who see themselves as immigrants, retarding or rejecting their integration threatens to keep them marginalized and to undermine civic solidarity. Integrating them, on the other hand, fosters civic solidarity.

The fourth idea is that integration can foster civic solidarity only if it requires reciprocity and mutual respect between newcomers and those who arrived before them. It follows that immigrant integration requires both an openness to all who are willing to become part of the national culture and a collective national willingness to be influenced by newcomers. Throughout US history, the process by which newcomers become part of American society has attracted many different labels with varying connotations. "Integration" is the term in broad use today, both in the United States and in similar discussions elsewhere in the world. "Assimilation"—a term widely used in earlier eras, notably the first half of the twentieth century—sometimes connotes pressure from the native majority for immigrants to cut ties with their cultures, languages, or societies of origin. This sort of pressure to conform reflects a greater willingness to accept immigrants from some countries than from others. If that happens, national borders become a proxy for the forms of discrimination that can make borders and equality irreconcilable. In contrast, viewing immigration as a transition to citizenship and fostering the integration of immigrants with reciprocity and mutual respect can broaden and deepen civic solidarity.[18]

The fifth idea that is essential if national borders are to reflect a commitment to meaningful equality is that integration is a long process, perhaps even taking multiple generations. This time dimension is consistent with the idea that reconciling borders with equality requires access to equality rather than immediate equality. Attempts to shape or measure integration in only one generation are short-sighted. What counts is not whether first-generation immigrants become integrated linguistically and participate in national culture. Doing so may involve great sacrifice and may even undermine the strength of family and community culture that will launch children into the broader community, where they can write their own immigrant success stories. The same long-term thinking applies to economic mobility, geographical distribution, and other dimensions of integration. The key is what happens in the second and third generations.

The sixth idea is a corollary to the emphasis on the integration of immigrants. Integrating immigrants allows equality that is fostered initially inside the national borders of the United States to extend beyond national borders by enabling or enhancing prosperity in sending countries. In this way, reconciling national borders with a national commitment to equality requires that the United States understand how its immigration and citizenship laws are related to transnational equality and inequality. The immigration-related policies of the United States can close or widen inequality between the United States and sending countries. For example, US international economic development initiatives can create economic opportunities in sending countries. The effect is to make migration from those countries seem less attractive or necessary to people who might otherwise try to come to the United States, and in turn to maintain the national border while fostering transnational equality.[19]

The Burdens of History

History makes it painfully clear that US immigration and citizenship laws have been decidedly unfaithful to these six ideas. One might even wonder if they are attainable or even realistically aspirational. Some might doubt that any scheme of national immigration and citizenship can ever be consistent with equality and individual dignity. The United States has made great strides in admitting and integrating immigrants over the past half-century, most significantly since 1965. But progress has been fitful, and significant problems remain, especially a system that both tolerates and exploits unauthorized migration.

A skeptical view of the potential of US immigration law to reflect a commitment to meaningful equality would cite the history of explicit racial, ethnic, and gender discrimination in immigrant admissions. This skepticism would also rely on another facet of history that directly links race to the question of whether immigrants are treated as Americans in waiting. This is the story of racial restrictions in citizenship laws.[20]

The end of the American Civil War made it possible for the first time to confirm the citizenship of African Americans based on birth in the United States. This was a central reason for the 1866 Civil Rights Act and the Fourteenth Amendment to the US Constitution in 1868. More generally, this kind of citizenship is often called birthright citizenship. The United States allows the acquisition of citizenship by birth on US territory through *jus soli*, a Latin phrase that literally means the law of land or ground. United States law also grants citizenship based on the other main approach to birthright citizenship that appears in worldwide surveys of citizenship laws. This is *jus sanguinis*, literally the law of blood. A child born outside the United States who has one or two US citizen parents may be a citizen at birth, depending on the specific facts.[21]

The adoption of the Fourteenth Amendment left citizenship unclear for persons who were born in the United States, but who were viewed as neither white nor African American. The two major questions concerned two groups of children born in the United States: children whose parents were American Indians or Asian immigrants. The US Supreme Court ruled in 1884 that American Indians were not citizens based on birth on US soil because they were not "subject to the jurisdiction" of the United States, as the citizenship clause of the Fourteenth Amendment requires. Indian tribes were sovereign nations for this purpose, the Court explained. But this restriction dissolved over the next 50 years as some American Indians acquired US citizenship through treaties, and Congress conferred citizenship on Indians through various statutes, most prominently the Snyder Act of 1924.[22]

The question of citizenship for the children of Asian parents reached the US Supreme Court in 1898. It held in *United States v. Wong Kim Ark* that persons born in the United States to Chinese parents were US citizens at birth under the common law of the United States, the Civil Rights Act of 1866, and the Fourteenth Amendment. Though Wong Kim Ark's parents were in the United States lawfully, the accepted reading of the Fourteenth Amendment today does not make citizenship turn on the parents' immigration status. Except for the children of diplomats, all children born on US soil are citizens.[23]

RACIAL RESTRICTIONS IN birthright citizenship paralleled similar laws that restricted the acquisition of citizenship by naturalization. In 1790, the first federal naturalization statute limited eligibility to "free white persons." It might surprise the modern reader that this rule may have seemed expansive at the time, but it opened up citizenship to Irish Catholics, Eastern European Jews, and other immigrants who were considered white for this purpose but did not come from the same Anglo-Saxon, Protestant stock as the dominant population.[24]

Only after the Civil War ended did persons who traced their ancestry to Africa receive birthright citizenship under the Fourteenth Amendment and eligibility to become citizens under the federal Naturalization Act of 1870. For Asian immigrants, however, the 1870 statute left naturalization eligibility unclear. Though the Supreme Court's decision in *Wong Kim Ark* guaranteed citizenship for their children based on birth in the United States, the Chinese Exclusion Act of 1882 slammed the door on naturalization by Chinese immigrants by providing: "hereafter no State court or court of the United States shall admit Chinese to citizenship." For all other immigrants from Asia, eligibility to naturalize remained in doubt.[25]

By the early twentieth century, a series of lower federal court decisions reflected a consensus that immigrants from the Middle East were eligible "free white persons." Mexican immigrants were allowed to naturalize in light of the conferral of US citizenship under the Treaty of Guadalupe-Hidalgo, but not necessarily because Mexican immigrants would be judged to be white absent that history. The essential logic of the only published court decision on Mexican naturalization eligibility was, as legal scholar Laura Gómez put it, that "Mexicans were white enough, despite not being truly white." In effect, those who could prove that they were not American Indians were allowed to naturalize.[26]

Soon afterward, two US Supreme Court decisions ruled on whether immigrants from South Asian and East Asian countries counted as white. In 1922, the Court ruled that Takao Ozawa, a Japanese immigrant, was not white and therefore was ineligible to naturalize. Ozawa did not contest the validity of the racial requirement, arguing instead that he was white by virtue of his assimilation into American culture and society. Rejecting his claim, the Court cited popular and scientific notions of race to conclude that a "person of the Japanese race" was not white. A year later, the Court held that Bhagat Singh Thind, "a high-caste Hindu, of full Indian blood" who was serving in the US Army at Fort Lewis, Washington, was not white. In the *Thind* decision, the Court turned away from invoking science and instead relied principally on popular notions of race and whiteness.[27]

These naturalization bars persisted longer than analogous restrictions on birthright citizenship, but one significant sign that US law was shedding some of its racist history was the erosion and repeal of the bars in the mid-1900s. The Nationality Act of 1940 opened up naturalization to "races indigenous to the Western hemisphere," a phrase intended to cover American Indians. Eligibility soon expanded to include immigrants from China in 1943, and from India and the Philippines in 1946. In 1952, Congress consolidated immigration and citizenship statutes into the Immigration and Nationality Act, which provided: "The right of a person to become a naturalized citizen of the United States shall not be denied or abridged because of race or sex or because such person is married." Only then were the last racial barriers to naturalization in US statutes repealed.[28]

ALONGSIDE CITIZENSHIP BARRIERS, federal law restricted Asian immigration. The Chinese exclusion laws (starting with the Page Act of 1875), the

Gentlemen's Agreement with Japan in 1907, the Asiatic barred zone in 1917, and the adoption of the national origins system in the 1920s all rested on a core assumption that Asian immigrants could not or would not integrate into American society. And even though President Teddy Roosevelt urged Congress to allow Japanese immigrants to naturalize, reflecting his concern with diplomatic relations with Japan, he wrote that allowing unlimited immigration would be "race suicide."[29]

These cross-currents notwithstanding, the non-assimilability theme remained strong. A notable example is the 1889 US Supreme Court decision in *Chae Chan Ping v. United States*, which declined to hear a challenge to the constitutionality of Chinese exclusion laws. This seminal decision is usually considered the source of the plenary power doctrine, which largely immunizes immigration law decisions by the legislative and executive branches of the federal government from constitutional challenges in the courts. Writing for a unanimous Supreme Court, Justice Stephen Field relied on the idea that Chinese immigrants could not or would not assimilate into American society: "[If Congress] considers the presence of foreigners of a different race in this country, who will not assimilate with us, to be dangerous to its peace and security...its determination is conclusive upon the judiciary."[30]

This connection between the admission of immigrants and their potential integration also led Congress to restrict immigration from southern and eastern Europe. These laws relied on a pseudo-scientific veneer drawn from the eugenics movement, which maintained that racial differences had an objective, measurable, and scientific basis. The influence of eugenics was most clearly evident in the 1911 report of the Dillingham Commission on immigration. Its argument for restrictions was that new waves of immigrants from southern and eastern Europe belonged to an unassimilable race that was intellectually inferior to previous generations from northern and western Europe. Even laws that barred some immigrants based on ideology and national security were based on perceptions that immigrants from southern and eastern Europe were un-American and untrustworthy.[31]

Embracing the Dillingham Commission report, some congressional leaders called for a literacy test that would require proof that an immigrant could read in his or her native language. Believing that literacy was lower among immigrants from southern and eastern Europe, advocates of a literacy test frequently cited illiteracy as a sign of inferior intelligence and thus inability to assimilate. The test became a legislative goal for those who wanted to control the nation's racial demography and keep undesirable immigrants from diluting white America's genetic pool. In 1917, Congress adopted a literacy requirement for admission. President Woodrow Wilson vetoed it, but Congress overrode the veto. Eugenics continued to permeate prevailing views on the integration of immigrants and immigrant admissions, soon leading to the adoption of the national origins system in the 1920s.[32]

The National Origins Act of 1924 limited immigration from southern and eastern Europe. It also broadened the exclusion of Asian immigrants by relying on the same racial restrictions on naturalization that rejected any notion that Asian immigrants were Americans in waiting. The statutory mechanism was to admit only nationalities that counted as "inhabitants in continental United States." The statute defined this phrase to exclude "aliens ineligible to citizenship and their descendants" and "the descendants of slave immigrants." After the Supreme Court decided *Ozawa* and *Thind*, this bar based on ineligibility to naturalize applied to anyone of Asian ancestry. The reference to slave ancestry reflected concerns in Congress that black immigrants from the Caribbean would not respect antimiscegenation statutes or other Jim Crow laws. This provision stopped almost all black immigration to the United States from the Caribbean, Latin America, and Africa.[33]

Race was also central to the treatment of Mexican migration as a flexible, temporary labor force starting in the early twentieth century, but the emphasis was not on restricting the number of immigrants and not even on formal regulation through immigration law. Rather, the central purpose was to manage workers—some coming as immigrants, some as temporary workers, and some outside the law—who could do needed work but could also be counted on to return to Mexico.[34]

The combined effect of the Asian exclusion laws, the national origins system, the management of a flexible, temporary Mexican labor force, the Great Depression, and World War II was a dramatic decline in the number of immigrants coming to America from the 1920s to the mid-1960s. Global upheavals reduced overall levels of immigration to the United States. At the same time, the discriminatory admission scheme established by the National Origins Act preserved the dominant culture of the United States as resolutely white, Anglo-Saxon, and Protestant.[35]

In this setting shaped by law, economics, and demography, US laws and policies favored immigrants who were viewed as Americans in waiting. The working assumption that they would assimilate easily into that dominant culture and ultimately would become citizens had deep roots in the 1800s. One of its expressions in law was the declaration of intent to become a citizen. From 1795 until 1952, these declarations, sometimes called first papers, were a prerequisite to naturalization. New immigrants could file them at any time after arrival—but only if they were racially eligible to naturalize. Those who filed declarations were known as intending citizens.[36]

Intending citizens were not citizens, but they enjoyed a favored status that included many of the rights of citizenship, including voting. This practice contrasts with noncitizen voting today, which exists in only a few scattered localities. In the early 1900s, noncitizen voting was commonplace, but not for all noncitizens. In many states and territories, voting by noncitizens was limited to those who filed declarations of intent. This pattern started with the Wisconsin Constitution of 1848, followed by the constitutions of Michigan in 1850 and Indiana in 1851. Acts of Congress allowed intending citizens to vote in the Dakota, Kansas, Minnesota, Nebraska, Nevada, Oklahoma, Oregon, Washington, and Wyoming Territories. Most of these territories maintained this practice after they attained statehood, and other states adopted it.[37]

Other laws and policies treated intending citizens like citizens for many purposes. An 1804 federal statute automatically conferred citizenship on the widows and children of intending citizens who died before naturalizing. In one prominent incident in 1853, the US government granted diplomatic protection to an intending citizen. Intending citizens were allowed to settle land under the Homestead Act of 1862. During the Civil War, military conscription included intending citizens—but not other noncitizens.[38]

This treatment of intending citizens as if they were citizens continued into the twentieth century. A 1907 law allowed them to get US passports if they had lived in the United States for three years. During World War I, intending citizens were the only noncitizens drafted into the military. A 1918 federal statute regulating service on US merchant or fishing vessels treated seamen who were intending citizens just like citizens. Under the federal Revenue Act of 1918, intending citizens could take advantage of a lower tax rate for citizens. In an era when other noncitizens were typically denied jobs on public works projects and other public employment, some state and local governments hired intending citizens on the same basis as citizens. In the period following World War I, many private employers promoted only citizens or noncitizens in the process of naturalizing.[39]

For intending citizens, immigration was a transition to citizenship, but no person who was barred from naturalization could become an intending citizen. With naturalization restricted to "free white persons," and expanded only in 1870 to "aliens of African nativity and to persons of African descent," only some immigrants were Americans in waiting. Citizenship did not guarantee integration, but ineligibility to naturalize inhibited or precluded integration.

For much of American history, race and ethnicity decided whether integration was assumed and fostered—or unthinkable and resisted. To tie this history back to the six ideas that are essential to reconciling the tension between borders and equality, these aspects of US immigration and citizenship laws thwarted the emergence of the sort of bounded egalitarian society that might justify such laws in the first place.[40]

THE LAWS THAT reflected and reinforced these attitudes would eventually change. This trend started gradually, with the growing reliance on workers from Latin America, especially Mexico. Though they had a variety of statuses under US immigration and citizenship laws, they collectively expanded the ethnic mix of the noncitizen presence in the United States and of the US population as a whole. As a parallel development, several generations of children born in the United States to Asian immigrant families became US citizens by birth. A significant number of Asian immigrants circumvented the national origins system's strict numerical caps after they were modified to not apply to spouses and children of US citizens. In 1952, Congress repealed the last statutory naturalization barriers based on race. Then, with the repeal of the national origins system in 1965, the immigrant admissions system finally abandoned explicit discrimination on grounds other than citizenship status itself.

Starting in the mid-1960s, the combination of the end of the Bracero program, new restrictive employment-based categories for immigrants, and numerical limits on Western Hemisphere immigration—against the backdrop of economic and political troubles in Latin America—led to a sharp increase in the number of unauthorized migrants in the United States. The post-1965 changes in the population of newcomers also had an important ethnic dimension, with the number of lawful immigrants from Asia and Latin America rising sharply.[41]

The end of the national origins system allowed small Asian immigrant communities to grow dramatically through new and expanded immigrant admission categories based on family ties, employment, and education. As for Latin America, shutting down the Bracero program led not only to an increase in unauthorized migration, but also to a sharp increase in lawful immigration. The newly capped categories for lawful immigrants from Latin America filled up. A growing number were admitted in the one category that remained uncapped: spouses and unmarried minor children of US citizens. The overall result was a steep rise in lawful immigration from Mexico in particular and Latin America in general at the same time that the unauthorized population grew.[42]

The ethnic mix of immigrants to the United States shifted radically in the years that followed. In the 1950s, about 56 percent of new lawful immigrants came from Europe, more than half of this group from just two countries: Germany and the United Kingdom. By the 1980s, only 11 percent came from Europe. In 2012, only about 8 percent came from Europe, compared with 42 percent from Asia, 38 percent from Latin America and the Caribbean, and 10 percent from Africa. These changes in ethnic composition occurred at the same time that overall immigration increased dramatically. In 1970, under 5 percent of the US population was foreign-born. In 2010, it was about 13 percent, or nearly 40 million people. Of the foreign-born, those from Latin America accounted for 53 percent, Asia for 28 percent, and Europe for 12 percent. With these changes, the integration of immigrants crossed new lines of race, ethnicity, language, and religion.[43]

A Circle of Skepticism

The dramatic expansion of Asian and Latin American immigration after 1965 might suggest that US immigration and citizenship laws have become more inclusive and more faithful to the non-discrimination and immigrant integration that are essential for reconciling national borders with equality. Moreover, millions of immigrants from southern and eastern Europe, cast in the late 1800s and early 1900s as racially inferior by multiple Congresses and the Dillingham Commission, became part of the broad success story of immigrant integration. That being acknowledged, admission to the United States as a lawful permanent resident today does not come with the treatment as Americans in waiting that white European immigrants enjoyed in the nineteenth century and the first half of the twentieth century.

Part of this trend is evident in naturalization. On the one hand, naturalization is easier and more routine than it is in many, perhaps most, other countries around the world. Many applicants for US citizenship perceive only minor obstacles to naturalization. At the same time, the requirements are more demanding, fees are higher, and fewer noncitizens naturalize than might under more welcoming or supportive policies. On a more conceptual and rhetorical level, legal and policy claims on behalf of permanent residents rarely rely on viewing them as Americans in waiting. Today, US laws and policies have moved away from treating intending citizens like citizens and away from viewing immigration as a transition to citizenship.[44]

This erosion of the idea of Americans in waiting should not be entirely surprising. Starting early in the twentieth century and then more vividly after

1965, the immigrant population changed in ways that profoundly challenged the American culture that had been dominant through the first two-thirds of the twentieth century. The new immigrants were from strange lands. There were many more of them, and modern communications and transportation allowed them to maintain closer home country ties than previous generations could. And a growing number were in the United States unlawfully.[45]

Against the backdrop of these pronounced changes in the immigrant population, some observers expressed concern that non-European newcomers fail to integrate into American society as well as immigrants from Europe once did. In the 1990s, a best-selling book by journalist Peter Brimelow called for America to return to its white, European roots, citing the inability of immigrants from Asia, Africa, and Latin America to integrate. Prominent political scientist Samuel Huntington argued in a book published in 2004 that immigration patterns threaten the American nation because of the failure of immigrants, especially from Latin America, to assimilate to a core Anglo-Saxon, Protestant culture. Criticism of this sort can be especially sharp when the focus is unauthorized migrants and disregard of immigration laws is cited as a sign of failure to integrate.[46]

Developments in national political culture starting in the mid-1960s added to this anxiety by closely linking immigration and citizenship with race and ethnicity. The overarching ideas of equality and non-discrimination that drove passage of the Civil Rights Act of 1964, the Voting Rights Act of 1965, and the end of the national origins system in the 1965 immigration amendments created a shared legislative legacy at a transformational time in national history. Profound shifts in the racial and ethnic composition of the immigrant population occurred just when domestic civil rights legislation opened up passionate debates involving race and ethnicity in the contexts of affirmative action, diversity, multiculturalism, and racial identity. Spilling beyond settings that seemed to be domestic, these topics came to overlap with immigration and citizenship debates. Language policy, bilingual education, and ethnic studies became battlegrounds for debates over the integration of immigrants, including unauthorized migrants.[47]

GIVEN THE LONG history of racial and ethnic exclusion in US immigration and citizenship law, some Latino, Asian, and African immigrants are especially likely to respond to an ambivalent welcome with reticence of their own in an unfortunate circle of reciprocal skepticism. It may seem surprising that naturalization rates are lower among some immigrant groups in spite of requirements that may not seem onerous, and it may seem natural to conclude that the reason is hesitation to naturalize and perhaps to integrate into American society. But what may seem on the surface like an immigrant's inherent resistance to integration may in truth be the skepticism on the part of America's dominant culture reflected back.

Essential to escaping this circle of skepticism that exists between some immigrants and some of American society is greater acceptance of immigrants in the United States, starting with noncitizens who are lawful permanent residents. If they are not treated with the expectation of naturalization, an important opportunity is lost to embolden them to reach outside their own communities and to foster their integration into the broader fabric of American society.

Treating immigrants as Americans in waiting is essential to counter the feeling among many Latin American, Asian, and African immigrants that no matter what they do, they will always remain strangers in the land—perpetual foreigners because of their names, skin color, languages, or accents. For many of today's Latino immigrants, the history of labor migration from the early twentieth century up through the predictable rise in unauthorized migration after 1965—with severe new limits on both temporary and permanent admissions from Latin America—have produced a natural sensitivity to being wanted not as Americans in waiting, but just as workers. This sensitivity is rooted in the feelings of marginalization and disposability that come from being largely excluded from the lawful immigration system while being tolerated outside the law.[48]

It was precisely the expectation that workers from Latin America during most of the twentieth century—and before them workers from Asia in the nineteenth century—would *not* assimilate that made them especially attractive to US employers and the mainstream of American society. Without meaningful integration that makes the line between immigrant and citizen permeable, reflects reciprocity and mutual respect, and recognizes that integration may take multiple generations, immigrants—especially those from Latin America, Asia, and Africa—will be excluded as outsiders. National borders will remain, but not the sort of borders that can reconcile the tension between borders and equality and thus justify those borders in the first place.[49]

Integration and Immigration Outside the Law

So far, this chapter has examined the tension between borders and equality. It has also explained what it would take for immigration and citizenship laws to reflect a commitment to meaningful equality. A core principle is openness without discrimination to the integration of immigrants over time. This openness is especially vital given a national history that has been burdened by bias and intolerance, even if immigration and citizenship laws no longer have their most odious features. Now I return to the question that opened this chapter: Are *unauthorized* migrants Americans in waiting? Or must a noncitizen in the United States be lawfully present before she can expect integration into American society?

The answer to these questions cannot rely simply on the idea that immigrant integration is essential if national borders are to be consistent with equality and individual dignity. This emphasis on integration reflects viewing immigration as a transition to citizenship, and it explains why lawful permanent residents have persuasive claims to be treated as Americans in waiting. But the idea that immigrant integration is essential does not explain why unauthorized migrants may or may not have the same claims. The question is why immigration law violations by unauthorized migrants should not extinguish their claims to integration.

My answer starts with *Plyler*, which addressed integration by emphasizing the importance of education for all children regardless of immigration status. The Court invoked *Brown v. Board of Education*, but its reasoning went beyond education. The Court celebrated social mobility generally and abhorred divisions of caste. Was this part of the *Plyler* reasoning broad enough to include unauthorized migrants who are not children? To be sure, pivotal to Justice Powell's decisive fifth vote for the Court's opinion was the idea that the children were innocent, having no choice in their parents' decisions to bring them to Texas and to stay unlawfully. On closer analysis, however, the reasons to treat some unauthorized migrants as Americans in waiting sweep broadly enough to include many adults. The Court's basic precepts on integration are not easily confined to children or to educational access. Understanding why they are broader than just children requires a closer look at the ideas of innocence and choice as well as the two main types of arguments for treating at least some unauthorized migrants—including adults—as Americans in waiting. They are arguments based on what I have called immigration as contract and immigration as affiliation.[50]

Of course, the claims of individual unauthorized migrants vary in strength. Factors like when they arrived, how long they have been in the United States, and what they have been doing will matter. My chief aim is more general: to identify the two general types of arguments for integration that unauthorized migrants might bring, while acknowledging that these arguments will be stronger in some cases than others.

THE CONCEPTUAL BASIS for the first type of argument is what I have called immigration as contract. It may seem natural to view children in *Plyler* as innocent and their parents as lawbreakers. But US immigration law has tolerated significant unauthorized migration to assure a supply of flexible, cheap labor, subject to discretionary, unpredictable, and inconsistent enforcement. A logical corollary is key to deciding if some unauthorized migrants are Americans in waiting in spite of their unlawful presence. A national policy of acquiescence means that unauthorized migrants come to the United States as part of a tacit arrangement that is mutually beneficial.[51]

In spite of the letter of the law, this arrangement amounts to an invitation extended by the combination of willing employers, limited enforcement, and legal mechanisms that allow unauthorized migrants to stay as a matter of government discretion. This is not the innocence that applies to children who make no choices at all. It is, however, the innocence that comes with accepting this invitation in order to provide for one's children and other loved ones within the expectations of a long-standing system of labor and migration that exposes them to employer exploitation and discretionary enforcement. Unauthorized migrants have come within a scheme of tolerance that enriches the United States and supports their claims to be treated as Americans in waiting.

The fundamental idea is that coming to America reflects reciprocity—immigrants' expectations of their new country, and what their new country and its inhabitants expect of them. This is not a contract in the formal legal sense of a binding agreement after back-and-forth bargaining. There may be no formally binding agreement and no bargaining at all. Instead, I use the term "immigration as contract" to refer more generally to a set of concepts of fairness and justice that are associated with contracts and sometimes with property rights. These ideas are often phrased in terms of promises, invitations, expectations, notice, and reliance.[52]

Contract-related concepts have formed a consistent thread in US immigration debates since the late nineteenth century. For example, the early US Supreme Court decisions rejecting constitutional challenges to the government's immigration decisions relied heavily on contract-based reasoning. In one landmark decision, the Court held in its decision in *Fong Yue Ting v. United States* that deportation decisions were just as insulated from constitutional challenges in the courts as admission decisions were. The Court explained that immigrants have no basis for complaint if the US government decides to deport them, because admission into the United States is a conditional, revocable license agreement that the government can revoke at any time.[53]

Today, one sometimes hears that immigrants "promise not to go on welfare" or that obeying the law is a condition of admission. Breaking that promise could lead to deportation, the reasoning goes. Thinking about immigration as a matter of promises, expectations, and other ideas related to contract can also push in the opposite direction and support arguments on behalf of noncitizens. For example, the 1996 Welfare Reform Act cut back on food stamps and other public benefits for noncitizens. Opponents charged that changing the rules to limit existing eligibility would unfairly upset immigrants' expectations. Similarly, some argue that it is unjust to change deportation laws retroactively after immigrants have relied on prior law and entered guilty pleas to minor criminal charges in order to avoid deportation. In 2001, the US Supreme Court endorsed this view by holding that statutes governing the removal of noncitizens from the United States can apply retroactively only when Congress clearly says so. Otherwise, the Court explained, changing the rules "would surely be contrary to 'familiar considerations of fair notice, reasonable reliance, and settled expectations.' "[54]

Of course, there is much room for debate about the actual terms of any immigration contract. Some might argue that federal immigration statutes set out the contract's terms. From this perspective, violating immigration laws by crossing the border without permission or overstaying a period of lawful admission breaches that contract. It would follow that unauthorized migrants have no contract-based claim to treatment as Americans in waiting. More generally, any discussion of contract-based arguments must consider the interests of those who are already in the United States, especially as citizens. If they withhold consent, then an essential element of contract is missing.

But analyzing immigration as contract requires delving deeper than the letter of immigration statutes and the fact that there is strong support for more vigorous immigration law enforcement. It is odd, and perhaps hypocritical, to claim that no consent or agreement exists and at the same time to enjoy enrichment within a national economy that has relied on a sizable unauthorized workforce. It is much more persuasive to view the true immigration contract as the combination of the invitations and expectations generated by US government policies that have historically tolerated unauthorized migration. Recognizing the need to integrate unauthorized migrants would honor their legitimate reliance on such de facto policies. In contrast, significant changes in the intensity of enforcement would upset that reliance.

Several rebuttals to this reliance on tolerance or acquiescence in unauthorized migration deserve discussion. Political philosopher Joseph Carens has argued that shortcomings in enforcement do not amount to what he calls complicity in unauthorized migration. Nor, he maintained, is complicity established just because some employers want to hire unauthorized workers. Carens may have been right to resist the complicity label, but government policy can generate legitimate expectations without complicity. Carens got closer to the heart of the matter when he explained that if unauthorized migration is determined "by structural factors beyond the state's control, the state cannot be held responsible for failing to prevent the entry and settlement of the irregular migrants." Though this statement seems persuasive if taken literally, the premise—that structural factors determining migration flows are beyond the state's control—seems questionable. Indeed, the very concept of control may be misleadingly simplistic.[55]

Many structural influences on migration flows are the product of deliberate government decisions, including domestic legislation and agency decisions on immigration, citizenship, and settlement, as well as patterns of border and interior enforcement. Migration also reflects international economic policy and various other aspects of international relations. By making a variety of decisions, governments shape populations and thus are involved in the many types of regulation and influence that make up immigration law. Some of these decisions are familiar examples of immigration law, such as admission categories. Others, like the Homestead Act, are immigration law in more subtle forms. Still others, like the consequences of a federal employer sanctions scheme that looks good on paper but is inherently ineffective, are essential features of immigration law in action.[56]

I am not suggesting that every state of affairs that is partly attributable to government action or inaction makes the government responsible for the array of outcomes that emerge. Nor am I saying that every such state of affairs justifies expectations that government policies will never change. Such broad assertions would be not only hard to cabin; they would also make government decision-making impossible. I offer a more modest position, based on two ideas.

The first idea is that the actual operation of law in action can amount to government policy. This is true even if that policy seems inconsistent with what is explicitly written in statutes and regulations. US government policy sets out a type of immigration contract. Even if migration is unauthorized, it justifies expectations based on a combination of acquiescence, tolerance, invitation, permission, or reliance. Many of the US government's approaches to enforcement have reflected workforce needs, rather than a consistent commitment to enforcement. A merchant who has expanded his customer base by consistently accepting late payments should be not allowed to insist long afterwards that late payments in the past violated the contract. A highly restrictive system of immigrant admissions that fails to meet the labor needs of the US economy and the highly discretionary application and enforcement of immigration law have been the main features of the invitation that unauthorized migrants accept by coming to the United States.[57]

The second idea is that when a government changes laws or policies, fairness requires that it consider how those changes adversely affect anyone who acted in reliance on the prior state of things. What should be done when unauthorized migrants have come to the United States within an economic system that enriches the country with their labor and an immigration law system that acquiesces in their presence, but the government then shifts course? Answering this question starts by seeing if the course has in fact shifted. For this purpose, the text of statutes is as unhelpful as it is for ascertaining the content of prior policy. But suppose that the government not only adopts new policies but musters the political will to implement them at the border and in the interior so that the enforcement rate is substantially higher than it has been historically. Though nothing about the past should block such changes, it is independently important to recognize the interests of unauthorized migrants who came under the old regime. Here, immigration as contract and the invitation and expectations are highly relevant because they support unauthorized migrants' fairness-based claims to be treated as Americans in waiting.

A SECOND TYPE of argument for treating unauthorized migrants as Americans in waiting is based on what I have called "immigration as affiliation." This is the idea that the law should acknowledge unauthorized migrants' ties and contributions to their communities in various forms that include work, tax payments, and civic participation. Their US citizen children may make (or will make) similar contributions. The reasoning that recognizes such affiliation is evident throughout US immigration law. Federal immigration law allows noncitizens to rely on their ties and contributions to avoid deportation, even if their presence has been entirely unlawful. Such discretionary relief from deportation is typically limited to noncitizens who have been in the United States for a certain period of time and have close relatives who are citizens or permanent residents. Ties and contributions are also central to the federal government's guidelines for exercising prosecutorial discretion not to remove an individual noncitizen.[58]

Affiliation-based arguments are open to serious objections, similar to those that might counter contract-based arguments. Skeptics generally emphasize that these ties reflect violations of law and therefore cannot convincingly support a need to integrate unauthorized migrants. But as with immigration as contract, the best lens for examining these objections is history, which prompts an analysis that parallels the analysis of unauthorized migrants' contract-based claims to integration. The shared element is that affiliation-based claims by unauthorized migrants to be treated as Americans in waiting are based on ties that are the known, predictable results of government decision-making. In this sense, immigration as contract argues for the legitimacy of the ties on which immigration as affiliation rests.

There are some subtle differences between affiliation and contract arguments to be treated as Americans in waiting. One difference involves the concept of innocence that typically animates discussion of unauthorized migrants who were children when their parents brought them to the United States. An affiliation-based claim that unauthorized migrants have acquired ties and have made contributions while living in the United States unlawfully seems to concede initial wrongdoing, and then to argue that it is offset later by virtuous behavior. In contrast, the argument that unauthorized migrants are here as a consequence of de facto government policy rebuts any implication of wrongdoing from the start. Another difference between affiliation and contract arguments is that affiliation arguments grow in strength as unauthorized migrants develop ties and make contributions to American society over time. This is true even if immigration as contract lends little support to integration claims by unauthorized migrants who arrive after a real shift to a new immigration system that takes enforcement much more seriously.[59]

The reasons for integrating unauthorized migrants based on contract and affiliation are not mutually exclusive. They overlap and complement each other, though the mix can vary according to the individual or group of unauthorized migrants. Based on some combination of contract- and affiliation-based arguments, many unauthorized migrants have been living and working in the United States long enough to be considered Americans in waiting. Viewing the integration claims of unauthorized migrants as a matter of immigration as contract is more relevant early in their lives in the United States. Over time, it becomes more accurate to view claims for integration as a matter of their ties, contributions, and other forms of affiliation. Both views of immigration combine to support claims based on fairness for the integration of unauthorized migrants, even if they are not children.

MORE THAN A generation ago, the *Plyler* Court raised "the specter of a permanent caste of undocumented resident aliens." It viewed education as crucial in preventing the creation of an underclass. This reasoning directly supported the Supreme Court's holding that no state or local government may deny any child in the United States access to public elementary or secondary education.[60]

In analyzing how this aspect of the Court's reasoning has remained central to debates about the integration of unauthorized migrants, I have explained the basic tension between borders and equality, the essential role of immigrant integration in reconciling that tension, and the reasons to integrate *unauthorized* migrants. This chapter stops short of discussing how these reasons to treat unauthorized migrants as Americans in waiting might lead to lawful immigration status or citizenship itself for some unauthorized migrants through legalization and other vehicles. Before reaching that topic, it is important to analyze the other connections among the three themes that were essential in *Plyler*. The next chapter starts by examining how the meaning of unlawful presence is related to the role of state and local governments.

4

Deciding Who Enforces

THE FEDERAL GOVERNMENT'S attempt to keep Arizona SB 1070 from going into effect quickly reached the Supreme Court, where oral argument took place on April 25, 2012. Speaking for the federal government, Solicitor General Donald Verrilli had barely opened with "Mr. Chief Justice, and may it please the Court," when Chief Justice John Roberts interrupted: "Before you get into what the case is about, I'd like to clear up at the outset what it's not about. No part of your argument has to do with racial or ethnic profiling, does it? I saw none of that in your brief." Verrilli replied, "That's correct" and added: "We're not making any allegation about racial or ethnic profiling in the case."[1]

In a sense, Verrilli's answer was accurate. The earliest challenges to SB 1070 came from a variety of individuals, labor unions, churches, community organizations, and chambers of commerce. These lawsuits argued not only that SB 1070 was preempted by federal law but also that it violated the rights of individuals under the equal protection clause of the Fourteenth Amendment, protections in the Fourth Amendment against unreasonable arrests and searches, and freedom of speech and association as guaranteed by the First Amendment. Some of these claims included allegations of profiling, discrimination, and other bias. In contrast, the federal government based its lawsuit entirely on preemption—the idea that Arizona, by enacting SB 1070, overstepped its lawmaking authority by intruding on exclusive federal power to regulate immigration.

If Verrilli's answer was technically accurate, it was far too simple and even misleading. This became awkwardly clear when he tried to bring up race and ethnicity a few minutes later. Starting to explain SB 1070's potentially disproportionate effects by race and ethnicity, Verrelli observed that two million Latinos live in Arizona, but only 400,000 at most are unauthorized migrants. But Justice Antonin Scalia cut him off: "What does this have to do with Federal immigration law? I mean, it may have to do with racial harassment, but I thought you weren't relying on that."[2]

When Scalia jumped in, Verrilli was trying to express a view of the state and local role in immigration that went beyond the pure question of who was the right decision-maker. He wanted to support his preemption argument by raising concerns about the effects of SB 1070 on racial and ethnic minorities. But Scalia essentially told Verrilli he could bring up race and ethnicity only to show profiling or other forms of discrimination, not to show preemption. And Roberts had already prompted Verrilli to take profiling and discrimination claims off the table. It is hard to know why Roberts asked his opening question, but these exchanges forced Verrilli's oral argument to separate the federal government's concerns about state involvement in immigration law from any concerns related to race and ethnicity. Verrilli was left to argue that the only potential defect had nothing to do with SB 1070's content, but rather its source—that it was a state law.

This exchange at the Supreme Court is important because it went to the heart of an issue that is central to today's debates about unauthorized migration: state and local enforcement authority. Can state and local governments take the initiative and do something about unauthorized migration if they believe that the federal government is not doing enough? This is partly a matter of constitutional law, for the US Constitution defines the roles of federal, state, and local governments. But this chapter discusses far more than what the Constitution or statutes allow or forbid by way of state and local enforcement authority. The more fundamental question is whether decisions about immigration and immigrants should be made in Washington, DC, in state capitols, in city council chambers, or by local cops on the street. At stake are basic values relating both to the institutions of government and to what it means to be a nation of immigrants.

STATE AND LOCAL involvement in immigration enforcement reached the US Supreme Court in two landmark cases in 2011 and 2012. The decisions addressed the constitutionality of two of the most prominent state laws, both from Arizona. The first was the Legal Arizona Workers Act (LAWA), which indirectly enforced federal immigration law by restricting work by unauthorized migrants in Arizona. LAWA did this by requiring all employers in the state to use the federal E-Verify database to check if their employees are allowed to work. Employers who violated LAWA could have their business licenses suspended or revoked. The second Arizona law was SB 1070, which involved state and local police directly in federal immigration enforcement. It required police to check the immigration status of individuals under some circumstances and to detain some unauthorized migrants. SB 1070 also created new state crimes for federal immigration violations.[3]

The federal government's challenge to SB 1070 was based on preemption, which is essentially the argument that a state or local government has overstepped its authority by doing something that is for the federal government to decide. Preemption appears to be concerned only with *who* decides. It seems not to be concerned with *what* is decided, for example, whether a law unlawfully discriminates and thus violates the equal protection clause of the Fourteenth Amendment. But as I will explain, there is much more to preemption and to defining the state and local role in addressing immigration and immigrants.

This chapter will explain that the most important purpose of preemption in immigration-related situations is to minimize problems with immigration enforcement. Because the immigration system makes enforcement highly discretionary, it matters a great deal who exercises that discretion. The most significant potential danger is that discretionary enforcement will be tainted by racial or ethnic discrimination that will escape detection and remedy. Limiting the state and local role in immigration law is a way of preventing discrimination in state and local enforcement before it might happen. As a corollary, preventing discrimination before it takes place allows courts to avoid the nearly impossible task that a discrimination lawsuit forces judges to undertake—ascertaining what particular state or local officials were thinking.

This sort of prophylactic preemption is part of an important category of legal rules—those that serve to prevent violations of the US Constitution that would be hard to detect, prove, or remedy after they occur. In other words, an important way to uphold constitutional values is to prevent serious but elusive constitutional violations. To take an example from outside immigration law, police officers are generally required to give so-called *Miranda* warnings when making arrests ("You have the right to remain silent...."). Even if nothing in the Constitution requires such warnings, their purpose and effect is to make it much more likely that suspects have practical, preventive protection against self-incrimination, involuntary confession, and other constitutional violations.[4]

Similarly, criminal statutes are unconstitutional if they are excessively vague. One reason for this rule is that a person might naturally refrain from doing something that is constitutionally protected, if she is afraid that she will be arrested, charged, and punished under the vague statute. For example, she might refrain from free speech protected by the First Amendment. Vague criminal laws leave considerable room for police to engage in law enforcement practices that effectively prevent individuals from doing something that is protected by the Constitution, yet might expose them to arrest. At the same time, such violations of First Amendment rights would be hard to remedy after they occur, because it is nearly impossible to know what individuals would have done if the vague laws did not exist. The Constitution prohibits vague criminal laws in order to prevent improper exercises of law enforcement authority.[5]

In the near half-century since the US Supreme Court decided *Miranda v. Arizona* in 1966, *Miranda* warnings have become routine in law enforcement. As with any preventive approach, the warnings apply even when the problem that they seek to prevent might not occur. Police give *Miranda* warnings even though it is uncertain whether self-incrimination or coerced confessions might occur in any given case. Likewise, courts strike down vague statutes even if police officers might not enforce them in ways that violate constitutional rights. The core justification for both *Miranda* warnings and the void-for-vagueness doctrine is the very uncertainty whether a violation will occur and, if it does, whether the violation will be detected and the remedy will be adequate.

By suggesting that a principal reason for preemption is to prevent improper decisions by state and local governments, I do not mean to romanticize federal decision-making. But if enforcing immigration law—either directly or indirectly—is entirely a federal job, then state or local pressures to do something about unauthorized migration need to be directed to Congress and federal agencies headquartered in Washington, DC. Sometimes by transparency or by procedure, and sometimes by sheer inertia, national politics and the processes of federal decision-making can more effectively temper those impulses that might lead to enforcement that is discriminatory or otherwise improper. If, however, state and local governments have broad enforcement prerogatives, then a wider variation in outcomes is likely, with problems that may go undetected and unchecked.

Limits on State and Local Enforcement

Many state and local governments have tried in the past generation to enforce federal immigration law indirectly or directly. *Plyler* was one of the first modern US Supreme Court cases to address the constitutionality of such laws. The winning argument for the *Plyler* children was that the Texas statute discriminated unconstitutionally. According to the Court, Texas could not justify a law that effectively kept the children from a public education. The specific defect in *Plyler* was that the statute violated the equal protection clause of the Fourteenth Amendment to the Constitution. The Court said in a footnote that it would not address the plaintiffs' other main argument—that federal law preempted the Texas statute. But a big part of its equal protection analysis was that states and localities have less authority than the federal government to treat people differently based on immigration status.[6]

Even if *Plyler* stands for the general idea that the state and local role is limited, it offers little guidance to courts on the constitutionality of state and local laws. Courts have generally rejected the argument that the Constitution requires equal treatment of unauthorized migrants and noncitizens who are in the United States lawfully. The *Plyler* Court's equal protection holding in favor of unauthorized migrants has never been applied beyond public elementary and secondary education. When challengers have succeeded with a constitutional challenge to a law that enforces immigration law directly or indirectly against unauthorized migrants, they typically have not won on equal protection. When they alleged violations of individual rights, they have focused on other rights—such as freedom of speech or association under the First Amendment to the US Constitution, or protections against unreasonable searches and seizures under the Fourth Amendment. But most often, successful constitutional challenges have instead targeted the decision-maker and have argued principally that the law is preempted.[7]

ON THE QUESTION of whether federal law preempts a state or local law relating to immigration or immigrants, a key modern precedent is *De Canas v. Bica*, a unanimous Supreme Court decision authored by Justice Brennan in 1976, six years before he wrote for the Court in *Plyler*. The *De Canas* case involved a California law, enacted in 1971, that penalized employers who "knowingly employ an alien who is not entitled to lawful residence in the United States if such employment would have an adverse effect on lawful resident workers." Violators could be fined $200 to $500. Preceding federal employer sanctions by 15 years, it was the first such law in the United States, soon followed by similar laws in 11 other states and the city of Las Vegas.[8]

The plaintiffs in *De Canas* were farmworkers who were lawfully in the United States and who worked for several farm labor contractors. The contractors told the workers that because enough other workers were available, the plaintiffs would be discharged and not rehired. The plaintiffs sued to get their jobs back, alleging that the contractors had replaced them with workers who were in the United States unlawfully. The pivotal issue was preemption: Did the California law encroach on federal immigration laws by penalizing employers for hiring unauthorized workers? They lacked federal permission to be in the United States or to work, but federal law imposed no analogous penalty on employers.[9]

Courts often explain that there are several types of preemption. First, a federal statute might say explicitly that state or local laws on a particular topic are preempted. This is known as "express preemption." Or, if there is no such express language in a statute, preemption might be "implied." There are two types of implied preemption. With either type, states and localities may not regulate at all, even if no federal law expressly addresses the issue in the case.

One type of implied preemption is "field preemption," which occurs when a state or local law addresses an area either where lawmaking authority is inherently and exclusively federal—such as foreign relations—or where federal regulation is so pervasive and comprehensive as to occupy the field. Another type of implied preemption is called "conflict preemption." Even when an entire field is not exclusively federal, preemption invalidates any state or local law that conflicts with federal law. A conflict exists if state or local law is inconsistent with federal law, or if it stands as an obstacle to accomplishing Congress's objectives. A conflict may be readily apparent if state and federal laws apply different standards.[10]

The Court in *De Canas* noted that no federal law expressly preempted the California statute. The long tradition of state employment laws ruled out the notion that employment laws are an inherent and exclusive federal domain. Nor did federal laws totally regulate employment by unauthorized migrants. So the Court addressed conflict preemption, observing that the California law would be preempted if it penalized employers for hiring a noncitizen who, though "not entitled to lawful residence in the United States," had federal permission to work. Because the way the statute would be applied was uncertain, the Court sent the case back to the California courts to see if they would interpret the statute to conflict with federal law or be consistent with it.[11]

In many court cases since *De Canas*, the decisive issue has been whether a state or local law relating to immigration or immigrants is preempted because it conflicts with federal law. One example is an early version of a local ordinance adopted in 2007 in Farmers Branch, Texas. The ordinance required renters to prove either US citizenship or "eligible immigration status," originally defined to mean eligibility for federal housing subsidies. Federal district judge Sam Lindsay explained that applying federal housing eligibility rules would prohibit housing rentals to international students and other noncitizens lawfully in the United States. He found that by restricting a lawfully present noncitizen's ability to rent housing, the local ordinance was preempted because it conflicted with federal law.[12]

A logical question is why it conflicts with federal law to restrict housing for lawfully present noncitizens. The answer comes from a 1915 US Supreme Court decision that *Farmers Branch* cited. An Austrian citizen named Mike Raich was lawfully in the United States and was working as a cook at William Truax's restaurant in Bisbee, Arizona. Truax wanted to fire him to comply with an Arizona requirement that if any employer had more than five employees, at least 80 percent of them had to be US citizens or noncitizens eligible to vote. (Statewide noncitizen voting was not unusual in this era.) Raich sued to keep his job. In *Truax v. Raich*, the Supreme Court struck down the Arizona law, explaining that a state cannot "deny to lawful inhabitants, because of their race or nationality, the ordinary means of earning a livelihood." If states or localities effectively discourage noncitizens who are lawfully present in the United States from living there, then they are regulating immigration in conflict with federal immigration law.[13]

The Mirror Image?

What if state and local restrictions on housing and employment target only noncitizens who are in the United States in violation of federal immigration law? May state and local governments adopt such laws if the laws are drafted to adopt or "mirror" the standards in federal law? The Legal Arizona Workers Act (LAWA) requires all Arizona employers to use the federal E-Verify database to confirm each employee's permission to work under federal law, so Arizona does not restrict work by noncitizens who have federal work permission. By mirroring federal law, LAWA avoided the fatal flaw in *Farmers Branch*. But was LAWA still preempted because it intruded in some other way on federal authority to regulate immigration?[14]

The US Chamber of Commerce and several other business and civil rights organizations sued to block LAWA. They argued that federal law expressly preempts state and local employer sanctions, or in the alternative that LAWA is preempted because federal law occupies the field or conflicts with LAWA. In 2011, the Supreme Court rejected these preemption arguments and upheld LAWA by a 5–3 vote in *Chamber of Commerce v. Whiting*, with Justice Kagan recusing herself.[15]

The Court first focused on the provision in federal law that expressly preempts state and local employer sanctions but makes an exception for "licensing and similar laws." It ruled that because LAWA penalizes violators by revoking business licenses, the exception applies, so there is no express preemption. The Court also considered whether LAWA might still be preempted, if not because of the express preemption provision, then because LAWA conflicts with federal immigration law. The plaintiffs argued that federal law left E-Verify optional, stopping short of zero-tolerance enforcement as a way of delicately balancing employer sanctions against other priorities, such as minimizing employer burdens, protecting employee privacy, and preventing employment discrimination. By making E-Verify mandatory and imposing stiffer penalties, the plaintiffs argued that LAWA reflects a different balance and thus conflicts with federal law. This, they reasoned, meant implied preemption.[16]

The Court rejected this argument. By emphasizing that LAWA targets only unauthorized workers, the Court seemed to agree with Arizona that because LAWA mirrors federal law, there is no implied preemption. But the lesson from this part of *Whiting* was unclear, because the Court's implied preemption analysis relied heavily on its express preemption analysis. That analysis was unique to the federal employer sanctions context with its express preemption provision and licensing law exception. *Whiting* left open whether other state or local laws that target unauthorized migrants are preempted.[17]

THE 5–3 SPLIT in *Whiting* reflected—but did not resolve—a basic difference between two approaches to state and local authority when it comes to immigration and immigrants. According to the mirror image theory, the key question is whether a noncitizen is violating federal immigration law. It does not matter that federal agencies might not actually deport or take any sort of action against any individual unauthorized migrant. A state or local law that targets unauthorized migrants does not conflict with federal law. In contrast, the three dissenters in *Whiting* looked beyond the question of whether state or local laws adopt the standards in federal immigration law. They emphasized that in practice, LAWA and federal employer sanctions produce different enforcement results. For the dissenters, the difference in outcomes signaled a conflict and thus preemption, even though the written laws mirror each other.

To further the analysis, it is useful to examine the successful preemption challenge to two local ordinances in Hazleton, Pennsylvania. They required anyone working or living in rental housing to prove US citizenship or lawful immigration status. The federal court of appeals for the Third Circuit found that the ordinances conflicted with federal law, and so were preempted, even though they mirrored the federal statute. The ordinance's fatal flaw was that the city would restrict housing and work for unauthorized migrants even if the federal government would not try to deport them.[18]

The conflict between federal and local law went beyond the possibility that local authorities, being less conversant with federal immigration law, would misinterpret or misapply it. The real problem was the gap between the city's enforcement of its ordinances and federal immigration enforcement. Writing for the Third Circuit, Chief Judge Theodore McKee noted that enforcement reflects many highly discretionary decisions. He wrote: "Stitched into the fabric of Hazleton's housing provisions…is either a lack of understanding or a refusal to recognize the complexities of federal immigration law." The federal government might or might not seek removal, and even if it does, an immigration judge may grant discretionary relief that confers lawful status. Emphasizing federal enforcement discretion, the decision in *City of Hazleton* rejected the notion that a local housing or employment law is consistent with federal law—and thus not preempted—if it relies on federal law to identify immigration law violators and then merely purports to fill a gap in federal enforcement. Instead, federal immigration law consists of both action and inaction, so no gap exists for state or local law to fill. The decision not to enforce in some situations is part of federal immigration law.[19]

Finding Immigration Law

The *Hazleton* analysis is far more consistent with reality than the mirror image theory. Restrictive lawful admissions, strong economic needs for workers, and selective enforcement have combined to make immigration law in action depend far more on the exercise of discretion than on the letter of federal immigration statutes. In theory, immigration law starts with Congress, but in practice it is made in the field. The city of Hazleton was enforcing immigration law indirectly by restricting housing and work for unauthorized migrants. In finding that federal law preempted the city's ability to do so, the Third Circuit emphasized several different ways in which unlawful presence is inconclusive—twilight statuses, avenues from unlawful to lawful status, and the predictable improbability of removal even when a noncitizen's presence is clearly unlawful. The core problem was that the city's immigration enforcement activity through its own discretionary decision-making would differ from federal immigration law in action.

One reasonable objection to this analysis is that federal law that is not set out in the text of a statute cannot have the power to preempt state or local law. This objection is the foundation of the mirror image theory, which focuses on the letter of the law. From this point of view, Hazleton's ordinances are not preempted if they use federal immigration law to limit access to housing and jobs in the city, and it is wrong to look beyond what is written in federal statutes to find inconsistencies between local and federal law. As long as the ordinances target only unauthorized migrants, it does not matter for preemption purposes that twilight statuses exist, that immigration status can change, or that removal is improbable. More generally, this argument supports broadening the circle of government actors with some kind of enforcement authority. By supporting an expansive view of the state and local role, this argument parallels the dissenters in *Plyler*, for whom the children's unlawful presence in the United States was the essential and deciding fact.

It is part of the lawmaking process, however, for any government to choose among a variety of modes for doing so. One traditional mode is a statute, but a government might make law in the form of agency regulations. Or the law might consist of the combined results in a body of court cases, or in policies and practices that reflect numerous decisions by officials in a federal administrative agency. This choice of mode reflects basic judgments inherent in the power to make law. A statute has the advantage of announcing a rule in advance, but it may be phrased so generally that its precise meaning is left to later agency or court decisions about specific applications. When Congress cannot come up with a statute that announces precisely what is both legislatively desirable and administratively feasible, it may allow individual discretionary decisions to create law in action incrementally.

If the purpose of preemption is to allow federal decision-making to override any inconsistent state or local laws, as the supremacy clause of the US Constitution requires, then state or local governments may not insist that the federal government adopt its laws in a particular form. Indeed, the very idea of implied preemption assumes that the federal government need not anticipate and foreclose every possible inconsistent state or local government decision, and that it need not enact a federal statute precisely addressing every issue where it may be important to assert federal prerogatives.

The idea that the power to make law includes the power to select the mode of law is a well-established principle of US law governing cases in federal court. When cases between adversaries from different states go to federal court, a basic question is whether state or federal law applies. Suppose a Maryland resident sues a Virginia resident for breach of a contract that was signed in Maryland, for services to be performed in Maryland. If a Maryland state court were to hear the case, it is clear that Maryland contract law would apply. But what happens if the case is in federal court? Can the federal court develop and apply its own federal contract law, disregarding contract law developed by the Maryland legislature and courts?

According to the landmark 1938 US Supreme Court decision in *Erie Railroad v. Tompkins*, a federal court in this scenario applies state law, regardless of whether it is a state statute or a state case precedent. Previously, federal courts generally applied state statutes, but not state judicial decisions. The core idea in *Erie* is that the federal government must respect state law, no matter what form that state law takes. It is not a legitimate concern of the federal government whether state law is found in a statute enacted by the legislature or a court decision by a judge. The state government that makes the law can choose the mode, because that choice is part of the very process of lawmaking.[20]

In preemption cases, the same idea applies in the opposite direction. Instead of allowing state law to displace federal law, as it does under *Erie*, the federal government's decisions—no matter what form they take—override state or local law. *Erie* involved state lawmaking by judges, whereas *Hazleton* involved federal lawmaking by executive branch agencies, but the idea is the same. Federal lawmaking power includes the power to choose whether Congress or the executive branch makes that law.

Courts seem to recognize the power of federal executive agency regulations to preempt state and local law. But a further issue is whether it matters that the federal prerogatives are set out in regulations with the force of law, or instead are less formal, such as memoranda to guide the exercise of prosecutorial discretion or simply a pattern of decisions to enforce or not enforce immigration law in particular situations. *Hazleton* reflects the view that for purposes of preempting state or local law, the federal government is free to set out federal immigration law not only in the letter of federal statutes or regulations, but also in federal patterns of discretionary enforcement.[21]

A logical objection is that informal executive branch decisions should not serve as the basis of preemption because they are not subject to the same deliberation or transparency as decisions by Congress or federal judges. They might not be, but that is not relevant to preemption. Instead, the issue is whether federal law exists and is inconsistent with state or local law. If both of these things are true, then objections about the quality of federal law should be directed toward Congress or the federal executive branch. Congress could curtail executive branch authority, but it has not, for many reasons that are inherent in a system of selective admissions and selective enforcement that has historically acquiesced in a large unauthorized population. Here again, the federal choice of one kind of decision-making process over another is part of federal authority over immigration or any other area of law.[22]

Another objection to allowing federal executive branch decisions to preempt state laws is based on the idea that an important function of state and local lawmaking authority is curbing federal executive power when Congress has not addressed an issue. It would follow that the exercise of enforcement discretion by federal executive agencies and officials should not be allowed to curtail state or local power to make laws. The problem with this objection is evident from looking more closely at what happens when a state or locality takes action that the federal executive branch would not. Suppose that the city of Hazleton targets unauthorized migrants whom federal immigration agencies would not. If a court allows the city of Hazleton to do this in a way that is inconsistent with federal agency priorities, then that court is assuming that Congress intended state and local laws to do so. That is possible, but it is at least as likely that Hazleton would be undermining authority that Congress has delegated to federal agencies. The operation of immigration law in practice strongly suggests that the exercise of federal executive discretion in enforcement supplies the real content of federal immigration law for the purpose of deciding what is inconsistent with state and local decisions.[23]

I ACKNOWLEDGE THAT complete analysis requires going further. *City of Hazleton* decided that the local ordinances were preempted because they conflicted with federal immigration law, which it found not just in the text of the Immigration and Nationality Act, but also in discretionary enforcement patterns. But the mere fact that state and local involvement in immigration enforcement targets a larger number of unauthorized migrants does not establish a conflict with federal law. This is the core argument of enforcement-minded states and localities—that it is entirely consistent with federal immigration law for state and local governments to step in and help out when the federal government is unable to enforce immigration law effectively.

To illustrate, assume that the federal government is highly unlikely to deport a noncitizen who is in the United States unlawfully. Federal law may still leave room for Hazleton or Arizona to make it harder for this noncitizen to earn a living or rent an apartment. If federal law allows local or state decisions to fill gaps in this way, there is no conflict and thus no preemption. Such openness to a state or local role is consistent with understandings of federalism in areas of law outside immigration law, where some degree of concurrent, overlapping, and even redundant federal and state regulation and enforcement are not unusual. Does federal law allow any such enforcement role for states and localities instead of sharply separating federal from state domains?[24]

Neither the federal appeals court in *City of Hazleton* nor the US Supreme Court in *Whiting* addressed this question, but it became central in the court challenges to Arizona's SB 1070. Going well beyond indirect enforcement in areas of traditional state regulation like work and housing, SB 1070 called for direct immigration enforcement by authorizing and sometimes requiring state and local police to detect and detain unauthorized migrants and then hand them over to federal immigration authorities. Section 2(B), sometimes referred to as the "show me your papers" provision, applies if a state or local law enforcement officer stops, detains, or arrests someone and reasonably suspects that the individual lacks lawful immigration status. If she cannot prove that she is in the United States lawfully, the officer must detain her while verifying her status with the federal government. SB 1070 also created new state crimes for working without authorization, for failure to comply with registration requirements in federal immigration law, and for encouraging or assisting unauthorized migration. Another section expanded state and local police authority to arrest individuals who might be deportable. Alabama, Utah, Georgia, and South Carolina soon enacted laws with similar provisions, plus additional requirements and prohibitions.[25]

Lawsuits challenged these laws as unconstitutional. Of these, the challenge to SB 1070 advanced most quickly through the courts. Soon after individual plaintiffs and nonprofit organizations sued, the federal government took the extraordinary step of trying to block the Arizona, Alabama, and Utah statutes. Its only argument was preemption. Because the federal government's challenge became the main vehicle in the courts, the dominant legal issue surrounding SB 1070 became preemption, not equal protection or other individual rights. Federal district judge Susan Bolton issued a preliminary injunction that kept four of SB 1070's key provisions from going into effect, and the Ninth Circuit Court of Appeals affirmed. Arizona's appeal soon reached the US Supreme Court, where the exchange between Chief Justice Roberts and Solicitor General Verrilli at oral argument confirmed the federal government's preemption focus.[26]

Rejecting the Mirror Image

The Supreme Court decided *Arizona v. United States* on June 25, 2012. Of the four provisions in SB 1070 challenged by the federal government, the Court struck down three. In an opinion by Justice Anthony Kennedy, the Court first invalidated the sections that created two new state crimes. One was section 3, which made it a state crime to not comply with federal registration requirements for noncitizens. Relying heavily on its 1941 decision in *Hines v. Davidowitz*, which invalidated a Pennsylvania state registration system for noncitizens, the Court found that federal registration occupied the field, leaving no room for state or local registration laws. The Court also invalidated the new state crime in section 5 for working without authorization. In contrast to its approach to registration requirements, the Court did not say that the federal government occupied the field of employer sanctions. Indeed, the Court had just held in *Whiting* that the federal government did not. But because Congress had deliberately declined to make unauthorized work a crime, section 5 conflicted with federal law and was therefore preempted. Applying similar reasoning, the Court also held that federal law preempted section 6, which would authorize any state or local police officer to arrest noncitizens without a warrant if they had committed an offense that made them removable. The Court explained that federal law allows state or local officers to make immigration arrests only in certain circumstances, so any broader arrest authority under section 6 would create a conflict.[27]

One crucial lesson from these parts of *Arizona v. United States* was that the Court rejected the mirror image approach that would allow state and local measures as long as they target only unauthorized migrants. It might have been plausible to read *Whiting* as endorsing the mirror image idea and allowing state and local restrictions on unauthorized migrants' access to work or housing, and possibly allowing some direct enforcement authority to arrest and detain unauthorized migrants. But *Arizona* effectively confined the mirror image idea to employer sanctions, where it could rely on the unique explicit opening that Congress left for state and local licensing laws.[28]

Central to the *Arizona* Court's rejection of the mirror image approach was not only a broad view of federal supremacy in immigration-related matters, but also the idea that the federal government's exercise of enforcement discretion counts as part of federal immigration law for preemption purposes. If a state law like SB 1070 enforces federal immigration law more fully than the federal government would—such as with extra state penalties for federal immigration violations—it conflicts with federal law and is preempted. This key aspect of *Arizona* led other federal and state courts to invalidate other mirror image state laws that targeted unauthorized migrants. Federal appeals courts ruled that federal law preempted analogous state law provisions in Alabama, Georgia, South Carolina, Utah, and Indiana. Likewise, a Louisiana state court held that federal law preempted a state law that made it a felony to drive without proof of lawful immigration status.[29]

ARIZONA V. UNITED STATES allowed one part of SB 1070—section 2(B)—to go into effect. This part of *Arizona* suggests several lessons for assessing whether state or local law conflicts with federal immigration law. Why did the Court invalidate section 6 but not section 2(B)? Both provisions would expand state and local police authority relating to arrests. Section 6 would authorize state and local arrests for some immigration violations. In contrast, section 2(B) applies more broadly, requiring an immigration status check and detention if a state or local law enforcement officer stops, detains, or arrests someone and reasonably suspects that the individual lacks lawful immigration status. These encounters will typically be encounters by state and local police in the normal course of law enforcement.[30]

Section 2(B) calls on state and local police to become involved with immigration enforcement less directly than state and local arrests under section 6 for federal immigration violations, but more directly than regulation of work or housing by LAWA and other state or local measures. In contrast to the traditional state role in regulating work and housing, immigration stopped being a traditional area of state regulation after the Civil War. By involving state and local governments in Arizona more directly in immigration enforcement, SB 1070, including section 2(B), exposed itself to more persuasive preemption challenges. The crucial question is why, given this move from indirect to direct involvement in enforcement, the Supreme Court allowed section 2(B) to go into effect. The answer requires the analytical step that *City of Hazleton* did not take, to explore the possibility that state and local laws on immigration or immigrants are not preempted just because states and localities fill gaps in federal law. Reaching different results is not a conflict if federal law allows the difference.

The strongest signs of such permission are federal laws that outline a state or local role. Key is section 1373(c) of title 8 of the United States Code, which requires the federal government to respond to state or local requests to check any individual's citizenship or immigration status. The Court in *Arizona* found that this section foresees these checks as routine follow-ups to normal arrests and stops by state and local police. This means that section 1373(c) eliminates any conflict between the status check requirement in section 2(B) and federal immigration law. The Court acknowledged that detention during the immigration status check could be so prolonged as to be unconstitutional. But it reasoned that because Arizona courts might interpret section 2(B) to eliminate this possibility, the provision could go into effect. The Court acknowledged that any of the numerous other constitutional challenges to SB 1070 might succeed on grounds other than preemption, such as equal protection, the Fourth Amendment, and the First Amendment. It also recognized that other lawsuits might be filed if the actual implementation of section 2(B) led to constitutional violations in specific situations, but the Court rejected the argument that section 2(B) was unconstitutional on its face.[31]

In evaluating the Court's decision to let section 2(B) take effect, I come back to the core question that decides whether state or local law is preempted: Does state or local involvement in enforcement conflict with federal immigration law? My answer involves two steps. The first looks more closely at discretion in immigration enforcement. The second considers in more fundamental terms why limits on state and local involvement in immigration enforcement are necessary.

A Closer Look at Enforcement Discretion

The *Arizona* Court was unconvinced by the federal government's argument that federal enforcement would be hampered if section 2(B) makes immigration status checks mandatory, even for noncitizens whom the federal government probably would not remove. According to the Court, nothing in federal law says that states and localities should refrain in low priority cases from asking the federal government for immigration status information under section 1373(c). Writing separately, Justice Samuel Alito agreed on this point, adding that the federal government still has discretion to do nothing with the knowledge that someone in state or local custody is in the United States illegally. As he put it, "the discretion that ultimately matters is not whether to verify a person's immigration status but whether to act once the person's status is known." As long as the federal government has this discretion, section 2(B) does not conflict with federal law, according to this analysis.[32]

The Court's view may seem logical, but its soundness depends on the practical role that state and local arrest discretion plays in federal immigration enforcement. Federal Bureau of Immigration and Customs Enforcement (ICE) agents are unlikely to arrest unauthorized migrants who represent a low enforcement priority. But under section 2(B), the routine state and local police discretion to conduct a traffic stop becomes the discretion to make an arrest that carries with it a mandatory duty under Arizona law to check immigration status. In practice, state and local police have the discretion to report an individual to federal authorities for potential deportation.

The crucial question is whether section 2(B) makes the state and local discretion to perform stops and arrests such an influential factor in immigration enforcement that state and local arrest practices are setting enforcement priorities. If state and local arrest discretion is the discretion that matters, then section 2(B)'s practical effect is to shape the federal enforcement caseload. But if Justice Alito is right, federal discretion to refrain from enforcement limits the ability of state and local police, through ordinary stop and arrests, to make immigration law on the ground.

ANSWERING THIS QUESTION requires an analysis of discretion. A logical starting point is the distinction between two broad types of discretion. The federal government exercises *macro*-discretion when agencies and officials set enforcement priorities and support them with funds and other resources. The federal government exercises *micro*-discretion when agencies and officials decide whether or not to pursue the removal of a noncitizen after she has been identified as unlawfully present or otherwise removable.[33]

Delving deeper than the micro-macro distinction reveals a taxonomy of discretion that reflects the stages of enforcement. First, Congress exercises legislative discretion when it enacts federal statutes defining who is to be admitted or removed, and thus who is in the United States lawfully or unlawfully. Legislation also sets penalties, including deportation, for immigration violations. Drafting and enacting legislation clearly reflects discretion, though it is not always viewed that way, perhaps because it is macro-discretion that does not name individuals.

In the second stage of discretion, a law enforcement officer decides to make a stop or arrest that puts an individual into contact with the immigration enforcement system and thus exposes him to potential deportation. For each of the over 11 million unauthorized migrants in the United States, the chances of arrest depend initially on how government officials exercise macro-discretion to decide the level of resources devoted to certain types of border or interior enforcement. Micro-discretion then comes into play, with decisions to pursue certain individuals.

In the third stage, the federal officials decide if they will press charges against a particular immigration violator who has come to their attention. A decision to seek deportation typically leads to a civil removal proceeding in immigration court with an immigration judge presiding. Federal officials might later exercise discretion to drop the matter, or they may move in the opposite direction by pressing criminal charges based on the immigration violation. The term "prosecutorial discretion," as used in immigration law today, usually refers to decisions in this third enforcement stage.[34]

The fourth stage of discretion is deciding if a specific violation has occurred and, if so, imposing a penalty. An immigration judge can decide to issue a removal order or to allow the noncitizen to remain. The judge might exercise discretion to grant asylum, cancellation of removal, or some other form of relief from removal. Or the Department of Homeland Security might acquiesce in a grant of discretionary relief that allows the noncitizen to stay in the United States.

The fifth stage of discretion shapes the ultimate outcome. A noncitizen who receives a formal order of removal may or may not actually leave the United States. The federal government exercises discretion to detain him to assure his physical deportation. Even if a noncitizen is in federal custody, the government can decide in its discretion to delay or avoid his deportation. For example, US government assistance may be required before he can get documents for travel to another country. Or if a noncitizen is not detained and absconds, federal authorities exercise discretion in how they try to find him.

IN *ARIZONA*, THE consensus on the Supreme Court was that because the federal government has ultimate discretion not to pursue deportation, SB 1070's section 2(B), though it turns state and local arrests into immigration arrests, does not undermine federal priorities. But identifying these five stages of discretion casts serious doubt on the Court's analysis. The central question is when discretion shapes immigration enforcement. The available statistics make clear that an individual unauthorized migrant's chances of arrest are very low. Once arrested, however, the chances are high that the federal government will move to deport or even criminally prosecute. Arrest discretion has by far the greatest effect on outcomes.

To identify the discretion that matters, I will focus on the year 2009. Because this was the last full federal fiscal year in which federal agencies played the dominant role in bringing unauthorized migrants into the immigration enforcement system, it permits a comparison of the stages of federal enforcement discretion. Before recent increases in the role of state and local police, the federal government historically controlled immigration enforcement discretion at nearly every stage, from legislation through outcome. Federal agencies made the overwhelming majority of arrests that led to removal proceedings. The estimated US unauthorized population in 2009 was 11.2 million. Government statistics on arrests are incomplete and do not separate interior from border arrests, but it is clear that arrests were a small fraction of the 11.2 million total, probably well under one million. Once violators were arrested, however, rough estimates suggest that between 65 to 95 percent were prosecuted, then had their cases decided, and were ultimately forced to leave the United States.[35]

These numbers suggest that arrest discretion matters far more at the arrest stage than at the prosecution stage. Section 2(B) and similar state laws magnify state and local stops and arrests into immigration enforcement events. If many state and local police bring unauthorized migrants into contact with federal immigration agencies, then state and local police will be the federal system's gatekeepers. In theory, federal agencies can let any arrestee go, as Justice Alito observed. But that ultimate discretion is limited in two important ways.

First, prosecutorial discretion after arrest is a federal response in an individual case after it is part of the caseload for potential removal from the United States. The more important fact is that state and local priorities and decision-makers have already shaped the caseload. Second, once state or local officers identify and detain an unauthorized migrant, any federal decision not to seek removal will prompt much more political exposure and criticism than the systemic, macro-level discretionary federal decisions that make arrests more or less likely in the first place. Imagine, for example, that police officers stop a van carrying several unauthorized migrants, but ICE decides not to take them into custody or not to seek their removal. By shaping the caseload and increasing exposure, section 2(B) limits the federal government's practical ability to set and implement enforcement priorities, such as focusing on the removal of noncitizens who may raise national security concerns or who have criminal convictions, or considering equities and hardships in individual cases.

I have now circled back to this basic question: What is wrong with state and local police dictating the caseload of federal immigration agencies and producing enforcement patterns that differ from what the federal government would achieve on its own? A strong state or local influence on immigration enforcement does not conclusively show a conflict that justifies preemption. One might argue instead that state or local variations are a feature of nation-wide enforcement under a federal umbrella.[36]

Ultimately, the language of federal immigration statutes does not provide a totally convincing answer one way or the other to this basic question. Federal statutes foresee some state and local role in immigration enforcement but leave unclear what that role is. In turn, a claim that a state or local law is preempted can be persuasive only if it reflects sound thinking about the risks when state and local governments get involved with immigration and citizenship. Central to this inquiry when the scope of express or implied preemption is unclear is the federal government's essential role in protecting some types of individual constitutional rights.

Finding the Right Decision-maker

In the oral argument in *Arizona v. United States*, Solicitor General Verrilli conceded a narrow view of preemption that separated the issue of state and local immigration authority in the abstract from the substance of the state or local decision. But this view of immigration-related preemption is too narrow. An approach that is far more grounded in US history reflects the same close link between process and content that emerged in *Plyler*, where concerns about state power to address immigration led the Supreme Court to find that the content of the Texas statute violated equal protection. In spite of the formal distinction between challenges to the *who* (such as preemption) or the *what* (such as equal protection) of an immigration decision, the relationship between *who* and *what* is essential to any sound assessment of a law or policy.

A persuasive preemption analysis must probe further into the reasons for concern about state or local decisions. Much of the constitutional concern is that overzealous enforcers will violate the rights of individuals. But what rights should preemption safeguard against violations at state or local hands? In theory, one possibility is an equal protection violation based on state or local discrimination against unauthorized migrants because they lack lawful immigration status. But state and local laws that disadvantage noncitizens because they are unlawfully present are very hard to challenge as equal protection violations.

The most notable successful equal protection challenge by noncitizens is the US Supreme Court's 1971 decision in *Graham v. Richardson*. Relying on both equal protection and preemption as alternative rationales, the Court struck down laws in Arizona and Pennsylvania that denied welfare benefits to lawful permanent residents. The equal protection reasoning was that "classifications based on alienage, like those based on nationality or race, are inherently suspect and subject to close judicial scrutiny." This wording seemed to invoke strict scrutiny, which is the most probing test of a statute's constitutionality.[37]

But the *Graham* plaintiffs were permanent residents. With the one exception of *Plyler*, no later published case from any appellate court in the United States has held that a state or federal law disadvantaging unauthorized migrants violates equal protection for that reason. Even for nonimmigrants who are lawfully present in the United States, courts are split on whether laws disadvantaging them are unlawfully discriminatory. For unauthorized migrants, courts require only that the law disadvantaging unauthorized migrants have a rational basis—a test that is hard to fail.[38]

One possibility is expanding current equal protection law so that it requires equal treatment for unauthorized migrants and noncitizens who are in the United States lawfully. This was an essential part of *Plyler*, but courts have limited this reasoning to children in public schools. It is unlikely that courts will find an equal protection violation just because the federal government draws a line that disadvantages individuals who are in the United States unlawfully. As a practical matter, challenges to state and local laws that disadvantage unauthorized migrants on account of immigration status generally do not argue that such line-drawing alone violates the US Constitution. Instead, they rely principally on preemption.[39]

In contrast, racial or ethnic discrimination is a more familiar claim. Challenges are stronger if a government distinction is superficially based on immigration law status but actually discriminates in another way, with immigration status serving as a proxy for something more sinister. A government might target a particular unpopular group or discriminate based on race or ethnicity to a degree that violates equal protection or Fourth Amendment protections against unreasonable searches and seizures.

The problem for challengers is amassing enough supporting evidence to meet the requirements for proving these constitutional violations. For example, the constitutional challenges to the Hazleton ordinances included allegations of racial and ethnic discrimination, supported by abundant evidence that the ordinances would disproportionately affect Latinos—not just unauthorized migrants, but also US citizens and lawfully present noncitizens. The Third Circuit decision in *Hazleton* discussed local and regional demographic shifts and the intimidation of local Latino residents. So did the prior district court decision in the same case by Judge Munley, who added a long appendix emphasizing the role of racial exclusion in US immigration history. But he found this evidence insufficient to sustain an equal protection challenge, and the plaintiffs did not appeal this ruling.[40]

The failure of the *Hazleton* plaintiffs' equal protection claim is not surprising. Equal protection demands more than showing that a government decision has a disproportionate effect by race, ethnicity, or national origin. The ordinances made no distinctions by race, ethnicity, or national origin, but well-established law demands proof of discriminatory intent in some form. Another possible argument is based on a federal civil rights statute, section 1981 of title 42 of the United States Code, which "provides that 'all persons' shall…have the same right to make and enforce contracts and have the full and equal benefit of all laws to the same extent enjoyed by 'white citizens.'" The legal challenge to the Hazleton ordinances included the argument that the ordinances violated this statute. Federal district judge Munley agreed, but the Third Circuit did not address this issue on appeal. It is not clear if this approach can operate effectively as a remedy for discrimination.[41]

The harm associated with state and local laws that target unauthorized migrants in an atmosphere of racial and ethnic tension may be difficult to prove with the specificity required for claims based on equal protection or section 1981. Moreover, discrimination claims, whether based on the equal protection clause or section 1981, require courts to identify specific victims of specific discriminatory practices, as well as blame specific culprits, perhaps as racists. These are high stakes, and judges may hesitate. Decisions will turn on a simple yes-or-no decision as to whether certain defendants have discriminated. This is deeply troubling if the risk of discrimination is real, but constitutional violations will be hard to detect and hard to remedy. What is called for, then, is a more systemic solution.[42]

PREEMPTION MAINTAINS A commitment to nondiscrimination in immigration law by limiting who decides, rather than by directly monitoring the content of their decisions. Suppose a judge is concerned that a state or local law puts police in a situation where they can exercise broad discretion to enforce immigration law in ways that rely improperly on race and ethnicity but are unlikely to be detected or corrected. This possibility of discrimination may persuade some judges to conclude that state and local governments have encroached on federal immigration authority. This is true even when proof of improper reliance on race or ethnicity is not enough to show that the state or local government has violated equal protection or other individual rights. From this perspective, it seems likely that the evidence of racial and ethnic discrimination amassed by the plaintiffs in *Hazleton* influenced the district court and appeals court decisions finding that the local ordinances were preempted. After all, both decisions discussed racial and ethnic tensions in the city together with the need to prevent local authorities from exercising discretion in ways that differed from federal enforcement.[43]

Imagine, for example, that a local sheriff targets unauthorized migrants for immigration enforcement if they are from Mexico, but not if they are from Ireland or Poland. Such improper bias by state and local agencies and officers may be hard to detect and prove. A complex set of factors influence arrest patterns, and any bias is likely to reflect multiple discretionary decisions made by a larger cast of characters. Concerns of this sort led the federal government to terminate its 287(g) agreement with the Maricopa County Sheriff's Office in 2011. Similarly, preemption—like *Miranda* warnings and the prohibition on vague criminal laws—is a way to prevent constitutional violations that will be difficult or impossible to detect or remedy after they occur. It makes good sense that preemption offers this sort of oblique constitutional protection against unlawful discrimination in state and local immigration enforcement.[44]

This link between the *who* and the *what* of SB 1070 sheds light on Solicitor General Verrilli's exchanges with Chief Justice Roberts and Justice Scalia during the oral argument in *Arizona v. United States*. The federal government relied only on preemption, arguing that it was the wrong government actor— the State of Arizona—that enacted SB 1070. And yet, a big part of that argument was that preemption was appropriate because SB 1070 would make unconstitutional racial or ethnic profiling more likely. That is why Verrilli tried to bring up the disproportionate impact on the Latino population of Arizona.

This relationship between preemption and individual constitutional rights explains the connection between the parallel federal and private lawsuits that tried to block immigration laws in Arizona, Alabama, South Carolina, and Utah. The federal government's challenges relied entirely on preemption, while the private plaintiffs cited a combination of preemption and individual rights. The private and federal government lawsuits seem different, but they are closely linked because evidence of equal protection violations can fortify a preemption claim. More generally, preemption is appropriate if an expanded state or local role substantially increases the risk of undetected or unremedied constitutional violations.

A Broad View of Enforcement Preemption

A preemption challenge to a state or local immigration law is an alternative to an equal protection challenge. When equal protection violations based on discriminatory intent are a serious concern but are hard to define and prove, a preemption challenge can shift who bears the practical risk that the truth is hard to ascertain. Plaintiffs would no longer need to prove that state and local governments intend to discriminate, as an equal protection challenge would require to succeed. Instead, preemption analysis would require state and local governments to allay concerns about allowing them to enforce immigration law. A broad view of preemption manages doubt differently, essentially shifting the burden of proof. In practical effect, a losing equal protection or Fourth Amendment challenge can become a winning preemption challenge.

Though some observers may see this broad view of preemption as a useful surrogate for equal protection and other content-based challenges, others may be troubled by this use of preemption. Some state or local laws will be preempted even though they might not lead to violations. Just as a critic of *Miranda* warnings may believe that they overreact to aggressive police practices, preemption may seem like an excessive and clumsy distraction from efforts to spot actual constitutional violations. Viewing preemption so broadly may seem to be a ruse that allows courts to circumvent the normal rules for an equal protection claim by re-labeling equal protection as preemption. This concern that fierce federal preemption of state and local immigration laws would be a cover for discrimination claims may have prompted Chief Justice Roberts and Justice Scalia to ask for confirmation at oral argument in *Arizona v. United States* that the federal government was not relying on racial and ethnic profiling in its constitutional challenge to SB 1070. The same concern may also have led the Supreme Court to let section 2(B) go into effect, deferring determinations about actual violations until more information emerged.

But there are compelling reasons for the broader view of preemption that would find that state and local laws like section 2(B) of SB 1070 are preempted because they arise in contexts where unconstitutional reliance on race or ethnicity is a real possibility and hard to detect, prove, or remedy. The first set of reasons emerges from understanding why the federal government took the extraordinary step of suing Arizona, Alabama, South Carolina, and Utah. By trying to regulate immigration directly by creating state penalties for federal immigration violations, these states posed a greater challenge to federal authority than state or local laws that address immigration indirectly by limiting housing or work. An expanded role in direct enforcement may allow state and local decision-makers to exercise more discretion. In turn, the risk of discrimination increases, but it may continue to elude remedy.

There is much more. In past periods of US history, various states and regions have tried to define who belongs in their communities and who does not. Most dramatic and significant was slavery itself. The US Supreme Court sided with what became the Confederacy in its 1857 decision in *Dred Scott v. Sandford*. The Court ruled that African Americans—whether free or slave—were not citizens of the United States. It took federal intervention in the American Civil War to reject this regional attempt to rely on race to define who belongs. Nearly a century later, in 1957, federal troops escorted the first students to desegregate Central High School in Little Rock, Arkansas.[45]

History shows that the federal government's efforts to maintain its exclusive role in immigration and citizenship go well beyond pure jurisdictional questions of identifying the right decision-maker. In defining the constitutional division of power between the federal government and states and localities, the *content* of state and local decisions also matters. Ever since the Civil War, one of the most essential functions of the federal government has been to make sure that regions, states, or localities are not allowed to decide who is an American in ways that rely improperly on race or ethnicity. This federal role is even more fundamental than the power to conduct foreign affairs that is sometimes identified as the basis for federal exclusivity in immigration law. The federal government's lawsuits against Arizona, Alabama, Utah, and South Carolina reflect its concern that these states have threatened the federal government's constitutional role—as it emerged from the Reconstruction Amendments following the American Civil War—to decide who belongs and who does not.

Justice Scalia dissented in *Arizona v. United States*. He would have upheld all of the challenged provisions of SB 1070. His opinion was based on viewing the nation as a "Union of sovereign States" and safeguarding the right of each state to "protect its sovereignty." Remarkably, the core of Scalia's analysis relied entirely on precedents before the Civil War. As examples of the state sovereignty reflected in SB 1070, he approvingly cited state laws from the first half of the nineteenth century, including state and local laws limiting the movement of free blacks during slavery. Scalia also expressed doubt that some states would have joined the new nation at its founding if they had foreseen how the Supreme Court would cite the federal power over immigration and citizenship to strike down most of SB 1070. True enough, but it is equally probable that some states would have stayed out of the union if they had foreseen the Emancipation Proclamation and the end of slavery.[46]

IN OTHER DECISIONS, the US Supreme Court has interwoven its consideration of the content of immigration-related laws with its assessment of whether the wrong decision-maker was involved. For example, *Plyler* was an equal protection decision, but it relied on the idea that the states have less power than the federal government to treat people differently based on immigration status. A similar connection between the content of law and the identity of the decision-maker is evident in *City of Hazleton*, where concerns about equal protection led to setting a limit on state and local authority.

Another example emerges from comparing two Supreme Court decisions from the 1970s. Five years after *Graham v. Richardson* struck down state laws that denied welfare benefits to lawful permanent residents, *Mathews v. Diaz* upheld federal rules that excluded some lawfully present noncitizens from Medicare. Distinguishing *Graham* as involving state law,

Diaz held that federal lines between citizens and some permanent residents are permissible even if state lines are not. *Diaz* did not say, however, that state laws addressing permanent residents are preempted. The decision's starting premise was that the federal government has more power than states to draw lines based on immigration status. Both *Plyler* and *Diaz* show how the greater power of the federal government led to rejecting an equal protection challenge.[47]

The Limits of Preemption

Earlier in this chapter, I acknowledged that preemption may sweep too broadly by striking down state and local measures out of concern about their content, even when evidence would not sustain a direct constitutional challenge to those measures based on violations of individual constitutional rights. From the opposite direction, preemption is open to criticism for doing too little. Legal scholar Harold Koh once observed that because preemption addresses the decision-making process without assessing the content of a law or policy, it is much weaker than equal protection in protecting noncitizens.[48]

Applying preemption to question *who* decides does not directly address improper reliance on race or ethnicity or other concerns about *what* is decided. If the wrong decision-maker—a state government—is involved, another with the proper authority—the federal government—might decide to adopt the same law or policy. For example, the US Supreme Court's *Chy Lung* decision in 1876 invalidated California's attempt to regulate immigration from China, and the first federal Chinese Exclusion Act came six years later. Soon after a federal court struck down most of California's Proposition 187, federal legislation in 1996 stiffened immigration enforcement and restricted public benefits for noncitizens. As another example, the federal government could use section 287(g) agreements to deputize state or local police to enforce federal immigration law in ways that they could not undertake independently. And Congress could allow states and localities to adopt the requirement in the Hazleton housing ordinance that renters prove they are in the United States lawfully.[49]

Even if section 2(B) of Arizona's SB 1070 is ultimately struck down in other lawsuits based the actual implementation of the provision, that ruling may do little to stop similar state and local activity as part of the federal Secure Communities program. Secure Communities, like section 2(B), allows all state and local arrests in the normal course of law enforcement to function as immigration enforcement arrests. Under both Secure Communities and section 2(B), state and local authorities can apply state and local priorities to affect arrest patterns and in other ways to exert substantial control over the federal government's immigration enforcement caseload. Any decision to strike down section 2(B) could simply shift debates to the federal level, where similar outcomes may become enshrined.[50]

This risk may seem greater after considering why the federal government relied only on preemption to challenge SB 1070, and did not allege equal protection violations, unlawful searches and seizures, or violations of freedom of speech and association. It would have been awkward for the federal government to argue more than preemption, since the federal Secure Communities program allows state and local police in Arizona to do much of what they would do under section 2(B). From the federal perspective, perhaps the only problem with section 2(B) was that it was a state law, not a federal one. In turn, it may not matter that section 2(B) is preempted if Secure Communities—a federal program immune from preemption challenges—leads to many of the same results.

These historical and modern examples underscore the danger in assuming that federal decisions are less discriminatory than state or local decisions. Moreover, pressure from regional, state, or local interests can push in many different, often unpredictable directions. Outside immigration, the states are the leaders in movements that would describe themselves as advancing civil rights. Perhaps most prominent in recent years has been the push for same-sex marriage. If decision-makers differ in ways that argue for some having more power than others, it must be based on more than simple assumptions about the political tendencies of federal versus state or local governments.[51]

THERE ARE, HOWEVER, systemic reasons to believe that federal decision-making is less likely to lead to discrimination that eludes detection and remedy. Preemption is valuable even if it is no guarantee that the same law will not be adopted as a federal measure. A focus on process over content—on preemption over equal protection—is a valuable pragmatic compromise as long as the immigration law system relies on unpredictable, inconsistent, and sometimes discriminatory discretion. With immigration enforcement as highly discretionary as it is today, the lack of transparency makes it hard to know if a government agency or official is relying on improper factors in exercising discretion.

The real questions are how to minimize discrimination, and when it does occur, how to identify, control, and correct it. These tasks become even more daunting, perhaps impossible, if weak preemption allows state and local governments to take the initiative. An expanded universe of state and local actors would be able to exercise discretion, and the difficulties of safeguarding against improper discretion would increase exponentially. Viewed pragmatically, the unfortunate but unavoidable lesson of history and human nature is that discrimination will occur and that it is essential to create structures that anticipate this regrettable fact.

Preemption works to shift decisions about immigration and citizenship out of state or local processes and into the national arena, sometimes in Congress but more frequently into federal executive branch agencies. State and local governments will have influence in those federal venues, but their ability to act unilaterally through state or local laws or policies is curtailed. Though some preempted state efforts have resurfaced as federal legislation, it is reasonable to assume that counterexamples are more plentiful, especially given the complexity of the federal decision-making process. During debate on the Illegal Immigration Reform and Immigrant Responsibility Act of 1996, Congress considered an amendment sponsored by congressman Elton Gallegly (R-CA) that would have authorized states to bar unauthorized children from public education. This is what Texas tried to do in 1975, and California in 1994. After strong opposition from the Clinton administration, the proposal was removed from the final version of the 1996 Immigration Act and was ultimately passed by the House as a separate bill. It never came up for a Senate vote. Robust preemption leads to greater deliberation in the federal arena with a more complex array of counterweights. This is more a matter of politics than law, but as such it is perhaps more meaningful.[52]

At first glance, robust preemption may seem to diminish transparency, if its real purpose is oblique—to safeguard against problems with the content of state and local decision-making. But preemption's principal effect—to focus decision-making at the federal level—is likely to mean more transparency. Public visibility and channels of communication in federal decision-making are more apparent than they are for 50 different states and countless local governments. If laws and policies addressing unauthorized migration must be decided nationally, then many laws and policies that raise concerns about discrimination that might raise constitutional or policy concerns might never be adopted. These political constraints on adopting enforcement priorities are especially crucial because there are few constitutional constraints on the content of federal laws on immigration and immigrants. And because one of the central features of US immigration law is a degree of discretion that is so unpredictable, inconsistent, and possibly discriminatory that it is difficult to reconcile with the rule of law, the challenge is to regain rational, rule-of-law control over immigration enforcement. Transparency and more process is the best way to do this.[53]

Even if the Secure Communities program might initially suggest that preempting section 2(B) of SB 1070 does not matter much, it actually illustrates the importance of preemption's emphasis on process. Even if Secure Communities delegates practical power to state and local police, it is delegation, rather than unilateral state or local action. Because it is a federal program, fixing or ending it is a national process. This is why federal programs like Secure Communities and section 287(g) agreements differ crucially from state and local initiatives in Arizona, Hazleton, and elsewhere. Requiring decisions in a larger national arena—either through direct federal action or delegated power to state and local governments under federal oversight—will provide greater confidence in avoiding enforcement-related discrimination.[54]

If state and local governments are constrained only by the requirement that they mirror the formal lines drawn by the letter of federal immigration law, they will have great latitude to exercise discretion in ways that discriminate. State and especially local decision-making is much more likely to be driven by specific groups that rise to positions of influence, especially in local partisan politics, without complex tempering by offsetting influences. One local sheriff in North Carolina explained his reasons for entering into a section 287(g) agreement with the federal government by describing Mexicans this way: " 'Their values are a lot different—their morals—than what we have here,' [the sheriff] said. 'In Mexico, there's nothing wrong with having sex with a 12-, 13-year-old girl.... They do a lot of drinking down in Mexico.'" It is much harder to imagine similar statements by federal officials in a position to make analogous decisions, even if some may harbor such feelings.[55]

ONE LESSON FROM the relationship between process and content in state and local immigration enforcement is that immigration preemption does not fit readily into general conceptual frameworks for preemption. In many areas of law, shared authority between the federal and state or local governments is often seen as normal, efficient, and beneficial.[56] But enforcement discretion is unusually important in immigration law, where detection and enforcement lead to a very severe penalty—removal from the United States—and the low rates of investigation, detection, apprehension, and prosecution are essential to the system itself. Because the overall system runs on discretion, it is of paramount importance *who* allocates enforcement resources, selects targets out of the huge unauthorized population, and balances enforcement against protections for individual rights. Even if databases for determining initially who is unlawfully present become more sophisticated and pervasive, enforcement discretion remains pivotal.[57]

The role of discretion in immigration law is so great that any sharing or delegation of power is inconsistent with basic rule-of-law concepts, especially reasonable expectations of predictability and prudent safeguards against arbitrary or discriminatory government decisions. This is especially true with immigration preemption, which is animated by a strong concept of anti-discrimination deeply rooted in US history. The Civil War casts a bigger shadow over some areas of law than others. Its influence is never greater than when some significant number of state and local governments try to exclude people from communities by race or ethnicity.[58]

Privatizing Enforcement

What are the implications of preemption for the involvement of private, non-governmental actors in immigration enforcement? The private enforcement role expanded dramatically in 1986, when Congress enacted the first federal law requiring employers to verify each employee's identity and permission to work. Employers can insulate themselves from liability by meeting their basic duty to examine a document or two that "reasonably appears on its face to be genuine." Doing more may expose them to discrimination claims. The gap between this minimal employer obligation to check documents and the general command that employers must discharge unauthorized workers vests broad discretion in employers to enforce immigration law against unauthorized workers.[59]

F. Ray Marshall, Secretary of Labor under President Jimmy Carter, once said that immigrants who come to the United States outside the law work "scared and hard." The "scared" part is especially true when an employer suspects that workers are unauthorized but has checked documents in the cursory manner required by law. Selectively checking or re-checking work authorization to get rid of troublemakers—or the constant implied threat to do so—can be an effective tool for an employer to discipline its workforce, especially because unauthorized migrants face formidable practical obstacles if they try to assert their workplace rights.[60]

Besides employer sanctions, the most widespread privatization of immigration enforcement involves the vast network of private prisons that detain noncitizens who are facing removal proceedings. Private detention comes into play only after unauthorized migrants are apprehended, so it may not seem to delegate federal authority in the same way as letting state and local police decide who comes into contact with federal immigration agencies, or letting employers fire unauthorized workers. But decisions by private prison companies raise concerns similar to those associated with employers and state and local governments. Something as basic as keeping detainees in solitary confinement for violations of prison rules can hamper the ability of unauthorized migrants to assert their rights when the government tries to deport them. As another example of private enforcement, some hospitals have physically transported noncitizens from the United States to their home countries when they cannot pay their bills, effectively deporting them without any government decision to do so.[61]

Private enforcement can also involve individuals or groups that have no particular connection to unauthorized migrants but take action to detect or even apprehend persons whom they believe to be in the United States unlawfully. When hundreds of thousands of Mexican Americans—many of whom were US citizens—were forced to leave Southern California in the 1930s, many of the instigators were persons with no formal government connection.[62]

Since the mid-2000s, the Minuteman Project and other militia or vigilante groups have patrolled the US-Mexico border. Criticized by some and lauded by others, these groups have attempted to draw national attention to surreptitious border crossings. They come armed to watch border regions, where they look for clandestine crossers and report them to the Border Patrol. These activities have pushed border crossers into even more dangerous and inhospitable terrain. Some of these groups have also expanded their efforts to monitor and report the employment of unauthorized migrants. Some governments may even actively support private enforcement. Perhaps inspired by border webcams set up by private groups like the TechnoPatriots, Texas governor Rick Perry ordered webcams installed along the border with Mexico to allow private monitoring of border crossings.[63]

Growing private enforcement magnifies the challenge of limiting improper or unlawful enforcement activity. Great caution is apt before letting private parties exercise discretion that goes a long way toward deciding whether an unauthorized migrant will be forced to leave the United States. The concerns that improper incentives, motives, and priorities by state and local agencies and officials may compromise the rule of law, especially even-handed enforcement, apply at least as strongly to private parties. These concerns also apply when federal employees act outside their official capacities to try to influence enforcement decisions.

I HAVE EXPLAINED in this chapter why it is important to apply preemption to limit the immigration enforcement authority of state and local governments. The main reason is to limit the ability of state and local governments to discriminate by enforcing against some unauthorized migrants on the basis of race or ethnicity in ways that would elude detection or remedy. The next question is whether and how the same preemption analysis might apply to state or local authority to support or integrate unauthorized migrants or to shield them from federal immigration enforcement. Is it consistent or self-contradictory to suggest a smaller state or local role when it comes to enforcement, but a larger role when a state or local law or policy runs the other way? The next chapter addresses these questions as part of a broader inquiry into the role of state and local governments in building communities.

5

Building Communities

JOSÉ MANUEL GODINEZ-SAMPERIO was nine years old when his family came to the United States from Mexico on tourist visas. They stayed after their authorized period of admission ran out. His family circumstances were meager, but he became the valedictorian of his high school class and an Eagle Scout, then attended the New College of Florida and the Florida State University College of Law on scholarships. While in law school, Godinez-Samperio volunteered as an intern at Gulf Coast Legal Services and Florida State's Center for the Advancement of Human Rights, and he cofounded the DREAM Bar Association, a group of students who aspire to be lawyers but are in the United States unlawfully. After graduating from law school, he passed the Florida bar exam, normally the last hurdle before being licensed to practice law. But the Florida Board of Bar Examiners asked the Florida Supreme Court for an advisory opinion on one question: "Are undocumented immigrants eligible for admission to the Florida Bar?"[1]

This question's apparent simplicity masks a host of complexities. The first is how a state's decision to license a lawyer who is unlawfully in the United States fits into the larger picture of state and local activity relating to immigration and immigrants. To admit an unauthorized migrant to the Florida bar would run counter to the efforts in Arizona, Hazleton, and other states and localities that have tried to enforce immigration law directly or indirectly against unauthorized migrants.

Viewed broadly, state and local activity runs on a spectrum from enforcement to measures that remain neutral or that try to neutralize federal immigration law enforcement. At any point on this spectrum, states and localities can involve themselves directly in federal immigration law by intervening in the core functions of classification, arrest, detention, and penalties, or they can involve themselves indirectly by restricting or facilitating access to housing, work, education, identification documents, and so forth.

Engagement with immigration and immigrants in other states and localities runs in the other policy direction, reflecting hesitation or skepticism
toward enforcement. Some state and local governments avoid any enforcement role. Other states and localities go further and insulate unauthorized
migrants from federal enforcement. These measures reflect efforts to include
unauthorized migrants in communities built through interactions in neighborhoods, schools, and workplaces. This part of the spectrum of state and
local activity connects the second essential theme in *Plyler*—the state and
local role—with the third theme—integration of unauthorized migrants.

This chapter has several main purposes. One is to explain why the preemption analysis that limits state and local enforcement should not apply in equal
measures to activities by state and local governments to recognize or foster the
integration of unauthorized migrants. Another is to show how various aspects
of federal, state, and local law recognize the integration of unauthorized
migrants into small-scale communities by affording them some legal rights
in spite of their unlawful status. These rights allow unauthorized migrants to
belong to the communities in which they live and work, illustrating the superficially paradoxical concept of alien citizenship. This chapter concludes by
explaining why the integration of unauthorized migrants into regional, state,
or local communities is consistent with the idea of national citizenship.[2]

State and Local Integration Measures

In *Plyler v. Doe*, the US Supreme Court said that all children, regardless of
immigration status, have the constitutional right, regardless of any state or
local restrictions, to attend public elementary and secondary schools. Even
if fully implemented, this guarantee has practical limits. Simply saying that
immigration status is formally irrelevant can only do so much to include children in public education. For example, families may believe that they will be
more exposed to immigration enforcement if a child's status becomes known,
but concealing her status may make it impossible for her to participate fully
in school life.[3]

The *Plyler* decision itself has faced various types of attack and erosion.
Part of California's Proposition 187 would have kept children out of public
schools, but a federal district court invalidated that provision, citing *Plyler*.
Other threats have been less direct but would still make it harder in practical
terms for unauthorized children to attend public schools. For example, civil
rights organizations have intervened repeatedly against school board requirements for Social Security numbers or identification documents, and against

the presence of federal immigration enforcement officers on school grounds. Another strategy for circumventing *Plyler* has been to restrict opportunities for children with a poor command of English, as a very imperfect proxy for targeting children without lawful immigration status.[4]

In 2011, Alabama enacted House Bill 56, part of which would have required public schools to keep records of the immigration status of newly enrolling children and their parents. Though the section's stated purpose was to measure the fiscal impact of unauthorized students, its immediate effect was a tripled absence rate for Hispanic children. A federal appeals court struck down this requirement, concluding that it would interfere significantly with the constitutional right of access to public schools guaranteed by *Plyler*. Overall, however, these efforts to undermine *Plyler* have been muted as compared to the indirect immigration enforcement efforts that have targeted work and housing. As Michael Olivas wrote, "there has been a conscious effort by immigrant restrictionists not to touch the third rail of schoolchildren."[5]

Even if the core of *Plyler* remains intact, its constitutional guarantee of access to public education loses traction once unauthorized children leave high school. This limitation on *Plyler* would not matter if these children could acquire lawful immigration status, which would be the effect of legislative proposals that have generally been dubbed the Development, Relief and Education for Alien Minors (DREAM) Act. No version of the DREAM Act has become law, but its broad support and active consideration in Congress was a major factor in the Obama administration's decision in 2012 to establish a program of temporary discretionary relief called Deferred Action for Childhood Arrivals (DACA) for many young noncitizens who would benefit from the DREAM Act. Implemented in August 2012, DACA grants a renewable two-year status with eligibility for work authorization. DACA does not open up any access to lawful permanent residence or other durable immigration status or citizenship, but federal law treats DACA recipients as lawfully present for all purposes except federal health care eligibility. The vast majority of states—but not all—will issue them driver's licenses.[6]

My immediate focus is not on ways that unauthorized migrants might acquire lawful immigration status, but rather on state and local efforts to provide unauthorized migrants with access to public higher education even if their presence in the United States is unlawful. As some of these prospective students are granted DACA, they can expect to escape some of the restrictions on the unauthorized, but the individual states' approaches to the integration of unauthorized students still merit discussion. Some states bar unauthorized migrants from admission to public colleges and universities, and others admit them but charge tuition at much higher nonresident rates. In contrast, about a dozen states allow unauthorized migrants to pay tuition at a more affordable resident rate if they have certain connections with the state. For example, in 2001 California enacted AB 540, which allows students who graduated from a California high school after attending it for three years to attend public colleges and universities at resident rates.[7]

Many factors can limit the effectiveness of state measures that support the integration of unauthorized migrants by opening up access to higher education. Insurmountable financial barriers, even with resident status for tuition, can make admission eligibility practically meaningless. Many unauthorized migrants come from low-income families. They do not have federal work permission. They are ineligible for financial aid from federal and almost all state sources, except for some state-funded aid in California, Texas, and New Mexico. Unauthorized students whose own resources are inadequate must rely on scarce private scholarships and loans.[8]

Due to these barriers, many unauthorized students who benefit from the constitutional guarantee in *Plyler* find that their education comes to an abrupt halt after high school, no matter how accomplished they are or how much potential they show. Typically, their parents sought work in the United States and brought their infants or small children along with them. As they grew up in US society, many did not know of their precarious legal status until they were teenagers. They may have first discovered their predicament when it came time to apply for a driver's license or a job, to consider attending college or vocational school, or to enlist in the military. For many students, this is a moment of disbelief and profound disappointment, and sometimes of deep resignation.

Barring access to public higher education has the direct effect of greatly limiting these students' life options, threatening to relegate them to the lives of economic disadvantage and marginalization that *Plyler* abhorred. State provisions that disregard immigration status in matters of admission, tuition rates, and financial aid can open up access to higher education, recognizing and fostering integration for unauthorized students. Of course, educational opportunity requires more than admission and financial aid. But by expanding access to higher education and thus increasing social and economic mobility, states recognize these students as future members of their communities—as Americans in waiting.[9]

SEVERAL LAWSUITS HAVE challenged various state laws that grant resident tuition rates to unauthorized students who have some connections to the state.

At least superficially, these lawsuits are the counterparts of the challenges to enforcement-minded state legislation, including the Arizona employer sanctions scheme that led to the Supreme Court decision in *Chamber of Commerce v. Whiting* and the provisions of SB 1070 that led to *Arizona v. United States*.[10]

The court challenges to resident tuition statutes relied mainly on two federal statutes enacted in 1996 and set out in title 8 of the United States Code. The first is section 1621, which generally makes unauthorized migrants ineligible for federal, state, or local public benefits. States may still allow unauthorized migrants to receive state or local public benefits, but they must do so "through the enactment of a State law after August 22, 1996, which affirmatively provides for such eligibility." States may not simply continue to apply a pre-1996 law. The other relevant federal statute is section 1623. It says that unauthorized students may not receive a state postsecondary education benefit on the basis of residence in a state, unless US citizens and nationals are eligible for the same benefit. In other words, states may not treat unauthorized residents of the state better than US citizens who live in other states.[11]

Opponents of resident tuition for unauthorized migrants sued in federal district courts in several states, and in California state court, raising two main arguments. The first was that sections 1621 and 1623, as federal statutes, expressly preempted state laws that would allow unauthorized migrants to pay resident tuition. The second argument was that even if these state laws are not expressly preempted, they are invalid as a matter of implied preemption because they conflict with federal laws addressing immigration. These preemption arguments outwardly resembled the arguments against state and local laws that try to restrict access to work and housing. The two opposing sides of the immigration debate seemed to trade positions, with the advocates for unauthorized migrants arguing for preemption in Hazleton and Arizona but against preemption in California. Like all legal concepts and theories, preemption showed that it has two edges.

None of the federal court challenges went far enough to decide if the state tuition statutes were preempted by section 1621 or section 1623. The reason was that no plaintiffs could allege that the unauthorized students' lower tuition bills had caused them an injury specific enough to allow them to file a lawsuit. In legal parlance, all of the federal courts found that none of the plaintiffs had standing to sue. In contrast, California state courts more readily let plaintiffs sue even if they may not meet the federal requirements for standing, so it came as no surprise that the California Supreme Court issued the first final judicial decision on the validity of state resident tuition for unauthorized students.[12]

In 2010, the California Supreme Court decided *Martinez v. Regents of the University of California*, which upheld AB 540's resident tuition rules. The court first concluded that AB 540 was valid under section 1621. Even assuming that resident tuition eligibility is a "benefit" under section 1621, California adopted it after 1996, as the section requires. *Martinez* also found that AB 540 did not need to meet the requirements that section 1623 imposes on state postsecondary education benefits for unauthorized migrants on the basis of state residence. The court explained that AB 540 does not rely on California residence. Nonresidents who graduate from a California high school after attending it for three years are eligible for AB 540 treatment, but they are not necessarily California residents. A student might have commuted across the state line to attend a California high school, or her family might have left California after she graduated. The court cited information from the University of California that most of its students using the nonresident tuition exemption in AB 540 were in the United States lawfully. The court also ruled against implied preemption, reasoning that sections 1621 or 1623 expressly allowed any state provision that the sections did not expressly preempt.[13]

THE STORY OF José Godinez-Samperio that opened this chapter is much like that of two other recent law graduates. All three freely disclosed that they were in the United States unlawfully, supplementing their applications for admission to the bar with letters of support from prominent figures in the legal and political worlds. One is Cesar Vargas, whose parents brought him to the United States when he was five years old. After graduating from law school and passing the bar exam, Vargas applied for admission to the New York State bar. Another is Sergio Garcia, who was 17 months old when his parents brought him into the United States without inspection at a port of entry. They took him back to Mexico when he was eight or nine. In 1994, when Garcia was 17 years old, his parents brought him back across the border, again without inspection, to live in the northern part of California's Central Valley. By then, his father was a permanent resident and filed an immigrant petition for him. When the petition was approved in 1994, Garcia started his wait in one of the longest lines for permanent residence.[14]

Garcia went to college, graduated from law school, and passed the California bar exam. The state Committee of Bar Examiners certified to the California Supreme Court that he met all of the requirements for a law license. The Committee also provided the court with information about Garcia's immigration status, prompting the court to pose several questions to the committee about his application and to invite friends of the court, or *amicus curiae*, to submit briefs. Some of the questions asked about the application of specific federal statutes. Another question asked much more broadly about "the legal and public policy limitations, if any, on an undocumented immigrant's ability to practice law." Also: "What, if any, other public policy concerns arise with a grant of this application?"[15]

One central line of statutory analysis was whether section 1621, which had been pivotal in the *Martinez* decision to approve AB 540, deprived California of the authority to admit Garcia to the practice of law. The "benefits" to which section 1621 applies include any professional license provided by a state "agency" or any benefit provided by "appropriated funds." But does the California Supreme Court count as a state agency, and is a law license provided by appropriated funds? If the answer to either question is yes, then California would need to enact a state law after August 22, 1996. Would a decision by a California Supreme Court to grant a law license count as such a law?[16]

Numerous organizations and individuals filed *amicus curiae* briefs, almost all favoring Sergio Garcia's admission. Two opposed it on the ground that he could not swear to uphold the law if his very presence violates federal immigration law. The third brief in opposition came from the federal government. It had taken no position on resident tuition in *Martinez*, but it opposed Garcia's bar admission, arguing that a law license is a public benefit covered by section 1621, and that admitting Garcia to the California bar would be conferring that benefit without enacting the required new state law.[17]

Ultimately, California Governor Jerry Brown signed legislation in October 2013 that expressly authorizes the admission to the practice of law of persons who are unlawfully present in the United States. The federal government withdrew its opposition, satisfied that this new statute met the new-law requirement in section 1621. On January 2, 2014, one day after the legislation took effect, the California Supreme Court issued an order permitting the Committee of Bar Examiners to admit Sergio Garcia to the practice of law. Important questions remain, however, about the status of unauthorized applicants in states without such legislation, and more generally about the federal government's position in these cases.[18]

THE FEDERAL GOVERNMENT'S position in *Garcia* appears consistent with its position in *Arizona v. United States*. In both cases, it asserted federal supremacy over immigration-related matters. One difference, however, is the statutory framework. When the state of Arizona defended SB 1070, it relied heavily on various federal statutes, especially section 1373(c). The state argued that this provision allows some state and local enforcement role, even outside specific grants of authority to state and local governments, such as under 287(g) agreements and Secure Communities. The federal government responded that section 1373(c) does not allow Arizona to engage in immigration law enforcement as fully as SB 1070 tried to authorize. In contrast, *Garcia* involved public benefits eligibility for unauthorized migrants as regulated by another federal statute, section 1621. The federal government initially argued that section 1621 did not allow the state of California to admit Garcia to the practice of law.

Though different federal statutes were involved, the situations in Arizona and California share some elements that are more fundamental. The basic issue is state authority to act in relation to unauthorized migrants. With neither federal statute clear or definitive in setting limits on state decision-making, it is at least as important to ask why the federal government chose to adopt its positions in these two cases. In *Arizona*, it sought to limit direct state involvement in immigration law enforcement. In *Garcia*, it tried to make it much more difficult for states to recognize or foster the integration of unauthorized migrants by opening up access to a profession. In both cases, the federal government asserted exclusive authority that severely limited state decision-making.

At least superficially, the symmetry appears to be sensible, and the federal government acted consistently by opposing state decisions in both cases. Relatedly, it might seem inconsistent to argue that SB 1070 is preempted, but at the same time to doubt that state laws are preempted if they give unauthorized migrants access to higher education and the licensed professions, or if they seek to neutralize or remain neutral on immigration law enforcement by federal authorities. But should the limits on state and local involvement in immigration enforcement also apply as strongly to state and local measures that try to integrate unauthorized migrants?

The answer is no. The inquiry should examine substance, not rely on symmetry. When the scope of implied or express preemption is uncertain, a far better approach—both as sound policy and as constitutional law—is limiting state and local enforcement, but allowing state and local measures to support the integration of unauthorized migrants. The reasons go back to the fundamental reasons to set boundaries on state and local involvement in immigration law enforcement. These boundaries help prevent constitutional violations, especially violations that involve improper reliance on race or ethnicity. History supports a presumption against letting state and local governments make decisions that could reflect or result in discrimination that is difficult to detect or remedy. Preemption is essential to keeping government decisions on immigration and immigrants faithful to core individual rights guaranteed in the US Constitution.[19]

A logical counterargument to treating enforcement and integration alike is that a similarly serious risk of constitutional violations is present when states and localities support the integration of unauthorized migrants whose very presence violates federal law. After all, any government decision that benefits one individual or group may cause a corresponding injury to another individual or group that does not get the same benefit. Allowing unauthorized migrants to attend a state university at lower resident tuition rates will either increase tuition for other students or reduce university revenues and thus the quality of the education provided. Similarly, one might argue that allowing unauthorized migrants to enter licensed professions increases competition for jobs and clients; these would be real constitutional harms. The argument would continue that preemption should invalidate state and local measures to integrate unauthorized migrants through education and work just as readily as it invalidates state and local involvement in enforcement.[20]

On balance, however, it seems wrong to characterize this effect—even assuming that it is real harm—as the risk of discrimination against these other students that would parallel the risk of racial or ethnic discrimination in state and local immigration enforcement. In the tuition and licensing scenarios, the harm is much more diffuse. It is nothing like targeting some persons for selective enforcement because they fit a police officer's image of an illegal alien. This difference in consequences is precisely why federal courts have consistently dismissed legal challenges without even reaching the substance of the case because the plaintiffs lack standing to sue. The pivotal distinction is one between diffuse harm and targeted exclusion from the community.

Admittedly, the distinction between harm and exclusion can be fuzzy, and the two ideas overlap. Exclusion is a type of harm. But exclusion by race or ethnicity is a special, notorious harm with far more serious, constitutional dimensions in the sensitive area of immigration and citizenship. At stake is something very fundamental—asking who belongs. It is pivotal that the legacy of the American Civil War was the emergence of national citizenship as an enduring guarantee against not only the battle cry of states' rights, but more fundamentally against racial exclusion.

In this way, preemption of state and local laws in the context of immigration and citizenship depends on the content of the measures under scrutiny. When state and local activity supports immigration enforcement, the risk of exclusion increases. Some of the targets will be US citizens and lawfully present noncitizens. Others will be unauthorized migrants, but that is just as troubling if race or ethnicity drives decisions to choose them for selective enforcement, given the broad role of discretion. In contrast, measures at the state and local levels to integrate unauthorized migrants run some risk of diffuse harm to US citizens, but it is not the harm of racial or ethnic exclusion. When it comes to assessing state and local authority, immigration enforcement and immigrant integration are not the same.

Recognizing Rights Based on Community Integration

Allowing unauthorized migrants access to higher education at resident tuition rates and to professional licensing may seem inconsistent with the fact that they are, by definition, in the United States unlawfully. But from the perspective of state and local governments dealing with people who live in the community, these impulses reflect the persuasive power of the arguments for integrating unauthorized migrants or, in other words, for treating them as Americans in waiting.

These forms of recognition rest on some bedrock assumptions about how the legal system treats unauthorized migrants. Even though state and local measures on both ends of the political spectrum have generated controversy—from SB 1070 at one end to integration and sanctuary provisions at the other—it is usually taken for granted that unauthorized migrants are not entirely without rights or legal recognition. They can marry and divorce. Unauthorized migrants can ask the courts to resolve a full range of civil disputes on matters ranging from family law to personal injuries to contracts. And to recall Justice Marshall's question in the *Plyler* oral argument, unauthorized migrants can count on fire protection. They can own property, tangible and intangible, including real estate. Some of this is reflected in specific state laws, such as provisions in state constitutions that confer rights on "persons" without mentioning immigration law status. More typically, however, these forms of recognition operate by custom and are even taken for granted.[21]

To be sure, the legal capacity of unauthorized migrants to do some of these things has been contested at times. In scattered jurisdictions in several states, local officials have required proof of lawful presence in the United States before issuing marriage licenses or granting child custody in divorce proceedings. In 2006, Arizona adopted a ballot initiative, Proposition 102, that disallows the award of punitive damages to unauthorized migrants who prevail in civil lawsuits. Some states detain some noncitizen criminal defendants without bond if they cannot prove their lawful presence in the United States.

The state of Alabama enacted a law in 2011 that would have nullified most contracts entered into by unauthorized migrants, but a federal appeals court ruled that federal law preempted the Alabama provision. In any event, these restrictions are outliers in a general pattern of federal, state, and local laws recognizing that unauthorized migrants have a significant bundle of rights. The unifying thread, as I will explain, is the integration of unauthorized migrants into small-scale communities within an immigration law system that tolerates a sizeable unauthorized population.[22]

AS A PROMINENT EXAMPLE, federal, state, and local laws recognize and foster the integration of unauthorized migrants in the workplace, where typical laws provide employees with some protections as to wages and hours, unionizing, health and safety, and discrimination. This array of laws may be unexpected. After all, immigration law forbids not only unlawful presence but also the hiring of unauthorized workers. But unauthorized migrants can sometimes call on employment law protections, rather than being relegated to legal oblivion.[23]

Such protections are not always available, however. To start with a case in which full protections were denied, I revisit one of the stories that opened Chapter 1. Hoffman Plastic Compounds, a company in Southern California, dismissed an employee going by the name of José Castro after discovering his involvement in union organizing. The National Labor Relations Board (NLRB) ruled that by dismissing Castro, Hoffman Plastic had violated federal labor law. The NLRB awarded Castro the standard remedy—back pay for the time that he would have worked if Hoffman Plastic had not fired him. But Castro was using a borrowed birth certificate, and he was in the United States and working unlawfully. In 2002, the US Supreme Court reversed the NLRB's back pay order in a 5–4 decision in *Hoffman Plastic Compounds, Inc. v. NLRB*. In an opinion by Chief Justice Rehnquist, the Court explained that an employee who works unlawfully cannot receive back pay from his employer, even if his employer fired him in violation of the National Labor Relations Act.[24]

One major question at the intersection of immigration law and employment law is what workplace rights and remedies against employers are available to unauthorized migrants. Some of the issues involve federal law, including the legal scheme in the National Labor Relations Act (NLRA) governing union organizing and collective bargaining. Other protections are set out in Title VII of the Civil Rights Act of 1964, which bans employment discrimination in various situations, and in the Fair Labor Standards Act, which establishes the minimum hourly wage and related guarantees. Other cases have arisen under state employment laws analogous to these federal schemes, under state worker compensation laws, and under state laws governing contracts and personal injuries.[25]

Taken as a whole, unauthorized migrants can sometimes assert these workplace rights, though of course there are practical obstacles to doing so. This body of law—like state authority to include unauthorized migrants in higher education and professional licensing—recognizes the integration of unauthorized migrants into communities. The California Supreme Court's *Martinez* decision on tuition at public colleges and universities and the California statute authorizing law licenses for unauthorized migrants shows how the law recognizes and fosters integration. Employment law similarly affords rights and remedies to unauthorized workers, in spite of what *Hoffman* seemed to suggest. Overall, significant parts of this body of law reflect the idea that given broad acquiescence in unauthorized migration, their integration into workplace communities can matter more than immigration status.

EMPLOYMENT LAW PROTECTS the rights of unauthorized workers in two general ways. Both combine the meaning of unlawful presence in the US immigration law system with the claims of unauthorized migrants to treatment as Americans in waiting. In the first approach, courts sometimes recognize that unauthorized workers have workplace rights and remedies because any other outcome will harm citizens and noncitizens who are working lawfully in the same workplace. This sort of relationship among workers is a strong sign that unauthorized workers are integrated into their workplaces. A leading example of this thinking is Justice Stephen Breyer's dissent in *Hoffman*. Writing for himself and three other justices, Breyer explained that if unauthorized workers lack effective workplace rights and remedies, employers will have an incentive to hire them instead of US workers.[26]

Breyer's dissent reflects a sound view of US immigration law. Employers in the many sectors of the US economy will rely heavily on unauthorized workers as long as the system of selective admissions and selective enforcement yields an inadequate lawful immigrant workforce. Suppose that employers can easily hire unauthorized workers in this setting of tolerance, and suppose also that employment law also allows employers to underpay those unauthorized workers or have them work under less favorable conditions. Then the consequence will be strong downward pressure on the wages and working conditions of US workers in the same workplace and industry. Of course, even if unauthorized workers have the same protections in theory as US workers, the practical obstacles to asserting those rights may be formidable. If they speak up, they may run a greater risk that the employer will somehow report them to federal authorities for arrest and possible removal. But Breyer's argument was that if unauthorized workers start out with diminished legal protections, such as ineffective remedies for violations of federal labor law, the chances are even greater that employers can use unauthorized workers to undermine US workers.[27]

Breyer's views did not prevail in *Hoffman*, but that case's holding has been relatively confined. It limits only back pay remedies for unlawfully discharging an unauthorized employee. Other aspects of federal labor law are closer in reasoning to Breyer's *Hoffman* dissent. A prominent example is *Agri Processor Co. v. NLRB*, a 2008 decision from the federal appeals court for the District of Columbia Circuit. The author of the majority opinion was Judge David Tatel, who had written the decision that the Supreme Court decision in *Hoffman* overturned. *Agri Processor* included unauthorized workers in workplace protections because allowing them to assert their workplace rights would help protect US citizens in the same workplace.

The case involved a labor dispute at a company by the name of "Agriprocessors," though the court case stated it incorrectly. Agriprocessors was one of the United States' largest suppliers of kosher meat, the same company that was the site of a major workplace raid in May 2008 by Immigration and Customs Enforcement agents. Employees at Agriprocessors's Brooklyn warehouse, frustrated with meager pay and benefits, and distrustful of company management, voted in September 2005 to join the United Food and Commercial Workers Union. Agriprocessors responded by refusing to negotiate with the union and urging its employees to sign on with a rival union. The employees went on strike, and about a dozen workers marched in the warehouse parking lot for three months. During the strike, Agriprocessors objected that the election was void because 17 of the 21 employees who had voted for the union were unauthorized migrants and therefore ineligible to vote.[28]

In the legal proceedings that followed, the core question was whether unauthorized workers count as employees in deciding if federal labor law obligates an employer to bargain with the union. The court said yes. Judge Tatel distinguished *Hoffman* as addressing only remedies, not the overall coverage of the National Labor Relations Act. He explained that protections for unauthorized workers can help all workers in a bargaining unit. No matter what their immigration status is, they share interests as to wages, benefits, skills, duties, working conditions, and supervision. It follows that NLRA elections for bargaining unit representatives should count the votes of both authorized and unauthorized workers.[29]

The Supreme Court's decision in *Hoffman* and the appeals court's decision in *Agri Processor* reflected sharply contrasting views of how immigration and employment laws combine to address unauthorized workers in the US economy. The *Hoffman* majority focused on the individual worker's violation of immigration law and found back pay to be unacceptable because it would tacitly excuse that violation. The focus was the individual, and the essential fact was the immigration law violation. In contrast, *Agri Processor* looked past the individual worker's immigration status, recognizing that unlawful presence does not prevent the widespread employment of unauthorized migrants, and concluding that protections for unauthorized workers would enhance protections for citizen and lawful permanent resident coworkers as a practical matter.

The unauthorized workers in *Agri Processor* won because they shared interests with a certain group of citizens who were their coworkers. This view was persuasive because these unauthorized workers were part of the small-scale community of the meatpacking plant where the unionization contest occurred. The integration and community membership in *Agri Processor* was much more immediate than in *Hoffman*, where the dissent expressed a systemic concern, across entire industries, that allowing unfair labor practices against unauthorized workers would hurt US workers, too. In *Agri Processor*, the closer proximity among coworkers in the same workplace made it easier to identify the US workers who would suffer if labor protections excluded unauthorized workers. Recognition as voters in union elections—as members of a workplace community—reflected the strength of these workers' claims to integration, in spite of their unlawful presence, within a selective and discretionary immigration enforcement system.[30]

EMPLOYMENT LAW ALSO protects the rights of unauthorized workers in a second type of case, where they are integrated into the larger workforce and their wrongdoing is less serious than their employer's. A focus on comparing wrongdoing was part of the reasoning in *Hoffman*. Both the Court's opinion and Breyer's dissent compared the violations committed by José Castro and Hoffman Plastic. In ruling that Castro was ineligible for back pay, the Court emphasized that his violation was more serious. He had not only worked unlawfully but also used false documents to get the job in the first place. Justice Breyer's dissent compared wrongdoing as well, but it underscored the seriousness of Hoffman Plastic's wrongdoing. That the company, by firing Castro, had committed "a crude and obvious violation of the labor laws" was central to Breyer's argument that allowing back pay against employers like Hoffman Plastic would deter them from hiring unauthorized workers in order to have a more compliant workforce.[31]

This comparison of wrongdoing is explicit in three cases from the state of New York, all from 2006. All three involved unauthorized migrants who suffered devastating injuries while working on construction sites. Gorgonio Balbuena, from Mexico, was hurt while pushing a wheelbarrow up a ramp. The fall left him with multiple skull fractures and other serious injuries. Balbuena's case was consolidated in court with a claim by Stanislaw Majlinger, a Polish citizen, who was working unlawfully in the United States after overstaying his admission on a visitor visa. Majlinger was installing siding on a building on Staten Island when the scaffold on which he was standing suddenly collapsed. He sustained serious injuries that left him unable to work. A second case addressed the claims of José Raimondo Madeira, a citizen of Brazil, who was earning $15 per hour as a construction worker when he fell from the roof of a building. He was disabled as a result, left able to walk only with great difficulty. In a third case, Christian Ambrosi, a native of Ecuador, fell from a temporary bridge above a sidewalk. He was trying to hoist up construction materials without any anchoring ropes or harnesses. He suffered permanent debilitating injuries.[32]

In all three cases, the employers violated New York State occupational safety statutes. If the injured men had been working legally, they could recover future lost wages. But all of the employers argued that the workers were ineligible for that remedy because they were working illegally. In the first case, the New York Court of Appeals ruled that Balbuena and Majlinger could claim lost wages. The court distinguished *Hoffman* because José Castro had "criminally provided his employer with fraudulent papers." The New York court reasoned that Balbuena's and Majlinger's employers were more blameworthy than Balbuena or Majlinger. Nothing indicated that either worker had ever presented false documents, or that their employers ever asked to see their documents at all. The other two cases applied the same reasoning but reached different results based on the different circumstances. A federal appeals court awarded lost wages to Madeira. Though he had worked illegally, his employer was more blameworthy for hiring Madeira knowing that he would do so. A different court denied Ambrosi's claim for lost wages because he used fraudulent documents to get hired. The *Ambrosi* court distinguished *Balbuena* and *Madeira* as cases involving employers who were more blameworthy because they never asked for documents.[33]

This focus on wrongdoing and willingness to see employers as more blameworthy than unauthorized migrants reflects the tolerance of unauthorized migration that is at the heart of the US immigration law system. At the same time, this tolerance and acquiescence in unauthorized migration is closely related to recognizing that unauthorized workers are integrated into the US economy in general and into workplaces in particular. These workers have predictably become part of the workforce. Working in the United States unlawfully is blameworthy only up to a point. In this setting, the employers in *Balbuena* and *Madeira* were especially blameworthy in both their federal employer sanctions violations associated with the initial hiring and the serious workplace safety violations that led to the workers' severe injuries. If not penalized and deterred, the thinking goes, these are the kind of employers whose behavior will harm all workers, including US citizens and noncitizens who are working lawfully.

EMPLOYMENT LAW IS just one area in which the integration of unauthorized migrants into some type of community is recognized even if they lack lawful immigration status. Also noteworthy are the protections under the Fourth Amendment to the US Constitution against unlawful searches and seizures. Consider what happened in February 2008 at an electronic assembly facility owned and operated by Micro Solutions Enterprise in Van Nuys, California. About 100 uniformed and armed Immigration and Customs Enforcement (ICE) agents entered the building and ordered all employees to stop working and gather in a large hallway. Agents blocked all exits and yelled at any worker who tried to use a cell phone. After separating out the workers who claimed to be US citizens or permanent residents from those who did not, the ICE agents took the women out of sight into the cafeteria while they kept the men in the hallway. The agents ordered the men to stand against the wall and searched them, shouting at any who tried to talk, then questioning and handcuffing the men. The scene in the cafeteria was even more confrontational, with agents screaming at the women.[34]

After detaining the employees for about an hour, the agents led them to buses outside, where they waited more than another hour before being driven to a detention facility. Only then were the employees allowed to visit bathrooms. As the night wore on, they were taken from a holding cell to be questioned individually once again, fingerprinted, and photographed. Agents did not advise employees of their rights at any time. After about 16 hours in the detention facility, they were finally brought a small amount of food, then received a larger meal a few hours later. Some were detained for well over 30 hours before being released.

Arrests like those in the Micro Solutions raid often uncover evidence that reveals an individual's immigration status. If the evidence shows that she is unlawfully present, the government typically introduces it in an immigration court hearing to prove that she should be removed from the United States. An immigration judge then decides if the noncitizen is removable and, if so, whether to grant discretionary relief if any is available. The noncitizen's attorney—if she has one—may file a motion to suppress the evidence because it was obtained in violation of the Fourth Amendment to the US Constitution or in violation of statutes and regulations that reflect similar principles.[35]

In criminal law, evidence that police obtain from a search or seizure that violates the Fourth Amendment must generally be disregarded—or as lawyers often say, "suppressed"—in any later prosecution. This is known as the exclusionary rule. It generally does not apply in immigration removal proceedings, according to the 1984 US Supreme Court decision in *INS v. Lopez-Mendoza*. Justice Sandra Day O'Connor's opinion for a 5–4 majority concluded that the "likely social benefits of excluding unlawfully seized evidence" were outweighed by the likely costs. O'Connor explained that even without evidence from the arrest, other proof of immigration status would lead to deportation in most cases. She added that excluding evidence would deter few federal officers from unlawful searches and seizures, that the federal government has internal mechanisms to deter violations, and that money damages and other private remedies would remain available. She noted the "unusual and significant" costs of requiring courts "to close their eyes to ongoing violations of the law."[36]

But *Lopez-Mendoza* left some wiggle room by allowing that the analysis might come out differently "if there developed good reason to believe that Fourth Amendment violations by INS officers were widespread." A clear majority of the Justices also seemed to agree that evidence would be excluded if obtained through "egregious violations of Fourth Amendment or other liberties." In turn, several federal appeals courts have suppressed evidence in removal proceedings because the source of the evidence was an egregious Fourth Amendment violation. The relevant court decisions vary in their reasoning, but they reflect a consensus that one type of egregious violation is an arrest or search that relies improperly on race or ethnicity.[37]

Even if evidence is not suppressed because it was obtained in an arrest or seizure that amounts to an egregious violation of the Fourth Amendment, it might be suppressed because the arrest or seizure violated similar federal regulations. In February 2009, one year after the Micro Solutions raid, immigration judge Ashley Tabaddor ruled that the federal government's efforts to remove the workers could not rely on evidence of the workers' unauthorized status obtained in the raid. Her rationale was that under federal regulations, even briefly detaining an individual requires federal agents to have a reasonable, individualized suspicion that she is unlawfully present in the United States. Judge Tabaddor found that the agents detained the workers without meeting this requirement.[38]

Whether through the egregious violation exception to *Lopez-Mendoza* or by application of federal regulations, the reasons for suppressing evidence that the government has obtained in violation of the Fourth Amendment have much in common with the reasons for protecting unauthorized migrants against violations of workplace protections. Unauthorized migrants work alongside citizens and permanent residents, and also live in the same neighborhoods and often in the same households. Both types of protection recognize the integration of unauthorized migrants into small-scale communities even though they are in the United States unlawfully. An unlawful arrest or search harms citizens and lawfully present noncitizens who live in the same home or neighborhood as unauthorized migrants, or who are employed at the same workplace.

In this context, the egregious violation exception in *Lopez-Mendoza* allows judges to safeguard these communities against racial and ethnic discrimination by responding to the problem of police who rely improperly on race or ethnicity. Similarly, employers who have committed especially serious wrongdoing against an unauthorized worker are more culpable than someone who violates immigration law. Employers should also be kept from injuring citizen workers in the same workplace. Just as employment law recognizes the integration of unauthorized migrants into workplace communities, the same approach makes sense when unauthorized migrants seek the protections of the Fourth Amendment.[39]

THESE PATTERNS OF rights outside of immigration law are consistent with provisions of immigration law that also reflect the integration of many unauthorized migrants into various communities. Examples include many of the ways that current law allows unauthorized migrants to acquire some form of lawful status based on their close connections with citizens and lawfully present noncitizens. One example is cancellation of removal. Applicants need to meet restrictive threshold eligibility requirements and then persuade an immigration judge to exercise discretion to grant cancellation under a demanding hardship standard. These obstacles are formidable, but an unauthorized migrant can become a lawful permanent resident through cancellation based on hardship to a child or other close relative who is a citizen or lawful permanent resident.[40]

More generally, allowing unauthorized migrants to assert various rights can be viewed in two overlapping ways. One possibility is a way of protecting citizens who may be directly affected by the government's treatment of unauthorized migrants. This perspective recognizes the integration of unauthorized migrants, especially their close relationships with citizens. But this rationale for recognition shifts attention away from the unauthorized migrants' own claims. In this vein, legal scholar Linda Bosniak has analyzed how the typical arguments made in 1994 by opponents of California's Proposition 187 emphasized US citizens' interests. Opponents argued, for example, that denying health care to unauthorized migrants would jeopardize the public health of all Californians. These pragmatic arguments had political value, since they could muster opposition to Proposition 187 while avoiding the question of whether unauthorized migrants had persuasive claims in their own right to health care.[41]

Though related to this emphasis on citizens' interests, the broader and more convincing explanation is that the law should recognize that unauthorized migrants are part of US society. The patterns of unauthorized migrants' rights examined in this chapter have emerged from the US immigration law system, with its selective admissions, selective enforcement, and vast discretion. One natural consequence of this system is that unauthorized migrants are integrated into communities, and many of them have compelling arguments to be treated as Americans in waiting. Some arguments are based on immigration as contract. They came by invitation to the United States to take part in an economic system that has historically acquiesced in a large unauthorized population. Other arguments are based on immigration as affiliation. No matter how justified or unjustified an unauthorized migrant's unlawful presence might have been at first, the ties that he acquires and the contributions that he makes over time should override any original transgression.

It may be tempting and superficially logical to relegate unauthorized migrants to a domain that is outside the law—not outside US territory, but as nonpersons outside the protection of the law. After all, immigration law says they should not be here. But as Linda Bosniak wrote soon after the enactment of the Immigration Reform and Control Act (IRCA) of 1986: "Undocumented immigrants live at the boundary of the national membership community. They have long occupied a unique, deeply ambivalent place in the United States." This statement is even more true today. This uneasy ambivalence leads, as it should, to ways for unauthorized migrants to assert their rights, even if they cannot always make claims on the same footing as US citizens or permanent residents.[42]

At the same time, these patterns also show how unauthorized migrants remain at the law's margins. Their rights and interests are recognized only in part. Even where they can take advantage of lower resident tuition rates, they are typically ineligible to work or to receive public financial aid. They can claim protections from some types of employer exploitation, but their remedies are incomplete, even assuming that they can press their claims without jeopardizing their jobs. They are only sometimes fully protected against law enforcement practices that violate the Fourth Amendment.

Recognition is also typically granted in narrow terms. It may be conferred as an exception, such as to the normal rule that the Fourth Amendment exclusionary rule does not apply in immigration removal proceedings. Or it may depend on the ad hoc and unpredictable evaluation of the facts, such as a comparison of employer and employee wrongdoing. Or rather than relying directly on the US Constitution, it may be based on the text of a statute, a regulation, or even internal agency guidelines, though constitutional ideas may heavily influence how such texts are interpreted.[43]

The obliqueness of unauthorized migrants' rights may seem odd and even perverse. But it is unsurprising as long as the immigration law system depends much more on scattered and unpredictable discretion than on the letter of the law as enacted by Congress. The partial and narrow recognition of rights accurately reflects these migrants' status as tolerated and even welcome lawbreakers. These oblique rights also allow decision-makers to avoid daunting questions about changes to the system of immigrant and temporary admissions and immigration law enforcement, and about granting lawful status and a path to citizenship for unauthorized migrants. By avoiding these questions, decision-makers can avoid giving answers that may be hard to undo.[44]

So the current system limps along, tolerating a large number of unauthorized migrants, whose claims based on integration have reached a critical mass in political and moral terms. The best solutions lie in reworking the immigration law system, providing lawful immigration status to some unauthorized migrants, and replacing broad discretion with the greater predictability and consistency that are the hallmarks of the rule of law. Only then will a chance at full membership replace various bundles of rights. But unless and until that happens, the best interim approach to reflect their integration into society is for unauthorized migrants to be protected by employment law, family law, and the law governing police behavior, to name just a few key areas. Though immigration law on the books denies their presence, the integration of unauthorized migrants into American society reemerges as the foundation of persuasive legal arguments in multiple areas of law.

Communities and Citizenship: Local, State, and National

So far, I have presented two basic ideas in this chapter. First, states and localities recognize and foster, as they should, the integration of unauthorized migrants through a variety of measures. Federal immigration regulation generally does not preempt these integration measures, even though it generally should preempt decisions by states and localities to involve themselves in immigration enforcement without express federal authorization. Second, the rights of unauthorized migrants in various federal and state legal schemes recognize and foster, as they should, the integration of unauthorized migrants into small-scale communities such as workplaces, neighborhoods, and families.

These two thoughts may seem at odds with the basic idea that US citizenship is national citizenship, not regional, state, or local citizenship. But this tension is more apparent than real. Recognizing and fostering the integration of unauthorized migrants into small-scale, often local, communities *is* consistent with the concept of national citizenship. The analysis starts with the idea that integration is essential to reconciling the basic tension between national borders and equality. Without integration, borders are functionally impermeable, even if they let in noncitizens. Integration allows borders to coexist with equality by offering immigrants some access to equality. In turn, integration has multiple dimensions, but two are of particular concern in considering the state or local role. First, where does integration take place? And second, what are the principles and idea of membership that govern integration?[45]

TO ANSWER THE first question, integration is fundamentally and inevitably local. It takes place in neighborhoods, schools, workplaces, and similar small-scale, localized venues for interaction with others. These are venues that are traditionally and constitutionally governed by state and local decision-making, not by the federal government. Everyday decisions about education and employment are local or state decisions as a general matter. If unauthorized migrants are to have access to higher education to recognize or foster their integration, state governments must provide that access. In neighborhoods, police protection combined with community trust in law enforcement should help integrate unauthorized migrants as long as the immigration law system is set up to tolerate a significant unauthorized population. But integration involves more than the relationship between immigrants and various governments. It also reflects how individuals and groups who have long been part of US society interact with immigrants in general, and with unauthorized migrants in particular. Several types of interactions especially deserve discussion.[46]

One issue on which engagement and dialogue are especially important is the economic impact of unauthorized migration. The belief that unauthorized migrants cause economic harm to some US citizens drives much of the policy debate about immigration outside the law. Assessments depend heavily on the frame of reference chosen. The consensus among economists appears to be that immigrants as a whole benefit the overall US economy. This is also true for unauthorized migrants, mainly because unauthorized migrants tend to take on different jobs, often at the lowest wages or under the harshest working conditions. As workers who generally complement rather than substitute for US workers, unauthorized migrants create new jobs for citizens more often than they displace citizens. Economists also generally agree that any negative effect that immigrants, including unauthorized migrants, have on wages and working conditions is mainly to the detriment of other immigrants in similar circumstances. There is also a likely positive effect on major parts of the public fiscal picture, such as Social Security, especially over time. Unauthorized workers pay substantially more into Social Security than they receive, largely because they are not eligible for benefits.[47]

Overall assessments of economic impact provide little comfort if unauthorized migrants take away jobs or depress wages that some citizens might otherwise get. Unauthorized migrants are not evenly spread out across the United States or across all economic sectors. Concentrations in particular regions, locales, or economic sectors may make the aggregate positive effect irrelevant for the US workers who are adversely affected. Moreover, the idea of unauthorized migrants doing complementary work—the work that citizens would not do—is not entirely convincing. Because citizens might take these jobs if wages were higher, it is misleading to say that this is work that citizens are unwilling to do. Or the unavailability of low-wage labor might prompt innovation that substitutes technology for workers, or prompt a shift to products that require less labor in the United States. Either way, an employer could reconfigure operations to employ a workforce consisting of citizens and lawful immigrants.

On the other hand, adopting these solutions may make employers uncompetitive. Paying higher wages may force the employer to outsource work or to conduct its own operations outside the United States. Or if these options are unworkable, for example in service industry jobs that are not moveable, higher wage costs could drive an employer out of business altogether. In broader perspective, there is also considerable evidence that any adverse effects on some US workers that might be attributable to unauthorized migrants are insignificant compared to larger trends in the domestic and international economy that have increased income inequality throughout the United States over the past generation. Workers in the United States have been hurt by several interrelated domestic and global economic trends outside immigration. These include the decline of labor unions, the privatization of government functions, the prevalence of temporary and part-time work, and the shift of manufacturing from middle America to overseas locations.

Regardless of whether economic impact is viewed overall or by locale, industry, occupation, or ethnic group, the perception that unauthorized migration hurts the American working class is a powerful political force. This reality continues a constant tension throughout US immigration history—that workers who are already here feel threatened by economic competition from newcomers. It can be tempting to ascribe any hostility among the American workers toward unauthorized migrants to prejudice or racism. But honest fear and insecurity play a role that no conscientious policymaker should ignore. As long as these concerns exist, they cannot be dismissed responsibly by relying simply on academic studies by economists.

Local perspectives make more vivid the hardships that fall on citizens whose wages decline or who lose their jobs as a consequence of competition from unauthorized workers. Much of the confrontation is felt locally in small-scale communities. This reality puts local decision-making in the best position to reconcile the integration of unauthorized migrants with the interests of all residents of a community. To take an example outside the employment context, the challenge of integrating children into public schools may be practically impossible to address with broad-scale, uniform national decision-making. It is daunting at the local level, of course, but at least there the hardships experienced by neighbors on all sides of policy debates become very real. Local school boards have the best chance to allocate scarce resources in ways that balance all interests, including those of community members who feel harmed by the unauthorized migrants in their midst.

JUST AS LOCAL perspectives can lead communities to consider more com-pletely how the integration of unauthorized migrants affects its other mem-bers, local perspectives can also shed new light on the hardships caused by enforcement. Immigration laws that may seem part of a reasonable enforce-ment scheme when viewed from Washington, DC, can seem extremely unjust when looking more closely at the person being deported or considering the effects on family members who are left behind.[48]

Former Representative Bill McCollum, a Republican from Orlando, Florida, and later Florida attorney general, was a leading sponsor of the 1996 legislation known as the Illegal Immigration Reform and Immigrant Responsibility Act (IIRIRA). One of the strongest enforcement measures ever adopted by Congress, among its purposes was to expand many grounds for deportability, make detention mandatory in many cases, limit discretion-ary relief, streamline deportation, and curtail court review of deportation decisions. Soon after IIRIRA became law, McCollum introduced a private bill to restore lawful immigration status to a permanent resident whose drug conviction had recently led to his deportation based on that very law. Like almost all private bills, it failed to pass, but more noteworthy is what might seem a striking turnaround for McCollum to take this public position in that case. And yet, it is unsurprising. Congressional offices are often supportive in constituent immigration matters, even if they are much less sympathetic leg-islatively. This difference is due in part to the desire to win favor with voters, but it also reflects the power of personal hardship stories.[49]

More generally, perceptions of unauthorized migration vary depending on whether the perspective is local, state, regional, or national. It can be easier to find common ground—or at least constructive disagreement—when focus-ing on individuals, families, and real-world situations, especially at the local level. The negative economic or emotional consequences of enforcement can prompt rethinking of such policies when the consequences are local. It can be easy to rail against unauthorized migrants when drafting federal legislation, but much harder when they are the people you have entrusted to take care of your food, your house, and your children. At the same time, local perspectives can make more real any harms that unauthorized migration may visit on dis-advantaged citizens. All of this underscores the value of local decision-making as a matter of building communities.[50]

I HAVE JUST EXPLAINED how integration is fundamentally local. A second, related question is to ask: What are the principles and the idea of membership that govern integration? The local nature of integration does not mean that citizenship itself is local. In fact, it is essential that integration—even if it takes place locally or in other small-scale settings—remains the national citizenship that emerged from the Civil War and the Fourteenth Amendment to the US Constitution. In deciding who belongs and who does not, the principles of national citizenship informed by the protections of the Constitution ensure that discrimination by race, ethnicity, religion, and gender has no influence. This is precisely why state and local decision-making is subject to preemption in order to prevent discrimination.

The alternative would be to imagine the integration of unauthorized migrants into communities of state and local citizenship. The danger is that integration into small-scale communities as sites of membership means that these communities will tolerate forms of discrimination that are inconsistent with constitutional protections for national citizenship. For example, immigrants could be forced to meet the expectations of a small town's culture. This might mean supporting the integration of unauthorized migrants only if they belong to the town's majority religion. The result would be a serious risk that the integration of unauthorized migrants—and of immigrants in general— will create local hierarchies along lines that are fundamentally incompatible with the aspirations of national citizenship.

Such a framework should recall Michael Walzer's memorable admonition that a world without national walls would soon become a world of a "thousand petty fortresses." If that happens, integration will be a hollow achievement. Though the integration of immigrants, including unauthorized migrants, necessarily occurs within state and local communities, it is essential that it is integration into national citizenship and that integration be informed by a national perspective. The commitment to equality and civil rights that has emerged in the context of national citizenship—especially but not only through a public culture informed by constitutional protections for individual rights—must govern the building of small-scale communities. In this important way, local integration and national citizenship are not only compatible but also mutually reinforcing, with local integration serving national citizenship.[51]

TWO FURTHER PRINCIPLES emerge from the idea of a framework of national citizenship for local integration. The first is that racial or ethnic discrimination has no place in the enforcement of immigration law. The most persuasive way to reconcile borders with the idea of equality is that national borders create a bounded sphere in which equality can flourish. This is true even if the very fact of borders creates inequality between people on opposite sides of the borderline. But this justification dissolves if discrimination infects either admission categories or the implementation of immigration law, including enforcement against unauthorized migrants.[52]

Second and just as importantly, the integration of unauthorized migrants may not be used to undermine or compromise the social, political, or economic position of US citizens on the basis of race or ethnicity. The same commitment to equality that shapes immigration law both on the books and in action must also shape how unauthorized migrants who join communities are allowed to affect citizens who are already part of those communities. Crucial here is the persistent concern that the arrival and integration of unauthorized migrants dilutes the rights and undermines the economic, social, and political position of African Americans in the United States. No matter what studies by social scientists might suggest, the perception remains, and with it the politically powerful sense of insecurity and disenfranchisement in local settings.[53]

One episode that posed this issue occurred in the aftermath of Hurricane Katrina in New Orleans in 2005. The federal government announced that laws and policies intended to curtail the hiring of unauthorized workers would be suspended for a period of time while the work got underway to rebuild the city. Many of the workers involved in the rebuilding effort were unauthorized, of whom many were Latinos. It is difficult to know how much the suspension increased the number of unauthorized workers, but the perception became widespread that these Latino workers were displacing African Americans.[54]

Of course, this perception was not new or unique to post-Katrina New Orleans. In October 1992, journalist Jack Miles offered a similar perspective in his article entitled "Blacks v. Browns" in *The Atlantic Monthly*. The effects of immigration on the wide range of African American communities is a complex and often controversial topic, but Miles's portrayal of a zero-sum game in which gains by unauthorized migrants who are predominantly Latino necessarily undermine African Americans is at least a profound cautionary tale about perceptions that are politically and socially influential. Some of the underserved or disadvantaged communities in the United States that can feel adversely affected by unauthorized migration have been marginalized for generations, especially those whose early history in this country was scarred by slavery.[55]

As with the concerns of the American working class of all races and ethnicities that has come to see its economic security reduced, effective responses will need to emerge at many levels of government. Some will be federal initiatives, including legislation. But other responses are inherently local, as they would have been in post-Katrina New Orleans, where the best accommodation of the many conflicting demands and interests had to be worked out on the ground.

_____

THE ROLE OF state and local governments has multiple facets. One is enforcement, which can be indirect as in *Plyler v. Doe*, or direct as in Arizona's SB 1070. States and localities can also act to recognize or foster integration, consistent with the need to integrate unauthorized migrants acknowledged by the US Supreme Court in *Plyler*. This chapter has explained why strict limits on state and local enforcement should not similarly limit the state and local role in the integration of unauthorized migrants, as long as that integration takes place within a framework of national citizenship. Room for state and local integration also is consistent with the recognition of the rights of unauthorized migrants in various areas of law, both federal and state, in spite of their unlawful presence.

The integration of unauthorized migrants is closely related not only to the state and local role, but also to the first theme at the core of *Plyler*—the meaning of unlawful presence. If the US immigration law system has acquiesced in a large unauthorized population, and if unauthorized migrants have strong claims to be treated as Americans in waiting, then does it make sense to go beyond the exceptional or narrow recognition of unauthorized migrants' rights to granting some unauthorized migrants a form of lawful status? This is the central inquiry for the next chapter.

6

Legalization and the Rule of Law

OVER THE PAST several decades, immigration policy has occasionally attracted close attention in the US Congress. There were times when broad legislative proposals seemed poised for serious consideration. In the late summer of 2001, for example, Congress was actively considering broad reform, including legalization. The probable support and opposition did not seem to follow strict partisan fault lines, much as the vote on the Immigration Reform and Control Act (IRCA) in 1986 did not. During Mexican president Vicente Fox's visit to Washington in September 2001, immigration policy was front and center among the topics that he and US president George W. Bush discussed. But the terrorist attacks of September 11, 2001, dramatically shifted public attention to national security in all things, including immigration law, putting off any broader reworking of the immigration system.[1]

By mid-decade, bipartisan cooperation on immigration-related issues—including support for legislation that included legalization—reawakened with broad-ranging proposals that progressed far into the legislative process. Proposals of this ambition came to be labeled as "comprehensive immigration reform." As IRCA had done in 1986, this new generation of proposals tackled several intertwined elements of immigration law and policy, including changes to admission categories, a greater emphasis on enforcement, and some kind of legalization to provide lawful immigration status for many unauthorized migrants.

Enacting any complex proposal of this sort would never be easy, but legislative coalitions that reflected a degree of bipartisanship seemed capable of bringing some version of comprehensive immigration reform to the president's desk. The political sands shifted, however, and those coalitions disappeared during the period that started with the 2008 presidential election campaign. Republican candidate John McCain adopted a near-exclusive emphasis on enforcement, reversing his earlier support for comprehensive reform. Throughout much of the United States, it became virtually impossible for political candidates to win Republican party primaries if they hinted at flexibility on immigration enforcement or at broader approaches to dealing with unauthorized migration. By mid-2008, it seemed a distant memory that Republican president George W. Bush had strongly favored a legalization program for unauthorized migrants.[2]

Though President Barack Obama listed immigration reform as a legislative priority when he first took office in 2009, much of the political energy in Washington, DC, during his first term went into the debate over health care reform. Then, persistent skirmishing and outright battles over budgets, taxes, and fiscal policy consumed much of the remaining oxygen inside the Beltway. In 2012, however, President Obama's reelection profoundly changed the landscape for immigration legislation. A central political lesson from the 2012 presidential campaign was that Obama's victory owed a great deal to his overwhelming support among Latino and Asian voters, due in large part to sharp differences between his immigration positions and those taken by the Republican Party and its nominee Mitt Romney. Obama promised to work toward comprehensive immigration reform in his second term.[3]

Back before the election, in the spring of 2012, the difference that immigration policy would make in the campaign was far from clear. Absent legislative activity on immigration during much of his first term and a steady increase in the number of deportations carried out by the Department of Homeland Security, much of Obama's support first waned, then turned into outright skepticism, among many Latino voters who had hoped for immigration reform. But in June 2012, with legislative progress stalled, the administration announced the Deferred Action for Childhood Arrivals (DACA) program, which provides a two-year period of protection from deportation and eligibility to work for many young people without lawful immigration status. As what seemed to some like a down payment on a limited legalization program, especially after Senate Republicans had blocked a vote on the DREAM Act in late 2010, DACA seemed to restore faith in President Obama's resolve to move forward on immigration. As a crucial consequence of this perception, DACA energized his support among Latino voters.[4]

In contrast, Mitt Romney's immigration policy views bore the unmistakable stamp of Kris Kobach, the architect of multiple state and local immigration enforcement measures over the preceding decade. In the second presidential debate, when Romney's efforts to recast himself as a moderate candidate were in full swing, he tried to distance himself from Arizona's SB 1070; Obama retorted that Romney's principal immigration advisor— Kobach—had written SB 1070.[5]

By the time the next Congress opened for business in January 2013, the legislative push for comprehensive immigration reform had already gathered steam. Bipartisan working groups in both the House and the Senate drafted legislation that would balance the many competing interests whose support would be required for passage. The Republican mainstream seemed to have undergone a conversion, with leaders such as Senator McCain reemerging as supporters of comprehensive immigration reform. The White House developed and floated its own plan but stopped short of formal introduction while the working groups in both houses continued to negotiate and draft their bills.[6]

On the contentious issue of temporary workers, business groups and organized labor reached what they called a historic compromise, at least in principle. And because the US Supreme Court's decision in *Arizona v. United States* in June 2012 erected a major roadblock to state and local enforcement, it became clear that the action would be in Washington, DC, not state capitols, county governing boards, or city councils. For the first time since the 1980s, there seemed to be momentum toward passing major federal legislation. In June 2013, a sweeping package of legislative changes passed the US Senate with the affirmative votes of 68 Senators, including 14 Republicans. The legislation then entered a more precarious period of consideration in the House of Representatives, where the Senate bill would be a tough sell to the Republican majority.[7]

One of the core questions for lawmakers is whether to provide access to lawful immigration status for some or all of the 11 or 12 million unauthorized migrants who are living in the United States. A familiar label for such programs is "legalization." Opponents have often called it "amnesty" as a term of derision, though some supporters accept or even embrace the amnesty label. The key issues for any legalization or amnesty include the following: Who is eligible, what must they do to get lawful status, what sort of status do they get, and does that status include a path to citizenship?[8]

Various legislative proposals reflect differing answers to these questions. To analyze what is at stake, I will start with proposals to make lawful status available to young unauthorized migrants who were brought to the United States as children. This chapter will then address other vehicles for conferring lawful status and explore ways to think about structuring legalization programs. More fundamentally, my goal in this chapter is to combine analysis of the meaning of unlawful presence and of the integration of unauthorized migrants to shed light on legalization (or amnesty) and the rule of law.

The DREAM Act

Proposed federal legislation, usually called the Development, Relief, and Education for Alien Minors (DREAM) Act, would address the predicament of young persons who were brought to the United States as children and are now unlawfully present. Recent Congresses have considered various versions of the DREAM Act over the past decade, all of which would eventually confer lawful permanent resident status. One version passed the US Senate in May 2006. In 2010, another won the support of a majority of Senators, but not the 60 needed to allow a vote on the bill. Yet another version was part of the legislation that passed the US Senate in June 2013.[9]

The DREAM Act would set several conditions for lawful status. Eligibility under the version considered by the Senate in 2011, for example, required that a noncitizen was under age 16 when she came to the United States, and under age 35 when the act became law. In addition to these age requirements, she had to have continuous residence in the United States. She had to earn a high school diploma or the equivalent in the United States, or have been admitted to a US college or university. Criminal convictions could disqualify. Eligible noncitizens could become conditional permanent residents, and then after two years attain full lawful permanent resident status by attending college or serving in the US military for two years.[10]

Starting in August 2012, the Deferred Action for Childhood Arrivals (DACA) program provided interim lawful status to most of the individuals who would benefit if some version of the DREAM Act were enacted. They can apply for a renewable two-year deferred action status that safeguards them from deportation and makes them eligible for work authorization based on financial need. The DACA eligibility criteria roughly parallel eligibility under versions of the DREAM Act, with some variations. The federal government decides as a matter of case-by-case discretion whether to grant relief under DACA. More fundamentally, DACA is not the DREAM Act; as an interim executive measure, it is limited in duration and provides no durable immigration status.[11]

In the legislation that passed the Senate in June 2013, the DREAM Act was just one part of a broad-scale legalization that would give a large number of unauthorized migrants a transitional status called Registered Provisional Immigrant (RPI). The DREAM Act legalization track would be much more generous than the legalization offered to other unauthorized migrants. After five years, these DREAM Act RPIs could not only become permanent residents but also apply immediately to naturalize as US citizens. A test of English and civics would be required, as well as enrolling in higher education or serving in the US military for four years. There would be no upper age limit for eligibility.[12]

ARGUMENTS FOR THE DREAM Act fall into two basic categories. Some arguments are policy-based appeals to fairness or justice. Other arguments are pragmatic—or consequentialist, some might say. The fairness arguments for the DREAM Act draw heavily on the meaning of unlawful presence within the highly discretionary US immigration law system, and on arguments for integrating unauthorized migrants and treating them as Americans in waiting. Some arguments for integration rely on what I have called "immigration as contract," acknowledging a tacit invitation to unauthorized migrants accept when they come to work in the United States, often bringing their families with them. The claims to be treated as Americans in waiting based on this background are at least as strong for their children as they are for the parents. Other arguments for integration rely on immigration as affiliation, which captures the view that unauthorized migrants' ties to individuals or communities in the United States deserve recognition. Here, the claims of the children are almost always stronger, since the United States is typically the only country that they know, having arrived at an early age and having remained.[13]

Unauthorized migrants who were brought to the United States as children have strong claims to integration that support concrete steps to grant them lawful status through the DREAM Act. The work of social scientists is important in showing how lawful status matters to this group of young noncitizens. For example, Roberto Gonzales and Leo Chavez have shown how the paradox at the core of these young people's lives—complete acculturation as Americans combined with unlawful status—profoundly influences them starting no later than their teen years. While their peers who are citizens or noncitizens with lawful immigration status start to drive, work, and think about college, young unauthorized migrants find that they cannot do some or all of these things, at least not legally. The result is a debilitating marginalization that starts with the most mundane details of daily life but ultimately imposes severe limits on their realistic horizons and expectations. The fairness argument is that it is morally essential, especially given their innocence, to lay the foundation for their integration by conferring lawful status.[14]

Pragmatic arguments for the DREAM Act overlap with fairness arguments but connect the meaning of unlawful presence with the integration of unauthorized migrants differently. For unlawful presence, these pragmatic arguments assume that the government has only limited control over the basic contours of unauthorized migration. Even with stiffer laws or more enforcement, unauthorized migration will be substantial, given ingrained tolerance of a large, flexible unauthorized workforce. Though this situation could change, the costs of intensifying enforcement and deporting the children who arrived here within the current immigration system are prohibitive. As the US Supreme Court put it in *Plyler*, the schoolchildren had a "permanent attachment" to the United States and were "unlikely to be displaced from our territory." Because the vast majority of the young unauthorized migrants will stay in the United States, as will their children, it is pragmatic for immigration status to reflect this reality.[15]

As for integration, pragmatic arguments emphasize that full integration is impossible without lawful immigration status. Research like the Gonzales-Chavez study suggests that hosting a large marginalized population would cause great harm to the national interest. In contrast, lawful status would nurture positive contributions to society by DREAM Act beneficiaries and their children and grandchildren. Requirements to attend college or serve in the military work specifically toward this goal. From this perspective, it is unsurprising that passage of the DREAM Act has been part of the strategic planning of the Department of Defense as a way to fill the ranks of an all-volunteer military.[16]

Arguments against the DREAM Act are also grounded in fairness, pragmatism, or a blend. Fairness objections start with the meaning of unlawful presence by stressing that unauthorized migrants, whether children or not, are by definition violating federal immigration law. Other fairness objections are anchored in rejecting integration, emphasizing that these noncitizens are not Americans in waiting and have no legitimate claims to integration based on either contract or affiliation. If there is an immigration contract, their parents broke it by breaking the law, and children have to live with their parents' choices. And even if these young people bear no blame, they should still leave now. As for immigration as affiliation, their ties are unworthy of recognition because they result from lawbreaking, especially because lawful status would give them access to scarce public resources. All of these fairness objections invoke the rule of law by insisting that unauthorized migrants must not cut in line ahead of immigrants who play by the rules. From this perspective, rejecting the DREAM Act reflects a triumph of the will to enforce immigration law and to deny illegitimate claims to belonging.

Pragmatic objections to the DREAM Act also connect the meaning of unlawful presence to the integration of unauthorized migrants. First, noncitizens who are unlawfully present pose a straightforward problem that the government can solve by apprehending and deporting them, or by making life so hard that they will leave. Such enforcement policies are needed, this argument continues, to uphold the system for lawful admission to the United States. Pragmatic objections emphasize that any need to integrate beneficiaries of the DREAM Act will diminish or disappear with effective immigration law enforcement, and that it is unsound and dangerously self-fulfilling to assume that any of them will stay indefinitely. Moreover, granting lawful status to individuals brought to the United States as children will create incentives for parents to come to the United States, in turn undermining enforcement. In contrast, tough enforcement makes deportation, including self-deportation, a pragmatic alternative to integrating young people who are in the United States illegally. Later in this chapter, I will further examine these arguments for and against the DREAM Act. To lay the groundwork for that discussion, it is important next to consider how these arguments might apply to other schemes that confer lawful status.

Birthright Citizenship

Under the citizenship clause of the Fourteenth Amendment to the US Constitution, all children born on US soil are citizens, regardless of their parents' immigration status. The only exception is for the children of diplomats. This interpretation of the clause has stood for over a century, though several modern scholars have challenged it as flawed. Other critics accept the constitutional rule as settled but argue that it is unwise as a matter of policy. Over the past several decades, Congress has considered but has never approved several constitutional amendments that would withhold citizenship from children born on US soil if their parents lack certain types of lawful status in the United States.[17]

The Fourteenth Amendment and the DREAM Act seem quite different. The former confers citizenship, while the latter would confer lawful immigration status. Birthright citizenship applies to children who happened to be born in the United States, while the DREAM Act applies to children who happened to be born outside the United States and were then brought into the country. But they have the same effect—giving a type of lawful status to someone who might otherwise lack it. This similarity becomes clear from imagining two variations on current US law.

First, suppose that the US Constitution did not confer citizenship based on birth on US soil. Under this approach—which is the law in many countries around the world—children born in the United States to parents who are unauthorized migrants would also be present unlawfully. Then the practical reach of a law like the DREAM Act would broaden significantly to serve as the vehicle to confer lawful status on these children. In the second variation, imagine that children brought to the United States at a young age would be naturalized automatically as citizens after a certain number of years in the United States. This would resemble a similar rule in current law that confers citizenship on children, mostly adoptees, brought to the United States by citizens or lawful permanent residents. This second variation—broader than current law by covering all children regardless of their parents' immigration status—would eliminate the need for the DREAM Act.[18]

These two imaginary laws show that the DREAM Act has the same practical effects as birthright citizenship and automatic naturalization. The reality that current law includes birthright citizenship—but not the DREAM Act or automatic naturalization of childhood arrivals—often divides children in the same family by a simple twist of fate. The younger ones, born after their parents arrived, are citizens, while older siblings in the so-called 1.5 generation are in the United States unlawfully.

Reflecting this practical overlap, the typical objections to birthright citizenship echo objections to the DREAM Act. Pragmatic objections assert that it undermines enforcement to grant birthright citizenship to all children born in the United States, because doing so rewards parents who enter or remain illegally. Fairness-based objections would deny that immigration law violators have any claims to integration, even if they were children when their parents brought them to the United States. It would undermine fairness and the rule of law to grant these children a benefit as precious as citizenship, which would allow them to sponsor their parents for admission. Though it is a myth that they can file immediately—citizens must be 21 years of age before they may file an immigrant petition for a parent—the basic objection remains that an automatic grant of citizenship allows lawbreakers to impose their children unilaterally on American society.[19]

Supporters of birthright citizenship generally assume that US citizenship matters, just as DREAM Act supporters assume that immigration status matters. Without birthright citizenship, the children of unauthorized migrants would likely be in the United States unlawfully. From this premise, the arguments for birthright citizenship mirror arguments for the DREAM Act. Fairness arguments emphasize that even if children (and their parents) are in the United States unlawfully, they remain innocent, because their parents came to America amid widespread tolerance of unauthorized migration and because they and their parents have contributed to American society. This line of argument emphasizes that they have persuasive claims to be treated as Americans in waiting, but that their full integration is impossible without US citizenship. Pragmatic arguments for birthright citizenship also parallel support for the DREAM Act. Most of these young people will remain in the United States indefinitely, given tolerance of unauthorized migration and enforcement that is highly selective and discretionary. The reasoning is that because deportation is improbable, conferring citizenship is essential to preventing their marginalization and fostering their contributions to society in the future.[20]

The Role of Children

The arguments supporting the DREAM Act and birthright citizenship share an emphasis on children. Their innocence—or absence of blame, guilt, or responsibility—was a big part of the rationale in *Plyler* for constitutionally guaranteed access to public elementary and secondary schools as against state or local restrictions. The innocence of children also arises in debates over birthright citizenship and the DREAM Act as an important reason to look beyond unlawful presence and to recognize the need for integration. A crucial question is whether legal and policy debates change when children are not involved. In my view, many of the same arguments that support citizenship or lawful immigration status for children apply in nearly full measure to unauthorized migrants who came to the United States as adults. The first step in explaining why is to understand the role of children in immigration policy more fully.[21]

One argument for the DREAM Act is that the need is paramount to integrate young people in the future. Similarly, birthright citizenship gives children the lawful status that is an essential platform for integration as they come of age in America. More fundamentally, both the DREAM Act and birthright citizenship give immigration and citizenship law a strong forward-looking perspective that emphasizes integration as a process that occurs over time, measured in generations. In these ways, the involvement of children expands the time horizon well into the future for assessing policy options. By doing so, the involvement of children makes current immigration status less significant.[22]

Children also highlight the role of the family. In many families, the parents lack lawful immigration status, but the children are citizens by birth in the United States. At least 9 million people in the United States are in such mixed-status families, with at least one unauthorized adult and one US citizen child. According to 2010 US Census data, 4.5 million of all the children who had been born in the United States, and thus were US citizens, had at least one unauthorized parent. Of all babies born in the United States in the one year from March 2009 to March 2010, an estimated 350,000, or 8 percent, had at least one unauthorized parent. Reflecting these demographics, one version of the DREAM Act would have given lawful immigration status to over 1.9 million individuals, but not to their unauthorized parents.[23]

By conferring lawful status on some family members, both birthright citizenship and the DREAM Act foster the integration of all family members, including those without lawful immigration status. Having US citizen children is insufficient by itself to block a parent's deportation. But children who have lawful status or citizenship may be the basis of discretionary relief from removal under current immigration law. Moreover, all children who are acculturated in the United States, but especially those with lawful status or citizenship, can serve as cultural brokers between their parents and mainstream society. A central aspect of this brokering role is translating between their parents and teachers, not only to and from the English language but also to and from the culture of the school system and US society in general.[24]

These implications of birthright citizenship and the DREAM Act can generate controversy, mainly because looking to the future and focusing on the US citizen children of unauthorized migrants may seem to distract from current violations of immigration law. But the role of children in debates over birthright citizenship and the DREAM Act is important to bear in mind in asking the next crucial question: Do arguments for the DREAM Act and birthright citizenship also support broad-scale legalization?

Broad-Scale Legalization Proposals

The Immigration Reform and Control Act (IRCA) of 1986 included two legalization programs that together allowed about 2.7 million unauthorized migrants to become lawful permanent residents. The total estimated unauthorized population when the legislation was enacted was around 3.2 million. Under the general legalization program, a noncitizen who had been in the United States unlawfully since January 1, 1982, had a period of 12 months from May 1987 to apply for temporary resident status. He then had three years to apply for lawful permanent resident status. This second step required continuous residence in the United States. A conviction for a felony or three misdemeanors was disqualifying. Applicants had to demonstrate minimal understanding of English, as well as knowledge of US history and civics, or they had to be enrolled in a course on these subjects. A waiver of these tests was available for applicants older than 65. The second legalization program in IRCA was open to unauthorized migrants who had worked 90 days in seasonal agriculture between May 1985 and May 1986. They could become lawful permanent residents with three more years of agricultural work. About 1.6 million unauthorized migrants became permanent residents under the general legalization program in IRCA, and another 1.1 million under the agricultural program.[25]

IRCA was controversial not just for legalization, but also for its other main features. These included stronger border enforcement, employer sanctions, provisions on discrimination related to employer sanctions, and a program to admit temporary agricultural workers. Some critics of IRCA's legalization provisions argued that the program invited fraudulent claims, and more fundamentally that it was an affront to the rule of law. From the opposite direction, other critics objected that IRCA legalization did not go far enough. For example, by requiring applicants to have been in the United States illegally for almost five years, the general legalization program excluded many unauthorized migrants who arrived after the cutoff date. A large number of those left out were closely related to an eligible applicant, but many of these individuals were able to stay in a type of twilight status. Eventually, many of these family members became lawful permanent residents after their relatives became permanent residents or citizens and filed immigrant petitions for them.[26]

Congress debated and rejected several legalization proposals in the decade before the 2012 presidential election. Like IRCA, these proposals would have offered lawful immigration status to a large number of the unauthorized migrants in the United States, though the number who would actually have applied under any given plan is speculative. Of these pre-2012 proposals, Senate Bill 1639, considered in 2007, came closest to enactment. Known as the AgJOBS Act of 2007, it would have established a new Z visa for unauthorized migrants. To qualify initially, applicants had to be working and living in the United States as of January 1 of that year. They would have to pay $1,000 and additional processing fees, provide biometric data, and stay employed. A criminal record would disqualify them. The initial Z visas would have been valid for four years, renewable by demonstrating "an attempt to gain an understanding of the English language and knowledge of United States civics." A noncitizen with a Z visa could become a permanent resident only after everyone else who had been waiting in line for two years when the program was adopted. Moreover, she would have to leave the United States to apply and pay another $4,000. She would then start the five years usually required to naturalize. To use some now-familiar phrasings, she would go to the back of the line, but she would have a path to citizenship.[27]

IN WIDENING ANALYSIS from the DREAM Act and birthright citizenship to include broad-scale legalization, the first question is whether all three ways of conferring status justify similar arguments in support and in opposition. The arguments for the DREAM Act and birthright citizenship seem to apply especially to children. In the same vein, the Supreme Court emphasized in *Plyler* that the children kept out of school had been brought to the United States by their parents. The Court put it this way: "Even if the State found it expedient to control the conduct of adults by acting against their children, legislation directing the onus of a parent's misconduct against his children does not comport with fundamental conceptions of justice." In turn, it may seem logical to favor birthright citizenship and the DREAM Act, but then to oppose broad-scale legalization. On closer examination, however, the arguments that support the DREAM Act and birthright citizenship also apply to broad-scale legalization. The reason is that arguments for all three approaches to conferring lawful status reflect similar views about two themes that were essential in *Plyler*: the meaning of unlawful presence in the US immigration law system and the need to integrate unauthorized migrants.[28]

First, on fairness, the innocence of children makes it seem especially compelling to give them lawful status, but many of the same understandings of unlawful presence and integration that support lawful status for children also apply to adults. The large unauthorized population that is the known product of the immigration law system consists mostly of adults—the system's very purpose is to have a flexible workforce. Moreover, adults suffer at least as much as their children from the unpredictability, inconsistency, and possible discrimination that are inherent in the current selective enforcement regime.[29]

It is also important to think about the role of children in immigration law and policy, and in turn about parents and children together in families. Shifting away from a stark choice between focusing on children and focusing on adults, and instead viewing immigration as a matter of families moving to the United States, the choice between the innocent child and the guilty parent seems artificial and misleading. Workers accept an invitation to work in the United States under trying and precarious conditions not only for themselves, but also for the future of their children. Though they have violated US immigration law in a way that their children have not, these circumstances should make it hard to view them as ordinary criminals or to define them by their immigration law violations alone. This broader view of unauthorized migration helps explain why *Plyler* called unauthorized migrants, including adults, "productive and law-abiding" even if they were in the United States unlawfully. Even if the Court showed special concern for the children as vulnerable members of an underclass, its overall concern extended to every member of the underclass created by US immigration policy. Though the holding in *Plyler* was limited to children and access to public elementary and secondary schools, the Court's reasoning treated what the federal government does in the context of economic realities as equal in significance to the formal letter of immigration law.[30]

Shifting to a pragmatic perspective, an important aspect of the meaning of unlawful presence is that deporting over 11 million people is impossible or at least extremely impractical. This reality reflects not only the quantum of enforcement resources that would be required, but also the economic and political costs of deporting a substantial part of the US labor force. These workers make significant contributions to the US economy, and they are highly integrated in other ways within local neighborhoods, workplaces, churches, and communities. An underground economy with an exploited population is an alternative to deportation, but it is much more pragmatic to offer lawful immigration status as a platform for unauthorized migrants to integrate and contribute to society. These pragmatic arguments, like fairness arguments, apply as strongly to adults as to children.

I should acknowledge that a potential problem with applying DREAM Act arguments to broad-scale legalization is the matter of numbers.[31] Even if the same reasoning supports both, broad-scale legalization would confer lawful status on a much larger number of unauthorized migrants. The overall number who acquire lawful status may limit the acceptability of legalization among lawmakers or the electorate. In substance, however, this objection does not question the logical relevance of DREAM Act arguments to broad-scale legalization. Instead, this objection questions whether legalization should be narrower than covering every unauthorized migrant in the United States, and if so, how to design coverage. I will address these issues after fully laying out the general case for broad-scale legalization.

MY LAST POINT in comparing arguments for the DREAM Act and for broad-scale legalization concerns political advocacy. Even if those who support both the DREAM Act and broad-scale legalization rely on the same general arguments for both types of proposals, they need to make tough choices in advocacy strategy. At times in the past decade when broad-scale legalization seemed legislatively attainable, the similarity in supporting arguments made it tempting to reach for broad-scale legalization rather than settle for the DREAM Act. But when the winds shifted in Congress and broad-scale legalization became less realistic, especially with greater partisan polarization, the DREAM Act reemerged as the primary goal, coming close to approval in the lame duck Congress in December 2010.

In such strategizing, the similarity between arguments for children and adults can easily get lost in the rhetoric. The temptation is real—perhaps irresistible—to emphasize the innocence of children brought to the United States at a young age. A related temptation, equally strong, is to spotlight the many young people who have excelled academically, many of them winning admission to selective colleges and universities. An example is the story of José Godinez Samperio, high school valedictorian, graduate of the Florida State University College of Law, and applicant for admission to the Florida bar. High school valedictorians are undoubtedly more appealing in the political arena than students who struggle to make it through school or who drop out. Similarly, arguments for the DREAM Act may appeal to a broader audience than arguments for broad-scale legalization, and it is understandable that DREAM Act advocacy features model young immigrants.

In substance, however, the same general fairness and pragmatic arguments for lawful immigration status apply to all young people, not just the honor students, and to adults as well. Individual variations may justify including some unauthorized migrants in legalization and excluding others, but these variations are matters of degree, not kind. As a related political shift, major organizations that had persistently lobbied for the DREAM Act, most prominently United We Dream, shifted position in late 2012 by abandoning their separate support for the DREAM Act and instead throwing their political weight behind broad-scale legalization, with the DREAM Act as just one component.[32]

The Rule of Law

The objections to the DREAM Act, birthright citizenship, broad-scale legalization, or any other mechanism that confers lawful immigration or citizenship status deserve serious consideration. A cluster of objections rejects the notion that any reasons to integrate override unlawful presence in the United States.

One objection denies the existence of any de facto policy to tolerate or encourage unauthorized migration and argues that immigration law violations must be taken more seriously. Noncitizens without lawful status are simply illegal aliens, and there is no obligation or policy reason to recognize, foster, or even to tolerate their integration. From an immigration-as-contract perspective, immigration violators have broken the contract by breaking the law, so enforcement shortcomings are no legitimate basis for disregarding violations. Moreover, the objection continues, enforcement deficiencies should not inhibit future policy options, including stiffer enforcement and a refusal to grant amnesty.[33]

A related objection views arguments for legalization as bootstrapping. Those who push for legalization cite past acquiescence and tolerance that brought unauthorized migrants to the United States, but objectors believe that legalization would institutionalize that acquiescence and tolerance. The lesson of IRCA, according to this view, is the need to get out of this perpetual cycle. Otherwise, legalization builds acquiescence and tolerance into the system, and then a new phase of acquiescence and tolerance becomes part of the argument for another legalization.

The heart of this objection is that any policy of acquiescence or tolerance that may have existed is irrelevant today and does not limit future policy options. Moreover, the strong turn toward enforcement, starting in the 1990s with Proposition 187, then the 1996 amendments to federal immigration statutes, and then continued enhancement of border and interior enforcement, reflects a deliberate policy shift that undercuts any claims that rely on earlier, weaker, enforcement patterns. History generates no moral or legal obligations or justifiable expectations to continue. The argument is that amnesty would continue this cycle because it will buoy hopes of future largesse, adding an incentive to come illegally now even if legalization has a cut-off date.[34]

TO ANALYZE THIS cluster of objections, first consider effects on future unauthorized migration. To be sure, adopting any legalization today will make a similar program seem more likely than if Congress does not adopt one. But any greater likelihood of future legalization may not cause more unauthorized migrants to come to the United States or increase the size of the unauthorized population. A central reason for most unauthorized migrants to come to the United States is to take advantage of opportunities to work and earn so much more that it is worth great risk and sacrifice to get here. The promise of future lawful status might matter, but short-term risks and rewards are far more influential. Any future legalization is remote, and many unauthorized migrants have no plan or expectation to stay permanently. If they knew that they could only stay in the United States for a few years and earn well, the chances are that they would still come.[35]

Breaking any cycle of acquiescence and legalization is not simply a matter of deciding that the history of unauthorized migration to the United States no longer matters. The past generates obligations, even if everyone were to agree that the future needs to be different. Moreover, a different future requires the resolve to change and a feasible plan. Without both a way to deal fairly with obligations generated by the immigration system over much of the twentieth century, as well as reason to believe that different future policies will go beyond press releases, immigration statutes, and budget appropriations to effect real change, it is only right to assume that the future will be the logical extension of the past.

This relationship between the past and the future generates two main challenges. One is to design a legalization program to address the claims that the US immigration law system has generated. The other is to change law and policy—going much further than IRCA's superficial efforts—to break the cycle of unauthorized migration followed by legalization. Meeting these two challenges requires serious thought about how the past led to the present, then about durable solutions for the future.

Discussing these challenges requires that I first address another, more basic objection to legalization. The concern that legalization will create an incentive—or at least eliminate a disincentive—for unauthorized migration has roots that are too deep to be dismissed quickly by citing the reasons that people migrate. Critics of legalization would maintain that even if it does not increase unauthorized migration or the unauthorized population, and even if it does not repeat, granting access to lawful status effectively endorses lawbreaking. Even if legalization does not necessarily cause lawbreaking, the very endorsement of lawbreaking is objectionable. Endorsements and symbols matter in the making and implementation of laws and policies, and in determining how much public support they have. The phrase that captures what is at stake is "the rule of law." From this perspective, any form of legalization or amnesty is wrong, because it reflects refusal to enforce immigration laws and thus undermines the rule of law itself.[36]

IN ASSESSING THIS argument, the challenge is giving content to the idea of the rule of law. In debating legalization—and unauthorized migration generally—both sides appeal to this idea but give it different meanings.

Here are four examples to show how widely interpretations of the rule of law can vary, depending on how a decision-maker views two of the *Plyler* themes: the meaning of unlawful presence and the integration of unauthorized migrants.[37]

First, consider whether a prior ruling that a noncitizen is unlawfully present and should be deported is binding today, or instead is open to reevaluation. The US Supreme Court decided a case raising this question in 2006. Humberto Fernandez-Vargas, a citizen of Mexico, first came unlawfully to the United States in the 1970s and settled in Utah. He was deported for immigration violations but reentered the United States several times, most recently in 1982. He stayed, started his own trucking business, and in 1989 had a son who was born with US citizenship. In 2001, Fernandez married his son's mother, also a US citizen. The federal government eventually caught Fernandez in 2003 and tried to reinstate the old deportation order.[38]

In 1996, Congress amended the Immigration and Nationality Act to allow the government to reinstate prior removal orders against any noncitizen who has reentered the country unlawfully after being issued a formal order of removal. The government need not ask an immigration judge to issue a second order to remove the noncitizen. The government wanted to apply this new law to Fernandez, but it took effect many years after he had reentered unlawfully in 1982. Should the new law apply to Fernandez? No, argued Fernandez, because an immigration statute cannot be applied retroactively unless it clearly so provides, which Congress had not done. Fernandez contended that it would be retroactive—and therefore unlawful—to reinstate his old deportation order by applying the 1996 statute to his 1982 reentry.[39]

The US Supreme Court rejected this argument. Writing for the majority, Justice Souter reasoned that by unlawfully reentering and remaining, Fernandez's violations continued up to his arrest in 2003. Reinstating his deportation order was not retroactive at all. It simply applied the 1996 statute to his time in the United States up to 2003. This decision reflects the view that Fernandez's deportation order and unlawful reentry in 1982 established a firm foundation for any consequences that Congress might later attach. In rule of law terms, the original finding was that Fernandez was unlawfully present and should be deported, and no later events eroded or undercut that decision.[40]

In contrast, Justice Stevens's dissent explained that unlawful reentry could be offset by the community ties that Fernandez developed while living in Utah for over 20 years. In an analysis consistent with viewing the immigration law system as one of selective, highly discretionary enforcement, Stevens noted that the government had not enforced the prior deportation order against

Fernandez. This predictable non-enforcement, which allowed Fernandez to continue to live in the United States, was more significant for Stevens than the deportation order itself. Stevens reasoned that the 1996 statute would be impermissibly retroactive if it used Fernandez's unlawful reentry in 1982 to reinstate his old deportation order. Treating the 1982 order as binding would be reaching back in time and ignoring everything that had happened since 1982. Put differently, a prior order is not binding in the same way that a finding in a prior civil lawsuit might bind the parties in any future lawsuit between them that raises the same issue. In rule of law terms, courts should not blindly follow past decisions to deport. Instead, later reassessments of a case may justify discretionary relief to recognize equities that have arisen since a deportation order.[41]

The second example involves discretionary relief. One form of such relief, known as cancellation of removal, gives immigration judges the discretion to grant lawful permanent resident status to individual unauthorized migrants who have close relatives who are US citizens or permanent residents, meet a very demanding hardship standard, and do not have disqualifying criminal convictions. In 1996, Congress restricted the availability of cancellation of removal for noncitizens who are unlawfully present. Whether this change promotes the rule of law depends on whether cancellation is viewed as normal or extraordinary. If unlawful presence is straightforward and the rule of law demands enforcement against immigration violators, it follows that limiting cancellation makes sense. Then cancellation should remain an extraordinary act of grace, because the consequence of making it more widely available is to increase the likelihood that a proper deportation will not occur. In fact, however, cancellation decisions are governed by legal rules and standards that reflect threshold criteria, hardship requirements, and other standards that yield consistent results. Because the law applied to the facts may show that discretionary relief is proper, cancellation of removal does not stray from the rule of law. Instead, making cancellation more broadly available allows legal rules and standards to offset the unpredictable and inconsistent patterns of discretionary enforcement that brought an individual into removal proceedings.[42]

A third example involves the process for reviewing an order that a noncitizen is to be removed from the United States. The side that loses in immigration court may appeal to the Board of Immigration Appeals (BIA), a 15-member administrative review body within the US Department of Justice. If the BIA decides for the noncitizen, DHS can ask the attorney general of the United States for further review through a process called "certification." If the BIA rules for the government, however, noncitizens who want to have that decision reviewed must pursue another route, by filing an appeal in federal court. In 1996, Congress limited the jurisdiction of federal courts to consider noncitizens' appeals of removal orders. One provision severely limited court review of removal orders based on criminal convictions. Another generally eliminated court review of immigration decisions that are designated by statute as a matter of government discretion. Another section required noncitizens to wait for a final decision before they could appeal any rulings on specific issues in their cases. Further restrictions made it hard to challenge widespread or systemic government practices, thus forcing appeals to proceed individually instead.[43]

Does it better serve the rule of law to streamline court review, or instead to expand it? If unlawful presence is easy to ascertain and leads clearly to specific consequences, then the availability and scope of court review should be narrow and focus on a single case at a time. From this perspective, broader inquiry in a class action lawsuit leads to unjustified delay and expense, and anything more than minimal review undermines the rule of law. But assume that an individual's immigration or citizenship status is unclear, or that the consequence of a clear immigration law violation is not necessarily removal, or that the identification, arrest, and detention of noncitizens is highly selective and discretionary. Then the rule of law demands that courts have broad review powers over all issues in individual cases, and over claims that allege systemic problems, such as discriminatory enforcement or prosecution patterns.[44]

A fourth example of how widely interpretations of the rule of law can vary involves the right to effective counsel in immigration court. Removal proceedings are considered civil rather than criminal, and no court has ruled that the US Constitution requires legal representation at no cost for all noncitizens in removal proceedings. Though these general rules seem settled, contentious issues remain. One is whether a lawyer must be provided in certain circumstances, such as removal proceedings for noncitizens with limited mental capacity. Another tough question arises when a noncitizen finds legal representation, but the lawyer does a bad job. In 2009, this second question about a right to effective counsel came to a head in *Matter of Compean*, which prompted the rare intervention of two attorneys general of the United States, one of whom reversed his predecessor.[45]

The case grew out of separate removal proceedings involving three noncitizens. After losing in immigration court, each tried to have his case reopened, arguing that his attorney had been ineffective by not presenting highly relevant evidence or by not filing an appellate brief. In the last months of the George W. Bush presidency, Attorney General Michael Mukasey exercised his review authority over all three cases. He ruled that because there is no constitutional right to counsel in removal proceedings, the Constitution also does not guarantee that any available counsel will be effective. Five months after President Barack Obama took office, Attorney General Eric Holder vacated Mukasey's decision, repudiating his predecessor's statement that there is no constitutional right to effective assistance of counsel in removal proceedings.[46]

Whether a right to effective assistance of counsel is a key element of the rule of law in immigration law depends on how one thinks about the immigration law system. If discretionary relief is an act of grace, and decisions to grant or deny relief are not susceptible to correction after comparing each situation to the facts, reasoning, and outcome in prior cases, then it is much harder to argue that the rule of law demands a right to effective counsel. As with judicial review, an attorney's persistence would seem dilatory rather than a serious claim of right. But because many unauthorized migrants are allowed to stay in the United States through cancellation of removal and other forms of discretionary relief, then even if a noncitizen is unlawfully present, that fact is just the start of the analysis. Decisions about discretionary relief are governed by standards that make it possible to decide if decisions are wrong. Without effective counsel, the chances increase that the initial decision to identify the noncitizen for immigration enforcement is the only decision that matters. The rule of law requires that legal standards apply to government decisions. To make sure that this is true in immigration law, recognizing a right to effective assistance of counsel is essential.

These four examples show that the idea of the rule of law is malleable. Some observers believe that unlawful presence is straightforward, so the rule of law demands swift enforcement and rejects any need to integrate unauthorized migrants. This perspective on the rule of law is also the foundation of the gradual intertwining of immigration law with criminal law, which goes back well into the nineteenth century but has intensified since the 1990s. If unlawful presence is the crucial fact and civil enforcement of immigration law seems inadequate, a natural move is to raise the rule-of-law stakes. One consequence has been the growing emphasis on prosecuting and punishing immigration violations as crimes and as national security risks. Criminalization has steadily accelerated since the 1990s, when Congress added several new immigration-related crimes and increased penalties for existing ones. The other major link between immigration law and criminal law has been the use of immigration penalties—most prominently, deportation—as an extra penalty for noncitizens who are convicted of crimes unrelated to their immigration status. The 1996 amendments to the federal immigration statutes significantly broadened the crime-based grounds for removal. And even when a conviction is not a formal ground for the removal of an unauthorized migrant, a conviction can prompt federal immigration agencies to prioritize enforcement against him.[47]

Faith in a clear line between legal and illegal can seem reassuring, especially if crime control and national security are said to be at stake. The problem with this view, however, is that it disregards both US immigration history and the current state of immigration law and policy. The immigration law system is one of selective admissions, selective enforcement, and vast unpredictable and inconsistent discretion. It is not just a matter of enforcing a simple legal-illegal line. This context is the foundation for unauthorized migrants' claims to integration and to being treated as Americans in waiting. This context also illuminates what the rule of law means in my four examples.[48]

Limits on cancellation of removal tend to undercut the rule of law, because cancellation is immigration law's way of rationally assessing when case-by-case legalization makes sense to help integrate unauthorized migrants. They may be in the United States unlawfully, but that is not determinative. Threshold eligibility rules, hardship requirements, and discretionary standards can be applied consistently, so that applicants can have reasonable expectations based on precedents. This approach allows the rule of law to prevail over unreviewable choices made by border inspectors or other government officials. Likewise, the opportunity to reexamine prior findings in immigration cases, a robust system of court review, and a constitutional protection against ineffective assistance of counsel all promote the rule of law by allowing immigration decisions to conform to legal standards, and over time to form a coherent body of guiding law.

In the same way, past and present immigration law suggest that there is little substance to rule-of-law objections to the DREAM Act, birthright citizenship, and broad-scale legalization. In fact, the opposite is true. The immigration law system, especially its reliance on vast discretion, jeopardizes the rule of law when it creates a large unauthorized population, then leaves it to unpredictable and inconsistent decision-making to identify who will be caught in the immigration enforcement apparatus. Just as cancellation of removal, judicial review, and effective counsel can bring the rule of law to immigration law, so can the DREAM Act, birthright citizenship, and broad-scale legalization. Respect for the rule of law in immigration law means identifying where granting lawful status is an appropriate way to restore some predictability and consistency to the US immigration system. Understanding how this might be accomplished requires a closer look at related episodes in immigration law history.[49]

Legalizations, Past and Present

Rule-of-law objections to providing lawful immigration or citizenship status to some persons who might otherwise be unauthorized migrants are closely related to a view of history that characterizes legalization as extraordinary. In fact, however, legalization schemes have been frequent and commonplace in US immigration law. The legalization scheme in the Immigration Reform and Control Act (IRCA) of 1986 was a milestone in US immigration history, but it would be a grave misunderstanding to believe that grants of lawful status have been rare. One of immigration history's essential features in the modern era has been the repeated emergence of ad hoc arrangements to grant lawful status to noncitizens. Even if these arrangements have not been called legalization or amnesty, that has been their practical effect. Though they may appear scattered and unsystematic, in fact they follow familiar and predictable patterns and reflect broad, powerful forces that come from the core of the immigration system.[50]

Unauthorized migrants have numerous ways to acquire lawful immigration status on an individual basis. The most specific arrangements involve case-by-case discretionary relief under federal statutes. Each year, several thousand noncitizens who lack lawful immigration status become lawful permanent residents through cancellation of removal. Immigration judges decide these cases by relying on various factors, especially work history, family ties to citizens and permanent residents, and the absence of criminal convictions. Congress established the current scheme in 1996, but its precursors go back to 1940.[51]

Another individual form of legalization is known as "registry." This concept has been part of federal immigration law since 1929. It responded to a conundrum created by the statute of limitations that had been part of federal immigration law since 1903. Once it was too late to deport noncitizens, what would be their status? To take these noncitizens out of limbo, and also to establish records for immigrants who had arrived before federal law required registration at a port-of-entry, the federal government registered them as permanent residents. The statute of limitations was later repealed, but registry continues to have a similar practical effect by conferring lawful status on noncitizens based on length of residence. Today, any noncitizen who has been in the United States since January 1, 1972, whether or not in lawful immigration status, can qualify for registry and can become a permanent resident unless she has disqualifying criminal convictions. With the cutoff date so far in the past, only 135 noncitizens became permanent residents through registry in fiscal year 2012, but registry still deserves mention as another example of an individualized legalization.[52]

Numerous other programs in US immigration law from the end of World War II to the present have provided lawful immigration status to a group of noncitizens who fell outside the admission categories set out in immigration law at that time. In 1945, President Truman ordered the use of regular admission slots for some of the displaced persons left stranded by World War II. When the Soviet Union put down the Hungarian revolution in 1956, hundreds of thousands fled Hungary, at first mainly to Austria, but also generating pressure for a US response. The Eisenhower administration allowed 30,000 Hungarian refugees to come to the United States. In both cases, the federal executive branch provided lawful immigration status when the letter of immigration law seemed to deny it.[53]

The Hungarian example differs from the usual understanding of legalization, in that the refugees were outside the United States when the government acted to grant them lawful status on an extraordinary basis. Other programs have operated inside the United States as a form of legalization. For example, the Chinese Confession program, which operated from 1955 until 1970, offered lawful permanent residence to Chinese immigrants if they confessed to immigrating originally under false pretenses, often by claiming to be the son or daughter of a US citizen. The administration of the program was highly politicized, with the Immigration and Naturalization Service using the information acquired through confessions to target noncitizen Chinese American leftists for deportation. In spite of this taint, the program is part of the history of legalizations, having conferred lawful status on an estimated 20,000 to 30,000 noncitizens who otherwise would have been deportable.[54]

Other programs have conferred lawful immigration status on persons who had arrived in the United States after fleeing unsettled political conditions in the Caribbean and Central America, but who might not have qualified for asylum under existing law. In 1965, Cuban president Fidel Castro announced that Cubans who wanted to leave Cuba to join relatives in the United States could do so by leaving from the port of Camarioca. Within several months, around 200,000 Cubans arrived in the United States by boat. The migration then expanded to include air flights to the United States. In 1966, Congress passed the Cuban Adjustment Act, which remains in effect today and allows Cubans to become lawful permanent residents after one year on US soil, regardless of their manner of arrival in the United States.[55]

In 1997, the Nicaraguan Adjustment and Central American Relief Act (NACARA) became law, reflecting Congress's recognition that the US government had limited the opportunities for migrants from Nicaragua, El Salvador, and Guatemala to apply for asylum in the United States. As a remedy, NACARA opened a path to lawful immigration status for large numbers of Nicaraguans, Salvadorans, and Guatemalans who had been unlawfully present. A similar limited legalization program is the Haitian Refugee Immigration Fairness Act (HRIFA). It was companion legislation to go with NACARA, driven by concerns that the US government was treating Haitian asylum seekers unfavorably as compared to those from other Western Hemisphere countries.[56]

THESE EXAMPLES REVEAL general patterns. One is that US immigration law has given lawful status to noncitizens based on their integration into American society, as evidenced by specific ties or the passage of time. Cancellation of removal and registry are examples. At other times, immigration law has given lawful status to noncitizens who are in the United States after fleeing dire circumstances in their home countries. In this category are asylum seekers, who benefit from a type of legalization.

It may seem odd to think of asylum as a legalization program, especially because it has become a frequent occurrence to grant asylum and then permanent residence. In fact, many asylum seekers arrive without papers, or are admitted but later lose their lawful status. Though many affirmatively apply for asylum, many others only raise asylum claims later, as a defense to removal from the United States. And yet, law and popular culture have come to accept that asylum seekers are unlike other unauthorized migrants. Asylum has come to seem like another category of lawful admission to the United States, and generally as consistent with the rule of law. This public perception of asylum seekers may explain some of the discomfort with any government efforts to detain them or otherwise to treat them more like unauthorized migrants.[57]

The reasons to grant lawful status to asylum seekers seem compelling. Accepting asylum seekers from some countries may be an appropriate corollary to US foreign policy. Granting asylum reflects not only an impulse to protect vulnerable people, but also a historical sense of responsibility and obligation that infuses international law protections for refugees. The United States has acknowledged that humanitarian obligations recognized by international conventions can override immigration violations. This judgment is crystallized in Article 33 of the 1951 Geneva Convention Relating to the Status of Refugees. This provision protects a refugee from being returned to wherever his life or freedom would be threatened on account of race, religion, nationality, membership in a particular social group, or political opinion. Article 31 of the Convention commits signatories to not penalize refugees for illegally entering a state of refuge. Moreover, the United States, like many other countries, goes beyond its international law obligations at both stages of the asylum process. The first is granting lawful status to asylum seekers who prove their claims even if they appear on US territory without legal authorization. The second is conferring lawful permanent residence and thus a path to citizenship.[58]

Many of the reasons for granting asylum also apply in some measure to other examples of legalization. I do not mean to say that the arguments for lawful status are more or less compelling for asylum seekers than they are for other types of unauthorized migrants. My point is more limited: that the decision to grant access to lawful immigration status to any group of unauthorized migrants—including asylum seekers—requires a close look at the strength of their claims. It is unconvincing to reject such claims at the outset as offensive to the rule of law, as if it is extraordinary to have programs that can confer lawful status on those who lack it. Such programs are rather commonplace. Moreover, when unauthorized migrants are in the United States as part of an immigration system that has historically tolerated them, arguments for legalization resemble the arguments for asylum more than it may seem at first.

CURRENT IMMIGRATION LAW protects several other groups of noncitizens in the United States even if they, like many asylum seekers, lack lawful status. They include unaccompanied minors and noncitizens who have suffered from human trafficking, from domestic violence, or from other crimes. These noncitizens have access to lawful status including permanent residence and citizenship. Unaccompanied minors may be eligible for Special Immigrant Juvenile Status (SIJS), which provides lawful status to children who have been abused, abandoned, or neglected. Survivors and victims of human trafficking can apply for T visas that allow them to become permanent residents after three years. Domestic violence can be a basis for a number of special provisions that grant lawful immigration status. Crime victims can apply for U visas that allow them to become permanent residents after three years. And on rare occasions, Congress has passed private bills for noncitizens whose circumstances were especially compelling but did not fit into any existing type of admission or discretionary relief.[59]

Efforts to define who is eligible for these forms of legalization raise many difficult questions. Some observers have criticized what they call a trend to legalize and offer lawful permanent resident status only to those who match up with some image of stereotypical victims. These critics question why federal agencies seem to grant T visas more readily to sex trafficking victims than to abused seamstresses in garment sweatshops or to abused strawberry pickers on farms, or why federal agencies seem more responsive to physical harm suffered by victims rather than to psychological coercion. Notwithstanding these debates, asylum seekers and other unauthorized migrants who seem virtuous or vulnerable enough, or whose protection serves law enforcement or other goals, can shed the illegal label and become lawful permanent residents. One analysis found that since IRCA was adopted in 1986, over one million persons have become permanent residents of the United States through legalization programs other than the two programs in IRCA.[60]

This history alone is not a persuasive argument for legalization programs. Again, the past need not control the future, but unless there is both a resolve and a feasible plan for change, the past remains highly relevant and suggests that the reasons for legalizations in the past may still be persuasive today. With legalization granted to a significant number of individuals who seem worthy, the line between the lawful and unlawful is just the start of analysis. The real question is how to evaluate the arguments for legalization in any given situation. The answer starts by understanding why this history of legalizations exists in the first place.

THE REASONS FOR the history of legalization in US immigration law are related to each other. They combine to show that legalization is neither an aberration nor an affront to the rule of law, but rather a principled way of applying the rule of law to control the discretion that has historically governed unauthorized migration. Many of these reasons suggest that legalization is appropriate today, and that it is logical for this historical pattern of legalizations to continue. Or, if US immigration law is to move away from a system that makes occasional legalization appropriate, then it is essential to confront the historical reasons for legalization and to change the immigration law system so that legalizations are no longer part of the natural cycle.

One reason for legalization programs and mechanisms is that sound immigration policy is very hard to formulate in advance. Statutes are fixed and drafted in general terms, and enacting them requires tough compromises. No matter what congressional legislation says, and no matter what apparent exactitude a statute brings to bear on the selection of immigrants, making policy on the ground is messier than drafting legislation. The vast discretion in the current immigration system, as applied to a large unauthorized population, is a way of responding more immediately and more sensitively to domestic and global economic trends. But this system also makes very vulnerable the millions of unauthorized migrants who live precariously at discretion's mercy. Over time, decisions by those who administer the system gives rise to valid expectations and claims that can make legalization in some narrow or broad form sensible and just.[61]

A second reason is closely related to the first. To create any possibility of a significant reduction in the unauthorized population of the United States through enforcement, a significant increase over current resource commitments would be necessary. Allocating these scarce resources is logistically and politically complex, especially given powerful global economic factors shaping the migration trends that enforcement must counter. Allowing a significant number of immigrants to come outside the law, and then periodically legalizing those with strong work histories, may be more flexible, accurate, efficient, and politically expedient than trying to identify the most desirable immigrants in advance. The contributions of some unauthorized migrants may be speculative initially but discernible at a later time, when they can be granted lawful immigration status.[62]

A third, overlapping reason for the historical pattern of legalizations reflects changing views of what immigration law is in the first place. Today the prevailing tendency is to think of it as a single, unified body of law, but it was created and enforced on a much more ad hoc basis in earlier historical periods. The current unitary view emerged most prominently in 1965, when Congress abolished the national origins system, which had controlled immigration on a country-by-country basis in order to preserve the ethnic composition of the US population. The 1965 amendments embraced the idea that a unitary body of law should apply uniformly to immigrant admissions. This drive to universality reflects noble principles, but immigration statutes of general application will respond inadequately to specific situations, such as refugee crises, historical relationships with particular countries, or regional economic patterns. If this inadequacy becomes conspicuous and groups of unauthorized migrants come or stay in the United States for especially compelling reasons, the reasons to grant lawful status have become irresistible.

Fourth, lines of demarcation throughout the law often change as realities shift. An analogy is the doctrine of adverse possession in property law, which says that someone who is not the owner of the property according to official land records can acquire title to the property by occupying and using it. The requirements vary from state to state, but they generally include physical use of the property. The occupier's possession of the land must be exclusive, or in other words, not shared with whoever holds the formal title. Possession must also not be expressly authorized by the formal title holder. The occupier's use of the land must be visible to neighbors, if not to the formal title holder. In some states, occupation must be under what is called "color of title," which means some pretense of official authorization. Lastly, adverse possession requires a minimum time period, which varies from five years in California to 20 years in some states. Occupation need not be constant; it may be periodic or seasonal. If all of these conditions are met, the person who used the land can acquire official title, typically through a court proceeding. Based on a policy of recognizing the most efficient use of land, adverse possession confirms that the line between lawful and unlawful is not always fixed.[63]

Similarly, unauthorized migrants are physically in the United States. Their visible unlawful presence seems to satisfy the requirement that occupation is not shared with or permitted by the owner. The color of title requirement may be satisfied by an unauthorized migrant's US citizen children, payment of US taxes, and eligibility for some government programs. And as for the time requirement, many unauthorized migrants are long-time residents. To take the analogy further, unauthorized migrants might be trespassers, but the owner has tolerated them in order to improve the property over a period of time. In this way, applying adverse possession to unauthorized migration relies partly on immigration as affiliation, based especially on contributions to the US economy through their work. Adverse possession is also conceptually akin to immigration as contract, by inferring some kind of agreement or tacit consent if a landowner does nothing about the occupier's unlawful presence.[64]

In looking for analogies to legalization in general legal principles, the doctrine of adverse possession is more helpful than another possibility: the idea of a statute of limitations. It seems intuitive that the reasons to enforce immigration law against violators may diminish over time. But the analogy to a statute of limitations only makes sense if the time period starts to run as soon as the noncitizen is in the United States unlawfully. Because an unauthorized migrant's unlawful presence continues, this statute of limitations analogy may be weak. If an unauthorized migrant's ties and contribution over time deserve recognition by conferring her lawful status, the doctrine of adverse possession is more pertinent.[65]

A fifth reason for the history of various legalizations is that concerns about legality and reliance on the legal-illegal line in immigration law have ebbed and flowed over time. A bright line can provide an attractively simple guide to separate virtue from vice. In many past eras, however, the line between lawful and unlawful immigration did not have the visceral power that it does today, especially in electoral politics. In earlier periods of US history, unauthorized migrants could come to be seen as legal without attracting the opposition or attention that legalization might in the current political climate. The fact that migrants were in the United States lawfully or unlawfully was much less significant than the work that they did.[66]

A sixth reason is the most troubling but inescapable. Race and ethnicity have shaped immigration enforcement for much of US history and have influenced how past legalization programs and mechanisms have tempered enforcement. Especially important is the inclination to think of certain workers—especially Mexican workers in much of the twentieth century—as a flexible labor force that could be kept at society's margins. In turn, active recruitment by employers and tolerance by the US government contributed to the unauthorized population's growth over the past 50 years. But as historian Mae Ngai has shown, case-by-case discretionary relief was available to European and Canadian immigrants in the mid-twentieth century. The thinking was that their illegal status was merely technical, curable through various procedural avenues. These included a "pre-examination" process that was the precursor to adjustment of status under current immigration law, as well as suspension of deportation, which became cancellation of removal today. Both of these routes allowed Europeans and Canadians to cure their immigration violations. These forms of relief were unavailable to Mexican, other Latin American, and Caribbean immigrants, whose illegality was perceived as more fundamental, intrinsic, and indelible.[67]

History shows how the United States has tolerated but marginalized unauthorized migrants, while at the same time its immigration law system has granted admission and legalization to favored groups. This history has two legacies. One is that refusal to look beyond the line between legal and illegal is to turn a blind eye to the many suspect influences that have shaped that line. The other legacy is that it would be politically and morally untenable to deny legalization on similar terms to other groups today.[68]

Designing Legalization

The next question is how best to design a legalization program so that it is an effective, durable response to the problems with US immigration law. The answer starts by considering the political context. Many supporters of legalization view it as the key component of any legislative package on immigration issues that they would support. But opponents view legalization—or amnesty, as they would call it—as the most objectionable sort of proposed legislation. Their objections grow even louder if legalization would treat unauthorized migrants more favorably than others who have applied through the admission process, or if legalization would include a path to citizenship.[69]

The central position that legalization occupies in current immigration debates is entirely understandable, for it responds to the most glaring consequence of the current system. Over 11 million people in the United States are meaningfully part of American society in spite of their immigration violations. There are strong reasons to recognize and foster their integration, and to afford them lawful status. Deciding how to treat the unauthorized migrants in the United States is the first step into a sensible future.

And yet, it is also unfortunate that legalization has become so central to the politics of immigration law. On the one hand, legalization is not unusual or unprecedented, or as radical as opponents make it out to be, so it raises the decibel level of opposition more than history supports. At the same time, legalization alone cannot accomplish as much as some of its supporters may believe. Legalization can only correct the shortcomings of immigration laws in the past. It does nothing to fix immigration laws going forward. To be sure, legalization affects future immigration patterns because it will expand the group of permanent residents and then of US citizens who can sponsor future immigrants. The Immigration Reform and Control Act (IRCA) of 1986 allowed several million unauthorized migrants to become lawful permanent residents who could sponsor other immigrants, especially if they later became citizens. But if legalization is enacted without addressing the real possibility that a new unauthorized population will establish itself, then the same issues will return in the next generation.[70]

Because of this combination of misconceptions about legalization, it carries a degree of political liability that is more intense than its actual consequences. To suggest what a legalization program as part of a legislative package with more durable effects might look like, consider this thought experiment. Imagine what supporters of legalization would be willing to accept by way of permanent changes to immigration laws, in exchange for abandoning proposals for a one-time broad-scale legalization. Put differently, what changes to immigration law might accomplish much of what one-time legalization might achieve?

The answer starts by noting that under current law, a noncitizen might not be able to become a permanent resident even if she qualifies in an immigration category. Fixing this feature of current law may seem eminently sensible, and it may be surprising that qualifying noncitizens who are married to US citizens face significant barriers to becoming permanent residents. But these obstacles are real—the combined result of two rules that apply to noncitizens who originally entered the United States unlawfully. One rule says that noncitizens cannot become permanent residents inside the United States if they did not go through inspection at a port of entry, so they must leave the United States and obtain their immigrant visa at a US embassy or consulate. But the other rule says that noncitizens who have been in the United States unlawfully for 180 days or longer may not return for three or ten years if they leave the United States. They can come back earlier if they get a waiver for extreme hardship, but until late 2012, they had to leave before they could start the uncertain and often lengthy process of applying for the waiver.[71]

One step in crafting an alternative to broad-scale legalization would be allowing noncitizens who qualify for an immigrant admission category to become permanent residents without leaving the United States, even if they originally entered unlawfully. Congress could achieve the same result by repealing the three- and ten-year bars for unlawful presence. This change would still require qualifying noncitizens to leave the United States to get their immigrant visas, but they could return immediately without a three- or ten-year wait or a waiver. Either approach would allow many noncitizens who qualify in existing admission categories to become lawful permanent residents. In late 2012, the Obama administration implemented a third, though only partial, solution by allowing many of those eligible for the waivers to apply from inside the United States rather than leave the United States first.[72]

Admittedly, any of these approaches would mean disregarding a prior immigration law violation, typically crossing the border unlawfully, that allowed the unauthorized migrant to form the relationships that now allow her to immigrate, for example through marriage or employment. But given the strength of many unauthorized migrants' claims to integration and lawful status, it makes sense to start with the unauthorized migrants who would be lawful permanent residents under current law except for their simple unlawful presence in the United States.

A second step toward a more durable—if narrower—alternative to broad-scale legalization would be making discretionary relief more available. The eligibility rules for cancellation of removal are especially important. Congress severely restricted eligibility in 1996, mainly by requiring a longer residence period, counting that period more strictly, and stiffening the pivotal hardship requirement. Applicants previously had to show extreme hardship, which could include hardship to themselves; now they must show excep-tional and extremely unusual hardship to a child, spouse, or parent who is a US citizen or permanent resident. Restoring the pre-1996 rules would give lawful status to a large number of unauthorized migrants, but far fewer than broad-scale legalization. Like allowing unauthorized migrants who qualify in an immigrant admission category to become permanent residents, broaden-ing eligibility for cancellation would benefit the unauthorized migrants who would have the most compelling cases within any broader legalization.[73]

Here I should address an apparent tension between this proposal to expand discretionary relief and my overall analysis of the US immigration law system as characterized by selectivity and discretion. Discretion that is so vast undermines the rule of law. How, then, can I suggest that a discretionary rem-edy—cancellation of removal—be made more widely available? The answer is that I have not argued against all discretion, but rather against discretion that undermines the rule of law because it is unpredictable, inconsistent, and potentially discriminatory. In contrast, discretionary relief for unauthorized migrants is consistent with the rule of law because decisions to grant or deny relief are governed by a complex body of law as to threshold qualifications, hardship standards, the exercise of discretion, and judicial review.

These first two alternatives to legalization—narrower but more durable than broad-scale legalization—might be less objectionable to skeptics, and less politically risky for public officials facing election challenges. They essen-tially provide lawful status to the unauthorized migrants who have the stron-gest cases based either on qualifying in an existing category or on other family ties to citizens and permanent residents. At least as importantly, these alterna-tives are more consistent with the most fundamental reason for legalization—to make changes to immigration law itself, rather than simply legalizing the current unauthorized population while doing nothing to change the immi-gration system going forward.

The third step in designing an alternative to broad-scale legalization starts by considering changes to the admissions system going forward—a task that I will undertake more fully in the next chapter. For now, take as an example that Congress expands lawful immigrant admissions for workers who do not have a college diploma. One core group to benefit from legalization should then be the workers who are in the United States unlawfully today, but who would have been able to come lawfully if the admissions system had been expanded in this way a number of years ago. In other words, this third step would try to select retrospectively, through legalization, the immigrants whom the admission system should have admitted earlier.

THE NEXT QUESTION is how best to implement the three types of changes that I have described as an alternative to broad-scale legalization. A basic design question is whether unauthorized migrants in these categories should be granted lawful status on a group basis, or through decisions in individual cases. In answering this question, administrative efficiency is important. If certain groups of people are likely to qualify for a type of immigration status despite individual variations, it is more efficient to grant the status categorically by applying general requirements, rather than by weighing the specific equities and hardships of each case.

The current system of refugee protection provides an analogy. Asylum applications by individuals at the border or inside the United States prompt a searching inquiry into the circumstances of the case. However, US law grants admission as refugees to applicants outside the United States based on the general type of case, not on the precise facts. The decision starts with a judgment that certain groups generally qualify, followed by an inquiry into whether the individual belongs to the group. Similarly, DHS designates entire nationalities for "temporary protected status" due to unrest, disaster, or other unsettled conditions.[74]

Another related concern is that it may be too difficult to have legal standards govern an open-ended, detailed, case-by-case inquiry by individual government officials. The design of any legalization program must provide confidence that outcomes are consistent with each other and are not influenced by inappropriate factors, ranging from regional variations to racial or ethnic bias. And if part of the inquiry's focus is an individual unauthorized migrant's integration into American society, there is, as Joseph Carens put it, "something presumptuous in imagining that one person can make nuanced judgments about how deeply another belongs to the society in which she lives." Put differently, it would be a mistake to infuse legalization with the very sort of vast discretion that historically has been a source of unpredictability and inconsistency in US immigration law.[75]

The Deferred Action for Childhood Arrivals (DACA) program offers some lessons for legalization design. The Obama administration announced DACA in June 2012, and DHS started to accept applications two months later, in August 2012. About one year before, DHS had issued several memoranda to guide the exercise of prosecutorial discretion. Though the new memos were more detailed than their predecessors, and though they led to some discretionary grants of relief from removal, they failed to have much consistent and uniform influence on enforcement activities in the field. During the period before DACA, rank-and-file ICE officers resisted implementation of the new prosecutorial discretion memos, and members of their union adopted a vote of no-confidence in ICE director John Morton and one of his chief deputies. After DACA began, the ICE officers' union unsuccessfully challenged it in court. Given this resistance in the field, it took the adoption of DACA as a formal program to limit unpredictable and arbitrary decisions and to bring some consistency and predictability to the nationwide pattern of prosecutorial discretion decisions. From this perspective, DACA significantly advanced the rule of law. The process became formalized, as compared to haphazard decision-making in individual cases.[76]

A related point is that much of the argument for legalization is that US policy has long tolerated—or even encouraged—substantial unauthorized migration by large groups. In turn, it makes sense not to focus on individuals, but rather to allow legalization in groups to smooth out random variations in individual circumstances that have little to do with the reasons for legalization in the first place. For example, case-by-case decisions to grant lawful status might benefit traditional breadwinners in formalized sectors of the economy, but it might also limit avenues to lawful status for caregivers in the home. For this reason, administering legalization by asking whether an unauthorized migrant fits into a defined group reduces unwarranted disparities by gender.

IN SHORT, A workable, fair approach to legalization that produces predictable and uniform results is best achieved by thinking about legalization applicants in groups defined by set criteria, with individual inquiry limited to asking if each applicant fits into a group. This is how the DREAM Act would treat children who were brought to this country at a young age by their parents, who have completed high school, and who will be contributing to America by attending college or serving in the military. The multiple advantages of thinking about legalization in groups argue for a core legalization program that would allow access to lawful immigration status for the groups of unauthorized migrants who would benefit from the changes that I have outlined. These would be unauthorized migrants who could acquire lawful permanent resident status except for the three- and ten-year bars, plus those who could apply for cancellation of removal under pre-1996 standards, plus those who could have been admitted to the United States if reworked admission categories had been part of US immigration law all along. This core legalization program would include a significant number of unauthorized migrants. The combined result would seem narrower than an IRCA-type broad-scale legalization, but in the long run its effects would be broader and more durable.

Broad-scale legalization without changes to permanent rules will simply reduce the unauthorized population initially, if only by relabeling people unlawful instead of lawful. Some new lawful residents will be able to sponsor close relatives, and in this sense legalization will lead to the lawful admission of some future immigrants who might otherwise be unauthorized migrants. But the unauthorized population will increase gradually after this quick drop.

The most obvious sign of these limitations of one-time legalization is the cutoff date that seems essential to any program. The legislation that passed the US Senate in June 2013 would have applied only to unauthorized migrants who were in the United States as of December 31, 2011. The idea that a program excludes people who became unauthorized migrants after a certain date makes clear that legalization deals principally with the past without proposing durable future solutions. The consequence of settling for one-time, broad-scale legalization will be to repeat the legacy of IRCA legalization in 1986—deferring the real issues, only to see them return a generation later in more vexing form.[77]

SEVERAL YEARS AGO at a public forum on immigration policy in Asheville, North Carolina, a member of the audience asked me a simple but wise question: "Everyone talks about comprehensive immigration reform. But what does comprehensive immigration reform really accomplish? What does it get us?" I have spent a lot of time thinking about this question, and I have come to this response: any sort of reworking of our immigration laws can only buy time to make the changes that really matter in the long run. The better approach to legalization is to consider it in the way the next generation would want us to. In this spirit, I have tried in this chapter to explain the best approach to legalization by drawing on two of the themes that were essential to *Plyler*—the integration of unauthorized migrants and the meaning of unlawful presence in the context of the US immigration law system's selectivity and vast discretion.

Many might object that enforcement is much tougher now than in past eras, that the past does not bind the future, and that today's decision-makers are free to change course. In the abstract, these statements about the federal government's freedom to make decisions must be correct. But it is essential to acknowledge that the authority to make decisions does not necessarily include authority to erase history, obligations, or justified expectations by sheer fiat. At the very least, this difference between going forward and acknowledging the past affirms the need for a process of change that is both fair and pragmatic. Justice requires protections for legitimate expectations generated by recognizing de facto tolerance of unauthorized migration. These protections call for avenues to lawful immigration status as a first step toward a fundamental restructuring of government responses to migration patterns.[78]

To close out this chapter, I should acknowledge that there is much more to say about how to break the cycle of repeated legalizations. What other sorts of changes to immigration law and to aspects of government law and policy beyond immigration law are necessary to achieve durable solutions? Examining these challenges is the task for the next and final chapter of this book.

7

Finding Answers

THIS BOOK OPENED with the idea that the three themes central to the 1982 US Supreme Court decision in *Plyler v. Doe* have remained at the heart of debates about immigration outside the law and continue to illuminate their substance. For anyone who hopes that a sound national policy will emerge to engage with unauthorized migration, it is essential to understand these themes—the meaning of unlawful presence, the role of state and local governments, and the integration of unauthorized migrants. They are instructive, not just alone, but also because they combine to raise issues that are even more fundamental.

In combination, the meaning of unlawful presence and the state and local role shed light on the authority to enforce immigration law. Connecting the state and local role with the integration of unauthorized migrants guides the building of communities that include noncitizens and citizens. And looking at the meaning of unlawful presence and the integration of unauthorized migrants illuminates the topic of legalization. Any durable efforts to address immigration outside the law must take seriously the lessons that emerge from the *Plyler* framework.

This chapter picks up where my analysis of legalization in Chapter 6 left off. I did not fully address questions about how to rework immigration law to avoid repeating the same debates over legalization a generation from now. The answers fall into two general categories: those within immigration law, and those that go beyond immigration law. One helpful way to get at both categories is to consider a topic that is indispensable in any thoughtful discussion of immigration policy. The topic is temporary workers.[1]

Temporary worker programs are an essential part of any discussion of immigration outside the law, because an alternative to deporting or legalizing unauthorized migrants is admitting them lawfully. In turn, one approach to lawful admissions is to admit temporary workers. More fundamentally, temporary worker programs illuminate the choices available in responding to unauthorized migration. This broader inquiry goes beyond temporary workers and unauthorized migrants, and even beyond immigration law itself, to address not only the US system for admitting immigrants, but also the US educational system and international economic development.

But People Came

United States law currently admits groups of temporary workers in several nonimmigrant categories. Some categories have annual numerical limits, and one is limited to agricultural workers. Two categories are especially relevant to unauthorized migration because they do not have university-level educational requirements. As a result, these categories include many temporary workers who resemble unauthorized migrants in education, training, and occupation. The H-2A category allows the admission of an unlimited number of agricultural workers, assuming that they and their employers meet various requirements. H-2B temporary workers are unrestricted by line of work, but only 66,000 are admitted annually, and employers must show that these workers will not displace or earn less than prospective employees who are US citizens or lawful permanent residents.[2]

US immigration law admits other temporary workers in categories that require more formal education or higher-level job responsibilities. These workers tend not to fit a prevalent unauthorized stereotype, but they, too, might be unauthorized migrants if these temporary admission categories did not exist. One such category admits H-1B nonimmigrants, who generally must have a four-year college degree or its equivalent. This category is capped at 65,000 new visas each year, with exceptions. Other nonimmigrant categories seem intended for international business, but they include temporary employees and offer advantages over the H-1B category for those who qualify. For example, L-1 intracompany transferees must have worked for the same employer for one year out of the past three, but they can stay in valid nonimmigrant status for a longer period and become permanent residents more easily than H-1B workers. The E-1 and E-2 nonimmigrant categories for traders, investors, and some of their employees may also include some noncitizens who otherwise might arrive or stay unlawfully.[3]

Most of the legislative proposals since the year 2000 for legalization as part of a package of changes in US immigration law would have expanded temporary worker admissions. A bill to establish a broad temporary worker program passed the US Senate in 2006, but it failed in the House of Representatives. The next year, a more limited temporary worker program was part of the comprehensive Kennedy-McCain bill, which narrowly failed to pass in the Senate.

The bill that the US Senate approved in June 2013 included two temporary worker programs. One would have admitted temporary agricultural workers in a scheme that resembled various versions of prior legislation known as the Agricultural Job Opportunities, Benefits, and Security Act (AgJOBS). The 2013 Senate bill would also have established a new program to admit temporary workers in other industries, and would also have modified the existing H-1B and H-2B programs.[4]

Supporters of temporary worker programs typically argue that the lawful admission scheme should supply the US economy with needed workers. Failure to do so impairs national economic competitiveness and has contributed to the growth of the unauthorized population. Compared to permanent immigration, the argument continues, temporary or circular migration is more responsive to employers' workforce needs—especially for jobs requiring little training or formal education. Temporary workers benefit the economy without the social, fiscal, or political impact of the same number of long-term immigrants. Supporters also maintain that many migrants want only temporary work sojourns, preferring regular return visits home in circular migration patterns, and that it would be unjustifiably paternalistic for the government to deny this option.[5]

Skeptics often emphasize the exploitation of temporary workers, observing that they are vulnerable to harsh and dangerous working conditions, wage theft, and other workplace injustices. A deeper concern stems from the inherent tension between the borders that are inherent in immigration law and the national commitment to equality that is central to political and civic culture in the United States. The harm to that equality is too great, the argument goes, if immigration law admits noncitizens only temporarily as workers without the path to citizenship that is essential to preventing their permanent marginalization.[6]

Further skepticism of temporary worker programs reflects perceived harms to US citizens or permanent residents. Some will benefit from temporary workers who complement what they do, but other citizens or permanent residents will suffer a decline in job prospects, wages, or working conditions. Again, the link between temporary worker programs and unauthorized migration is crucial. Unauthorized migration may have similar effects, but some skeptics argue that these harms can become especially entrenched through temporary worker programs. From this point of view, temporary worker programs are not an acceptable alternative to unauthorized migration; the United States should admit noncitizens for permanent residence with a path to citizenship, or not admit them at all.[7]

THE OUTCOME OF debates between supporters and skeptics of temporary worker programs is evident in the design of temporary worker programs. Some choices involve what a worker must show to qualify—education, training, or work experience. Other questions involve the terms of admission—the initial stay, possible renewal, mandatory departure before renewal, and allowed total stay. Other issues include workplace rights and protections, ability to change jobs or employers while maintaining immigration status, and admission and work authorization for family members. It is also necessary to decide how the admission of temporary workers fits with other aspects of immigration law. For example, will prior immigration violations by a noncitizen block his admission as a temporary worker? Can a temporary worker become a permanent resident or citizen later? Can a temporary worker renew his status if he has applied and is waiting to become a lawful permanent resident?

Beyond these specific rules and conditions of admission lie other design choices. One is whether programs should be restricted to certain occupations or industries, and how to check compliance with such limits. Another is whether to make temporary admissions sensitive to regional needs, and how to make sure that the admitted workers meet those needs. And if only some employers may participate, how will they be chosen? Related questions are how to divide decision-making authority among Congress and federal administrative agencies, and whether state and local governments will have a role. Another issue is whether and how to respond to short-term conditions, perhaps with flexibility to set admission levels and respond to workforce needs in occupations, industries, or regions. And who will identify and respond to employer violations such as noncompliance with admission requirements or unlawful working conditions and wages? If workers overstay or otherwise violate their terms of admission, will the enforcers be US government agencies, employers, or even persons or institutions in their countries of origin?

Other issues are more fundamental. Should US law's treatment of temporary workers differ from its treatment of other noncitizens admitted temporarily, such as students? Another question is whether to handle temporary worker admissions from different countries differently, perhaps in bilateral or multilateral agreements with specific countries, rather than as part of a unitary body of immigration law.

The answers to these many questions can reflect a variety of possible perspectives on temporary worker programs. One perspective considers temporary workers as substitutes for unauthorized workers. A second evaluates the effects of temporary worker programs and unauthorized migration as similar forces in the US economy—benefiting many citizens and permanent residents, but perhaps disadvantaging others. A third perspective compares the roles that temporary worker admissions and unauthorized migration play in international economic development. A fourth assesses temporary admissions and unauthorized migration in the context of citizenship and of the integration of immigrants. Each of these four perspectives says something different about temporary workers, and in combination they yield a variety of lessons for responding to unauthorized migration.

Temporary Admissions and Immigration Outside the Law

It is only natural to compare temporary admissions with a closely related aspect of US immigration law—the admission of noncitizens as lawful permanent residents. But it is at least as accurate to see temporary workers as offering an alternative to unauthorized migration in the context of the US labor market. This relationship is especially apt for low-wage workers with little formal education or training, who fill the ranks of unauthorized migrants and of lawful temporary workers admitted as H-2A and H-2B nonimmigrants. These are also the workers who would be admitted temporarily under the bill that passed the US Senate in June 2013, part of which would have established a "blue card" program for temporary agricultural workers and a new "W" visa for temporary workers in general.[8]

It seems logical that admitting more temporary workers would likely curtail the number or flow of unauthorized migrants. This perspective also draws support from the long history of US government acquiescence in a sizable unauthorized population. From the early 1900s until the 1960s, a period when the line between legal and illegal had not yet acquired today's political valence, unauthorized migration and temporary farmworker admissions under the Bracero program coexisted as alternatives for supplying US employers with cheap labor that was temporary and flexible. By the time the Bracero program ended in 1964, it had brought in between 4 and 5 million Mexican workers, more than 400,000 in some years.[9]

Also in the 1960s, a new admission scheme limited the number of new lawful permanent residents from Latin America, but by then northward migration patterns had established work in the United States as both economically and socially customary. After the Immigration Reform and Control Act (IRCA) of 1986 bolstered enforcement, temporary worker programs grew but have stayed relatively small. Restrictions built into the current temporary worker categories preclude their use to admit many of the workers who are now unauthorized migrants. The annual cap for H-2B admissions falls far short of employer demand for willing workers. Many jobs do not qualify for H-2B treatment because the work is not temporary, even if the worker comes only for a limited period of time. Over 50,000 H-2A agricultural workers have been admitted annually since 2007, but this is a small group compared to the total agricultural labor force, which numbered about 750,000 workers in 2011. With both permanent and temporary admissions curtailed since the mid-1960s, unauthorized migration has increased dramatically.[10]

IF TEMPORARY WORKER programs are to be part of an acceptable response to unauthorized migration, they cannot replicate the vulnerability to workplace exploitation and abuse that unauthorized workers face. Analysis of workplace protections for temporary workers should start by comparing them to the protections available for unauthorized migrants and to the fuller protections for lawful permanent residents. Even if protections are weaker for temporary workers than for citizens or permanent residents, temporary workers would seem better protected than unauthorized workers, but the actual picture is mixed and complex.

The 2002 US Supreme Court decision in *Hoffman Plastic Compounds v. NLRB* limited the eligibility of unauthorized workers for back pay, which is a key remedy for employer violations of federal labor law governing union organizing and collective bargaining. In theory, unauthorized workers have many other workplace protections and remedies, especially for other aspects of organizing and collective bargaining, and for many wage-related claims. But the gap between theory and practice can be especially wide. If unauthorized workers assert their rights—or even complain informally—they can put themselves and their families in serious jeopardy of job loss and immigration enforcement. The inherently precarious position of unauthorized workers suggests that expanding temporary worker programs to include workers who are currently unauthorized would reduce overall workplace exploitation.[11]

And yet, a crucial form of protection for unauthorized migrants is quitting to seek other work. Finding a new job can be hard, especially because they will need to prove work authorization, and even more difficult in occupations and industries where the worksite and living quarters are isolated, making it hard to communicate with prospective employers. Ineligibility for unemployment insurance and for other safety net benefits also limits the mobility of unauthorized workers within the labor market. Nevertheless, their ability to find another job can limit what employers get away with. To be sure, lawful temporary workers also can quit, but under current law they give up their lawful status the moment they are no longer in the job that they were admitted to do. By quitting, they give up something very significant—their lawful status—whereas unauthorized migrants do not have that status to lose.[12]

Viewed in this light, lawful temporary workers are more tied to their jobs and employers than unauthorized workers are. Abuses rampant within the H-2A and H-2B programs include onerous debts owed to recruiters, failure to pay wages for work performed, denial of access to medical care for on-the-job injuries, squalid housing conditions, and blacklisting of workers who complain about wages and working conditions. It is not uncommon for employers of lawful temporary workers to hold the workers' identification documents and to threaten them with deportation if they complain about their wages and working conditions. The lack of mobility under current law may leave H-2A and H-2B workers at least as vulnerable as unauthorized workers to employer abuse and exploitation.[13]

Of course, labor mobility for temporary workers is only a partial response to employer abuse. Also important is a much more effective level of government enforcement against offending employers. If temporary worker programs are to be part of an acceptable and effective response to unauthorized migration, both labor mobility for temporary workers and strengthened government enforcement of workplace protections will be essential.[14]

IN EVALUATING WHETHER temporary worker programs can respond effectively to unauthorized migration, a different but equally important issue is whether either type of immigration is truly temporary. The suspicion of permanence may generate skepticism of temporary worker programs as a response to unauthorized migration. As compared to unauthorized migrants, however, temporary workers may come and go in migration patterns that are more circular. Temporary workers may stay for a long time, but on average they may not stay as long as unauthorized migrants, for whom a perilous and costly trip to his country of origin and back may be too daunting to undertake. Especially if enforcement is more intense on the border than in the interior, he may decide to stay longer in the United States. For those who are concerned about the permanence of unauthorized migration, temporary workers may be a preferred alternative, even if some stay long-term.[15]

A related way to compare temporary workers with unauthorized migrants examines the possibility that noncitizens in either group will become lawful permanent residents. When the federal government chooses noncitizens who are outside the United States for admission as lawful permanent residents, it selects them in advance, based on credentials but not on any track record in the United States. If and when temporary workers become permanent residents, the selection process may be better informed if it is delayed until some point in time after admission, when their employment record and other aspects of the integration into American society will be known.[16]

Because US immigration law provides some unauthorized migrants with various ways to become lawful permanent residents, it also defers the selection process. Eligibility to become a permanent resident through cancellation of removal generally requires ten years of continuous physical presence in the United States. The bill that passed the US Senate in 2013 would have made unauthorized migrants wait 10 years in Registered Provisional Immigrant (RPI) status before allowing adjustment of status to lawful permanent resident. If the only goal were to have the most informed process for finding workers, it may be best to tolerate significant unauthorized migration and periodically offer lawful status to workers based on their employment history or other contributions to US society. Temporary worker programs might provide a similarly informed selection process, but the probationary period for cancellation of removal or legalization may be even longer and perhaps better informed as a result.[17]

Domestic Economic Impact

To shift to a second perspective, any analysis of temporary worker programs as a response to unauthorized migration must also consider how both temporary and unauthorized workers affect the distribution of wealth and opportunity inside the United States. From this domestic economic perspective, would it be better to have more temporary workers and fewer unauthorized migrants? They have this in common: many citizens and permanent residents benefit when having more workers or lower wages dampens the cost of goods and services. Moreover, both temporary workers and unauthorized migrants may help create jobs and other opportunities for citizens and permanent residents.

The role of temporary workers in the US economy resembles the role of unauthorized migrants. Without temporary workers, the cost of doing business in the United States may rise and may force companies or industries to restructure, cutting jobs done by US citizens and permanent residents, or to forgo expansion plans. Or, high costs can force companies to move some or all of their operations outside the United States or to die out altogether. The potential benefits of temporary worker programs pose the challenge of making sure that they respond in a timely and rational way to economic conditions. The 2013 Senate bill would have established a new federal agency, the Bureau of Immigration and Labor Market Research, to make basic decisions about temporary worker admissions. Whether or not such institutional arrangements emerge, admitting temporary workers and tolerating unauthorized migrants are both ways to make the US economy more robust overall than it otherwise would be.[18]

But all immigration redistributes wealth and poverty by enhancing the economic well-being of some, while diminishing the well-being of others. On the negative side, temporary workers, like unauthorized migrants, can harm citizens and permanent residents who are vulnerable to economic displacement, including wage stagnation, declining work conditions, or outright job loss. These effects can be uneven in different regions of the United States. Moreover, a revenue imbalance generally arises because the federal government collects more in taxes from unauthorized migrants than it pays out, while states and localities pay out more than they collect.[19]

CAN TEMPORARY WORKER programs manage these distributional effects more effectively and more fairly than a system that tolerates significant unauthorized migration? The goal is to make sure that neither temporary workers nor unauthorized migrants exacerbate inequalities in US society. Unless temporary worker programs respond well to this challenge, it may be hard to include them in a sound response to unauthorized migration.

Unauthorized migration operates outside direct government regulation, so direct management seems inherently more difficult. In contrast, the current system of temporary admissions is designed to minimize adverse effects on US workers. For example, the number of H-1B workers admitted to the United States is capped. Employers must attest that they are offering the job at the prevailing wage or actual wage paid to similar individuals (whichever is higher), and that working conditions for the noncitizen will not undercut the working conditions of similarly employed workers. Employers who want H-2A and H-2B workers must go farther and secure a formal finding by the US Department of Labor that workers will receive the prevailing wage and that no citizens or permanent residents are able and willing to do the work. The proposal that passed the Senate in 2013 would have imposed more demanding requirements on employers, such as more recruiting of US workers before hiring temporary workers. It would also have limited H-1B or L-1 workers to half of an employer's workforce.[20]

If, however, current temporary worker programs are superior to unauthorized migration in minimizing harms to US citizens and permanent residents, it is likely not because of efforts to regulate the initial placement of workers in jobs. These controls are so imperfect that some adverse effects seem to be unavoidable and even inherent in letting employers hire temporary workers. Impact varies by employer and employee, by locality and region, and by government entity—local, state, federal. But the core incentive to hire temporary workers remains that employers often prefer them to US workers, who in turn suffer lost wages or lost jobs. The more fundamental solution is not to prevent the hiring of temporary workers who collectively benefit much of society even if they may adversely affect part of it. Instead, the daunting but ultimately more promising challenge is redistributing the benefits to individuals, economic sectors, geographic areas, or levels of government that are vulnerable to harm.[21]

A first step in any redistribution is measuring and capturing benefits. Current law collects an extra $1,500 from employers when they file initial petitions or extensions for H-1B temporary workers or hire one from another US employer. Fees paid by employers could generate much higher revenues. The 2013 Senate bill would have required employers to pay significantly higher fees on a sliding scale if 30 percent or more of the workforce consists of H-1B workers. A related option is screening employers more selectively for participation, perhaps through an auction or other market vehicles for the government to sell permits that employers could use to hire temporary workers. This approach would give employers an incentive to hire US workers whenever possible, and it would create a fund to offset both specific effects on US workers as well as general public costs associated with temporary workers. Similar vehicles for capturing and redistributing the benefits from temporary workers could be effective across a wide array of nonimmigrant categories and groups of US workers. Assistance to offset the negative impact of international trade offers instructive analogies. International trade has similar effects, especially when cheaper goods arrive from foreign sources. Lower prices for imports will benefit many consumers and businesses, but may also dry up the market for domestic production.[22]

The essential second step is redistributing these benefits. Under current law, the fees from H-1B visas go to the National Science Foundation and the Department of Labor, primarily for job training for citizens and permanent residents, for college scholarships for low-income students in engineering, math, and computer science, and for K-12 science enrichment programs. This basic idea of using fees for training makes sense, though many of the

US citizens and permanent residents who are adversely affected by temporary workers are unlikely to be attending college at all. If properly designed, redistribution mechanisms could operate more effectively as part of temporary worker programs than they could in the unregulated context of unauthorized migration. But if the idea is that this advantage over unauthorized migration makes temporary worker programs a superior alternative, much more must be done than current law undertakes to mitigate adverse effects on US citizens and permanent residents.[23]

To be meaningful, measures to mitigate these harms must go well beyond fees generated by federal immigration statutes. Effective responses must also go far beyond simply rejecting temporary workers and cracking down on the unauthorized. Essential are remedies for those who suffer a reduction in wages or outright job loss. This means that an essential aspect of both temporary worker programs and responses to unauthorized migration is investment in education and training, especially for lower income citizens, both to prevent job loss and to soften the blow if it occurs.[24] A proposal in the mid-2000s by Representative Sheila Jackson Lee would have required recruitment, including in minority communities, of US citizens and permanent residents before any job could be filled by a temporary worker. It also would have imposed a 10 percent surcharge on all petitions for temporary worker status to fund job creation and training programs for unemployed US citizens. Without careful thought about distributing the overall economic benefits from temporary workers and unauthorized migrants to those who suffer harm, the likely result is substantial political resistance to both temporary workers and unauthorized migrants from individuals, communities, industries, and regions that feel economically threatened.[25]

International Economic Development

A third perspective on temporary worker programs and unauthorized migration considers both as responses to economic development outside the United States. Temporary worker programs may be superior to unauthorized migration in this context, but once again the structure of the programs matters a great deal. Any comparison must start by acknowledging that the relationship between immigration law and international economic development goes both ways. Temporary worker programs and unauthorized migration both influence—and are influenced by—international economic development.

Of course, not all migration, and not all immigration outside the law, occurs from so-called developing countries to developed ones. Many unauthorized migrants move between developing countries. That said, most unauthorized migration to the United States comes from countries that are less economically prosperous. In this context, many temporary workers and unauthorized migrants—like migrants in general—send money back to their countries of origin, where the funds are essential. These remittances buoy the national economy as a whole. They also offset the absence of available credit for individuals and families, helping to build houses, educate children, start and grow small businesses, and more. Beyond sending remittances, temporary workers and unauthorized migrants may be well-positioned to address problems in their countries of origin through nonmonetary contributions based on their time in the United States. If they return to those countries with enhanced experience, ranging from language to occupational skills to entrepreneurial know-how, they vitally augment the education, training, and experience that are available there. In addition, temporary workers and unauthorized migrants—like all emigrants—provide a safety valve for economic or political discontent and unrest.[26]

International economic development concerns explain the dominant approach of some countries that actively promote the emigration of temporary workers. As a prominent example, the Philippine government has a long-standing practice of training workers who emigrate for temporary employment, helping them find work in other countries while maintaining home country ties with the Philippines, and facilitating remittances and their eventual return and integration into the domestic economy. This general model explains the emigration management policies of many governments, as well as the limits on their capacity or their readiness to protect their nationals in other countries for fear of jeopardizing their work prospects and remittances.[27]

A blend of permanent resident immigration to the United States, temporary worker programs, and tolerance of unauthorized migration can foster interrelated aspects of international economic development—especially remittances, return of human capital, and safety valves. This latitude may allow the US government to reduce direct aid or investment, to stabilize friendly regimes, or in extreme cases, to avoid more drastic measures like US military intervention—such as in Haiti in 1994—to resolve a crisis driving emigration to the United States.

Lawful temporary workers may find it easier than unauthorized migrants to travel back and forth and thus to stay active in their countries of origin. Frequent lawful travel may keep a worker from putting down deep roots in the United States. The result may be stronger remittance flows and other forms of home-country engagement. On the other hand, unauthorized migrants suffer from the acute impermanence that comes from living in jeopardy of arrest and deportation. In comparing temporary workers and unauthorized workers from an international economic development perspective, certainty is elusive and would require more empirical research than is available now.

COMPARING TEMPORARY WORKER programs and unauthorized migration as a matter of international economic development raises yet another important question about both temporary workers and unauthorized migrants: Should temporary workers from different countries be treated differently? For instance, should it be easier for temporary workers to come to the United States lawfully from Mexico than from other countries? If temporary worker programs are meant to respond to unauthorized migration from specific countries, it may be most effective to design such programs for those countries. A concrete example would be a program for Mexican temporary workers as part of an initiative to strengthen the Mexican economy and limit unauthorized migration from Mexico, which is the source of almost 60 percent of the unauthorized population of the United States.[28]

The issue of country-specificity is complex. Delving deeper starts with an idea inherent in an international economic development perspective—that immigration policy is a form of foreign policy, and foreign policy is a way of making immigration policy. In turn, this relationship requires another look at the inherent tension between national borders and a national commitment to equality. The very idea of national borders is in tension with a national culture that values equality, because borders and immigration law distinguish citizens from noncitizens. One way to ease this tension is to treat noncitizens equally, regardless of race or ethnicity, and to tolerate discrimination on no basis other than citizenship itself. A closely related principle is that immigration law must treat all citizens equally. These two ideas are intertwined; racial or ethnic discrimination against noncitizens is virtually certain to discriminate against citizens who are closely related to them. But the definition of equality is complex. Would US policy violate these equality principles by making it easier for temporary workers to come lawfully from some countries than from others? Perhaps yes, if temporary admissions are simply a variation on permanent admissions. If, however, the purpose of temporary admissions is to respond to unauthorized migration, then programs that favor certain countries may be more justified.[29]

Probing this issue calls for a look at the evolution of equality principles in immigration law during the twentieth century. One of the conceits of the past generation has been the belief that justice in immigration is the product of equality produced by the even-handed application of a set of universal principles. But the relationship between equality and universal principles in the immigration context is more nuanced. The belief in universal principles is a legacy of the struggle to end the national origins system. When operated from 1921 to 1965, its aim was to maintain the ethnic mix of the US population as it was at the turn of the twentieth century by strongly preferring European immigrants, especially from northern and western Europe. During the same era, a bilateral agreement between the United States and Mexico established the Bracero program starting in 1942, reflecting and reinforcing perceptions of Mexico as a source of workers, but not of Americans in waiting.[30]

The 1965 amendments to the Immigration and Nationality Act replaced the national origins system with a scheme that seemed to admit immigrants regardless of their country of origin. These amendments reflected a faith in uniform criteria and the related assumption that immigration law is a unitary body of law governed by principles that are neutral and applied universally. Today, it seems only natural to look back at the abolition of the national origins system as a hard-won triumph for the idea that a system for choosing immigrants should be based on law, not politics or prejudice. Closely related was the successful push in 1964 by the farmworker movement to end the Bracero program and its perceived abuse and exploitation of workers. The Civil Rights Act in 1964, the Voting Rights Act in 1965, and the 1965 immigration law reforms all seemed part of a long overdue embrace of equality.[31]

But with the end of the Bracero program, the major avenue for temporary worker admissions from Mexico disappeared, and it became much harder for immigrants from Latin America in general and Mexico in particular to come to the United States. Before 1965, immigrants from the Western Hemisphere had to meet financial self-sufficiency and other qualitative requirements, but their overall number was not capped. The 1965 amendments replaced the national origins system with a system that treated all countries equally, but this logic led to a series of laws that imposed an overall worldwide numerical limit on immigration in the family- and employment-based preference categories. In 1976, Congress capped the number of immigrants from any single country to 20,000 per year. The 20,000 cap had an important exception for "immediate relatives"—defined as spouses and unmarried minor children of citizens, and parents of citizens who are 21 years old—but these changes had two dramatic consequences.[32]

One was a steady rise in unauthorized migration. The other was waiting periods that are long for immigrants in many categories and even longer for immigrants from certain countries. Especially when the affected immigrants are from countries with a long history of sending workers to the United States, the question arises: What does it mean to apply universal principles and to treat countries equally? Is it faithful to equality to have uniform numerical ceilings that apply to all countries, regardless of a country's population or its geographic, historical, or economic ties to the United States?[33]

An international economic development perspective may make country-specific temporary worker policies seem less problematic and perhaps even natural. The reason is that international economic development initiatives are traditionally ad hoc arrangements with particular countries that are not limited by any expectation of uniform arrangements with all. Similarly, the conditions that affect emigration from a particular country may be unusually sensitive to US economic activity or policies, especially when such ties are geographic, historical, or economic.

Some country-specific arrangements are already part of current immigration law, though typically as exceptions. For example, the E nonimmigrant category admits traders, investors, and some employees on generous terms, if the United States has a trade or investment treaty with their country of nationality. Trade agreements with Chile and Singapore offer their citizens temporary admission on terms that vary from the general body of US immigration law. The North American Free Trade Agreement is a potential vehicle for temporary admissions from Canada and Mexico, though at present it does not facilitate low-wage worker admissions, and its categories requiring more education or training do not vary from immigration law generally.[34]

If well-designed with regard to international economic development, temporary worker programs may be essential to any sound response to unauthorized migration. To realize this potential, however, the programs must facilitate the return of funds and know-how, and they must maintain the safety valve aspect of emigration. This may require administering temporary worker programs more like economic development initiatives and less like part of a universal system of immigration admissions. Legislation may matter less, and executive agency decisions may matter more. Governments and private persons outside the United States may have more influence and possibly some enforcement power. The roles of courts and other institutions that traditionally apply legal rules of general application may diminish.[35]

Ad hoc, country-specific decisions—likely driven by executive branch initiative—raise questions about how to achieve transparency and establish checks on improper or unwise decisions. Standards and expectations may depend on the frame of reference. If temporary worker programs are compared to the admission of lawful permanent residents, then ad hoc, country-specific, executive branch decisions may seem unpredictable. But such decision-making may seem transparent, regulated, predictable, and consistent if temporary workers are compared to the highly discretionary regulation of unauthorized migration within the current immigration law system.

CONSIDERING TEMPORARY WORKERS as part of an international economic development response to unauthorized migration yields general lessons for dealing with unauthorized migration. One is that economic development initiatives are an essential part of any effective response. The selective, discretionary immigration law system that has led to a large unauthorized population is ultimately the reflection of international economic forces. In the global economy, immigration mediates between great wealth and great poverty. Remittances represent just one example. Flows of capital and goods—such as those fostered by the North American Free Trade Agreement (NAFTA)— create social networks and economic pressures that inevitably prompt people to move as well.[36]

Reducing unauthorized migration requires robust economies in sending countries, so that people have reasons to stay and prosper at home. The opportunity to buy houses and build businesses can keep people in their home countries even if wages are lower than those they could earn by emigrating. Migration patterns within the European Union are instructive. As sociologist Douglas Massey has explained, full economic integration in the European Union has retarded migration to wealthy countries. Especially important have been funds to support structural adjustments in credit markets in poorer countries that were joining the Union. For the United States, if economic conditions elsewhere make millions of people feel that they have no choice but to leave home to pursue what seem to be better lives—or basic survival—in this country, then emigration pressures can lead to substantial unauthorized migration.[37]

Citizenship and Integration

There is a fourth perspective on temporary worker programs as a lens to understand the best responses to unauthorized migration. This one is rooted in one of the most frequent criticisms of temporary worker programs: that they are the source of a troubling and corrosive inequality in the receiving society. The problem is that temporary workers, and unauthorized migrants, too, are relegated to second-class status: needed and tolerated as workers, but not fully accepted. The frequency and intensity of concerns about workplace conditions are only part of this dissonance. Even if wages, hours, and work-place conditions—and enforcement mechanisms—were the same for tem-porary workers as for citizens and lawful permanent residents, inequality is inherent in any system that assumes that workers are temporary. The same is true for unauthorized migrants. Limiting the future participation of both groups of noncitizens effectively bars them from society's mainstream.

Temporary worker programs can be an attractive alternative to unau-thorized migration, but only if they offer more satisfactory responses to this problem of inequality. How might temporary worker programs do this? The answer requires understanding how the initial admission of noncitizens into the United States is related to their integration into US society and their acquisition of US citizenship. Again, this inquiry not only shows how tem-porary worker programs can be part of a response to unauthorized migration; it also says a great deal about unauthorized migration in general.

In an earlier book, *Americans in Waiting*, I explained the compelling rea-sons to treat newcomers to the United States as Americans in waiting by admit-ting them as permanent residents, adopting policies that foster immigrant integration, and providing a clear, presumed path to citizenship. Making the line between immigrants and citizens permeable in this way is closely related to avoiding discrimination against noncitizens on any basis other than citi-zenship itself. Both are essential aspects of reconciling the tension between borders and equality. It is troubling that legalization proposals that Congress has seriously considered in recent years would force unauthorized migrants to wait many years before becoming eligible for citizenship, but proposals that would absolutely bar the path to citizenship are even more troubling.[38]

As a corollary, *Americans in Waiting* also criticized the steady trend over the twentieth century to widen the gap between permanent residents and cit-izens, and to abandon the expectation that lawful immigrants will integrate fully into American society. In past periods of US history, it was customary to view immigration as a transition to citizenship and immigrants as Americans in waiting, but the beneficiaries of this attitude were white, European immi-grants. As immigrants came from a wider array of countries, this attitude faded. Though racial barriers to immigration eroded, being an immigrant car-ried diminished expectations of belonging and US citizenship.[39]

These views about immigration as a transition to citizenship admittedly stand in some tension with the view of temporary worker programs that I express here—that temporary worker programs, if properly designed, have potential as part of a sound response to unauthorized migration. Admittedly, temporary worker programs suggest that noncitizens are unlike citizens and that the line between them may be hard to cross. In fact, however, US law can admit temporary workers as a partial response to unauthorized migration while also striving to give immigrants meaningful access to equality by treating them as Americans in waiting.

IF TEMPORARY WORKER programs are to be consistent with immigration as a transition to citizenship, then coming to America as a temporary worker must include some kind of path to citizenship. One way to think about that path is to view each temporary worker not just as an individual, but also as potentially part of a family. Doing so makes relevant the rules that confer citizenship on all children born on US soil, regardless of their parents' citizenship. Birthright citizenship under the Fourteenth Amendment is a backstop against the marginalization of temporary workers' families.[40]

More generally, the acquisition of citizenship by a temporary worker's family through the birth of children eases any tension between temporary workers and the idea of equality. Policymakers tend to overemphasize the adult generation, reflecting both the myopia of electoral politics and the difficulties of predicting how the children of immigrants will fit into American society. But moving away from a snapshot view of justice—and toward a sense of time measured in generations—makes temporary worker programs more compatible with the idea of Americans in waiting. Even if integration in one generation is too much to expect, two or three may be enough. Time makes the line between immigrants and citizens permeable.

Viewing temporary worker programs in light of their implications for citizenship and integration is consistent with seeing temporary workers as a matter of international economic development. Both perspectives allow time to soften injustices that might otherwise make temporary workers unacceptable as an alternative to unauthorized migrants. Just as birthright citizenship for children makes corrosive inequality less inherent in temporary worker programs, time also allows temporary worker programs to foster more benign migration patterns as part of international economic development. If opportunities in their home countries give temporary workers some meaningful choices—to stay in the United States, to return to their home countries, or to go back and forth—then temporary workers become more viable as a response to unauthorized migration.

A citizenship and integration approach also reprises the question of whether temporary worker programs are exploitative. The ability to change jobs and having legal protections in the workplace combined with government enforcement of employment law can limit employer abuse, but a more fundamental type of exploitation is inherent in being seen and treated as a worker, not as a person. Such fundamental exploitation may seem more irreducible, but it need not be entirely so. Curbing it can do much to make temporary workers an acceptable alternative to unauthorized migration. Citizenship law matters a great deal in this setting. The United States has a significant number of temporary workers, but again it matters a great deal that their children born on US soil are automatically citizens. In many other countries around the world, the children of temporary workers are not citizens at birth, and naturalization is difficult. Even if temporary workers are treated exactly the same in every other way, the US scheme is less exploitative because the admission of the workers, though temporary in their generation, can lead to future integration.[41]

Integration over time also raises this question: What does it mean for temporary worker programs to be temporary? Though part of this question is whether the programs themselves are temporary, it is much more important to ask what future possibilities these programs open up for individual workers and their families. If temporary admission of individual workers can be transitional for their families, then temporary worker programs can be consistent with viewing immigration as a transition to citizenship. Fostering the integration of families goes a long way toward reducing the concern that temporary worker programs are an unacceptable response to unauthorized migration because they are offensive to equality.

Besides citizenship for children born on US soil, what else might foster transition for temporary workers and their families? First, it is crucial that the spouses and children of temporary workers be allowed to come with them and to work. Current US law hampers the economic viability of the families of H-2A and H-2B temporary workers by allowing their spouses and unmarried minor children to come to the United States, but not to work. Second, it is important to allow temporary workers to become lawful permanent residents routinely after several renewals of temporary worker status, at least if they have formed close ties in the United States. Significantly, the modified and new temporary worker programs in the bill that passed the US Senate in 2013 would generally have let the spouses and unmarried minor children of temporary workers accompany them and let spouses work. It also would have made the transition to permanent resident status much easier than under current law.[42]

The Question of Permanence

So far in this chapter, I have assessed both temporary workers and unauthorized migration from four different perspectives, in order to explore how to design temporary worker programs so that they do not replicate the problems of unauthorized migration. Those problems include relegating temporary workers to a troubling second-class status, and allowing reliance on temporary workers to relegate some citizens and permanent residents to the same sort of second-class status. If, and only if, temporary worker programs can be severed from these fundamental defects, then they can serve as part of an effective and acceptable response to unauthorized migration.

Now I need to acknowledge a major objection to this inquiry into temporary worker programs as an alternative to unauthorized migration. The changes that would make them a constructive response to unauthorized migration address their shortcomings in ways that seem to make temporary migration more permanent. This means that such solutions undercut one of the main attractions of temporary worker programs as an alternative to unauthorized migration—the ability to meet the economy's labor needs without simply raising the number of lawful permanent immigrants to the United States. This concern with overall numbers will lead to political resistance to immigration in general if newcomers are seen as burdens in the short term, even if they contribute substantially in the long term.

One possible rebuttal to this objection is that even if almost all temporary workers and their families stay in the United States indefinitely, programs to admit temporary workers still have virtues. They reflect a different approach to selecting new permanent residents by imposing a probationary period of temporary status. But even if this response is accurate, any system that treats temporary workers as potential permanent residents—and then as potential citizens—is open to the charge that it is really a system of permanent admissions. Skeptics might argue that it is more honest and transparent to evaluate whether and how to increase the number of lawful permanent residents admitted to the United States.

THE BEST WAY to address this question of permanence is by designing a temporary worker program with incentives and choices. The distinction between incentives and coercion can be elusive, since any form of coercion can be cast as an incentive, and vice versa. But the distinction can be drawn coherently, if roughly, in ways that can allow temporary worker programs to be part of an effective response to unauthorized migration.

Consider possible measures to make it likely that many, if not most, temporary workers remain temporarily. At one extreme is an exclusive emphasis on enforcement that means arresting, detaining, and then deporting any worker who overstays. Closely related are measures to make the lives of over-staying workers hard enough that they will leave. A less coercive system might achieve similar results by requiring workers to post a financial bond or by withholding some earned wages until they return to their countries of origin. An approach with the same effects, but which may seem more like an incentive, is a financial bonus for leaving.[43]

A better approach would focus less on getting workers to leave and more on creating opportunities that draw them back to the countries and communities from which they came. This difference is imprecise but important. An exclusive focus on enforcing the terms of temporary worker admission, even if measures might fairly be cast as incentives, may be too costly or difficult to implement effectively. Moreover, a policy that is focused on enforcement, no matter if enforcement is hard or soft, is a reminder that these workers are brought in and tolerated just to work. Such a policy also resurrects the problem of creating a second-class status in a society that purports to embrace a commitment to equality.

This better approach works simultaneously toward two goals, even if they first appear to be in some tension with each other. One goal is to respond to the economy's needs with temporary workers rather than increased permanent admissions. The second goal is to keep temporary workers from becoming a servant underclass. The tension between these goals—and the way to resolve that tension—is captured in the idea that temporary workers should have a path to citizenship. This idea may seem counterintuitive, but any sound immigration policy must pursue these two goals simultaneously.

Doing so requires giving temporary workers some reasons to leave the United States that are not incentives or penalties tied directly to the individual worker or his work. The emphasis should instead be on international economic development initiatives that help to create general conditions in locales of origin that will give temporary workers, as a group, strong reasons to return, thus keeping migration temporary or circular for many of them. Some sending countries, notably but not only the Philippines, already try actively to entice emigrants to return. Programs by the US government could have the same aim. Some initiatives could concentrate on specific communities that have historically sent significant numbers of migrants to the United States and have built up strong migration networks over generations.[44]

The same policies that foster integration into American society can also enhance a migrant's position in her country of origin if she decides to go back. This happens when she acquires assets or skills in the United States. Ties to the country of origin can play a similar dual role. Such ties can provide the foundation for integration in the United States, but they can also make return migration easier and more likely. Crucial is enticing temporary workers to return to their countries of origin, but so is allowing them to integrate and succeed in the United States if they decide to stay.⁴⁵

Working without self-contradiction toward both temporary migration and integration, and toward creating a realistic path to citizenship for temporary workers, means turning both temporary work and permanent immigration into normal, government-fostered choices for individual migrants. The common element is treating temporary workers with dignity by offering them real choices. Doing so may be difficult and may even seem utopian, but the undertaking can start by respecting something obvious yet often overlooked—that many who come to the United States have no initial intent to stay permanently. Many do stay, but the first decision is typically to leave home temporarily, often under dire circumstances that push migrants to leave.⁴⁶

This approach—temporary workers with a path to citizenship—has its limits. It would be troubling to turn the acquisition of permanent residence by temporary workers into the dominant approach to selecting immigrants and thus future citizens. It would better enhance US society's capacity to integrate newcomers and to maximize their contributions if most immigrants arrive as permanent residents. As I explained more fully in *Americans in Waiting*, the welcome that is inherent in treating newcomers as future citizens makes them much more likely to integrate in ways that satisfy them and those who came to the United States before them. But it is not objectionable if some temporary workers become lawful permanent residents by exercising a choice. Overall, this approach to temporary worker programs from a citizenship and integration perspective would make them far more viable as part of a sound response to unauthorized migration.

Immigration Law and Beyond

So far in this chapter, I have explained how temporary worker programs can be a key part of any effective response to unauthorized migration. The challenge, however, is designing them well to serve this purpose and to avoid the problems that have consistently plagued such programs in the past. They would need to provide adequate workplace protections and play a constructive role in international economic development. They should include a path to citizenship, but alongside international economic development initiatives that give temporary workers a real choice to return to their countries of origin.

Looking closely at temporary worker programs reveals many core truths about unauthorized migration itself. Effective responses to unauthorized migration require a sharp awareness that it is a powerful force within the US economy. It is also crucial to appreciate that unauthorized migration plays a key role in international economic development. It is equally imperative to consider how unauthorized migrants fit into the patterns by which immigrants integrate and become US citizens.

Two further, more general lessons about unauthorized migration emerge from looking at temporary worker programs as both a lens and an alternative. One, grounded in pragmatism, is that moving to constructive responses to unauthorized migration is largely a search for second-best solutions that are better than the status quo. Temporary worker programs may be far from ideal from many perspectives, even if improved in the ways that I have suggested. And yet, they may help find the most realistic way out of the current dilemma.[47]

A second general lesson is that the challenges and opportunities associated with unauthorized migration—and with immigration in general—do not necessarily spring from immigration origins, nor do they have immigration solutions. What determines the success or failure of immigration policy is both more global and more local than it first appears. Effective approaches require a keen sensitivity to the multinational context that prompts migration across national borders, to the domestic interests of US citizens whom immigration most directly affects, and to the foundation laid by national history. Unauthorized migration is both a consequence and a cause of these fundamental forces.

THE NEXT STEPS are to apply these two general lessons—finding pragmatic solutions and thinking beyond immigration law—and to consider unauthorized migration from the same perspectives that I have applied to evaluate temporary worker programs: as a domestic economic force, as an aspect of international economic development, and as influencing integration and citizenship. But before considering these issues, I should revisit the topic of immigration enforcement, for it is an essential element in any search for answers.

Back in 1986, IRCA was a finely balanced legislative compromise that included stronger enforcement. On top of stricter border controls came the first federal employer sanctions scheme, which in turn allowed the same legislation to adopt broader changes, including legalization and revised temporary worker programs. In the generation since IRCA, it has remained difficult—perhaps impossible—to win votes for legalization and other reforms without agreeing to devote more resources to enforcement. In

2013, the Senate voted to condition the ability of unauthorized migrants to acquire lawful permanent resident status on the federal government meeting various enforcement goals, including a massive infusion of resources into the US-Mexico border.[48]

The impulse to accompany changes to the immigration system with an enhanced commitment to enforcement is entirely natural. The idea is that if the system changes in far-reaching ways, then the rules of the new system should be enforced. But the multiple perspectives that I have examined in this chapter show that enforcement—even though it will always matter—never should be the entire discussion. Much more fundamental is deciding what rules are being enforced and what system is being administered.

The seductive misconception is thinking that drastically increasing the resources devoted to enforcement is the one pivotal change that will ensure a new beginning. But this one-dimensional approach reflects blind faith in the line between legal and illegal, and a belief that laws must be enforced no matter how ultimately unenforceable. Simplistic solutions may win some votes in short-term election cycles, but the essential foundation for the rule of law is having laws that are actually enforceable in the broader context of the US economy and US society as a whole. Enforcement must take place with the predictability and consistency that have been impossible within a system that has come to tolerate a large unauthorized population.[49]

Ultimately, focusing on enforcement while ignoring larger forces that lie at the root of migration patterns is just as ineffective as responding to drugs only with more prisons, or to conflict only with more troops. Durable solutions lie in changes to the system for admitting immigrants and temporary workers, international economic development initiatives, and changes to domestic education and domestic economic policy. Without these broader changes, enforcement may intensify for some period of time, but it will remain inconsistent and unpredictable within some version of the current system.

DISCUSSING THE ROLE of temporary workers and unauthorized migrants in the domestic economy suggests a strong need to rethink the overall scheme for lawful admission of noncitizens to the United States to better meet the labor needs of the US economy. The US labor market has a strong demand for workers who lack a college degree—but who often have or easily can acquire valuable skills. Significantly, this is precisely the group of potential migrants for whom lawful admission to the United States is very limited under current law. In a system that would be more responsive to the US economy, they could be admitted as permanent residents, who by definition have a path to citizenship under current law, or as temporary workers with an opportunity to become permanent residents later.[50]

As with temporary workers, expanded work-related admissions may lead to reasonable perceptions that the overall gains to the US economy will be distributed unevenly, and that some citizens and permanent residents will suffer the most adverse effects. And as with temporary workers, the best solutions are not in limiting admissions, but rather in redistributing some of the overall benefits and in addressing the more fundamental flaws in the US system for education and training that leave these US workers vulnerable in the first place.

Another important change is relaxing or repealing numerical limits that currently cap immigrant admissions in many categories on a country-by-country basis. These limits make the waiting lists for intending immigrants from certain countries—notably Mexico—longer than for those from other countries. The bill approved by the Senate in 2013 would have maintained per-country limits but raised them from 7 percent to 15 percent of the total number of immigrant visas available in any given year. The same legislation would also have exempted employment-based admission categories. Immigrants from Mexico and the Philippines, who are waiting in long lines in the family-based preferences, would benefit most from these changes to the per-country cap. Amendments of this sort would reflect a commitment to equality in immigration law more effectively than simply capping admissions from every country in the world at the same number.[51]

Besides understanding immigration as a domestic economic force, any restructuring of admissions as part of a response to unauthorized migration must take integration and citizenship seriously. Especially important is recognizing that immigrant workers have families and aspirations outside the workplace. Laws and policies that view immigrants only as workers or other economic contributors run two overlapping risks. One is to strive only for short-term benefits that are easily measured. The other is to underestimate contributions that may be evident only as newcomers integrate into US society over several generations. It is a misleading assumption to believe that immigrants in employment-based categories that require advanced educational degrees will necessarily contribute more to US society in the long run. Immigrants who are admitted in the family-based categories—many of whom happen to have advanced degrees—may contribute at least as much economically in the long run, especially if their children and grandchildren achieve success. One noteworthy reason is that families may provide an especially strong platform for integration into US society.[52]

Other crucial responses to unauthorized migration involve international economic development. The core aim should be to support the economies of countries of origin, so that all intending migrants have a more realistic choice to stay home instead of coming to the United States. If a sending country's economy becomes robust enough to provide opportunities for the country's population, then the push to emigrate will diminish. Moreover, the migration that continues will become more likely to stay within the lawful admission scheme for immigrants or temporary workers. Return migration from the United States may also increase, moderating the size of the unauthorized population and making higher admission ceilings more acceptable politically. Return migration back to South Korea, Poland, and Ireland was significant in the 1990s and 2000s, when those economies began offering attractive prospects to their expatriates. In Ireland, later declines in the economy dampened this return trend, but the basic point remains that the economies in sending countries strongly influence who comes to America both lawfully and unlawfully, and how long they stay.[33]

One other possibility requires attention. If immigration to the United States diminishes or return migration away from the United States increases, then many of the jobs now performed by unauthorized migrants may go unfilled. If this happens, then economic development in sending countries will do more than reduce unauthorized migration. An additional consequence will be a need to align the US economy with the labor force that it can expect to have. That realignment may require restructuring, mechanization, outsourcing, or some combination of these and other approaches. The fundamental challenge would then be how to educate and train workers for an evolving US economy that can no longer rely on a flexible pool of cheap labor, including many unauthorized migrants. Here, too, the focus must be on the US educational system.

NOW IT IS time to circle back to a question that I deferred at the end of Chapter 6: How should broad-scale legalization be designed to fit best into an overall response to unauthorized migration? I explained how legalization should start with noncitizens who already qualify for lawful permanent resident status under existing law, and with unauthorized migrants who have close citizen or permanent resident relatives and have lived in the United States for the seven years that pre-1996 law required for cancellation of removal. This would amount to a limited legalization program for those with the closest or most long-standing ties in the United States.

The next issue is whether legalization should include a much larger group of unauthorized migrants in the United States. Legalization itself does little to solve fundamental problems with the US immigration system. Without other changes that address the origins of the current situation, a large unauthorized population is likely to reemerge. Many of these potential changes emerge from focusing on temporary worker programs, permanent admissions changes, domestic education, economic policy, and international economic development. What role does legalization play in this new beginning?

Suppose a response to unauthorized migration reworks the admissions system moving forward and changes the composition of the future immigrant population. But what if these changes had been part of US immigration law all along? What if the immigration system had not relied so heavily on selective admissions, selective enforcement, and vast discretion? If so, then many of today's unauthorized migrants might have been admitted to the United States lawfully. So viewed, these unauthorized migrants are logical candidates for legalization. Conceptually, legalization should amount to the retroactive application of changes that Congress adopts to temporary worker and permanent admissions. In a legalization program that takes this approach, the cutoff date becomes much less significant than it would be in a program that does nothing about future immigration.

This approach is generally evident in the legislation that the US Senate approved in 2013. Its legalization provisions would have provided lawful status under different terms to three groups of unauthorized migrants. Most favored would be DREAM Act beneficiaries, who would be eligible for permanent resident status after five years and eligible for naturalization as soon as they become permanent residents. Many in this group may qualify in an existing admission category, or would have the strongest case for cancellation of removal under pre-1996 requirements. Others may qualify under the revised admission categories in the 2013 Senate bill. Another favored group would be agricultural workers, who would be eligible immediately for interim lawful status and then for permanent resident status five years later. After five years as permanent residents, they would be eligible to apply for naturalization. This group would resemble the agricultural workers who would be admitted in the future under a new program for temporary agricultural workers. In this way, the bill would approach legalization as the retroactive admission of unauthorized migrants who arrived before the changes.[54]

Under this proposed legislation, a third tier of unauthorized migrants would need to wait the longest for permanent residence and citizenship, pay the largest monetary penalties and fees, and meet the most demanding requirements. But here, too, the rationale is that the practical effect reflects retroactive application of changes to the admission system. Many of the unauthorized migrants who would benefit from this part of the Senate proposal would, if they were outside the United States today, qualify for lawful permanent resident status in new employment-based immigration categories or for admission to expanded temporary worker programs.[55]

By combining a broad-scale legalization program with revised admissions, this part of the Senate proposal tried to find responses to immigration patterns that are in the national interest, are consistent with the realities of the US and global economies, and reflect fundamental notions of justice for both US citizens and newcomers. The answers reach the current unauthorized population through legalization, but they also recognize that one-time legalization is not part of the long-term solution. The system for admitting immigrants and temporary workers, international economic development initiatives, developments in the US educational system, and broader economic and demographic factors will be far more influential.

———————

IMMIGRATION IS ONE of the most important areas of American public policy, for it literally determines who "we" are. Some of the most urgent questions about immigration involve immigration outside the law. The dramatic increase over the past several decades in the number of noncitizens who live and work in the United States without lawful status has led to broad chasms between opposing views on immigration and has made the task of a national conversation especially daunting. But without hard work on all sides to make that conversation productive, this new American dilemma will persist, in even more divisive forms, to burden our children and grandchildren.

Working toward a productive national conversation will require the sort of broader and deeper understanding of unauthorized migration that starts with *Plyler*. The three themes that were essential to the US Supreme Court's decision in *Plyler* show, individually and in combination, that workable, durable, and politically viable responses will require forthright engagement with the larger forces that generate and shape migration patterns. It is far from clear if the ethos of *Plyler v. Doe* remains vibrant in today's America. But *Plyler* represents the noblest aspects of the US Constitution and more generally of the United States as a nation of immigrants—a nation with borders, but also a nation committed to a sense of equality and human dignity.

Notes

INTRODUCTION

The Children

1. From "The Dry Salvages," in Four Quartets 25 (New York 1943). With these lines, Professor Caleb Foote of the School of Law at the University of California, Berkeley (Boalt Hall) began his commencement address to the Class of 1978, my graduating class.

2. On controversy at that time, see, e.g., Vernon M. Briggs, Mexican Immigrants and the Labor Market, 49 Texas Bus. Rev. 85 (1975); Wilson McKinney, Wetbacks Flooding San Antonio Area, San Antonio Express/News, June 11, 1972, at 3-H; Mike Kingston, Illegal Aliens I, Brown Wave Engulfs North Texas, Del Rio News-Herald, May 23, 1971, at 4A. On the court cases' background, see the definitive account in Michael A. Olivas, No Undocumented Child Left Behind: *Plyler v. Doe* and the Education of Undocumented Schoolchildren (N.Y.U. Press 2012). See also Barbara Belejack, A Lesson in Equal Protection: The Texas Cases That Opened the Schoolhouse Door to Undocumented Immigrant Children, Tex. Observer, July 13, 2007, at 14; Michael A. Olivas, *Plyler v. Doe*, the Education of Undocumented Children, and the Polity, in Immigration Stories 197, 197–220 (David A. Martin & Peter H. Schuck eds., Foundation Press 2005).

3. Tex. Educ. Code Ann. § 21.031 (Vernon Supp. 1981). On the statute's origins, see Olivas, No Undocumented Child, supra note 2, at 9; In re Alien Children Education Litigation, 501 F. Supp. 544, 555 & n.19 (S.D. Tex. 1980).

4. The estimate is from Doe v. Plyler, 458 F. Supp. 569, 574–575, 577 (E.D. Tex. 1978). On the school districts' responses, see Olivas, No Undocumented Child, supra note 2, at 9–10.

5. 347 U.S. 483 (1954).

6. Compare San Antonio Independent School District v. Rodriguez, 411 U.S. 1, 28–39 (1973); with Serrano v. Priest, 18 Cal. 3d 728, 765–767, 557 P.2d 929, 950–952 135 Cal. Rptr. 345, 366–368 (1976).

7. 457 U.S. 202 (1982). On the *Brown* analogy, see Olivas, No Undocumented Child, supra note 2, at 12.

8. Roos warded off immigration raids that may have been meant to intimidate the plaintiffs' families. See Olivas, No Undocumented Child, supra note 2, at 14–15.

9. Doe v. Plyler, 458 F. Supp. 569 (E.D. Tex. 1978). On Judge Justice, see Frank R. Kemerer, William Wayne Justice: A Judicial Biography (Univ. of Texas Press 1991); Douglas Martin, William Wayne Justice, Noted Judge, Dies at 89, N.Y. Times, Oct. 15, 2009, at B11; Lynn E. Blais, William Wayne Justice: The Life of the Law, 77 Tex. L. Rev. 1, 2 (1998). On Roos' strategy, see Olivas, No Undocumented Child, supra note 2, at 17–18.

10. In re Alien Children Educ. Litig., 501 F. Supp. 544 (S.D. Tex. 1980).

11. Under § 101(a)(3) of the Immigration and Nationality Act, which is the principal federal immigration statute, an "alien" is any individual who is not a US citizen or national. For criticism of the terms "alien" or "illegal alien," see Flores v. USCIS, 718 F.3d 548, 551, n.1 (6th Cir. 2013); Joseph Nevins, Operation Gatekeeper and Beyond: The War on "Illegals" and the Remaking of the US-Mexico Boundary, 139–149 (Routledge 2010); Kevin R. Johnson, "Aliens" and the U.S. Immigration Laws: The Social and Legal Construction of Nonpersons, 28 U. Miami Inter-Am. L. Rev. 263, 272–281 (1996). In 2013, the Associated Press limited its use of "illegal immigrant" to direct quotes, and the New York Times strongly urged its reporters to consider alternatives. See Christine Haughney, The Times Shifts on "Illegal Immigrant," but Doesn't Ban the Use, N.Y. Times, Apr. 24, 2013. For misgivings about "undocumented," see Martinez v. The Regents of the University of California, 50 Cal. 4th 1277, 1288, 241 P.3d 855, 862, 117 Cal. Rptr. 359, 367–368 (2010); Kris R. Kobach, Reinforcing the Rule of Law: What States Can and Should Do to Reduce Illegal Immigration, 22 Geo. Immigr. L.J. 459, 460 n.4 (2008).

On terminology and metaphors, see Thomas Alexander Aleinikoff, David A. Martin, Hiroshi Motomura, & Maryellen Fullerton, Immigration and Citizenship: Process and Policy, 452–453 (7th ed. West 2012); Kamal Sadiq, Paper Citizens: How Illegal Immigrants Acquire Citizenship in Developing Countries, 22–23 (Oxford Univ. Press 2009); Douglas S. Massey & Karen A. Pren, Unintended Consequences of US Immigration Policy: Explaining the Post-1965 Surge from Latin America, 38 Pop. & Dev. Rev. 1, 5–8 (2012); Keith Cunningham-Parmeter, Alien Language: Immigration Metaphors and the Jurisprudence of Otherness, 79 Fordham L. Rev. 1545 (2011); Hiroshi Motomura, Immigration Outside the Law, 108 Colum. L. Rev. 2037, 2038 n.1 (2008); Gerald L. Neuman, Aliens as Outlaws: Government Services, Proposition 187, and the Structure of Equal Protection Doctrine, 42 UCLA L. Rev. 1425, 1440–1442 (1995).

12. On the law as creating unauthorized migration, see Catherine Dauvergne, Making People Illegal: What Globalization Means for Migration and Law, 15 (Cambridge

Univ. Press 2008). I owe thanks to Stephen Lee for calling to my attention the use of "immigration outside the law" in Select Commission on Immigration and Refugee Policy, Final Report and Recommendations of the Select Commission on Immigration and Refugee Policy with Supplemental Views by Commissioners, 10 (1981).

13. Martinez v. Bynum, 461 U.S. 321, 325–330 (1983), held that residence requirements for public school attendance are constitutional.

14. The Department of Justice appeared at the hearing on the plaintiffs' preliminary injunction motion, then later filed a motion to participate as a friend of the court, or *amicus curiae*. See Doe v. Plyler, 458 F. Supp. at 572–573. On the shift in 1981, see Brief for the United States as Amicus Curiae, Plyler v. Doe, 457 U.S. 202 (1982), 1981 WL 390001, at *5, *24–26 (1981); Olivas, No Undocumented Child, supra note 2, at 19; Linda Greenhouse, What Would Justice Powell Do? The *"Alien Children"* Case and the Meaning of Equal Protection, 25 Const. Comment. 29, at 31 n.10 (2008); Elizabeth Hull, Undocumented Alien Children and Free Public Education: An Analysis of *Plyler v. Doe*, 44 U. Pitt L. Rev. 409, 416–417 (1982–83); Stuart Taylor, U.S. Bars Challenge to a Law Restricting Schooling for Aliens, N.Y. Times, Sept. 8, 1981, at A1.

15. On the deliberations, see Greenhouse, What Would Justice Powell Do?, supra note 14, at 34–46; Mark Tushnet, Justice Lewis F. Powell and the Jurisprudence of Centrism, 93 Mich. L. Rev. 1854, 1862–1873 (1995); Olivas, No Undocumented Child, supra note 2, at 26–29; Earl M. Maltz, The Chief Justiceship of Warren Burger, 1969–1986, at 56–57 (2000).

16. Belejack, A Lesson in Equal Protection, supra note 2. See also Greenhouse, What Would Justice Powell Do?, supra note 14, at 30–34; Michael A. Olivas, Immigration-Related State and Local Ordinances: Preemption, Prejudice, and the Proper Role for Enforcement, 2007 U. Chi. Legal F. 27, 39; David G. Savage & Maura Reynolds, More Early Roberts Files Are Released, L.A. Times, Aug. 12, 2005, at A14 (citing Memorandum from John G. Roberts Jr. and Carolyn B. Kuhl to Atty. Gen. William French (June 15, 1982) (on file with The National Archives)).

17. See Editorial, Teaching Alien Children Is a Duty, N.Y. Times, June 16, 1982, at A30; *Plyler*, 457 U.S. at 243 (Burger, C. J., dissenting); Peter H. Schuck, The Transformation of Immigration Law, 84 Colum. L. Rev. 1, 54–58 (1984); Michael J. Perry, Equal Protection, Judicial Activism, and the Intellectual Agenda of Constitutional Theory: Reflections on, and Beyond, *Plyler v. Doe*, 44 U. Pitt. L. Rev. 329, 337–341 (1983); Dennis J. Hutchinson, More Substantive Equal Protection? A Note on *Plyler v. Doe*, 1982 Sup. Ct. Rev. 167, 174–191.

18. 457 U.S. at 210 n.8. For the view that *Plyler* should or could have been decided on preemption grounds, see Olivas, No Undocumented Child, supra note 2, at 87–103; Schuck, Transformation, supra note 17, at 57.

19. See *Plyler*, 457 U.S. at 210; *Plyler*, 457 U.S. at 243 (Burger, C. J., dissenting); Hiroshi Motomura, Americans in Waiting: The Lost Story of Immigration and Citizenship

in the United States, 77–78 (Oxford Univ. Press 2006); Linda Bosniak, Persons and Citizens in Constitutional Thought, 8 Int'l J. Const. L. 9, 14 (2010). The State of Texas devoted half of its brief to arguing that "[i]llegal aliens are not within the scope of the equal protection clause." Brief for the Appellant, Plyler v. Doe, 457 U.S. 202 (1982), No. 80–1538, 80–1934, 1981 WL 389967, at *14–22.

20. See Gerald Gunther, Foreword: In Search of Evolving Doctrine on a Changing Court: A Model for a Newer Equal Protection, 86 Harv. L. Rev. 1, 8 (1972). Compare Grutter v. Bollinger, 539 U.S. 306, 326–329 (2003); Adarand Constructors, Inc. v. Peña, 515 U.S. 200, 237 (1995); Adam Winkler, Fatal in Theory and Strict in Fact: An Empirical Analysis of Strict Scrutiny in the Federal Courts, 59 Vand. L. Rev. 793, 795 (2006).

21. 457 U.S. at 224.

22. For examples of intermediate scrutiny, see United States v. Virginia, 518 U.S. 515, 518 (1996); Personnel Adm'r of Mass. v. Feeney, 442 U.S. 256, 273 (1979); Craig v. Boren, 429 U.S. 190, 197 (1976). On Powell's views, see Greenhouse, What Would Justice Powell Do?, supra note 14, at 50.

23. 457 U.S. at 228–230. For a statement of Texas's position, see Mark White, Attorney General of Texas, Letter to the Editor, Of Aliens' Children, Education and Hypocrisy, N.Y. Times, Nov. 25, 1981, at A22.

24. 457 U.S. at 244–253 (Burger, C. J., dissenting).

25. See John Doe No. 1 v. Georgia Dep't of Pub. Safety, 147 F. Supp. 2d 1369, 1372–1376 (N.D. Ga. 2001); Tarango v. State Indus. Ins. Sys., 25 P.3d 175, 182–183 (Nev. 2001); State v. Cosio, 858 P.2d 621, 626–627 (Alaska 1993); American G.I. Forum v. Miller, 218 Cal. App. 3d 859, 867–868 (1990); Linda S. Bosniak, Membership, Equality, and the Difference that Alienage Makes, 69 N.Y.U. L. Rev. 1047, 1124–1126 (1994); Motomura, Immigration Outside the Law, supra note 11, at 2043, 2075–2076. A counterexample is Buck v. Stankovic, 485 F. Supp. 2d 576, 582 (M.D. Pa. 2007, which cites *Plyler* to invalidate state law requiring proof of lawful presence for a marriage license.

     On the holding's narrow reach, see Olivas, No Undocumented Child, supra note 2, at 27, 30; Gabriel J. Chin & Marc L. Miller, The Unconstitutionality of State Regulation of Immigration Through Criminal Law 61 Duke L.J. 251, 271 n.92 (2011);Nina Rabin, Mary Carol Combs, & Norma González, Understanding *Plyler's* Legacy: Voices from Border Schools, 37 J.L. & Educ. 15, 15 (2008); Greenhouse, What Would Justice Powell Do?, supra note 14, at 47; Tushnet, Justice Lewis F. Powell, supra note 15, at 1873. Of course, the Court's membership has changed completely since 1982.

26. Teaching Alien Children Is a Duty, supra note 17, at A30.

27. See Denise Gamino, A Giant of Texas History, Austin American-Statesman, Oct. 15, 2009, at A01; Kemerer, William Wayne Justice, supra note 9, at 248–249.

28. See 457 U.S. at 246 (Burger, C. J., dissenting); Lawrence Downes, Op-Ed., What Part of "Illegal" Don't You Understand?, N.Y. Times, Oct. 28, 2007, at WK11.

29. See 457 U.S. at 215, 226.

30. Compare 457 U.S. at 225 with 457 U.S. at 244–246 (Burger, C. J., dissenting).

31. See Chamber of Commerce v. Whiting, 131 S. Ct. 1968 (2011); Arizona v. United States, 132 S. Ct. 2492 (2012). For arguments for state and local enforcement, see Kris W. Kobach, The Quintessential Force Multiplier: The Inherent Authority of Local Police to Make Immigration Arrests, 69 Alb. L. Rev. 179, 181 (2005).

32. On uniformity, see *Plyler*, 457 U.S. at 225; Huyen Pham, The Inherent Flaws in the Inherent Authority Position: Why Inviting Local Enforcement of Immigration Laws Violates the Constitution, 31 Fla. St. U. L. Rev. 965, 995 (2004). On discrimination, see, e.g., Huyen Pham, The Private Enforcement of Immigration Laws, 96 Geo. L.J. 777, 781 (2008); Michael J. Wishnie, State and Local Police Enforcement of Immigration Laws, 6 U. Pa. J. Const. L. 1084, 1104 (2004); Chapter 4 in this volume. On community trust, see Wishnie, State and Local Enforcement, supra, at 1087.

33. See *Plyler*, 457 U.S. at 222 (quoting Brown v. Board of Education, 347 U.S. 483, 493 (1954)). The Court cited other education decisions: Meyer v. Nebraska, 262 U.S. 390, 400 (1923); Abington School District v. Schempp, 374 U.S. 203, 230 (1963); Wisconsin v. Yoder, 406 U.S. 205, 221 (1972). See also *Plyler*, 457 U.S. at 218–219, 222; Kenneth L. Karst, The Supreme Court 1976 Term: Forward: Equal Citizenship under the Fourteenth Amendment, 91 Harv. L. Rev. 1, 6 (1977).

34. On legalization, see Aleinikoff, Martin, Motomura, & Fullerton, Immigration and Citizenship, supra note 11, at 1103–1119, 1138–1146; David A. Martin, Eight Myths about Immigration Enforcement, 10 N.Y.U. J. Legis. & Pub. Pol'y 525, 527–531 (2007). For an argument that legalization should include a path to citizenship, see, e.g., Editorial, One Argument, 12 Million Holes, N.Y. Times, Jan. 18, 2008, at A20. See also Chapters 3 and 6 in this volume. Compare *Plyler*, 457 U.S. at 252–253 (Burger, C.J., dissenting).

35. Schuck, Transformation, supra note 17, at 3–7, 54–58. See also Olivas, No Undocumented Child, supra note 2, at 8, 23–26. My views loosely reflect a "realistic approach to morality," though this useful concept is capacious enough to include many notions of why an approach may be more realistic than ideal. See Joseph Carens, Realistic and Idealistic Approaches to the Ethics of Migration, 30 Int'l Migr. Rev. 156 (1996).

36. On the unauthorized population in 1982, see Jeffrey S. Passel, The Size and Characteristics of the Unauthorized Migrant Population in the U.S.: Estimates Based on the March 2005 Current Population Survey, 3 (Pew Hispanic Ctr. 2006). For estimates that are more recent, see Michael Hoefer, Nancy Rytina, & Bryan C. Baker, Estimates of the Unauthorized Immigrant Population Residing in the United States: January 2011, at 1 (Dept. of Homeland Sec. 2012); Jeffrey S. Passel, D'Vera Cohn, & Ana Gonzales-Barrera, Population Decline of Unauthorized Immigrants Stalls, May Have Reversed: New Estimate 11.7 Million in 2012, at 9 (Pew Hispanic Ctr. 2013); Robert Warren & John Robert Warren, Unauthorized

Immigration to the United States: Annual Estimates and Components of Change, by State, 1990 to 2010, 47 Int'l Migr. Rev. 296, 298 (2013); Ruth Ellen Wasem, Unauthorized Aliens Residing in the United States: Estimates Since 1986, at 3 (Cong. Research Serv. 2012). For the unauthorized percentage of the foreign-born US population, see Passel, Cohn, & Gonzales–Barrera, Population Decline, supra. On length of US residence, see Hoefer, Rytina, & Baker, Estimates of the Unauthorized Immigrant Population, supra, at 3; Wasem, Unauthorized Aliens, supra, at 12; Unauthorized Immigrants: Length of Residency, Patterns of Parenthood, 3–4 (Pew Hispanic Ctr. 2011). On the total US population, see US Census Bureau, Total Population: All Ages Including Armed Forces Overseas: National Monthly Population Estimate, Row 769, Column B.

37. On the *Brown-Plyler* comparison, see Olivas, No Undocumented Child, supra note 2, at 30; Schuck, Transformation, supra note 17, at 54.

CHAPTER I

Undocumented or Illegal?

1. See Transcript of Oral Argument, Plyler v. Doe, 457 U.S. 202 (1982) (No. 80–1538), Landmark Briefs and Arguments of the Supreme Court of the United States: Constitutional Law 1981 Term Supplement 609, 626–627 (Philip Kurland & Gerhard Casper eds., 1983); Barbara Belejack, A Lesson in Equal Protection: The Texas Cases That Opened the Schoolhouse Door to Undocumented Immigrant Children, Tex. Observer, July 13, 2007, at 14.

2. Hoffman Plastic Compounds, Inc. v. NLRB, 535 U.S. 137, 140 (2002). For a fuller account, see Catherine L. Fisk & Michael J. Wishnie, The Story of Hoffman Plastic Compounds, Inc. v. NLRB: Labor Rights Without Remedies for Undocumented Immigrants, in Labor Law Stories, 399, 408 (Laura J. Cooper & Catherine L. Fisk eds., Foundation Press 2005).

3. Plyler v. Doe, 457 U.S. 202, 207–208 n.4, 226 (1982).

4. 457 U.S. at 219.

5. 457 U.S. at 219 n.18. For a contrary view, see, e.g., Kris W. Kobach, Attrition Through Enforcement: A Rational Approach to Illegal Immigration, 15 Tulsa J. Comp. & Int'l L. 155 (2008). "Unlawful presence" is also a narrower term of art under Immigration and Nationality Act (INA) § 212(a)(9)(B)–(C), 8 U.S.C. § 1182(a)(9)(B)–(C).

6. On the complexities of ascertaining immigration status, see Lenni B. Benson, Separate, Unequal, and Alien: Comments on the Limits of *Brown*, 49 N.Y.L. Sch. L. Rev. 727, 732–734 (2004–2005).

7. See Guillermina Jasso, Douglas S. Massey, Mark R. Rosenzweig, & James P. Smith, Illegal to Legal: Estimating Previous Illegal Experience among New Legal Immigrants to the United States, 42 Int'l Migr. Rev. 803 (2008).

8. For an overview of nonimmigrant admission categories, see Thomas Alexander Aleinikoff, David A. Martin, Hiroshi Motomura, & Maryellen Fullerton, Immigration and Citizenship: Process and Policy, 382–451 (7th ed. West 2012).

9. The deportability grounds are in INA § 237, 8 U.S.C. § 1227. For the definition of immediate relative, see INA § 201, 8 U.S.C. § 1151. On permanent resident status, see INA § 101(a)(20), 8 U.S.C. § 1101(a)(20). Since 1921, "lawful immigrant" has meant the same thing as "permanent resident." See Act of May 26, 1924, ch. 190, § 3, 43 Stat. 153, 154–55, Act of May 19, 1921, ch. 8, § 2, 42 Stat. 5, 5. On adjustment of status, see INA § 245(a), 8 U.S.C. § 1255(a).

10. On naturalization rates, see Nancy Rytina, Estimates of the Legal Permanent Resident Population in 2011, at 1 (Dept. of Homeland Sec. 2012); James Lee, U.S. Naturalizations: 2012, at 1 (Dept. of Homeland Sec. 2013); 2011 Yearbook of Immigration Statistics, 52, table 20 (Dept. of Homeland Sec. 2012); Jeanne Batalova, Spotlight on Naturalization Trends (Migration Policy Inst. 2009); Aleinikoff, Martin, Motomura, & Fullerton, Immigration and Citizenship, supra note 8, at 111–114. On loss of permanent resident status, see Aleinikoff, Martin, Motomura, & Fullerton, Immigration and Citizenship, supra note 8, at 561. On crime-based deportability, see INA § 237(a)(2), 8 U.S.C. § 1227(a)(2).

11. See INA § 212(a)(9)(B), 8 U.S.C. § 1182(a)(9)(B); Aleinikoff, Martin, Motomura, & Fullerton, Immigration and Citizenship, supra note 8, at 595–601.

12. FY 2011 approval rates were 84 percent in the Mexico District, 54 percent in the Bangkok District, 50 percent in the Rome District. The Field Office in Cuidad Juarez, Mexico, receives about 75 percent of the total annual caseload. See Dept. of Homeland Sec., Citizenship and Immigration Services Ombudsman, I–601 Waivers of Inadmissibility: Does the Current Process Work? When Is Hardship Extreme? Do Alternative Models Exist?, Highlights from the First Annual USCIS Ombudsman's Office Conference, Oct. 20, 2011.

13. See INA § 240A(b), 8 U.S.C. § 1229b(b). Another provision known as *registry* confers permanent resident status by operating like a statute of limitations for persons who lack immigration law status but have been in the United States since January 1, 1972. See INA § 249, 8 U.S.C. § 1259; Aleinikoff, Martin, Motomura, & Fullerton, Immigration and Citizenship, supra note 8, at 672–673. I exclude registry from this analysis of the meaning of unlawful presence because an extremely small number of noncitizens take advantage of it. Chapter 6 in this volume discusses registry.

14. *Plyler*, 457 U.S. at 226. For a prominent example of an administrative decision granting relief under prior law, see In re O–J–O–, 21 I. & N. Dec. 381, 382–383 (BIA 1996). The 1996 reformulation was largely a reaction to *O–J–O–*, see H.R. Conf. Rep. 104–828, 104th Cong. 2d Sess. 230 (1996); Aleinikoff, Martin, Motomura, & Fullerton, Immigration and Citizenship, supra note 8, at 756–757.

15. On the number of applicants waiting in lines, see Annual Report of Immigrant Visa Applicants in the Family-sponsored and Employment-based Preferences Registered at the National Visa Center as of November 1, 2012 (Department of State 2012). It is unknown how many of these 4.4 million are among the 11 million unauthorized migrants in the United States. See Claire Bergeron, Going to the Back of the Line: A Primer on Lines, Visa Categories, and Wait Times, 7 (Migration Policy Inst. 2013).

16. See David A. Martin, Twilight Statuses: A Closer Examination of the Unauthorized Population, 1 (Migration Policy Inst. 2005).

17. See INA § 244, 8 U.S.C. § 1254a; see also David A. Martin, Thomas Alexander Aleinikoff, Hiroshi Motomura, & Maryellen Fullerton, Forced Migration: Law and Policy, 951–959 (2d ed. West 2013).

18. On parole generally, see INA § 212(d)(5), 8 U.S.C. § 1182(d)(5); Aleinikoff, Martin, Motomura, & Fullerton, Immigration and Citizenship, supra note 8, at 518–521. On humanitarian parole, see David A. Martin, A Defense of Immigration-Enforcement Discretion: The Legal and Policy Flaws in Kris Kobach's Latest Crusade, 122 Yale L.J. Online 167, 178–180 (2012); Aleinikoff, Martin, Motomura, & Fullerton, Immigration and Citizenship, supra note 8, at 518–521.

19. See Secretary Napolitano Announces Humanitarian Parole Policy for Certain Haitian Orphans, Dept. of Homeland Sec., Jan. 18, 2010; Julia Preston, Immigration Policy Aims to Help Military Families, N.Y. Times, Aug. 1, 2010, at A15. On the three- and ten-year bars, see earlier in this chapter.

20. 457 U.S. at 226. See also Arizona v. United States, 132 S. Ct. 2492, 2499 (2012).

21. See 2009 Yearbook of Immigration Statistics 91, table 33, 93, table 35, 95, table 36 (Dept. of Homeland Sec. 2010); Hiroshi Motomura, The Discretion That Matters: Federal Immigration Enforcement, State and Local Arrests, and the Civil-Criminal Line, 58 UCLA L. Rev. 1819, 1829–1830 & nn. 44–48 (2011). For more on Secure Communities, see Chapters 2 and 4 in this volume.

22. See, e.g., INA § 275, 8 U.S.C. § 1325 (illegal entry); INA § 276, 8 U.S.C. § 1326 (illegal reentry).

23. See Leon Wildes, The Nonpriority Program of the Immigration and Naturalization Service Goes Public: The Litigative Use of the Freedom of Information Act, 14 San Diego L. Rev. 42 (1976–1977). See also Leon Wildes, The Operations Instructions of the Immigration Service: Internal Guides or Binding Rules?, 17 San Diego L. Rev. 99 (1979–1980); Leon Wildes, The Deferred Action Program of the Bureau of Citizenship and Immigration Services: A Possible Remedy for Impossible Immigration Cases, 41 San Diego L. Rev. 819 (2004).

On prosecutorial discretion generally, see Aleinikoff, Martin, Motomura, & Fullerton, Immigration and Citizenship, supra note 8, at 778–788; Martin, A Defense of Immigration-Enforcement Discretion, supra note 18, at 181–186; Motomura, The Discretion That Matters, supra note 21, at 1826–1842; Kate M. Manuel & Todd Garvey, Prosecutorial Discretion in Immigration

Enforcement: Legal Issues (Cong. Research Serv. 2013); Shoba Sivaprasad Wadhia, Sharing Secrets: Examining Deferred Action and Transparency in Immigration Law, 10 U. New Hampshire L. Rev. 1 (2012); Michael A. Olivas, Dreams Deferred: Deferred Action, Prosecutorial Discretion, and the Vexing Case(s) of DREAM Act Students, 21 Wm. & Mary Bill of Rts. J. 463, 475–492 (2012); Shoba Sivaprasad Wadhia, The Role of Prosecutorial Discretion in Immigration Law, 9 Conn. Pub. Int. L.J. 244 (2010).

24. A key example is Memorandum from Doris Meissner, Comm., Immigration and Naturalization Serv., on Exercising Prosecutorial Discretion 2 (Nov. 17, 2000). See generally Adam B. Cox & Cristina M. Rodríguez, The President and Immigration Law, 119 Yale L.J. 458, 517–518 (2009).

25. See Memorandum from John Morton, Asst. Sec., US Immigration & Customs Enforcement, on Civil Immigration Enforcement: Priorities for the Apprehension, Detention, and Removal of Aliens (June 30, 2010); Aleinikoff, Martin, Motomura, & Fullerton, Immigration and Citizenship, supra note 8, at 780–788.

26. See Memorandum from John Morton, Asst. Sec., US Immigration & Customs Enforcement, on Prosecutorial Discretion: Certain Victims, Witnesses, and Plaintiffs (June 17, 2011); Memorandum From John Morton, Asst. Sec., US Immigration & Customs Enforcement, on Exercising Prosecutorial Discretion Consistent with the Civil Immigration Enforcement Priorities of the Agency for Apprehension, Detention, and Removal of Aliens (June 17, 2011); Memorandum from John Morton, Asst. Sec., US Immigration & Customs Enforcement, on Guidance Regarding the Handling of Removal Proceedings of Aliens with Pending or Approved Applications or Petitions (Aug. 20, 2010). See generally Olivas, Dreams Deferred, supra note 23, at 492–519. See also Memorandum from Peter S. Vincent, Principal Legal Advisor, US Immigration & Customs Enforcement, on Guidance Regarding U Nonimmigrant Status (U visa) Applicants in Removal Proceedings or with Final Orders of Deportation or Removal (Sept. 25, 2009); Memorandum from William J. Howard, Principal Legal Advisor, US Immigration & Customs Enforcement, on Prosecutorial Discretion (Oct. 24, 2005), at 8; Memorandum from William J. Howard, Principal Legal Advisor, US Immigration & Customs Enforcement, on Exercising Prosecutorial Discretion to Dismiss Adjustment Cases (Oct. 6, 2005).

27. See Press Release, Dept. of Homeland Sec., DHS Establishes Interim Relief for Widows of U.S. Citizens (June 9, 2009); Pub. L. No. 111–83, § 568(c), 123 Stat. 2142, 2186 (2009).

28. See Memorandum from Janet Napolitano, Secretary of Homeland Sec., to David V. Aguilar, Acting Commissioner, US Customs & Border Prot., Alejandro Mayorkas, Director, US Citizenship & Immigration Servs., & John Morton, Director, US Immigration & Customs Enforcement, on Exercising Prosecutorial Discretion with Respect to Individuals Who Came to the United States as Children (June 15, 2012).

29. See 457 U.S. at 207–08 n.4; Pub. L. No. 99–603, 100 Stat. 3359 (1986); INA §§ 101(a)(H)(ii)(a), 210, 245A, 274A. On IRCA legalization, see also Chapter 6 in this volume. On SAW legalization, see INA § 210, 8 U.S.C. § 1160; Aristide R. Zolberg, A Nation by Design: Immigration Policy in the Fashioning of America, 358–371 (Harvard Univ. Press 2006); Carl Hampe, Intent of Congress Behind Certain Provisions of the Immigration Reform and Control Act, 2 Geo. Immigr. L.J. 499, 502 (1988). Employer sanctions had the delayed effective date of December 1, 1988, for seasonal agricultural workers. See INA § 274A(i)(3)(A), 8 U.S.C. § 1324a(i)(3)(A), repealed, Pub.L. 104–208, § 412(c), 110 Stat 3009–668 (1996).

30. See Ruth Ellen Wasem, Alien Legalization and Adjustment of Status: A Primer, 5 (Cong. Research Serv. 2010); Jeffrey S. Passel, The Size and Characteristics of the Unauthorized Migrant Population in the U.S.: Estimates Based on the March 2005 Current Population Survey, 3 (Pew Hispanic Ctr. 2006); 1993 Statistical Yearbook of the Immigration and Naturalization Service, 179 (Dep't of Justice 1994). See also Chapter 6 in this volume. On family members, see US Immigr. & Naturalization Serv., Immigration Reform and Control Act: Report on the Legalized Alien Population, 7 (1992). Later legislation granted temporary status until family members could obtain permanent residence through existing immigration categories. Immigration Act of 1990, § 301, Pub. L. No. 101–649, 104 Stat. 4978, 5029–5030.

31. See Paul Feldman, Texas Case Looms over Prop. 187's Legal Future, L.A. Times, Oct. 23, 1994, at A1; Lucy Hood, Educating Immigrant Students, Carnegie Rep., Spring 2007, at 2, 6–8. See also Michael A. Olivas, No Undocumented Child Left Behind: *Plyler v. Doe* and the Education of Undocumented Schoolchildren, 7–8 (N.Y.U. Press 2012); Katherine Leal Unmuth, Texas Case Opened Schools to Illegal Migrants, Dallas Morning News, June 11, 2007; Mary Ann Zehr, Amid Immigration Debate, Settled Ground: High Court's School Access Ruling Endures as a Quiet Fact of Life, Case Touched Many Parts of Community, 26 Educ. Wk., June 6, 2007.

32. See, e.g., Nicaraguan Adjustment and Central American Relief Act (NACARA), Pub. L. No. 105–100, §§ 201–204, 111 Stat. 2160, 2193–201 (1997); Haitian Refugee Immigration Fairness Act of 1998, Pub. L. No. 105–277, §§ 901–904, 112 Stat. 2681–538 to –542 (1998). Chapter 6 in this volume discusses these programs as well as proposed 2013 legislation. See S. 744, § 2305, 113th Cong., 1st Sess. (2013).

33. Such sentiments drove legislation like the Hinder the Administration's Legalization Temptation Act (HALT Act), H.R. 2497, 112th Cong. (1st Sess. 2011), which would have drastically curtailed DHS authority to grant deferred action and other discretionary reprieves from removal, as well as the lawsuit filed by the ICE officers' union asserting that DACA is unlawful. See Crane v. Napolitano, 2013 WL 1744422 (N.D. Tex. Apr. 23, 2013). On DACA, see Chapter 6 in this volume.

34. See Matthew Frye Jacobson, Whiteness of a Different Color: European Immigrants and the Alchemy of Race, 22–31, 68–73 (Harvard Univ. Press 1999).

35. See Peter Behrens, Op–Ed: It's About Immigrants, Not Irishness, N.Y. Times, Mar. 17, 2012, at A21. The total foreign-born US population was 9.7 percent in 1850 but then increased and remained above 13 percent from the 1860 census through the 1920 census. See Campbell J. Gibson & Kay Jung, Historical Census Statistics on the Foreign-born Population of the United States: 1850–2000, at 1, 4–5, 17–18 & tables 1, 22, 23 (US Census Bureau 2006). The US Census Bureau does not report analogous pre-1850 data.

36. On the composition of the Union Army, see John Whiteclay Chambers, To Raise an Army: The Draft Comes to Modern America, 48–49, 53–54 (Free Press 1987); David L. Valuska & Christian B. Keller, Damn Dutch: Pennsylvania Germans at Gettysburg, 16–43 (Stackpole Books 2004); Benjamin Apthorp Gould, 2 Investigations in the Military and Anthropological Statistics of American Soldiers, 26–29 (Riverside Press 1869).

37. On the racial aspects of admission to statehood, see Eric Biber, The Price of Admission: Causes, Effects, and Patterns of Conditions Imposed on States Entering the Union, 46 Am. J. Legal Hist. 119, 166–168 (2004); Juan F. Perea, A Brief History of Race and the U.S.-Mexican Border: Tracing the Trajectories of Conquest, 51 UCLA L. Rev. 283, 299–301 (2003); John D. Leshy, The Making of the Arizona Constitution, 20 Ariz. St. L.J. 1, 7–23 (1988). On settlement as immigration history, see Kerry Abrams, The Hidden Dimension of Nineteenth-Century Immigration Law, 62 Vand. L. Rev. 1353, 1356 (2009).

38. See Rupert N. Richardson, Adrian Anderson, Cary D. Wintz, & Ernest Wallace, Texas: The Lone Star State, 49–79 (10th ed. Pearson Prentice Hall 2009); Martha Menchaca, Recovering History, Constructing Race: The Indian, Black, and White Roots of Mexican Americans, 198–203 (Univ. of Texas Press 2001). On tensions during this period between Mexico and the United States and American settlers, see Laura Gómez, Manifest Destinies: The Making of the Mexican American Race, 17–21 (N.Y.U. Press 2008); Joseph Nevins, Operation Gatekeeper and Beyond: The War on "Illegals" and the Remaking of the U.S.-Mexico Boundary, 21–29 (Routledge 2010).

39. See Treaty of Peace, Friendship, Limits, and Settlement between the United States of America and the Mexican Republic (Treaty of Guadalupe-Hidalgo), July 4, 1848, U.S.-Mex., art. VIII–X, 9 Stat. 922, 929–930; Amy S. Greenberg, A Wicked War: Polk, Clay, Lincoln, and the 1846 U.S. Invasion of Mexico, 3–110 (Knopf 2012); Sean Wilentz, The Rise of American Democracy: Jefferson to Lincoln, 559–576, 594–614 (W. W. Norton 2005); Perea, A Brief History of Race and the U.S.-Mexican Border, supra note 37, at 288–297. See also Roger Daniels, Coming to America: A History of Immigration and Ethnicity in American Life, 96–97 (2d ed. Perennial 2002); Roger Daniels, Guarding the Golden Door: American Immigration Policy and Immigrants since 1882, at 62–63, 142 (Hill & Wang 2004); Patricia Nelson Limerick, The Legacy of Conquest: The Unbroken Past of the American West, 228–232 (W. W. Norton 1987); Mae M.

Ngai, Impossible Subjects: Illegal Aliens and the Making of Modern America, 50–51 (Princeton Univ. Press 2004); Earl Shorris, Latinos: A Biography of the People, 35, 37 (W. W. Norton 1992). On differences between federal and state citizenship for the residents of the ceded territories, see Gómez, Manifest Destinies, supra note 38, at 41–45. For estimates of the affected population, see Richard Griswold del Castillo, The Treaty of Guadalupe Hidalgo: A Legacy of Conflict, 62–66 (Univ. of Oklahoma Press 1990).

40. See Tomas Almaguer, Racial Fault Lines: The Historical Origins of White Supremacy in California, 17–24 (Univ. of California Press 1994); Limerick, The Legacy of Conquest, supra note 39, at 238–241; Ngai, Impossible Subjects, supra note 39, at 51–52; Daniel J. Tichenor, Dividing Lines: The Politics of Immigration Control in America, 89 (Princeton Univ. Press 2002).

41. On the challenges of surveying the U.S.-Mexico boundary, see Michael Dear, Why Walls Won't Work: Repairing the U.S.-Mexico Divide, 2–14 (Oxford Univ. Press 2013). On the emergence of a binational border area that straddled the political boundary between the United States and Mexico, see Dear, Why Walls Won't Work, supra, at 37–49.

42. See Act of Mar. 26, 1790, ch. 3, § 1, 1 Stat. 103, 103. On early-twentieth-century understandings of race, see Immigration Comm., Reports of the U.S. Immigration Commission: Dictionary of Races or Peoples, S. Doc. 61–662, at 17 (1911). On the racial identity of Irish, see Michael M. Topp, Racial and Ethnic Identity in the United States, 1837–1887, in The Columbia Documentary History of Race and Ethnicity in America, 223–228 (Ronald H. Bayor, ed., Columbia Univ. Press 2004). The scholarship on the American Civil War is voluminous. See, e.g., Wilentz, The Rise of American Democracy, supra note 39, at 521–796; James M. McPherson, Battle Cry of Freedom: The Civil War Era (Oxford Univ. Press 1988).

43. See Homestead Act of 1862, ch. 75, 12 Stat. 392, 392 (repealed 1976); Daniel J. Tichenor, Strange Bedfellows: The Politics and Pathologies of Immigration Reform, 5 Labor: Studies in Working-Class History of the Americans, 39, 43 (2008); Aziz Rana, The Two Faces of American Freedom, 184–187 (Harvard Univ. Press 2010); Abrams, Hidden Dimension, supra note 37, at 1401. On declarations of intent and the treatment of intending citizens, see Hiroshi Motomura, Americans in Waiting: The Lost Story of Immigration and Citizenship in the United States, 172 (Oxford Univ. Press 2006); see also Chapter 2 and 3 in this volume.

44. On recruitment by states and territories, see Tichenor, Strange Bedfellows, supra note 43, at 43. On the hierarchy of work based on race, see Rana, The Two Faces of American Freedom, supra note 43, at 186–193. The Burlingame Treaty Is Treaty of Trade, Consuls and Emigration between China and the United States, signed at Washington, July 28, 1868, Art. V, 137 Consolidated Treaty Series 469. On Chinese immigration in this period and reactions to it, see Almaguer, Racial Fault Lines, supra note 40, at 154–182; Gabriel J. Chin, *Chae Chan Ping* and *Fong Yue Ting*: The Origins of Plenary Power, in Immigration Stories, 7–29 (David

A. Martin & Peter H. Schuck eds., Foundation Press 2005); Roger Daniels, Asian America: Chinese and Japanese in the United States since 1850, at 9–66 (Univ. of Washington Press 1988); Daniels, Coming to America, supra note 39, at 239–243; Daniels, Golden Door, supra note 39, at 11–26; Andrew Gyory, Closing the Gate: Race, Politics, and the Chinese Exclusion Act, 212–259 (Univ. of North Carolina Press 1998); Bill Ong Hing, Making and Remaking Asian America Through Immigration Policy 1850–1990, at 19–26 (Stanford Univ. Press 1993); Erika Lee, At America's Gates: Chinese Immigration during the Exclusion Era, 1882–1943, at 23–46 (Univ. of North Carolina Press 2003); Limerick, The Legacy of Conquest, supra note 39, at 261–269; Charles J. McClain, In Search of Equality: The Chinese Struggle Against Discrimination in Nineteenth-Century America, 9–76, 201–206 (Univ. of California Press 1994); Jean Pfaelzer, Driven Out: The Forgotten War Against Chinese Americans (Random House 2007); Lucy E. Salyer, Laws Harsh as Tigers: Chinese Immigrants and the Shaping of Modern Immigration Law, 8–18, 43–58 (Univ. of North Carolina Press 1995); Ronald Takaki, Strangers from a Different Shore: A History of Asian Americans, 79–131 (updated & rev. ed. Little Brown 1998); Tichenor, Dividing Lines, supra note 40, at 87–108.

On the Golden Spike, see 9 San Francisco Newsletter & Calif. Advertiser No. 15, Transcontinental Railroad Postscript Supplement 4 (May 15, 1869). See also John Hoyt Williams, A Great and Shining Road: The Epic Story of the Transcontinental Railroad, 265 (Univ. of Nebraska Press 1996); James McCague, Moguls and Iron Men: The Story of the First Transcontinental Railroad, 327 (Harper & Row 1964) (reporting that four Chinese and four Irish workers laid the last two rails).

45. On hostility toward Chinese immigrants in this period, see Pfaelzer, Driven Out, supra note 44. Other Western states enacted laws directed against Chinese laborers, see, e.g., An Act to protect free white labor against competition with Chinese coolie labor, and to discourage the immigration of the Chinese into this territory, 1864 Wash. Sess. Laws 56, 56 § 1. See also Abrams, Hidden Dimension, supra note 37, at 1387–1388 nn. 173, 174.

46. Act of Mar. 3, 1875, ch. 141, 18 Stat. 477. On anti-Chinese hostility in the California gold country, see Pfaelzer, Driven Out, supra note 44, at 3–46. On the Page Act, see Pfaelzer, Driven Out, supra note 44, at 89–120; Kerry Abrams, Polygamy, Prostitution, and the Federalization of Immigration Law, 105 Colum. L. Rev. 641, 690–715 (2005); Sucheng Chan, The Exclusion of Chinese Women, 1870–1943, in Entry Denied: Exclusion and the Chinese Community in America, 1882–1943, at 94, 94–146 (Sucheng Chan ed., Temple Univ. Press 1991); Kevin R. Johnson, The Huddled Masses Myth: Immigration and Civil Rights, 126 (Temple Univ. Press 2004); Lee, At America's Gates, supra note 44, at 30–31; Leti Volpp, Divesting Citizenship: On Asian American History and the Loss of Citizenship Through Marriage, 53 UCLA L. Rev. 405, 458–469 (2005). See also US Cong., Joint Special Committee to Investigate Chinese

Immigration, 44th Cong., 2d Sess., S. Rep. No. 689, at viii (1877); Calif. Const., Art. XIX Sec. 4 (1879).

47. See Treaty Regulating Immigration from China, Nov. 17, 1880, art. I., 22 Stat. 826; Act of May 6, 1882, ch. 126, 22 Stat. 58. The 1882 legislation came after President Arthur vetoed a 20-year ban. See An act to execute certain treaty stipulations relating to the Chinese, S. 196(71), 47th Cong. (1882); 13 Cong. Rec., S. 2551 (Apr. 4, 1882) (veto message). For renewals and extensions, see Act of Apr. 27, 1904, ch. 1630, § 5, 33 Stat. 392, 428; repealed by Act of Dec. 17, 1943, ch. 344, § 1, 57 Stat. 600, 600.

48. On Japanese immigration in this period and reactions to it, see Daniels, Asian America, supra note 44, at 100–129; Daniels, Coming to America, supra note 39, at 250–258; Daniels, Golden Door, supra note 39, at 41–45; Roger Daniels, The Politics of Prejudice: The Anti-Japanese Movement in California, and the Struggle for Japanese Exclusion, 1–15 (Univ. of California Press 1977); John Higham, Strangers in the Land: Patterns of American Nativism 1860–1925, at 166, 171–172 (Rutgers Univ. Press 1955); Hing, Asian America, supra note 44, at 26–29, 53–55; Ngai, Impossible Subjects, supra note 39, at 39–40; Tichenor, Dividing Lines, supra note 40, at 123; Yuji Ichioka, The Issei: The World of the First Generation Japanese Immigrants, 1885–1924, at 1–90 (Free Press 1988).

49. See Peter Margulies, Taking Care of Immigration Law: Presidential Stewardship, Prosecutorial Discretion, and the Separation of Powers, 94 B.U. L. Rev. 105, 152–158, (2014); Elihu Root, The Real Questions under the Japanese Treaty and the San Francisco School Board Resolution, 1 Am. J. Int'l L. 273, 274–276 (1907); Motomura, Americans in Waiting, supra note 43, at 31–32.

50. See Act of May 19, 1921, ch. 8, §§ 2(a)(6), 3, 42 Stat. 5, 5–7; Act of May 26, 1924, ch. 190, § 4(a), 43 Stat. 153, 155. On the period from 1921 through 1924, see Daniels, Golden Door, supra note 39, at 47–49, 54–57; Higham, Strangers in the Land, supra note 48, at 308–311; Jacobson, Whiteness of a Different Color, supra note 34, at 68–135; Desmond King, Making Americans: Immigration, Race, and the Origins of the Diverse Democracy, 39–41, 200–228 (Harvard Univ. Press 2000); Ngai, Impossible Subjects, supra note 39, at 21–23, 25–27, 28–29; Tichenor, Dividing Lines, supra note 40, at 143–148.

51. See U.S. Pub. L. 73–127, § 8(a)(1), 48 Stat. 456 (1934); Ichioka, The Issei, supra note 48, at 244–254; Ngai, Impossible Subjects, supra note 39, at 27; Daniels, Golden Door, supra note 39, at 67–68; Hing, Asian America, supra note 44, at 31, 33, 61–62; Rick Baldoz, The Third Asiatic Invasion: Migration and Empire in Filipino America, 1898–1946, at 177–181 (N.Y.U. Press 2011); Bill Ong Hing, Defining America Through Immigration Policy, 49–50 (Temple Univ. Press 2004).

52. See Tichenor, Strange Bedfellows, supra note 43, at 55; Gómez, Manifest Destinies, supra note 38, at 140.

53. See Marc Reisner, Cadillac Desert: The American West and Its Disappearing Water, 109–110, 131–132, 150–152, 238–239 (Penguin rev. ed. 1993); John H. White,

Jr., The American Railroad Freight Car: From the Wood-Car Era to the Coming of Steel, 270–271 (Johns Hopkins Univ. Press 1993); Motomura, Americans in Waiting, supra note 43, at 129–130; Nevins, Operation Gatekeeper, supra note 38, at 42–45 (discussing the labor shortage in the United States caused by domestic migration to northeastern states, limitations on Japanese immigration, US entry into World War I, and restrictive immigration legislation in 1917 that exempted Mexicans).

54. On northward migration, see Daniels, Golden Door, Why Walls Won't Work, supra note 39, at 62–63; Douglas S. Massey, Jorge Durand, & Nolan J. Malone, Beyond Smoke and Mirrors: Mexican Immigration in an Era of Economic Integration, 26–33 (Russell Sage Found. 2002); Shorris, Latinos, supra note 39, at 42; Nevins, Operation Gatekeeper, supra note 38, at 40–41.

On enforcement on the US-Mexico border, see Dear, Why Walls Won't Work, supra note 41, at 64 66; Kelly Lytle Hernández, Migra!: A History of the U.S. Border Patrol (Univ. of California Press 2010); John Torpey, The Invention of the Passport: Surveillance, Citizenship, and the State, 118 (Cambridge Univ. Press 2000); Nevins, Operation Gatekeeper, supra note 38, at 32–33, 68. On Chinese immigrants in Mexico in this period, see Robert Chao Romero, The Chinese in Mexico, 1882–1940 (Univ. of Arizona Press 2010). On Angel Island, see Erika Lee & Judy Yung, Angel Island: Immigrant Gateway to America (Oxford Univ. Press 2010).

55. See Act of May 28, 1924, Pub. L. No. 68–153, ch. 204, 43 Stat. 205, 240.

56. On the selective application of exclusion grounds and eligibility for discretionary relief, see Tichenor, Strange Bedfellows, supra note 43, at 43; Ngai, Impossible Subjects, supra note 39, at 56–90.

57. See Immigration Act of February 20, 1907, § 39, Pub. L. No. 59–96, ch. 1134, 2d Sess., 34 Stat. 898, 909; Immigration Commission, Reports of the Immigration Commission: Abstracts of the Reports of the Immigration Commission with Conclusions and Recommendations and Views of the Minority, S. Doc. No. 61–747, at 690–691 (1911), quoted in Kitty Calavita, The Immigration Policy Debate: Critical Analysis and Future Options, in Mexican Migration to the United States: Origins, Consequences, and Policy Options, 151, 155–159 (Wayne Cornelius & Jorge Bustamante eds., Center for U.S.-Mexican Studies, Univ. of California 1989). See also Tichenor, Strange Bedfellows, supra note 43, at 44; Martha Gardner, The Qualities of a Citizen: Women, Immigration, and Citizenship, 1870–1965, at 209 (Princeton Univ. Press 2005).

58. See Nevins, Operation Gatekeeper, supra note 38, at 130–133; Kitty Calavita, U.S. Immigration Law and the Control of Labor: 1820–1924, at 133–37, 148–150 (Academic Press 1984); David Bacon, Illegal People: How Globalization Creates Migration and Criminalizes Immigrants, 208–209 (Beacon Press 2008).

59. The Bracero program ended on December 31, 1964, with the expiration of the authority granted by the Act of Dec. 13, 1963, Pub. L. No. 88–203, § 1, 77 Stat. 363, 363. See Kitty Calavita, Inside the State: The Bracero Program, Immigration,

and the I.N.S. (Routledge 1992); Daniels, Golden Door, supra note 39, at 89–91, 142; Leonard Dinnerstein & David M. Reimers, Ethnic Americans: A History of Immigration, 131–134 (4th ed. Columbia Univ. Press 1999); Massey, Durand, & Malone, Beyond Smoke and Mirrors, supra note 54, at 34–41; Ngai, Impossible Subjects, supra note 39, at 138–166. On the historical pattern, see Gerald P. López, Don't We Like Them Illegal?, 45 U.C. Davis L. Rev. 1711, 1742–1773 (2012); Hiroshi Motomura, Immigration Outside the Law, 108 Colum. L. Rev. 2037, 2047–2055 (2008); Motomura, Americans in Waiting, supra note 43, at 129–135; Gerald P. López, Undocumented Mexican Migration: In Search of a Just Immigration Law & Policy, 28 UCLA L. Rev. 615, 640–674 (1981).

60. On employer control and preferences, see Jennifer Gordon, Tensions in Rhetoric and Reality at the Intersection of Work and Immigration, 2 U.C. Irvine L. Rev. 125, 136–137 (2012); Roger Waldinger & Michael I. Lichter, How the Other Half Works: Immigration and the Social Organization of Labor, 155–180 (Univ. of California 2003); Limerick, The Legacy of Conquest, supra note 39, at 243–251; Tichenor, Dividing Lines, supra note 40, at 151, 167–175, 211; Nevins, Operation Gatekeeper, supra note 38, at 43. The H-2A program is based on INA § 101(a)(15)(H), 8 U.S.C. § 1101(a)(15)(H). On the idea that the exploitability and exclusion of workers are "effectively their passport," see Kitty Calavita, Immigrants at the Margins: Law, Race, and Exclusion in Southern Europe, 74 (Cambridge Univ. Press 2005).

61. See 32 Killed in Crash of Charter Plane; California Victims Include 28 Mexican Workers Who Were Being Deported, N.Y. Times, Jan. 29, 1948, at 5. See also Diana Marcum, Names Emerge from Shadows of 1948 Crash, L.A. Times, July 9, 2013; http://www.check-six.com/Crash_Sites/Deportee_1948_crash.htm. See also Joe Klein, Woody Guthrie: A Life, 349–350 (Knopf 1980). Here are their names: Miguel Negrete Álvarez, Tomás Aviña de Gracia, Francisco Llamas Durán, Santiago García Elizondo, Rosalio Padilla Estrada, Tomás Padilla Márquez, Bernabé López Garcia, Salvador Sandoval Hernández, Severo Medina Lára, Elías Trujillo Macias, José Rodríguez Macias, Luis López Medina, Manuel Calderón Merino, Luis Cuevas Miranda, Martin Razo Navarro, Ignacio Pérez Navarro, Román Ochoa, Ramón Paredes Gonzalez, Guadalupe Ramírez Lára, Apolonio Ramírez Placencia, Alberto Carlos Raygoza, Guadalupe Hernández Rodríguez, Maria Santana Rodríguez, Juan Valenzuela Ruiz, Wenceslao Flores Ruiz, José Valdívia Sánchez, Jesús Meza Santos, Baldomero Marcas Torres.

62. This information tracked the news story, see 32 Killed in Crash of Charter Plane, supra note 61. For fuller discussion of the vulnerability of temporary workers to employer exploitation, see Chapter 7 in this volume.

63. See Hernández, Migra!, supra note 54. See also Nevins, Operation Gatekeeper, supra note 38, at 67. On deportations during the 1930s, see generally Francisco E. Balderrama & Raymond Rodríguez, Decade of Betrayal: Mexican Repatriation in the 1930s (2d ed. Univ. of New Mexico Press 2006); Nevins, Operation Gatekeeper, supra note 38, at 37–38.

64. On the dominant image, see Leo R. Chavez, The Latino Threat: Constructing Immigrants, Citizens, and the Nation, 23–26 (Stanford Univ. Press 2008). On selective enforcement, see Calavita, Immigration Policy Debate, supra note 57, at 155–159 (chronicling the historical nexus between US immigration policies and Mexican migration); Nevins, Operation Gatekeeper, supra note 38, at 39, 44. On the significance of this history of immigration law enforcement, see also Chapter 3 in this volume.

65. See generally Motomura, The Discretion That Matters, supra note 21, at 1826–1842; Cox & Rodríguez, The President and Immigration Law, supra note 24, at 511–514.

66. Jasso, Massey, Rosenzweig, & Smith, Illegal to Legal, supra note 7, at 835.

67. See Massey, Durand, & Malone, Beyond Smoke and Mirrors, supra note 54, at 41; Calavita, Inside the State, supra note 59, at 142–143; Tichenor, Dividing Lines, supra note 40, at 209–211

68. On the connections between the civil rights movement and immigration law, see Mary L. Dudziak, Cold War Civil Rights: Race and Image of American Democracy, 152–248 (Princeton Univ. Press 2000); Motomura, Americans in Waiting, supra note 43, at 130–132; Gabriel J. Chin, The Civil Rights Revolution Comes to Immigration Law: A New Look at the Immigration and Nationality Act of 1965, 75 N.C. L. Rev. 273, 296 (1996).

69. Remarks at the Signing of the Immigration Bill, Liberty Island, New York, in Public Papers of the Presidents of the United States: Lyndon B. Johnson 1037, 1038–1039 (1966). In 1958, then Senator John F. Kennedy called for an end to the national origins system in his book *A Nation of Immigrants*. See John F. Kennedy, A Nation of Immigrants, 75 (rev. & enl. ed. Harper and Row 1964). For a firsthand account, see Edward M. Kennedy, The Immigration Act of 1965, 367 Annals Am. Acad. Pol. & Soc. Sci. 137 (1966). See also Daniels, Golden Door, supra note 39, at 129–144; King, Making Americans, supra note 50, at 236–253; Massey, Durand, & Malone, Beyond Smoke and Mirrors, supra note 54, at 40; Ngai, Impossible Subjects, supra note 39, at 243; Tichenor, Dividing Lines, supra note 40, at 196–216.

70. See Civil Rights Act of 1964, Pub. L. No. 88–352, 78 Stat. 241; Voting Rights Act of 1965, Pub. L. No. 89–110, 79 Stat. 437 (codified as amended at 42 U.S.C. § 1973–1973bb–1); Motomura, Americans in Waiting, supra note 43, at 134.

71. On the Western Hemisphere limit, see Act of Oct. 3, 1965, Pub. L. No. 89–236, §§ 8, 21(e), 79 Stat. 911, 916, 921; S. Rep. 89–748, 89th Cong., 1st Sess. 1965, at 3336; H.R. Rep. 94–1553, 94th Cong., 2d Sess. 1976, at 6074. Motomura, Americans in Waiting, supra note 43, at 134; Gabriel J. Chin, The Civil Rights Revolution, supra note 68, at 298; Daniels, Golden Door, supra note 39, at 133; Select Commission on Immigration and Refugee Policy, U.S. Immigration Policy and the National Interest: Staff Report of the Select Commission on Immigration and Refugee Policy, 208 (1981); Johnson, Huddled Masses, supra note 46, at 25–26; Ngai,

Impossible Subjects, supra note 39, at 254–261; John A. Scanlan, Immigration Law and the Illusion of Numerical Control, 36 U. Miami L. Rev. 819, 830 (1982). For later legislation imposing caps, see Act of Oct. 20, 1976, Pub. L. 94–571, § 3, 90 Stat. 2703; Pub. L. No. 95–412, 92 Stat. 907 (1978); Pub. L. No. 96–212, 94 Stat. 102 (1980). The current version is in INA § 202(a)(2), 8 U.S.C. § 1152(a)(2). See also H.R. Rep. 94–1553, 94th Cong., 2d Sess. 1976, at 6076.

72. On increased immigration from Latin America, see also Chapter 3 in this volume.

73. See Department of State, Visa Bulletin for May 2013. The 2013 Senate bill would have treated spouses and minor children of permanent residents like the spouses and minor children of US citizens. See S. 744, § 2305, 113th Cong., 1st Sess. (2013).

74. See Department of State, Visa Bulletin for May 2013. See generally Bergeron, Going to the Back of the Line, supra note 15; Ruth Ellen Wasem, U.S. Immigration Policy on Permanent Admissions, 11–14 (Cong. Research Serv. 2012). The 2013 Senate bill would have raised the per-country limits from the current 7 percent of the worldwide cap to 15 percent. See S. 744, § 2306, 113th Cong., 1st Sess. (2013).

75. See Randall Monger & James Yankay, U.S. Legal Permanent Residents: 2012, at 2, table 1 (Dept. of Homeland Sec. 2013); 2011 Yearbook of Immigration Statistics, supra note 10, at 5, table 1, 18, table 6; Wasem, Permanent Admissions, supra note 74, at 6–11. Other categories of immigrants include spouses and minor children, so more than 65 percent of permanent residents qualify through family ties. See Hiroshi Motomura, The Family and Immigration: A Roadmap for the Ruritanian Lawmaker, 43 Am. J. Comp. L. 511, 535–538 (1995).

76. See INA § 201(d)(1)(A), 8 U.S.C. § 1151(d)(1)(A); 2011 Yearbook of Immigration Statistics, supra note 10, at 65, table 25; Jacqueline Hagan, Nichola Lowe, & Christian Quingla, Skills on the Move: Rethinking the Relationship Between Human Capital and Immigrant Labor Market Incorporation, 38 Work & Occupations 149, 152 (2011); Wayne A. Cornelius, Controlling "Unwanted" Immigration: Lessons from the United States, 1993–2004, 31 J. Ethnic & Migr. Stud. 775, 788–790 (2005).

77. See Randall Monger, Nonimmigrant Admissions to the United States: 2012, at 3, table 1 (Dept. of Homeland Sec. 2013); 2011 Yearbook of Immigration Statistics, supra note 10, at 65, table 25. On temporary worker programs generally, Aleinikoff, Martin, Motomura, & Fullerton, Immigration and Citizenship, supra note 8, at 428–35. On the unauthorized U.S. workforce, see Jeffrey S. Passel & D'Vera Cohn, Unauthorized Immigrant Population: National and State Trends, 2010, at 17 (Pew Hispanic Ctr. 2011).

78. The Bracero program ended on December 31, 1964, with the expiration of the authority granted by the Act of Dec. 13, 1963, Pub. L. No. 88–203, 77 Stat. 363. See Calavita, Inside the State, supra note 59. On its influence on current immigration, see Calavita, Immigration Policy Debate, supra note 57, at 155–160; López, Undocumented Mexican Migration, supra note 59, at 664–672, 707–708.

79. On self-sustaining migration, see Motomura, Americans in Waiting, supra note 43, at 48–49, 134–135, 178–179; Douglas S. Massey, Luin Goldring, & Jorge Durand, Continuities in Transnational Migration: An Analysis of Nineteen Mexican Communities, 99 Am. J. Sociology 1492, 1496–1503 (1994); Douglas S. Massey, Rafael Alaron, Jorge Durand, & Humberto González, Return to Aztlan: The Social Process of International Migration from Western Mexico, 115 (Univ. of California Press 1987). On the increase in immigration from Mexico, see Massey, Durand, & Malone, Beyond Smoke and Mirrors, supra note 54, at 41–47; Arthur F. Corwin & Johnny M. McCain, Wetbackism since 1964: A Catalogue of Factors, in Immigrants—and Immigrants: Perspectives on Mexican Labor Migration to the United States, 67, 68 (Arthur F. Corwin ed., Greenwood Press 1978).

80. On the migration industry, see Rubén Hernández León, Conceptualizing the Migration Industry, in The Migration Industry and the Commercialization of International Migration, 24 (Thomas Gammeltolt-Hansen & Ninna Nyberg Sorensen eds., Routledge 2012); David Spener, Clandestine Crossings: Migrants and Coyotes on the Texas-Mexico Border (Cornell Univ. Press 2009); Ted Conover, Coyotes: A Journey Through the Secret World of America's Illegal Aliens (Vintage 1987). On the development of Mexico's northern border cities, see Dear, Why Walls Won't Work, supra note 41, at 46–48; M. Angeles Villarreal, U.S.-Mexico Economic Relations: Trends, Issues, and Implications, 7–9 (Cong. Research Serv. 2011); Ginger Thompson, Chasing Mexico's Dream Into Squalor: The Dividing Line: Misery on the Border, N.Y. Times, Feb. 11, 2001, at 11; Sandy Tolan, The Border Book; Hope and Heartbreak, N.Y. Times, July 1, 1990, at 617; William Stockton, Mexico's Grand "Maquiladora" Plan, N.Y. Times, Jan. 19, 1986, at 34; Richard J. Meislin, Mexican Border Plants Beginning to Hire Men, N.Y. Times, Mar. 19, 1984, at D8.

81. On enforcement generally, see Doris Meissner, Donald M. Kerwin, Muzaffar Chishti, & Claire Bergeron, Immigration Enforcement in the United States: The Rise of A Formidable Machinery (Migration Policy Inst. 2013). See also Michael Jones-Correa, Contested Ground: Immigration in the United States, 8–11 (Migration Policy Inst. 2012); Adam B. Cox & Eric A. Posner, The Second-Order Structure of Immigration Law, 59 Stan. L. Rev. 809, 845–46 & nn.133–134 (2007).

82. Pub. L. No. 104–208, 110 Stat. 3009.

83. On the relationship between potential future change in enforcement and arguments for and against legalization, see Chapter 6 in this volume.

84. On state employer sanctions, see Select Commission on Immigration & Refugee Policy, Staff Report, supra note 71, at 565; Stephen Lee, Private Immigration Screening in the Workplace, 61 Stan. L. Rev. 1103, 1111 & n.18 (2009). On the Texas Proviso, see Act of June 27, 1952, Pub. L. No. 82–414, § 274, 66 Stat. 163, 228–29; Daniels, Golden Door, supra note 39, at 121; Tichenor, Dividing Lines, supra note 40, at 194.

85. On the employers' role, see Stephen Lee, Workplace Enforcement Workarounds, 21 Wm. & Mary Bill of Rts J. 549 (2012); Lee, Private Immigration Screening, supra note 84. On harboring, see Eisha Jain, Immigration Enforcement and Harboring Doctrine, 24 Geo. Immigr. L.J. 147 (2010). Crimes related to unauthorized employment include 42 U.S.C. § 408(a)(7) (false representation of a Social Security number); 18 U.S.C. § 1546(a) (possession or use of a false immigration document).

86. See INA § 274A(b)(1)(A), 8 U.S.C. §1324a(b)(1)(A); Collins Foods Int'l, Inc. v. U.S. INS, 948 F.2d 549, 554 (9th Cir. 1991); INA § 274B(a)(6), 8 U.S.C. § 1324b(a)(6); Immigration Reform: Employer Sanctions and the Question of Discrimination (General Accounting Office 1990).

87. See INA § 274A(e)–(f), 8 U.S.C. § 1324a(e)–(f); Kitty Calavita, Employer Sanctions Violations: Toward a Dialectical Model of White-Collar Crime, 24 L. & Soc'y Rev. 1041, 1046–55, 1057, 1060 (1990); Cornelius, Controlling "Unwanted" Immigration, supra note 76, at 786–87; Wayne A. Cornelius, The U.S. Demand for Mexican Labor, in Cornelius & Bustamante, supra note 57, at 25, 43–44; Tichenor, Dividing Lines, supra note 40, at 243; Immigration Enforcement: Weaknesses Hinder Employment Verification and Worksite Enforcement Efforts, 34–40 (Government Accountability Office 2005); Peter Brownell, The Declining Enforcement of Employer Sanctions (Migration Policy Inst. 2005). On unauthorized workers by industry and occupation, see Passel, The Size and Characteristics of the Unauthorized Migrant Population, supra note 30, at 9–14.

88. See Lack of Worksite Enforcement and Employer Sanctions: Hearing Before the Subcomm. on Immigration, Border Security and Claims of the H. Comm. on the Judiciary, 109th Cong. 7 (2005) (statement of Richard M. Stana, Director, Homeland Security and Justice, US Government Accountability Office); Immigration Enforcement: Preliminary Observations on Employment Verification and Worksite Enforcement Efforts, report GAO–05–822T (Government Accountability Office 2005); Cornelius, Controlling "Unwanted" Immigration, supra note 76, at 785–786. On the low level of activity from 1999 to 2004, see Michele Wucker, Lockout: Why America Keeps Getting Immigration Wrong When Our Prosperity Depends on Getting It Right, 114 (Public Affairs 2006).

In fiscal year 2002, the federal government arrested 510 unauthorized workers and employers in workplace raids. Worksite arrests rose to 1,292 in fiscal year 2005 and then leapt to 4,940 in 2007. US Immigration and Customs Enforcement, Worksite Enforcement Fact Sheet (Apr. 30, 2009). Large-scale raids resulted in the arrests of 1,297 workers at six branches of meat processor Swift & Co. in December 2006, and of 350 workers at a New Bedford, Massachusetts, leather goods factory in March 2007. See Yvonne Abraham & Brian R. Ballou, 350 Are

Held in Immigration Raid: New Bedford Factory Employed Illegals, US Says, Boston Globe, Mar. 7, 2007, at 1A.

89. On the Postville raid and the trend toward criminal prosecution of unauthorized migrants, see Ingrid V. Eagly, Prosecuting Immigration, 104 Nw. U. L. Rev. 1281 (2010). See also Immigration Raids: Postville and Beyond: Hearing before the Subcomm. On Immigration, Citizenship, Refugees, Border Security, and International Law of the H. Comm. on the Judiciary, 110–198, at 1–2 (2008) (statement of Rep. Zoe Lofgren, Chairwoman, Subcomm. on Immigration, Citizenship, Refugees, Border Security, and International Law); Julia Preston, 270 Immigrants Sent to Prison in Federal Push, N.Y. Times, May 24, 2008, at A1; see TRAC Immigration, Prosecutions for 2008: Referring Agency: Department of Homeland Security Immigration and Customs Enforcement. Compare Adam Nossiter, Nearly 600 Were Arrested in Factory Raid, Officials Say, N.Y. Times, Aug. 27, 2008, at A16.

90. On audits of employers' personnel files, see Julia Preston, Illegal Workers Swept from Jobs in Silent Raids, N.Y. Times, July 10, 2010, at A1; Neil A. Lewis, In Search for Illegal Workers, Immigration Officials Will Audit 1,000 More Companies, N.Y. Times, Nov. 20, 2009, at A14; Julia Preston, Immigrant Crackdown Leads to 1,800 Pink Slips, N.Y. Times, Sept. 30, 2009, at A1; Aleinikoff, Martin, Motomura, & Fullerton, Immigration and Citizenship, supra note 8, at 964–965. For mandatory E-Verify for federal contractors and subcontractors, see Executive Order 13465, 73 Fed. Reg. 33,285 (2008); 73 Fed. Reg. 67,651 (2008). On E-Verify errors, see Aleinikoff, Martin, Motomura, & Fullerton, Immigration and Citizenship, supra note 8, at 965–972; Marc Rosenblum, E-Verify: Strengths, Weaknesses, and Proposals for Reform (Migration Policy Inst. Feb. 2011); Kathy Kiely, Employer-Verification Proposal Draws Fire: Provision Part of Immigration Bills' Debate, USA Today, May 25, 2007, at 7A. On opposition to E-Verify and database checks generally, see Miriam Jordan, E-Verify Bill Against Illegal Workers in Doubt, Wall St. J., Sept. 20, 2011, at A6; Elizabeth E. Joh, Discretionless Policing: Technology and the Fourth Amendment, 95 Cal. L. Rev. 199, 230–232 (2007).

91. In the past two decades, Congress has expanded the categories of crimes that can lead to the deportation of noncitizens, including long-time permanent residents. On competing priorities, see Mariano-Florentino Cuellar, The Political Economies of Immigration Law, 2 U.C. Irvine L. Rev. 1, 46–50 (2012); Ming H. Chen, Where You Stand Depends on Where You Sit: Incorporating Undocumented Workers in Federal Workplace Agencies, 33 Berkeley J. of Emp. & Lab. L. 227, 250–253 (2012); Stephen Lee, Monitoring Immigration Enforcement, 53 Ariz. L. Rev. 1089, 1096–1105 (2011). On taxes, see Paying Taxes, and Fearing Deportation, N.Y. Times, Feb. 2, 2009, at A9; Francine J. Lipman, Bearing Witness to Economic Injustices of Undocumented Immigrant Families: A New Class of "Undeserving Poor," 7 Nev. L.J. 736, 743–751 (2007); Francine J. Lipman, The Taxation of Undocumented

Immigrants: Separate, Unequal, and Without Representation, 9 Harv. Latino L. Rev. 1, 18–48 (2006).

92. Historian Ronald Takaki once wrote, "the border existed only when Mexican labor was not needed." Ronald Takaki, A Different Mirror: A History of Multicultural America, 334 (Little, Brown 1993), quoted in Nevins, Operation Gatekeeper, supra note 38, at 137. See also Bacon, Illegal People, supra note 58, at 79; Wucker, Lockout, supra note 88, at 102–103; Catherine Dauvergne, Making People Illegal: What Globalization Means for Migration and Law, 19, 25 (Cambridge Univ. Press 2008). See also Julia Preston, Huge Amounts Spent on Immigration, Study Finds, N.Y. Times, Jan. 8, 2013, at A11.

93. See Meissner, Kerwin, Chishti, & Bergeron, supra note 81, at 23–33; Sheryl Gay Stolberg, Advocates of an Immigration Overhaul Question a Border Deployment, N.Y. Times, May 27, 2010, at A22; Dan Frosch, Aug. 1 Set as Date for Troops to Go to Border, N.Y. Times, July 20, 2010, at A12; Marc Lacey, Date for Buildup at Border Comes, But the National Guard Does Not, N.Y. Times, Aug. 2, 2010, at A9; Mark Smith, Reno Pledges Aid to Secure Borders/Del Rio Border Patrol Area Will Benefit Most, Houston Chron., Jan. 7, 1995 at A1; John Dillin, US Beefs up Border Patrol after Protests from States about Costs of Immigration, Christian Science Monitor, Feb. 7, 1994, at 1; David LaGesse, Texas to Get 300 More Border Agents, Dallas Morning News, Jan. 6, 1995, at 36A. On the federal budget for 2010, see US Department of Homeland Security, Budget-in-Brief: Fiscal Year 2011, at 17.

94. Woody Guthrie, Deportee: Plane Wreck at Los Gatos. On the federal misdemeanor, INA § 275, 8 U.S.C. § 1325. On sending offenders back, see John M. Broder, The Immigration Debate: The States; Governors of Border States Have Hope, and Questions, N.Y. Times, May 17, 2006, at A16; Rachel L. Swarns, Tight Immigration Policy Hits Roadblock of Reality, N.Y. Times, Jan. 20, 2006, at A12.

95. See Cindy Chang, Immigration Cases Take Bigger Toll on U.S. Courts: They Make up More than 40% of Federal Prosecutions, Human Rights Watch Says, L.A. Times, May 22, 2013, at Late Extra 1. On the trend toward criminal prosecution of border crossers, see Eagly, Prosecuting Immigration, supra note 89, at 1321–1336; Jennifer M. Chacón, Managing Migration Through Crime, 109 Colum. L. Rev. Sidebar 135, 139–140, 142–143 (2009). On Operation Streamline, see Eagly, Prosecuting Immigration, supra note 89, at 1327–30; Joanna Jacobbi Lydgate, Comment, Assembly-Line Justice: A Review of Operation Streamline, 98 Calif. L. Rev. 481 (2010); Walter Ewing, Border Patrol to Roll Out New "Get Tough" Policy on Unauthorized Immigrants, Immigr. Impact (Jan. 19, 2012); Authority of U.S. Customs and Border Protection Agents: An Overview (Immigr. Policy Center 2012).

96. See generally National Research Council, Options for Estimating Illegal Entries at the U.S.-Mexico Border (Alicia Carriquiry & Malay Majmundar eds., Nat'l Acad.

Press 2012); Manuela Angelucci, U.S. Border Enforcement and the Net Flow of Mexican Illegal Migration, 60 Econ. Dev. & Cultural Change 311 (2012).

97. On crossing strategies, see Eric Lipton & Julia Preston, As U.S. Plugs Border in Arizona, Crossings Shift to South Texas, N.Y. Times, June 17, 2013, at A1; Noah Gilbert, California: 25 Arrested off Coast in Suspected Smuggling Case, N.Y. Times, Dec. 10, 2012, at A20; Randal C. Archibold, As Mexico Border Tightens, Smugglers Take to Sea, N.Y. Times, July 18, 2009, at A11; Pia M. Orrenius, The Effect of U.S. Border Enforcement on the Crossing Behavior of Mexican Migrants, in Crossing the Border: Research from the Mexican Migration Project, 281, 287– 296 (Jorge Durand & Douglas S. Massey eds., Russell Sage Found. 2004). On the perils of crossing, see Jacqueline Maria Hagan, Migration Miracle: Faith, Hope, and Meaning on the Undocumented Journey, 59–81 (Harvard Univ. Press 2008); Luis Alberto Urrea, The Devil's Highway: A True Story (Little, Brown 2004).

The fee paid to a smuggler to cross the US-Mexico border reportedly rose in inflation adjusted terms from about $600 to $1,000 in 1990 to $2,500 in 2010. See Carriquiry & Majmundar, supra note 96, at 2–14. On the number of migrants who have died crossing the border, see US Border Patrol, Southwest Border Deaths by Fiscal Year, http://www.cbp.gov/linkhandler/cgov/border_security/border_ patrol/usbp_statistics/usbp_fy12_stats/border_patrol_fy.ctt/border_patrol_ fy.pdf; A Continued Humanitarian Crisis at the Border: Undocumented Border Crosser Deaths Recorded by the Pima County Office of the Medical Examiner, 1990–2012 (Binational Migration Institute 2013); Meissner, Kerwin, Chishti, & Bergeron, Immigration Enforcement, supra note 81, at 33–35; Cornelius, Controlling "Unwanted" Immigration, supra note 76, at 783.

98. On the percentage of overstays, see David A. Martin, Eight Myths about Immigration Enforcement, 10 N.Y.U. J. Legis. & Pub. Pol'y 525, 544 (2007). On enforcement increasing the unauthorized population, see Massey, Durand, & Malone, Beyond Smoke and Mirrors, supra note 54, at 128–133; Cornelius, Controlling "Unwanted" Immigration, supra note 76, at 782; Belinda I. Reyes, U.S. Immigration and Policy and the Duration of Undocumented Trips, in Crossing the Border: Research from the Mexican Migration Project, 299, 310–319 (Jorge Durand & Douglas S. Massey eds., Russell Sage Found. 2004).

99. See Michael Hoefer, Nancy Rytina, & Bryan C. Baker, Estimates of the Unauthorized Immigrant Population Residing in the United States: January 2011, at 1 (Dept. of Homeland Sec. 2012); Jeffrey S. Passel, D'Vera Cohn, & Ana Gonzales-Barrera, Population Decline of Unauthorized Immigrants Stalls, May Have Reversed: New Estimate 11.7 Million in 2012, at 9 (Pew Hispanic Ctr. 2013); Robert Warren & John Robert Warren, Unauthorized Immigration to the United States: Annual Estimates and Components of Change, by State, 1990 to 2010, 47 Int'l Migr. Rev. 296, 298 (2013); Ruth Ellen Wasem, Unauthorized Aliens Residing in the United States: Estimates Since 1986, at 3 (Cong. Research

Serv. 2012). On the relationship between migration from Mexico to the United States and economic and demographic trends, see Meissner, Kerwin, Chishti, & Bergeron, Immigration Enforcement, supra note 81, at 142–143. On opportunities in Mexico and diminishing emigration, see Francisco Alba, Mexico: The New Migration Narrative (Migration Policy Inst. 2013); Damien Cave, Better Lives for Mexicans Cut Allure of Going North, N.Y. Times, July 6, 2011; Damien Cave, In Mexican Villages, Few Are Left to Dream of U.S., N.Y. Times, Apr. 2, 2013, at A1.

100. On the political aspects of voting for fences, see Pratheepan Gulasekaram, Why a Wall?, 2 U.C. Irvine L. Rev. 147, 149, 173–176 (2012); Martin, Eight Myths, supra note 98, at 545. On the entrenchment of the idea that robust border enforcement is essential, see John D. Skrentny & Micah Gell-Redman, Comprehensive Immigration Reform and the Dynamics of Statutory Entrenchment, 120 Yale L.J. Online 325, 333–337 (2011). On border enforcement generally, see Dear, Why Walls Won't Work, supra note 41, at 107–125; Dauvergne, Making People Illegal, supra note 92, at 157, 162–163; Kamal Sadiq, Paper Citizens: How Illegal Immigrants Acquire Citizenship in Developing Countries, 192 (Oxford Univ. Press 2009); Massey, Durand, & Malone, Beyond Smoke and Mirrors, supra note 54, at 45–47, 84–98; Peter Andreas, Border Games: Policing the U.S.-Mexico Divide, 85–87, 89–96, 106–12 (Cornell Univ. Press 2000); Calavita, Immigrants at the Margins, supra note 60; Nevins, Operation Gatekeeper, supra note 38, at 8; Cornelius, Controlling "Unwanted" Immigration, supra note 76, at 789; Gloria Valencia-Weber & Antoinette Sedillo Lopez, Stories in Mexico and the United States about the Border: The Rhetoric and the Realities, 5 Intercultural Hum. Rts. L. Rev. 241, 253–272 (2010); Daniel Ibsen Morales, In Democracy's Shadow: Fences, Raids, and the Production of Migrant Illegality, 5 Stan. J. C.R. & C.L. 23, 26 (2009); Mary Fan, When Deterrence and Death Mitigation Fall Short: Fantasy and Fetishes as Gap-Fillers in Border Regulation, 42 L. & Soc'y Rev. 701 (2008); Bill Ong Hing, The Dark Side of Operation Gatekeeper, 7 U.C. Davis J. Int'l L. & Pol'y 121 (2001).

On costs, see Brian Bennett, A Border Spending Surge: Security Measures in the Immigration Bill Would Be a Boon for Private Companies and Border States, L.A. Times, July 8, 2013, at 1; US Government Accountability Office, Secure Border Initiative Fence Constructions Costs (2009); Denise Gilman, Obstructing Human Rights: The Texas-Mexico Border Wall, 12 (Working Group on Human Rights and the Borderwall 2008); Julia Preston, Some Cheer Border Fence as Others Ponder Cost, N.Y. Times, Oct. 20, 2011, at A17; Chad C. Haddal et al., Border Security: Barriers along the U.S. International Border, 27–28 (Cong. Research Serv. 2009). In 2011, the federal government dropped a major project to add video cameras, radar, sensors, and other technologies along the border. See Julia Preston, Homeland Security Cancels "Virtual Fence" after $1 Billion Is Spent, N.Y. Times, Jan. 15, 2011, at A11.

101. See Juliet Stumpf, Fitting Punishment, 66 Wash. & Lee L. Rev. 1683, 1684 (2009).

102. See S. 744, § 3101, 113th Cong., 1st Sess. (2013).

103. See Julia Preston, Employers Fight Tough Measures on Immigration, N.Y. Times, July 6, 2008, at A1; Dauvergne, Making People Illegal, supra note 92, at 167; Cuellar, Political Economies, supra note 91, at 25–26; Martin, Eight Myths, supra note 98, at 544–545; Nevins, Operation Gatekeeper, supra note 38, at 13. On the evolution of enforcement strategies, see Aleinikoff, Martin, Motomura, & Fullerton, Immigration and Citizenship, supra note 8, at 921–985. On acquiescence in unauthorized immigration, see also Raquel E. Aldana, The Subordination and Anti-Subordination Story of the US Immigrant Experience in the Twenty-First Century, 7 Nev. L.J. 713, 729–730 (2007).

On dependence on unauthorized workers, see Passel & Cohn, Unauthorized Immigrant Population, supra note 77, at 17; Passel, The Size and Characteristics of the Unauthorized Migrant Population, supra note 30, at 9–14; Cristina M. Rodríguez, Guest Workers and Integration: Toward a Theory of What Immigrants and Americans Owe One Another, 2007 U. Chi. Legal Forum 219, 223; Alejandro I. Canales, Mexican Labour Migration to the United States in the Age of Globalization, 29 J. Ethnic & Migr. Stud. 741, 754–56 (2003).

104. Max Frisch, Überfremdung I, in Schweiz als Heimat? Versuche über 50 Jahre 219, 219 (Suhrkamp Verlag 1991) ("[M]an hat Arbeitskräfte gerufen, und es kommen Menschen.").

105. On the trade-offs, see Cuellar, Political Economies, supra note 91, at 6–7, 15, 21–22, 36–37, 42–44; Skrentny & Gell-Redman, Comprehensive Immigration Reform, supra note 100, at 328–329. On choosing workers, see Cox & Posner, Second-Order, supra note 81, at 844–849. For a response, see Hiroshi Motomura, Choosing Immigrants, Making Citizens, 59 Stan. L. Rev. 857, 869 (2007).

106. For more on remittances and other aspects of unauthorized migration from an international economic development perspective, see Chapter 7 in this volume.

107. On the effects of economic realignment in Mexico starting in the mid-1980s, particularly in making employment more precarious and broadening the emigrant population to the United States to include new regions and social groups, see Canales, Mexican Labour Migration, supra note 103, at 743–747. See generally Bill Ong Hing, Ethical Borders: NAFTA, Globalization, and Mexican Migration (Temple Univ. Press 2010); M. Angeles Villarreal & Marisabel Cid, NAFTA and the Mexican Economy (Cong. Research Serv. 2008).

CHAPTER 2

What State and Local Role?

1. See William Finnegan, Sheriff Joe, 85 New Yorker, Jul. 20, 2009, at 42, 44–45, 51.

2. See Press Release, Arpaio Orders Move of Hundreds of Illegal Aliens to Their Own Tent City, Maricopa County Sheriff's Office, Feb. 3, 2009; Jana Bommersbach, Goldwater's Group Goes after Arpaio, Phoenix Magazine, Sept.

2009, at 26; Sheriff Joe Arpaio Setting up Separate Tent City for Illegals, Phoenix Bus. J., Feb. 3, 2009; Shackling Immigrants in Arpaio's America, Int'l Herald Trib., Feb. 7, 2009, at 6; Sue Anne Pressley, Sheriff's Specialty: Making Jail Miserable; Arizona Lawman Draws Spotlight, Scrutiny with Tent City, Chain Gangs and Posse, Wash. Post, Aug. 25, 1997, at A1.

3. See Joe Arpaio & Len Sherman, Joe's Law: America's Toughest Sheriff Takes on Illegal Immigration, Drugs, and Everything Else That Threatens America (AMACOM 2008). Arpaio later denied writing parts of the book. See Fernanda Santos, Confronted in Court with His Own Words, Sheriff Denies Profiling, N.Y. Times, July 25, 2012, at A11. On the costs of lawsuits, see Corey Rangel & Maria Tomasch, Your Tax Dollars: How Much Does It Cost to Defend the Maricopa County Sheriff's Office?, ABC15.com, May 13, 2011. See also Finnegan, Sheriff Joe, supra note 1, at 45.

On the federal investigation, see U.S. DOJ Civil Rights Division, United States Investigation of the Maricopa County Sheriff's Office Findings Letter, Letter Memorandum from Thomas E. Perez, Assistant US Attorney Gen., to Mr. Bill Montgomery, Cnty. Attorney for Maricopa Cnty., Ariz., Dec. 15, 2011; Marc Lacey, U.S. Says Arizona Sheriff Shows Pervasive Bias Against Latinos, N.Y. Times, Dec. 16, 2011, at A1; Nicholas Ricardi, Grand Jury Investigating Ariz. Sheriff, L.A. Times, Jan. 9, 2010, at A14; Let's Thank Feds for Entering Fray, Ariz. Republic, Jan. 10, 2010, at B10.

On the congressional and grand jury investigations, see J. J. Hensley & Yvonne Wingett, U.S. Grand Jury Examining MCSO, Ariz. Republic, Jan. 8, 2010, at A1; Daniel González & Dan Nowicki, Sheriff Faces a Second Inquiry, Ariz. Republic, Mar. 12, 2009, at 1; Randal Archibold, Lawmakers Want Look at Sheriff in Arizona, N.Y. Times, Feb. 14, 2009, at A12; Michael Kiefer, J. J. Hensley & Yvonne Wingett Sanchez, How Fed's Arpaio Case Unraveled, Ariz. Republic, Sept. 2, 2012, at A1.

4. See Press Release, Department of Justice Files Lawsuit in Arizona Against Maricopa County, Maricopa County Sheriff's Office, and Sheriff Joseph Arpaio, Office of Public Affairs, Department of Justice, May 10, 2012. On the federal government's termination of its agreement with the Maricopa County Sheriff's Office, see Statement by Secretary Napolitano on DOJ's Findings of Discriminatory Policing in Maricopa County, Department of Homeland Security Press Release, Dec. 15, 2011; see also Jeremy Duda, Homeland Security Revokes 287(g) Agreements in Arizona, Ariz. Capitol Times, June 25, 2012. For further developments, see Case Against Sheriff Joe Arpaio Can Move Forward, Assoc. Press, Dec. 13, 2012. The private lawsuit decision is Melendres v. Arpaio, 2013 WL 2297173 (D. Ariz. May 24, 2013); see also Fernanda Santos, Judge Finds Violations of Rights by Sheriff, N.Y. Times, May 24, 2013, at A14.

5. See Finnegan, Sheriff Joe, supra note 1, at 49–51.

6. See A Star Turn for a Sheriff on Fox TV, N.Y. Times, Jan. 5 2009, at B1; Lawmakers Want Look at Sheriff In Arizona, N.Y. Times, Feb. 14, 2009, at A12; Immigration

and the Law: Still Going after Them: America's Toughest Sheriff Is Still Hunting Illegals, Economist, Oct. 24, 2009, at 84.

7. See Ariz. Rev. Stat. Ann. §§ 23–211, 212, 212.01.

8. See Ariz. Rev. Stat. Ann. §§ 23–211, 212, 212.01; Chamber of Commerce v. Whiting, 131 S. Ct. 1968 (2011).

9. S.B. 1070, 49th Leg., 2d Reg. Sess. (Ariz. 2010), as amended by H.B. 2162, 49th Leg., 2d Reg. Sess. (Ariz. 2010). Section 1 continues: "The provisions of this Act are intended to work together to discourage and deter the unlawful entry and presence of aliens and economic activity by persons unlawfully present in the United States." See SB 1070 as amended § 2(H), Ariz. Rev. Stat. Ann. § 11–1051(H).

10. See Arizona v. United States, 132 S. Ct. 2492 (2012); SB 1070 as amended § 2(B), Ariz. Rev. Stat. Ann. § 11–1051(B).

11. See SB 1070 as amended §§ 3, 5, 6, Ariz. Rev. Stat. Ann. §§ 13–2929(A), 13–3883(A) (5)5(C), Ariz. Rev. Stat. Ann. §§ 13–1509(A), 13–2928(C); INA § 274A, 8 U.S.C. § 1324a.

12. See Anna Gorman, A Voice for Tough Immigration Laws, L.A. Times, May 13, 2010, at A1; John Hanna, Kan. Lawyer Is Architect of Many Immigration Laws, San Diego Union-Trib., May 10, 2010; Julia Preston, A Professor Fights Illegal Immigration One Court at a Time, N.Y. Times, July 21, 2009, at A10. On NSEERS, see 67 Fed. Reg. 52584; Thomas Alexander Aleinikoff, David A. Martin, Hiroshi Motomura, & Maryellen Fullerton, Immigration and Citizenship: Process and Policy, 526–528, 1020–1021, 1031–1035 (7th ed. West 2012). On state and local enforcement efforts generally, see S. Karthick Ramakrishnan & Pratheepan Gulasekaram, The Importance of the Political in Immigration Federalism, 44 Ariz. St. L.J. 1431, 1450, 1456–1457, 1475–1476 (2013).

13. On the vetoes, see HB 2807, 48th Leg., 2d Sess. (2008); HB 2577, 47th Leg., 2d Sess. (2006), Randal C. Archibold, Arizona Governor Vetos Bill Aimed at Illegal Immigration, N.Y. Times, June 7, 2006 at A21. On the debate and protests, see Randal C. Archibold, Pre-emption, not Profiling, in Challenge to Arizona, N.Y. Times, July 8, 2010, at A15; Randal C. Archibold, In Border Violence, Perception Is Greater Than Crime Statistics, N.Y. Times, June 20, 2010, at A18. On boosting political support, see Ronald J. Hansen, Politics, Age Sway Opinions on Immigration Law, Ariz. Republic, Jul. 25, 2010, at A18. On the vote count, see State of Arizona Official Canvass, Arizona Secretary of State, 2010 General Election (Nov. 29, 2010).

14. On the intent to fill gaps, see Press Release, Office of the Governor, Statement by Governor Jan Brewer on the signing of Senate Bill 1070, Apr. 23, 2010; Letter from Janet Napolitano, Governor of the State of Ariz., to Hon. Jim Weiers, Speaker of the House, July 2, 2007; see also Peter Skerry, Many Borders to Cross: Is Immigration the Exclusive Responsibility of the Federal Government?, 25 Publius 71, 72–73 (No. 3 1995).

15. See Michael Hoefer, Nancy Rytina, & Bryan C. Baker, Estimates of the Unauthorized Immigrant Population Residing in the United States: January 2011, at 5 & table 4 (Dept. of Homeland Sec. 2012); Jeffrey S. Passel, D'Vera Cohn, & Ana Gonzales-Barrera, Population Decline of Unauthorized Immigrants Stalls, May Have Reversed: New Estimate 11.7 Million in 2012, at 26, table A1 (Pew Hispanic Ctr. 2013); Jeffrey S. Passel & D'Vera Cohn, Unauthorized Immigrant Population: National and State Trends, 2010, at 14 & table 4, 15 & table 5, 17 (Pew Hispanic Ctr. 2011); Robert Warren & John Robert Warren, Unauthorized Immigration to the United States: Annual Estimates and Components of Change, by State, 1990 to 2010, 47 Int'l Migr. Rev. 296, 298, 317 (2013).

16. On the federal-state revenue imbalance, see Natl. Res. Council, The New Americans: Economic, Demographic, & Fiscal Effects of Immigration, 254–296 (James P. Smith & Barry Edmonston eds., Nat'l Acad. Press 1997).

17. See Hoefer, Rytina, & Baker, Estimates of the Unauthorized Immigrant Population, supra note 15, at 3 & table 1, 5 & tables 3, 4. On rapid local growth in immigrant (including unauthorized) population, see Owen Furuseth & Heather A. Smith, Localized Immigration Policy: The View from Charlotte, North Carolina, a New Immigration Gateway, in Taking Local Control: Immigration Policy Activism in U.S. Cities and States, 173 (Monica W. Varsanyi ed., Stanford Univ. Press 2010); Jill H. Wilson, Audrey Singer, & Brooke DeRenzis, Growing Pains: Local Response to Recent Immigrant Settlement in Suburban Washington, DC, in Varsanyi, Taking Local Control, supra, at 193. See also Jeffrey S. Passel & D'Vera Cohn, U.S. Unauthorized Immigration Flows Are Down Sharply since Mid-Decade, 3 (Pew Hispanic Ctr. 2010); U.S. Census Bureau, Place of Birth for the Foreign-Born Population: Census 2000 Summary File, Table North Carolina; Steven A. Camarota & Nora McArdle, Where Immigrants Live: An Examination of State Residency of the Foreign Born by Country of Origin in 1990 and 2000, table 1 (Center for Immigr. Studies 2003).

18. Brief for Petitioners, at 3, Arizona v. United States, 132 S. Ct. 2492 (2012) (No. 11–182).

19. See Ramakrishnan & Gulasekaram, The Importance of the Political, supra note 12, at 1435, 1440, 1467, 1479; S. Karthick Ramakrishnan & Tom Wong, Partisanship, Not Spanish: Explaining Municipal Ordinances Affecting Undocumented Immigrants, in Varsanyi, Taking Local Control, supra note 17, at 73. Ramakrishnan and Gulasekaram contrast their findings with a "demography-based explanation for state and local involvement," for which they cite Cristina Rodríguez, The Significance of the Local in Immigration Regulation, 106 Mich. L. Rev. 567 (2008); Clare Huntington, The Constitutional Dimension of Immigration Federalism, 61 Vand. L. Rev. 787 (2008); Alex Kotlowitz, Our Town, N.Y. Times, Aug. 5, 2007 (Magazine), at 6–30.

20. See Chapter 1 in this volume; Stephanie Marudas, Interview with Douglas Massey: Measuring the Effects of US policy on Latin American Migration

Patterns, Amn. Acad. of Pol. & Soc. Sci. News, July 6, 2010. On San Diego as an anomaly in that it is a predominantly Anglo community in a border area, see Joseph Nevins, Operation Gatekeeper and Beyond: The War on "Illegals" and the Remaking of the US-Mexico Boundary, 95 (Routledge 2010).

21. See H 56, §§ 27(a) 28(a)(1), (d)(3), (d)(4), § 30(b), (d), Beason-Hammon Alabama Taxpayer and Citizen Protection Act, Pub. Act No. 535, 2011 Al. ALS 535 (Ala. 2011); Illegal Immigration Reform and Enforcement Act of 2011 (HB 87), 151st Ga. Gen. Assem. (2011) (codified in scattered sections of Ga. Code Ann. tits. 13, 16, 17, 35, 36, 42, 45, 50); Act of May 5, 2011, Pub. L. No. 171, 2011 Ind. ALS 171 (codified in scattered sections of Ind. Code titles 4, 5, 6, 11, 12, 22, 34, 35); S.B. 20, 2011–2012 Gen. Assem., 119th Sess. (S.C. 2011) (codified in scattered sections of S.C. Code tits. 6, 8, 16, 17, 23, 41); 2011 Utah Laws 18 (H.B. 116) Utah Code Ann. § 63G–12–201 to 212. § 76–9–1003. See also H.B. 488, 2012 Leg., Reg. Sess. (Miss. 2012).

22. See Marc Laccy & Katharine Q. Seelye, Recall Election Claims Arizona Anti-Immigration Champion, N.Y. Times, Nov. 10, 2011, at A22; Jay Reed, Immigration & Alabama's Workforce, Alabama Construction News 4–6 (Oct.–Nov. 2011); Rick Jervis & Alan Gomez, Tough Immigration Law Raises Fears in Alabama, USA Today, Oct. 19, 2011 at A1; Patrik Jonsson, Why Republicans Are Doing an About-face on Tough Alabama Immigration Law, Christian Science Monitor, Nov. 16, 2011; Kate Brumback, Georgia Immigration Law Upsets Restaurants, Farmers, Assoc. Press, Nov. 15, 2011.

23. 36 U.S. (11 Pet.) 102, 132, 141 (1837). See also Gibbons v. Ogden, 22 U.S. (9 Wheat.) 1, 203, 235 (1824). See generally Gerald L. Neuman, The Lost Century of American Immigration Law (1776–1875), 93 Colum. L. Rev. 1833 (1993). See also Kunal Parker, State, Citizenship, and Territory: The Legal Construction of Immigrants in Antebellum Massachusetts, 19 Law & Hist. Rev. 583 (2001).

24. Act of Feb. 28, 1803, ch. 10, 2 Stat. 205, 205; Act of Mar. 2, 1819, ch. 46, 3 Stat. 488, 488; Act of Feb. 19, 1862, ch. 27, 12 Stat. 340, 340.

25. Homestead Act of 1862, ch. 75, 12 Stat. 392, 392 (repealed 1976); see also Aziz Rana, The Two Faces of American Freedom (Harvard Univ. Press 2010); Kerry Abrams, The Hidden Dimension of Nineteenth-Century Immigration Law, 62 Vand. L. Rev. 1353, 1401 (2009). On settlement, see also Chapter 1 in this volume. On declarations of intent and the favored treatment of intending citizens, see also Chapter 3 in this volume.

26. See Neuman, Lost Century, supra note 23, at 1835–84; Aristide R. Zolberg, A Nation by Design: Immigration Policy in the Fashioning of America, 74–76 (Harvard Univ. Press 2006). See also Mary Sarah Bilder, The Struggle over Immigration: Indentured Servants, Slaves, and Articles of Commerce, 61 Mo. L. Rev. 743, 793–798 (1996); Gabriel J. Chin, Regulating Race: Asian Exclusion and the Administrative State, 37 Harv. C.R.–C.L. L. Rev. 1, 12 (2002); James W. Fox, Jr., Citizenship, Poverty, and Federalism: 1787–1882, 60 U. Pitt. L. Rev. 421, 559–565 (1999).

27. See Chapter 1 in this volume. See also Abrams, Hidden Dimension, supra note 25, at 1406–1408.

28. See Abrams, Hidden Dimension, supra note 25, at 1363, 1401, 1410–1411.

29. See Hiroshi Motomura, Americans in Waiting: The Lost Story of Immigration and Citizenship in the United States, 21–25 (Oxford Univ. Press 2006).

30. 60 U.S. 393 (1857). See Peter H. Schuck & Rogers M. Smith, Citizenship without Consent: Illegal Aliens in the American Polity, 66–76 (Yale Univ. Press 1985); Rogers M. Smith, Civic Ideals: Conflicting Visions of Citizenship in U.S. History, 253–71 (Yale Univ. Press 1997). See also Chapter 3 in this volume.

31. On the children of diplomats, see 8 C.F.R. §101.3(a)(1).

32. See Act of Mar. 3, 1875, ch. 141, §§ 3, 5, 18 Stat. 477, 477; Act of Aug. 3, 1882, ch. 376, § 2, 22 Stat. 214, 214; Act of Feb. 26, 1885, ch. 164, § 1, 23 Stat. 332, 332; Act of Mar. 3, 1891, ch. 551, § 1, 26 Stat. 1084, 1084. On the national origins system, see Chapter 1 in this volume.

33. See Smith v. Turner (Passenger Cases), 48 U.S. (7 How.) 283, 409, 410–12, 447, 463–464 (1849), invalidating Act of Apr. 20, 1837, ch. 238, §§ 2,3, 1837 Mass. Laws 270, 270; Act of Mar. 30, 1798, ch. 67, § 5, 1797 N.Y. Laws 93, 94.

34. Henderson v. Mayor of the City of New York, 92 U.S. 259, 270, 275 (1876).

35. See Chy Lung v. Freeman, 92 U.S. 275, 279–281 (1876).

36. The State of New York imposed international quarantines until 1921. See Compagnie Francaise de Navigation a Vapeur v. Louisiana State Bd. of Health, 186 U.S. 380, 387 (1902); Morgan's S.S. Co. v. Louisiana Bd. of Health, 118 U.S. 455, 465–466 (1886). On the state role in naturalization, see Act of Mar. 26, 1790, ch. 3, § 1, 1 Stat. 103. See also Charles Gordon, Stanley Mailman, Stephen Yale-Loehr, & Ronald Y. Wada, Immigration Law and Procedure § 94.01[2][c] (2013); Nancy Morawetz, Citizenship and the Courts, 2007 U. Chi. Legal F. 447, 452.

37. For a California state precursor to the Page Act, see Act of Mar. 18, 1870, ch. 230, 1870 Cal. Stat. 330, 330–331, "An Act to prevent the kidnapping and importation of Mongolian, Chinese, and Japanese females, for criminal or demoralizing Purposes." See Abrams, Hidden Dimension, supra note 25, at 1395–1396. On the 1906 statute, see Gordon, Mailman, Yale-Loehr, & Wada, Immigration Law and Procedure, supra note 36, at § 94.01[2][c] (2013). On the chain of events from state anti-Chinese laws to federal Chinese exclusion, see Motomura, Americans in Waiting, supra note 29, at 21–26.

38. See Plyler v. Doe, 457 U.S. 202, 215–216, 225 (1982); 457 U.S. at 237–238 n.1 (Powell, J., concurring).

39. See Legislative Analyst's Office, The California Economy (1995).

40. See Illegal Aliens, Ineligibility for Public Services, Verification and Reporting, Proposition 187, §§ 2, 3, 4, 5, 6, 7, 8. There were an estimated 1.47 million unauthorized migrants in California in 1990, and 2.05 million in 1995. See Warren & Warren, Unauthorized Immigration to the United States, supra note 15, at 317, table S3; Office of Policy and Planning, U.S. Immigration and Naturalization

Service, Estimates of the Unauthorized Immigrant Population Residing in the United States: 1990–2000, at 8 (2003).

41. On self-deportation, see Janet Boss & Carol Kasel, Proposition 187 Feedback and Fallout, Rocky Mountain News, Nov. 21, 1994, at 3N; Angela M. Banks, The Curious Relationship Between "Self–Deportation" Policies and Naturalization Rates, 16 Lewis & Clark L. Rev. 1149 (2012). On the effects on the Republican Party, see Adam Nagourney, In California, G.O.P. Fights Steep Decline, N.Y. Times, July 22, 2012, at A1; John M. Broder, California Republican Party Finds Itself Deep in Pit, N.Y. Times, Sept. 17, 2002, at A22.

42. See League of United Latin Am. Citizens v. Wilson, 908 F. Supp. 755 (C.D. Cal. 1995).

43. On the national significance of state efforts, see Ramakrishnan & Gulasekaram, The Importance of the Political, supra note 12, at 1435, 1445; Nevins, Operation Gatekeeper, supra note 20, at 87. On the states' lawsuits, Bill Stall & Patrick J. McDonnell, Wilson Urges Stiff Penalties to Deter Illegal Immigrants, L.A. Times, Aug. 10, 1993, at A1; California v. United States, 104 F.3d 1086, 1090–1091 (9th Cir. 1997), cert. denied, 522 U.S. 806 (1997); Arizona v. United States, 104 F.3d 1095 (9th Cir.), cert. denied, 522 U.S. 806 (1997); New Jersey v. United States, 91 F.3d 463, 468–469 (3d Cir. 1996); Padavan v. United States, 82 F.3d 23, 28 (2d Cir. 1996); Chiles v. United States, 69 F.3d 1094, 1097 (11th Cir. 1995), cert. denied, 517 U.S. 1188 (1996). See also Zolberg, A Nation by Design, supra note 26, at 403–404; Tony Perry, State's Immigration Suit Against U.S. Dismissed: Courts: Wilson Vows to Continue Fight to Have Federal Government Cover Costs of Dealing with Illegal Aliens, L.A. Times Feb. 14, 1995, at 3; California Sues U.S. Government Over Costs Tied to Illegal Aliens, N.Y. Times, May 1, 1994, at A24.

44. On stiffer border enforcement, see Chapter 1 in this volume.

45. See Pub. L. No. 104–132, 110 Stat. 1214; Pub. L. No. 104–208, 110 Stat. 3009; INA § 235(b)(1), 8 U.S.C. § 1225(b)(1) (expedited removal); INA § 236(c), 8 U.S.C. § 1226(c) (mandatory detention); INA § 238(b), 8 U.S.C. § 1228(b) (administrative removal); INA § 240A, 8 U.S.C. § 1229b (cancellation of removal); INA § 241(a)(5), 8 U.S.C. § 1231(a)(5) (reinstatement of removal); INA § 242(a)(2), 8 U.S.C. § 1252(a)(2) (limits on judicial review).

46. See Personal Responsibility and Work Opportunity Reconciliation Act of 1996, § 411(d), Pub. L. No. 104–193, 110 Stat. 2105 (1996), 8 U.S.C. § 1621(d); Ruth Ellen Wasem, Noncitizen Eligibility for Federal Public Assistance: Policy Overview and Trends, 1–2 (Cong. Research Serv. 2012).

47. On the fate of Proposition 187, see League of United Latin American Citizens v. Wilson, 997 F. Supp. 1244, 1261 (C.D. Cal. 1997); Michael A. Olivas, No Undocumented Child Left Behind: *Plyler v. Doe* and the Education of Undocumented Schoolchildren, 41–42 (N.Y.U. Press 2012); Patrick J. McDonnell, Prop. 187 Talks Offered Davis Few Choices, L.A. Times, July 30, 1999, at A3.

48. See Proposition 200, 2004 Ballot Propositions, Arizona Secretary of State, §§ 3, 4, 6; Richard Marosi, Arizona Stirs Up Immigration Stew, L.A. Times, Nov. 6, 2004, at A11; Charlie LeDuff, Immigration Measure Taps Frustrations in Arizona, N.Y. Times, Oct. 26, 2004, at A14; Richard Marosi, Decade Later, Prop. 187 Has an Echo in Arizona, L.A. Times, Oct. 23, 2004, at A1. The voting requirements were upheld in part and struck down in part in Gonzales v. Arizona, 677 F.3d 383 (9th Cir.) (en banc), aff'd sub nom. Arizona v. Inter Tribal Council of Arizona, Inc., 133 S.Ct. 2247 (2013).

49. See James Sterngold, San Bernardino Seeking "Relief," S.F. Chron., June 11, 2006, at A4; Cindy Chang, California City Council Rejects Anti-Immigration Legislation, N.Y. Times, May 16, 2006, at A21. On the proposal's influence, see Editorial, Hazy Days of Immigration, N.Y. Times, July 20, 2006, at A20; Ashley Powers, Law Aimed at Migrants Faces Hurdle, L.A. Times, June 27, 2006, at B3.

50. Hazleton, Pa., Illegal Immigration Relief Act Ordinance §§ 2C, 2F, Ordinance 2006–18 (Sept. 12, 2006). See generally Lozano v. City of Hazleton, 496 F. Supp. 2d 477, 484 (M.D. Pa. 2007), aff'd, 620 F.3d 170 (3d Cir. 2010), vacated, 131 S. Ct. 2958 (2011), on remand, 724 F.3d 297 (3d Cir. 2013); Matt Birkbeck, No Data on Immigrants, Mayor Admits: Hazleton's Lou Barletta Testifies on City's Ordinance on Illegals, Allentown Morning Call, Mar. 15, 2007, at A1; Tom Brune, Laying Down the Law: Hazleton, Pa., Says Yes to a Law Banning Illegal Workers, Newsday, July 18, 2006, at A19; Benjamin Fleury-Steiner & Jamie Longazel, Neoliberalism, Community Development, and Anti-Immigrant Backlash in Hazleton, Pennsylvania, in Varsanyi, Taking Local Control, supra note 17, at 157; Jill Esbenshade, Benjamin Wright, Paul Cortopassi, Arthur Reed, & Jerry Flores, The "Law and Order" Foundation of Local Ordinances: A Four-Locale Study of Hazleton, PA, Escondido, CA, Farmers Branch, TX, and Prince William County VA, in Varsanyi, Taking Local Control, supra note 17, at 255.

51. See Hazleton Illegal Immigration Relief Act Ordinance, supra note 50, § 4E; Lozano v. City of Hazleton, 496 F. Supp. 2d at 484.

52. See Villas at Parkside Partners v. City of Farmers Branch, 701 F. Supp. 2d 835, 835–841 N.D. Tex. 2010), aff'd, 675 F.3d 802 (5th Cir. 2012), rehearing en banc granted, 688 F.3d 801 (5th Cir. 2012); Garrett v. City of Escondido, 465 F. Supp. 2d 1043, 1047–1048 (S.D. Cal. 2006); Escondido, Cal., Ordinance No. 2006–38 R (Oct. 18, 2006); Valley Park, Mo., Ordinances 1721 (housing) (repealed) and 1722 (employment) (Feb. 5, 2007); Gray v. City of Valley Park, 567 F.2d 976, 979–980 (8th Cir. 2009); Riverside, N.J., Illegal Immigration Relief Act, Ordinance 2006–16 (July 26, 2006), later rescinded, see Ken Belson & Jill P. Capuzzo, Towns Rethink Laws Against Illegal Immigrants, N.Y. Times, Sept. 26, 2007, at A1. See also Comite de Jornaleros v. City of Redondo Beach, 657 F.3d 936 (9th Cir. 2011), cert. denied, 132 S. Ct. 1566 (2012). See generally Esbenshade, Wright, Cortopassi, Reed, & Flores, Law and Order Foundation, supra note 50; Cristina Rodríguez, Muzaffar Chishti,

& Kimberly Nortman, Testing the Limits: A Framework for Assessing the Legality of State and Local Immigration Measures, 30 (Migration Policy Inst. 2007); Jill Esbenshade, Division and Dislocation: Regulating Immigration Through Local Housing Ordinances, 3 (Am. Immigr. Law Found. 2007). David Bacon, Illegal People: How Globalization Creates Migration and Criminalizes Immigrants, 128 (Beacon Press 2008); Kristina M. Campbell, The High Cost of Free Speech: Anti-Solicitation Ordinances, Day Laborers, and the Impact of "Backdoor" Local Immigration Regulations, 25 Geo. Immigr. L.J. 1 (2010); Monica W. Varsanyi, City Ordinances as "Immigration Policing by Proxy": Local Governments and the Regulation of Undocumented Day Laborers, in Varsanyi, Taking Local Control, supra note 17, at 135; Michael S. Danielson, All Immigration Politics is Local: The Day Laborer Ordinance in Vista, California, in Varsanyi, Taking Local Control, supra note 17, at 239. For arguments for attrition, see Kris W. Kobach, Attrition Through Enforcement: A Rational Approach to Illegal Immigration, 15 Tulsa J. Comp. & Int'l L. 155, 160 (2008); Mark Krikorian, Downsizing Illegal Immigration: A Strategy of Attrition Through Enforcement, Backgrounder, 1, 1–6 (Center for Immigr. Studies 2005).

53. See Careen Shannon, Regulating Immigration at the State Level: A Focus on Employment, 3 Albany Gov't L. Rev. 218, 223–225 (2010); Marc R. Rosenblum & Leo B. Gorman, The Public Policy Implications of State-Level Worksite Migration Enforcement: The Experiences of Arizona, Mississippi, and Illinois, in Varsanyi, Taking Local Control, supra note 17, at 115. See Ariz. Rev. Stat. Ann. §§ 23–211, 212, 212.01; Okl. Stat. Ann. § 25–1313; See Miss. Code Ann. § 71–11–3 (Mississippi Employment Protection Act) (making it a felony for any person to accept or perform work knowing or in reckless disregard of the fact that individual is not authorized to work under federal immigration law). See Beason-Hammon Alabama Taxpayer and Citizen Protection Act, Pub. Act No. 535, 2011 Al. ALS 535 (Ala. 2011); Utah St. § 63G–12–301 to 212.

54. On admissions, see Michael A. Olivas, Dreams Deferred: Deferred Action, Prosecutorial Discretion, and the Vexing Case(s) of DREAM Act Students, 21 Wm. & Mary Bill Rts. J. 463, 470–471 & table 2 (2012); Robbie Brown, Five Public Colleges in Georgia Ban Illegal-Immigrant Students, N.Y. Times, Oct. 14, 2010, at A30; Julianne Hing, Georgia's Statewide Undocumented Students College Ban Fails, Colorlines, Mar. 30, 2012. On tuition, see Olivas, Dreams Deferred, supra, at 470–471 & table 2 (citing Ariz. Rev. Stat. Ann. § 15-1803; Colo. Rev. Stat. Ann. § 24-76.5-103; Ga. Code Ann. § 20-3-66(d); Ind. Code Ann. § 21-14-11; O.R.C. 3333.31(D), (E); University of North Carolina Board of Governors 700.1.4[G]). An exception is California, see later in this chapter. For a thorough overview, see Olivas, Dreams Deferred, supra, at 464–471.

55. See REAL ID Act of 2005, Pub. L. No. 109–13, 119 Stat. 302, 311–312 (codified at 49 U.S.C.A. § 30301 (West 2008); Final Report of the National Commission on Terrorist Attacks Upon the United States 384 (2004); see also Charlie

Savage, Some Fear Law Would Create a National ID Card, Boston Globe, Apr. 26, 2005, at A1. States that did not require proof of lawful immigration status included Maryland, North Carolina, and Tennessee. See generally Maria Pabón López, More Than a License to Drive: State Restrictions on the Use of Driver's Licenses, 29 S. Ill. U.L.J. 91 (2004); Hinda Seif, "Tired of Illegals": Immigrant Driver's Licenses, Constituent Letters, and Shifting Restrictionist Discourse in California, in Varsanyi, Taking Local Control, supra note 17, at 275; Yilu Zhao, Illegal Aliens Travel to Other States for Driver's License, N.Y. Times, Mar. 2, 2003, at 14 WC–5.

56. See Gonzales v. City of Peoria, 722 F.2d 468, 475 (9th Cir. 1983); INA §§ 274, 275, 276, 8 U.S.C. §§ 1324, 1325, 1326.

57. See U.S. Census Bureau, State & County QuickFacts, http://quickfacts.census.gov/qfd/states/04/0454050.html; U.S. Census Bureau, 1980 Census of Population, Characteristics of Population, Number of Inhabitants Arizona 4–12, table 5; Gonzales v. City of Peoria, 537 F. Supp. 793, 794 (D. Ariz. 1982), aff'd, 722 F.2d 468 (9th Cir. 1983), overruled in part on other grounds by Hodgers-Durgin v. De La Vina, 199 F.3d 1037 (9th Cir. 1999).

58. See Gonzales v. City of Peoria, 722 F.2d at 472, 478–479.

59. See 722 F.2d at 474–476. See also Ker v. California, 374 U.S. 23, 31 (1963); Miller v. United States, 357 U.S. 301, 305 (1958); Johnson v. United States, 333 U.S. 10, 15 & n.5 (1948); United States v. DiRe, 332 U.S. 581, 589 (1948). See also United States v. Bowdach, 561 F.2d 1160, 1168 (5th Cir. 1977). The court was careful to observe that the US Constitution requires probable cause for an arrest, and that Arizona law allows law enforcement officers to make misdemeanor arrests based on probable cause. 722 F.2d at 476–477; see also US Const. Amends. IV, XIV; 42 U.S.C. § 1983.

60. See INA §§ 212(a)(6)(A)(i), 237(a)(1)(B)–(C), 8 U.S.C. §§ 1182(a)(6)(A)(i), 1227(a)(1)(B)–(C). Deportability grounds, set forth in INA § 237(a), 8 U.S.C. § 1227(a), apply only to noncitizens who have been admitted. See generally Aleinikoff, Martin, Motomura, & Fullerton, Immigration and Citizenship, supra note 12, at 583–584. See also INA § 266, 8 U.S.C. § 1306 (making willful failure to register as an alien a federal misdemeanor). On overstayers, see Ruth Ellen Wasem, Nonimmigrant Overstays: Brief Synthesis of the Issue (Cong. Research Serv. 2010); David A. Martin, Eight Myths about Immigration Enforcement, 10 N.Y.U. J. Legis. & Pub. Pol'y 525, 544 (2007); Modes of Entry for the Unauthorized Migrant Population, 3 (Pew Hispanic Ctr. 2006).

61. See United States v. Watson, 423 U.S. 411, 417, 96 S. Ct. 820, 824–825, 46 L.Ed.2d 598 (1976) (probable cause); Terry v. Ohio, 392 U.S. 1, 19, n.16, 88 S. Ct. 1868, 1879 n.16, 20 L.Ed.2d 889 (1968). United States v. Arvizu, 534 U.S. 266, 273, 122 S. Ct. 744, 750, 151 L.Ed.2d 740 (2002). See generally Aleinikoff, Martin, Motomura, & Fullerton, Immigration and Citizenship, supra note 12, at 995–996. On how the connections between criminal law and immigration law affect state and local immigration authority, see Ingrid V. Eagly, Criminal Justice for Noncitizens: An

Analysis of Variation in Local Enforcement, 88 N.Y.U. L. Rev. 1126 (2013); Juliet P. Stumpf, States of Confusion: The Rise of State and Local Power Over Immigration, 86 North Carolina L. Rev. 1557, 1600–1615 (2008).

62. Compare Assistance by State & Local Police in Apprehending Illegal Aliens, 20 Op. Off. Legal Counsel 26, 32 (1996) with Non–Preemption of the Auth. of State & Local Law Enforcement Officials to Arrest Aliens for Immigr. Violations, 26 Op. Off. Legal Counsel 1, 1–2 (2002). See also United States v. Santana–Garcia, 264 F.3d 1188, 1193 (10th Cir. 2001); United States v. Vasquez–Alvarez. 176 F.3d 1294, 1296–97 (10th Cir. 1999); United States v. Salinas–Calderon, 728 F.2d 1298, 1301–02 & n.3 (10th Cir. 1984). On Kris Kobach's role, see Eric Schmitt, Administration Split on Local Role in Terror Fight, N.Y. Times, Apr. 29, 2002, at A1; Ramakrishnan & Gulasekaram, The Importance of the Political, supra note 12, at 1456 n.87. See generally Aleinikoff, Martin, Motomura, & Fullerton, Immigration and Citizenship, supra note 12, at 1078–1086; Michael John Garcia & Kate M. Manuel, Authority of State and Local Police to Enforce Federal Immigration Law (Cong. Research Serv. 2012).

63. See generally Jennifer Chacón, A Diversion of Attention? Immigration Courts and the Adjudication of Fourth and Fifth Amendment Rights, 59 Duke L.J. 1563, 1586–1598 (2010).

64. See Andrea Guttin, The Criminal Alien Program: Immigration Enforcement in Travis County, Texas, 4 (Immigration Policy Center Feb 2010); Fact Sheet: Criminal Alien Program, U.S. Immigr. & Customs Enforcement (Mar. 29, 2011), available at http://www.ice.gov/news/library/factsheets/cap.htm. For a critical examination of CAP's operation in one Texas city, see Trevor Gardner II & Aarti Kohli, The C.A.P. Effect: Racial Profiling in the ICE Criminal Alien Program (Warren Inst. 2009).

65. See INA § 287(g), 8 U.S.C. § 1357(g). See also INA § 103(a)(10), 8 U.S.C. § 1103(a)(10); U.S. Immigration & Customs Enforcement, Delegation of Immigration Authority Section 287(g) (2008); Office of the Inspector General, The Performance of 287(g) Agreements 83–85 (Dept. of Homeland Sec. 2010). See generally Randy Capps, Marc R. Rosenblum, Cristina Rodríguez, & Muzaffar Chishti, Delegation and Divergence: A Study of 287(g) State and Local Immigration Enforcement, 21 (Migration Policy Inst. 2011); Aleinikoff, Martin, Motomura, & Fullerton, Immigration and Citizenship, supra note 12, at 946, 1076–1077; Lisa M. Seghetti, Karma Ester, & Michael John Garcia, Enforcing Immigration Law: The Role of State and Local Law Enforcement, 17–21 (Cong. Research Serv. 2009). On the phase-out, see News Release, FY 2012: ICE Announces Year-End Removal Numbers, Highlights Focus on Key Priorities and Issues New National Detainer Guidance to Further Focus Resources, U.S. Immigr. & Customs Enforcement, Dec. 21, 2012.

66. See Homeland Security Advisory Council, Task Force on Secure Communities: Findings and Recommendations, 7 (Dept. of Homeland Sec.

2011); Activated Jurisdictions, Department of Homeland Security, Aug. 22, 2012; Task Force on Secure Communities: Findings and Recommendation (Dept. of Homeland Sec. 2012); see also Adam B. Cox & Thomas J. Miles, Policing Immigration, 80 U. Chi. L. Rev. 87, 88, 96–97 (2013).

67. See 8 U.S.C. § 1373(a). It was upheld against constitutional challenge in City of New York v. United States, 179 F.3d 29 (2d Cir. 1999). For more on this part of § 1373, see later in this chapter. See Fact Sheet: Law Enforcement Support Center, Dept. of Homeland Sec., May 29, 2012.

68. See La. Rev. Stat. Ann. § 14:100.13(C); S.C. Code Ann. § 16–23–530(A), (C).

69. See earlier in this chapter.

70. See generally Pablo A. Mitnik & Jessican Halpern-Finnerty, Immigration and Local Governments: Inclusionary Local Policies in the Era of State Rescaling, in Varsanyi, Taking Local Control, supra note 17, at 51; Pratheepan Gulasekaram & Rose Cuison Villazor, Sanctuary Policies & Immigration Federalism: A Dialectic Analysis, 55 Wayne L. Rev. 1683 (2009); Seghetti, Ester, & Garcia, Enforcing Immigration Law, supra note 65; Rose Cuison Villazor, What Is a "Sanctuary"?, 61 SMU L. Rev. 133, 142–143, 148–149, 151–154 (2008); Hiroshi Motomura, Immigration Outside the Law, 108 Colum. L. Rev. 2037, 2075–2083 (2008); Department of Justice, Office of the Inspector General, Audit Division, "Cooperation Of SCAAP Recipients in the Removal of Criminal Aliens From The United States"(redacted public version 2007); Rodríguez, The Significance of the Local, supra note 19, at 600–605; Huyen Pham, The Constitutional Right Not to Cooperate? Local Sovereignty and the Federal Immigration Power, 74 U. Cin. L. Rev. 1373 (2006); Orde F. Kittrie, Federalism, Deportation, and Crime Victims Afraid to Call the Police, 91 Iowa L. Rev. 1449, 1466–1475 (2006); Peter H. Schuck & John Williams, Removing Criminal Aliens: The Pitfalls and Promises of Federalism, 22 Harv. J.L. & Pub. Pol'y 367, 459 (1999). On the residence of the foreign-born, see Mitnik & Halpern-Finnerty, Immigration and Local Governments, supra, at 54.

71. See Special Order No. 40 (Nov. 27, 1979), available at www.lapdonline.org/get_informed/pdf_view/44798; San Francisco Bd. of Supervisors Res. 1087–1085 (Dec. 23, 1985); San Francisco Admin. Code, ch. 12H.1, 12H.2 (Oct. 24, 1989). See generally Rose Cuison Villazor, "Sanctuary Cities" and Local Citizenship, 37 Fordham Urb. L.J. 573, 583–589 (2010). On sanctuary for Salvadorans and Guatemalans, see Villazor, What Is a "Sanctuary"?, supra note 70, at 139–143.

72. See 8 U.S.C. § 1373(c); Seattle Mun. Code § 4.18.015(A) (2003). See Or. Rev. Stat. § 181.850 (originally adopted in 1987) (providing that no Oregon law enforcement agency "shall use agency moneys, equipment or personnel for the purpose of detecting or apprehending persons whose only violation of law is that they are persons of foreign citizenship present in the United States in violation of federal immigration laws"); Legis. Resolve 27, 23d Leg., 1st Sess., 2003 Alaska Sess. Laws at LR 27 (a state agency or instrumentality may not "use state resources or institutions

for the enforcement of federal immigration matters, which are the responsibility of the federal government"). Compare New Mexico Governor Orders State Law-Enforcement Officers to Inquire about Arrestees' Immigration Status, 88 Interpreter Releases 493 (2011) (rescinding a 2005 Executive Order barring state law enforcement officers from inquiring about a person's immigration status solely to determine whether the person is violating federal civil immigration law).

73. Teresa Watanabe, Beck Affirms Rule about Immigrants, L.A. Times, Dec. 20, 2009, at A41; Seattle Ordinance No. 121063 (Feb. 7, 2003). See also Michele Waslin, Immigration Enforcement by State and Local Police: The Impact on the Enforcers and Their Communities, in Varsanyi, Taking Local Control, supra note 17, at 97, 106–107; Kittrie, Federalism, Deportation, supra note 70, at 1475–1477, 1480–1484.

74. For exceptions allowing enforcement cooperation, see San Francisco Admin. Code, ch. 12H.2–1; Seattle Mun. Code § 4.18.015(B) (2003). On the political pressure on state and localities to engage in immigration enforcement against serious criminal offenders in spite of a general non-inquiry policy, see Jesse McKinley, San Francisco at Crossroads over Immigration, N.Y. Times, June 13, 2009, at A12; Rachel Gordon, Stance on Illegal Youths Is Revised, S.F. Chron. May 11, 2011, at A1; Villazor, "Sanctuary Cities" and Local Citizenship, supra note 71, at 585–589. For state laws barring limits on enforcement cooperation, see e.g., S.B. 1070, 49th Leg., 2d Reg. Sess. § 2A (Ariz. 2010). On limits on state restrictions on E-Verify, see United States v. Illinois, 2009 WL 662703 (Mar. 12, 2009). For state laws limiting the ability of local efforts to shield noncitizens from federal immigration enforcement, see, e.g., Beason-Hammon Alabama Taxpayer and Citizens Protection Act, § 5(a), Pub. Act. No. 535, 2011 Al. ALS 535 (Ala. 2011); Ga. St. § 36–80–23(b).

75. See, e.g., Michele Waslin, The Secure Communities Program: Unanswered Questions and Continuing Concerns, 12–16 (Immigr. Policy Ctr. 2010).

76. On the Tenth Amendment and commandeering, see generally United States v. Printz, 521 U.S. 898, 919–933 (1997); New York v. United States, 505 U.S. 144, 155–183 (1992). For policies limiting immigration detainers, see California TRUST Act, A.B. 4, Cal. Govt. Code §§ 7282, 7282.5; New York City Admin. Code 1, §§ 9–131,14–154; Bd. of Supervisors of the Cnty. of Santa Clara, State of California, Board of Supervisors' Policy Manual § 3.54, Civil Immigration Detainer Requests; Cook County Ordinance § 46–37(a); Chicago Municipal Code §§ 2–173–05, 2–173–042; N.Y. City Administrative Code § 9–131; City of Berkeley, California Council, Regular Meeting Annotated Agenda (Oct. 30, 2012); D.C. Acts 19–442, Immigration Detainer Compliance Amendment Act of 2012.

77. On tuition, see Tex. Educ. Code Ann. § 54.052; Cal. Educ. Code § 68130.5; Utah Code Ann. § 53B-8-106; N.Y. Educ. Law § 355(2)(h)(8); Wash. Rev. Code Ann. § 28B.15.012; Okla. Stat. Ann. tit. 70, § 3242; 110 Ill. Comp. Stat. Ann. 305/7e-5; Kan. Stat. Ann. § 76-731a; N.M. Stat. Ann. §21-1-4(g); Neb. Rev. Stat. Ann. § 85-502; Md. Code. Ann. Educ. § 15-106.8; Conn. Gen. Stat. § 10a-29; S. 5.0, R.I.

Board of Governors for Higher Education, September 26, 2011; Ore. H.B. 2787 (2013), Ore. Laws 2013, c. 17, § 4; Colorado S.B. 33, Colo. Laws 2013, ch. 156, § 1, codified at Colo. Rev. Stat. 23–7–110. For overviews, see Olivas, Dreams Deferred, supra note 54, at 470–471 & table 2. See also Laws & Policies Improving Access to Higher Education for Immigrants (Nat'l Immigr. L. Ctr. 2013). On court challenges to AB 540 and similar provisions, see Chapter 5 in this volume. The California DREAM Act is Cal. Educ. Code §§ 66021.6, 66021.7, 68130.7, 69508.5, 76300.5.

78. See generally Doug McIntyre, Editorial: Time for Straight Talk on the Facts, Daily News, Feb. 12, 2012, at A1; Monica W. Varsanyi, Documenting Undocumented Migrants: The *Matrículas Consulares* as Neoliberal Local Membership, 12 Geopolitics 299, 304–307, 311–312 (2007); Andorra Bruno & K. Larry Storrs, Consular Identification Cards: Domestic and Foreign Policy Implications, the Mexican Case, and Related Legislation, 1–4 (Cong. Research Serv. 2005); Monica Rohr, More Countries Offering Emigrant ID Cards: "Matrícula Consular" Popular, Controversial, Boston Globe, Nov. 10, 2003, at A2; Jennifer Mena, Conferring Legitimacy, This Card Draws a Crowd, L.A. Times, Sept. 27, 2004, at B3; "Matrícula" Debate Rages Quietly: Secrecy, Security Fears Cloak Administration Debate on Mexican ID, Dallas Morning News, Jul. 7, 2003, at 1A.

79. On the REAL ID Act's restrictions on driver's licenses, see earlier in this chapter. On New York, see Erika Hayasaki, Driver's License Plan Dropped, L.A. Times, Nov. 15, 2007, at A16.

80. See Azam Ahmed & Karoun Demirjian, Credit Offered to Illegal Residents: Bank Target Workers Without Documents, Chicago Trib., Feb. 15, 2007, at 1; E. Scott Reckard et al., Banking on Illegal Immigrants: A Move to Issue Credit Cards to People Without Social Security Numbers Draws Anger and Praise, L.A. Times, Feb. 14, 2007, at A1; Miriam Jordan & Valerie Bauerlein, Bank of America Casts Wider Net for Hispanics, Wall St. J., Feb. 13, 2007, at A1; We the People: Helping Newcomers Become Californians vii, x, 33–34 (State of California, Little Hoover Comm'n 2002). On the significance of documents, see generally Craig Robertson, The Passport in America: The History of a Document (Oxford Univ. Press 2010); Susan B. Coutin, Nations of Emigrants: Shifting Boundaries of Citizenship in El Salvador and the United States of America, 49–50, 101–103, 119 (Cornell Univ. Press 2007); Jane Caplan & John Torpey, Introduction to Documenting Individual Identity: The Development of State Practices in the Modern World, 1, 5 (Jane Caplan & John Torpey eds., Princeton Univ. Press 2001); Gérard Noiriel, The French Melting Pot: Immigration, Citizenship, and National Identity, 45 (Geoffroy de Laforcade trans., Univ. of Minnesota Press 1996); John Torpey, The Invention of the Passport: Surveillance, Citizenship, and the State, 10–17 (Cambridge Univ. Press 2000); Dean Spade, Documenting Gender, 59 Hastings L.J. 731, 761 (2008).

81. On New Haven, see City of New Haven, New Haven's Elm City Resident Cards—Fact Sheet; Jeff Holtz, This Summer's Surprise Hit: An Elm City ID, N.Y. Times, Sept. 16, 2007, at 6CT; Jennifer Medina, New Haven Approves Program to Issue Illegal Immigrants IDs, N.Y. Times, June 5, 2007, at B6. On San Francisco, see Phillip Matier & Andrew Ross, Gavin's Green Goals for New Stadium Made Niners See Red, S.F. Chron., June 7, 2009, at B1; Heather Knight, Hundreds Wait for Hours to Buy ID Card, S.F. Chron., Jan. 16, 2009, at B1; Jesse McKinley, ID Cards for Residents Pass a Vote in California, N.Y. Times, Nov. 15, 2007, at A20; Cecilia M. Vega, City Making Clear Illegals Can Obtain Services Here, S.F. Chron., 3 Apr. 2008, B1; on Oakland, see Matthai Kuruvila, Council Votes to Proceed Planning for ID Cards, S.F. Chron., June 4, 2009, at B4. On Trenton, see Kirk Semple, In Trenton, Issuing IDs for Illegal Immigrants, N.Y. Times, May 17, 2010, at A17; Editorial, Trenton Gets It Right, N.Y. Times, May 23, 2010, at WK7. On Los Angeles, see Ian Lovett, IDs for Illegal Immigrants Take a Step in Los Angeles, N.Y. Times, Oct. 17, 2012, at A23.

82. See National Conference of State Legislatures, 2012 Immigration-Related Laws and Resolutions in the States (Jan. 1–Dec. 31, 2012).

CHAPTER 3

Americans in Waiting?

1. See Hiroshi Motomura, Americans in Waiting: The Lost Story of Immigration and Citizenship in the United States (Oxford Univ. Press 2006).

2. See Frank Swoboda, Unions Reverse on Illegal Aliens; Policy Seeks Amnesty, End to Sanctions, Wash. Post, Feb. 17, 2000, at A1; Michele Wucker, Lockout: Why America Keeps Getting Immigration Wrong When Our Prosperity Depends on Getting It Right, 112–113 (Public Affairs 2006).

3. See Karin Brulliard, AFL–CIO Aligns with Day-Laborer Advocates, Wash. Post, Aug. 10, 2006, at A5; Steven Greenhouse, Labor Federation Forms a Pact with Day Workers, N.Y. Times, Aug. 10, 2006, at A18; Shawn Neidorf, Friend, Not Foe; Unions Step up Campaign to Strengthen Workplace Rights for Illegal Immigrants, Chicago Trib., Aug. 31, 2003, at 5.

4. See Urgent Message from Pablo Alvarado, Director of NDLON, regarding SB 1070, Jornalero News: Official News Blog of the National Day Laborer Organizing Network (Apr. 16, 2010) (emphasis in original).

5. See Jorge-Mario Cabrera, May 1st Voices Ring in New Day in America, Huffington Post (May 3, 2010); William Perez, We ARE Americans: Undocumented Students Pursuing the American Dream, 149–150 (Stylus Publishing 2009).

6. Plyler v. Doe, 457 U.S. 202, 218–219 (1982); see also 457 U.S. 207–208, 213, 216 n.14, 221–222; 457 U.S. at 234 (Blackmun, J., concurring); 457 U.S. at 239 (Powell, J., concurring); Motomura, Americans in Waiting, supra note 1, at 160–161.

7. 457 U.S. at 221, 222 n.20, 223. On Reconstruction-era restrictions on education for African Americans as a way to deny full citizenship, see generally James D. Anderson, The Education of Blacks in the South, 1860–1935, at 1–109 (Univ. of North Carolina Press 1988).

8. See Chapter 1 in this volume.

9. See generally Hiroshi Motomura, Who Belongs?: Immigration Outside the Law and the Idea of Americans in Waiting, 2 UC Irvine L. Rev. 359 (2012).

10. See Catherine Dauvergne, Making People Illegal: What Globalization Means for Migration and Law, 123–124 (Cambridge Univ. Press 2008).

11. On borders, see, e.g., David Miller, On Nationality, 96 (Oxford Univ. Press 1995); John Rawls, The Law of Peoples (Harvard Univ. Press 1999); Michael Walzer, Spheres of Justice: A Defense of Pluralism and Equality, 35–42 (Basic Books 1983); Rainer Bauböck, Citizenship and Free Movement, in Citizenship, Borders, and Human Needs, 343, 358–364 (Rogers M. Smith ed., Univ. of Pennsylvania Press 2011); Matthew Gibney, Liberal Democratic States and Responsibilities to Refugees, 93 Am. Pol. Sc. Rev. 169, 174 (1999); Stephen Macedo, The Moral Dilemma of U.S. Immigration Policy: Open Borders Versus Social Justice, in Debating Immigration, 63, 69–75 (Carol M. Swain ed., Cambridge Univ. Press 2007).

12. See Sarah Song, What Does It Mean to Be an American?, Daedalus, Spring 2009, at 31, 31–32.

13. Walzer, Spheres of Justice, supra note 11, at 39.

14. See Motomura, Americans in Waiting, supra note 1, at 152–153; Randall Hansen, The Poverty of Postnationalism: Citizenship, Immigration, and the New Europe, 38 Theory & Soc'y 1 (2009); Dauvergne, Making People Illegal, supra note 10, at 21.

15. Cf. Joseph Nevins, Operation Gatekeeper and Beyond: The War on "Illegals" and the Remaking of the US-Mexico Boundary, 10 (Routledge 2010).

16. On a similar idea, see Donald Galloway, Strangers and Members: Equality in an Immigration Setting, 7 Can. J.L. & Jur. 149, 161–172 (1994); Donald Galloway, Liberalism, Globalism, and Immigration, 18 Queen's L.J. 266, 301–302 (1993); Catherine Dauvergne, Beyond Justice: The Consequences of Liberalism for Immigration Law, 10 Can. J.L. & Jur. 323, 328–332 (1997); Catherine Dauvergne, Amorality and Humanitarianism in Immigration Law, 37 Osgoode Hall L.J. 597, 604–606 (1999). On when immigration law discriminates by treating different countries differently, see Chapter 7 in this volume.

17. On approaching constitutional rights in immigration law as a matter of the rights of affected citizens, see Adam B. Cox, Citizenship, Standing, and Immigration Law, 92 Cal. L. Rev. 373, 374 (2004); Hiroshi Motomura, Whose Immigration Law?: Citizens, Aliens, and the Constitution, 97 Colum. L. Rev. 1567, 1584–1586, 1601–1602 (1997); Hiroshi Motomura, Whose Alien Nation?: Two Models of Constitutional Immigration Law, 94 Mich. L. Rev. 1927, 1946–1952 (1996).

18. See Song, What Does It Mean to Be an American?, supra note 12, at 34–35.

19. On "brain drain," compare Michael A. Clemens, What Do We Know about Skilled Migration and Development (Migration Policy Inst. 2013); Michele Pistone & John J. Hoeffner, Stepping Out of the Brain Drain: Applying Catholic Social Teaching in a New Era of Migration (Lexington Books 2007); Fernando R. Teson, Brain Drain, 45 San Diego L. Rev. 899 (2008); with Jagdish N. Bhagwati, The Brain Drain Tax Proposal and the Issues, in Taxing the Brain Drain (Jagdish N. Bhagwati & Martin Partington eds., North-Holland 1976); Lisa Leiman, Should the Brain Drain Be Plugged? A Behavioral Economics Approach, 39 Tex. Int'l L.J. 675 (2004).

20. See Motomura, Americans in Waiting, supra note 1, at 73–75.

21. See INA § 301, 8 U.S.C. § 1401; Thomas Alexander Aleinikoff, David A. Martin, Hiroshi Motomura, & Maryellen Fullerton, Immigration and Citizenship: Process and Policy, 38–50 (7th ed. West 2012). See also Chapter 2 in this volume.

22. See Elk v. Wilkins, 112 U.S. 94, 109 (1884), Act of June 2, 1924, ch. 233, 43 Stat. 253; INA § 301(b), 8 U.S.C. § 1401(b). See generally Angela R. Riley, Indians and Guns, 100 Geo. L.J. 1675, 1702 (2012); Aleinikoff, Martin, Motomura, & Fullerton, Immigration and Citizenship, supra note 21, at 50–51.

23. 169 U.S. 649, 694–696 (1898). See also Erika Lee, At America's Gates: Chinese Immigration During the Exclusion Era, 1882–1943, at 103–105 (Univ. of North Carolina Press 2003); Lucy E. Salyer, Laws Harsh as Tigers: Chinese Immigrants and the Shaping of Modern Immigration Law, 98–99 (Univ. of North Carolina Press 1995); Lucy E. Salyer, Wong Kim Ark: The Contest over Birthright Citizenship, in Immigration Stories, 51–85 (David A. Martin & Peter H. Schuck eds., Foundation Press 2005). On birthright citizenship, see also Chapter 6 in this volume.

24. See Act of Mar. 26, 1790, ch. 3, § 1, 1 Stat. 103, 103; Chapter 1 in this volume. On the definition being viewed as broad, see Daniel J. Tichenor, Strange Bedfellows: The Politics and Pathologies of Immigration Reform, 5 Labor: Studies in Working-Class History of the Americans 39, 56 (2008).

25. See Act of July 14, 1870, ch. 254, § 7, 16 Stat. 254, 256; Act of May 6, 1882, ch. 126, § 14, 22 Stat. 58, 61.

26. On the eligibility of immigrants from the Middle East, see Dow v. United States, 226 F. 145, 145–148 (4th Cir. 1915); In re Halladjian, 174 Fed. 834, 835–845 (C.C.D. Mass. 1909); Matter of Najour, 174 Fed. 735, 735 (N.D. Ga. 1909). See generally John Tehranian, Whitewashed: American's Invisible Middle Eastern Minority (N.Y.U. Press 2009); John Tehranian, Compulsory Whiteness: Toward a Middle Eastern Legal Scholarship, 82 Indiana L.J. 1 (2007). On Mexican immigrants, see In re Rodriguez, 81 F. 337 (W.D. Tex. 1897); Martha Menchaca, Naturalizing Mexican Immigrants: A Texas History, 129–159 (Univ. of Texas Press 2011); Laura Gómez, Manifest Destinies: The Making of the Mexican American Race, 138–142 (N.Y.U. Press 2008); Martha Menchaca, Recovering History,

Constructing Race: The Indian, Black, and White Roots of Mexican Americans, 281–285 (Univ. of Texas Press 2001).

27. Ozawa v. United States, 260 U.S. 178, 189, 197–199 (1922); United States v. Thind, 261 U.S. 204, 206, 210, 214–215 (1923). For a lower federal court case applying both *Ozawa* and *Thind*, see United States v. Cartozian, 6 F.2d 919, 919–22 (D. Ore. 1925). See also Ian F. Haney-López, White by Law: The Legal Construction of Race, 67–77, 80–86 (N.Y.U. Press 1996); Yuji Ichioka, The Issei: The World of the First Generation Japanese Immigrants, 1885–1924, at 219–226 (Free Press 1988); Matthew Frye Jacobson, Whiteness of a Different Color: European Immigrants and the Alchemy of Race, 223–245 (Harvard Univ. Press 1999); Charles J. McClain, In Search of Equality: The Chinese Struggle Against Discrimination in Nineteenth-Century America, 70–73 (Univ. of California Press 1994); Mae M. Ngai, Impossible Subjects: Illegal Aliens and the Making of Modern America, 41–45 (Princeton Univ. Press 2004); Salyer, Laws Harsh as Tigers, supra note 23, at 13; Rogers M. Smith, Civic Ideals: Conflicting Visions of Citizenship in U.S. History, 369–370, 446–447 (Yale Univ. Press 1997); Ronald Takaki, Strangers from a Different Shore: A History of Asian Americans, 208–209 (updated & rev. ed. Little, Brown 1998). On naturalization by Asian immigrants before *Ozawa*, see Noah Pickus, True Faith and Allegiance: Immigration and American Civic Nationalism, 67, 108 (Princeton Univ. Press 2005).

28. See Act of Mar. 24, 1934, ch. 84, § 8, 48 Stat. 456, 462; Act of Oct. 14, 1940, ch. 876, § 303, 54 Stat. 1137, 1140; Act of Dec. 17, 1943, ch. 344, § 3, 57 Stat. 600, 601; Act of July 2, 1946, ch. 534, § 1, 60 Stat. 416, 416; Act of June 27, 1952, Pub. L. No. 82–414, ch. 477, § 311, 66 Stat. 163, 239 codified at INA § 311. See generally Motomura, Americans in Waiting, supra note 1, at 73–75. Filipinos had been able to travel freely to the United States as noncitizen US nationals, but as Asians they could not naturalize. Two days after Filipinos became eligible to naturalize, the Philippines became an independent nation under a 12-year transition set out in the Tydings-McDuffie Act of 1934. See U.S. Pub. L. 73–127, § 8(a)(1), 48 Stat. 456, 462 (1934). See also Chapter 1 in this volume.

29. See Act of May 19, 1921, ch. 8, §§ 2(a), 3, 42 Stat. 5, 5–7 (repealed 1952); Act of May 26, 1924, ch. 190, § 11, 43 Stat. 153, 159–160 (repealed 1952). See also John Higham, Strangers in the Land: Patterns of American Nativism 1860–1925, at 308–311 (Rutgers Univ. Press 1955). On Teddy Roosevelt, see Peter Margulies, Taking Care of Immigration Law: Presidential Stewardship, Prosecutorial Discretion, and the Separation of Powers, 94 B.U. L. Rev. 105, 152–158 (2014); Gabriel J. Chin, Regulating Race: Asian Exclusion and the Administrative State, 37 Harv. C.R.-C.L. L. Rev. 1, 19 (2002).

30. See Chae Chan Ping v. United States (The Chinese Exclusion Case), 130 U.S. 581, 606 (1889); Motomura, Americans in Waiting, supra note 1, at 15–37; 126–132.

31. See US Congress, Immigration Commission, 1 Abstracts and Reports of the Immigration Commission (1911). On eugenics and race, see Higham, Strangers in

the Land, supra note 29, at 31–38, 151–152, 271–277; Jacobson, Whiteness, supra note 27, at 77–90; Kevin R. Johnson, The Huddled Masses Myth: Immigration and Civil Rights, 113–114 (Temple Univ. Press 2004); Desmond King, Making Americans: Immigration, Race, and the Origins of the Diverse Democracy, 50–81, 127–195 (Harvard Univ. Press 2000); Ngai, Impossible Subjects, supra note 27, at 24–25; Alejandro Portes & Ruben G. Rumbaut, Immigrant America, A Portrait, 172–175 (3d ed. Univ. of California Press 2006); Salyer, Laws Harsh as Tigers, supra note 23, at 124, 130; Daniel J. Tichenor, Dividing Lines: The Politics of Immigration Control in America, 42–43, 77–78, 115, 127–132, 140–144, 160 (Princeton Univ. Press 2002). On ideology and national security, see, e.g., Act of Oct. 16, 1918, ch. 186, § 2, 40 Stat. 1012, 1012; Aleinikoff, Martin, Motomura, & Fullerton, Immigration and Citizenship, supra note 21, at 612–614; Harlan Grant Cohen, Note, The (Un)favorable Judgment of History: Deportation Hearings, The Palmer Raids, and the Meaning of History, 78 N.Y.U. L. Rev. 1431, 1451–1466 (2003); Higham, Strangers in the Land, supra note 29, at 229–263; Edwin P. Hoyt, The Palmer Raids 1919–1920: An Attempt to Suppress Dissent (Seabury Press 1969); King, Making Americans, supra, at 19–27, 85–126; William Preston, Jr., Aliens and Dissenters: Federal Suppression of Radicals 1903–1933, at 208–237 (Harvard Univ. Press 1963); Salyer, Laws Harsh as Tigers, supra note 23, at 233–239; Tichenor, Dividing Lines, supra, at 140; Pickus, True Faith and Allegiance, supra note 27, at 107–123.

32. See US Congress, Immigration Commission, 1 Abstracts and Reports of the Immigration Commission, 24, 47–48 (1911); Act of Feb. 5, 1917, ch. 29, § 3, 39 Stat. 874, 875–878. See also Roger Daniels, Guarding the Golden Door: American Immigration Policy and Immigrants since 1882, at 31–34, 46 (Hill & Wang 2004); Higham, Strangers in the Land, supra note 29, at 101, 112, 162–165, 191, 195, 202–203; Bill Ong Hing, Making and Remaking Asian America Through Immigration Policy 1850–1990, at 32 (Stanford Univ. Press 1993); King, Making Americans, supra note 31, at 78–79; Tichenor, Dividing Lines, supra note 31, at 81–83, 124–127, 133, 136–141.

33. On the citizenship-based admission bar, see Chapter 1 in this volume. See Act of May 26, 1924, ch. 190, §§ 11(d), 28(c), 43 Stat. 153, 159, 168. See also King, Making Americans, supra note 31, at 39–40, 155–159; Bill Ong Hing, Immigration Policies: Messages of Exclusion to African Americans, 37 Howard L.J. 237, 246 (1994); Vilna Bashi, Globalized Anti-Blackness: Transnationalizing Western Immigration Law, Policy, and Practice, 27 Ethnic & Racial Stud. 584, 590–591 (2004).

34. See Motomura, Americans in Waiting, supra note 1, at 48–49, 128–130, 134–135, 178–179; Hiroshi Motomura, Immigration Outside the Law, 108 Colum. L. Rev. 2037, 2049–2053 (2008); Douglas S. Massey, Jorge Durand, & Nolan J. Malone, Beyond Smoke and Mirrors: Mexican Immigration in an Era of Economic Integration, 26–34 (Russell Sage Found. 2002). See also Chapter 1 in this volume.

35. On the decline in the number of immigrants from the 1920s to the mid-1960s, see 2011 Yearbook of Immigration Statistics, 5, table 1 (Dept. of Homeland Sec. 2012).

36. See Act of Jan. 29, 1795, ch. 20, 1 Stat. 414; Act of Jan. 29, 1795, ch. 20, 1 Stat. 414. See generally James W. Fox, Jr., Citizenship, Poverty, and Federalism: 1787–1882, 60 U. Pitt. L. Rev. 421, 429–435 (1999); Frank George Franklin, The Legislative History of Naturalization in the United States: From the Revolutionary War to 1861, at 49–71, 167–168, 175–176, 215–300 (Univ. of Chicago Press 1906); James H. Kettner, The Development of American Citizenship, 1608–1870, at 232–286 (Univ. of North Carolina Press 1978); Gerald L. Neuman, Strangers to the Constitution: Immigrants, Borders, and Fundamental Law, 64 (Princeton Univ. Press 1996); Pickus, True Faith and Allegiance, supra note 27, at 16–63; Peter H. Schuck & Rogers M. Smith, Citizenship Without Consent: Illegal Aliens in the American Polity, 51 (Yale Univ. Press 1985); Smith, Civic Ideals, supra note 27, at 159–168; Tichenor, Dividing Lines, supra note 31, at 53–54; John S. Wise, A Treatise on American Citizenship, 57–58 (Edward Thompson Co. 1906). See Chapters 1 and 2 in this volume; Motomura, Americans in Waiting, supra note 1, at 8–9, 116–123.

37. See Americans in Waiting, supra note 1, at 116–119; Virginia Harper-Ho, Noncitizen Voting Rights: The History, the Law and Current Prospects for Change, 18 Law & Ineq. 271, 273–283 (2000); Kettner, The Development of American Citizenship, supra note 36, at 102–103, 123; Neuman, Strangers to the Constitution, supra note 36, at 63–71; Jamin B. Raskin, Legal Aliens, Local Citizens: The Historical, Constitutional and Theoretical Meanings of Alien Suffrage, 141 U. Pa. L. Rev. 1391, 1401–1417 (1993); Gerald M. Rosberg, Aliens and Equal Protection: Why Not the Right to Vote?, 75 Mich. L. Rev. 1092, 1093–1100 (1977). See Mich. Const. of 1850, art. VII, § 1; Ind. Const. of 1851, art. II, § 2; Dakota Territorial Gov. Act, ch. 86, § 5, 12 Stat. 239, 241 (1861); Kansas-Nebraska Act, ch. 59, §§ 5, 23 (1854); Nevada Territorial Gov. Act, ch. 83, § 5, 12 Stat. 209, 211 (1861); Okla. Territorial Gov. Act, ch. 182, §§ 5, 26 Stat. 81, 84 (1890); Wash. Territorial Gov. Act, ch. 90, § 5, 10 Stat. 172, 174 (1853); Wyoming Territorial Gov. Act, ch. 235, § 5, 15 Stat. 178, 179–180 (1868); Alexander Keyssar, The Right to Vote: The Contested History of Democracy in the United States, 32–33, 104–105, 136–138, 359–361, app. table A.12 (Basic Books 2000); Higham, Strangers in the Land, supra note 29, at 214; Gerald L. Neuman, "We Are the People": Alien Suffrage in German and American Perspective, 13 Mich. J. Int'l L. 259, 297–299 (1992); Raskin, Legal Aliens, supra, at 1406–1408; Brian C. Riopelle, Note, Revitalization of the "Intending Citizen" Status: Rights of Declarant Aliens after IRCA, 28 Va. J. Int'l L. 987, 995 (1988). See also Minor v. Happersett, 88 U.S. 162 (1874). For state statutes allowing voting by intending citizens, see Ala. Const. of 1868, art. VII, § 2; Ark. Const. of 1868, art. VIII, § 2; Fla. Const. of 1868, art. XIV, § 1; Ga. Const. of 1868, art. II, § 2; Mo. Const. of 1865, art, II, § 18; Tex. Const. of

1876, art. VI, § 2; Idaho Territory Rev. Stat. § 1860 (1873); La. Const. of 1879, art. 185; N.D. Const. of 1889, art. 5, § 121.

38. On widows and children, see Act of Mar. 26, 1804, ch. 47, § 2, 2 Stat. 292, 293; Franklin, Legislative History of Naturalization, supra note 36, at 115. On diplomatic protection, see Letter from Secretary of State William L. Marcy to Chevalier Hulseman, Sept. 26, 1853, H.R. Exec. Doc. No. 1, 33d Cong., 1st Sess., 30, 40 (1853), discussed in Alexander Porter Morse, A Treatise on Citizenship, by Birth and by Naturalization, 68–71 (Little, Brown 1881); Frederick Van Dyne, Citizenship of the United States, 70–73 (Lawyers' Co-operative Publishing Co. 1904); 1 Charles Cheney Hyde, International Law Chiefly as Interpreted and Applied by the United States, 687–688 n.2 (Little, Brown 1922); Maximilian Koessler, Rights and Duties of Declarant Aliens, 91 U. Pa. L. Rev. 321, 324–325 (1942–1943); Neuman, Alien Suffrage, supra note 37, at 306; Riopelle, Revitalization, supra note 37, at 990–994; Frederick Van Dyne, A Treatise on the Law of Naturalization of the United States, 67–68 (F. Van Dyne 1907). On the Homestead Act, see 12 Stat. 392, 392 (1862); 7 Charles Gordon, Stanley Mailman, & Stephen Yale-Loehr, Immigration Law and Procedure § 96.02[02] (2013).

39. On military service, see John Whiteclay Chambers II, To Raise an Army: The Draft Comes to Modern America, 51, 59 (Free Press 1987); Higham, Strangers in the Land, supra note 29, at 214; Neuman, Alien Suffrage, supra note 37, at 306; Riopelle, Revitalization, supra note 37, at 990. On passports, see Act of Mar. 2, 1907, ch. 2534, § 1, 34 Stat. 1228, 1228, discussed in Hyde, International Law, supra note 38, at 688; Neuman, Alien Suffrage, supra note 37, at 305–306; Van Dyne, Naturalization, supra note 38, at 74. On seamen, see Act of May 9, 1918, ch. 69, § 1, 40 Stat. 542, 544, discussed in Hyde, International Law, supra note 38, at 633; Van Dyne, Naturalization, supra note 38, at 74–76, repealed by Act of Oct. 14, 1940, subch. V, § 504, 54 Stat. 1172–1173. On tax rates, see Higham, Strangers in the Land, supra note 29, at 161–162, 248 (apparently referring to Revenue Act of 1918, Pub. L. No. 254, ch. 18, § 210, 40 Stat. 1057, 1062); U.S. Department of the Treasury, Bureau of Internal Revenue, Bulletin "B" Income Tax Withholding, Revenue Act of 1918, at 20–21. On public employment, see Kansas Gas & Electric Co. v. City of Independence, 79 F.2d 32, 36 n. 3 (10th Cir. 1935) (citing National Industrial Recovery Act, 40 U.S.C. § 406). See generally In re Kleibs, 128 Fed. 656, 656 (Cir. S.D.N.Y. 1904); In re Moses, 83 Fed. 995, 996 (Cir. S.D.N.Y. 1897); Maloy v. Duden, 25 Fed. 673, 673–675 (Cir. S.D.N.Y. 1885); Koessler, Declarant Aliens, supra note 38, at 323.

40. See Act of July 14, 1870, ch. 254, § 7, 16 Stat. 254, 256. See also Kettner, American Citizenship, supra note 36, at 246; Koessler, Declarant Aliens, supra note 38, at 321; Neuman, Alien Suffrage, supra note 37, at 297, 325; Riopelle, Revitalization, supra note 37, at 989–990; Van Dyne, Naturalization, supra note 38, at 54–84; Motomura, Americans in Waiting, supra note 1, at 116–119, 123–24.

41. See Motomura, Americans in Waiting, supra note 1, at 132–135; Daniels, Golden
    Door, supra note 32, at 123, 137, 151; Hing, Asian America, supra note 32, at 36,
    48–49, 66–68; Christian Joppke, Immigration and the Nation-State: The United
    States, Germany, and Great Britain, 27–28 (Oxford Univ. Press 1999); King, Making
    Americans, supra note 31, at 241–242; Ngai, Impossible Subjects, supra note 27, at
    261–263. On post–1965 unauthorized migration, see Chapter 1 in this volume.

42. See Chapter 1 in this volume; on Asian immigration, compare Daniels, Golden
    Door, supra note 32, at 135; Hing, Asian America, supra note 32, at 39–41; David
    M. Reimers, Still the Golden Door: The Third World Comes to America, 74–91
    (2d ed. Columbia Univ. Press 1992); with Gabriel J. Chin, The Civil Rights
    Revolution Comes to Immigration Law: A New Look at the Immigration and
    Nationality Act of 1965, 75 N.C. L. Rev. 273, 303–345 (1996). On prior occupa-
    tional categories, see Act of June 25, 1948, ch. 647, § 6, 62 Stat. 1009, 1012. On
    immigration from Latin America, see Douglas S. Massey & Karen A. Pren,
    Unintended Consequences of US Immigration Policy: Explaining the Post-1965
    Surge from Latin America, 38 Pop. & Dev. Rev. 1, 1–8, 17–21 (2012); Massey,
    Durand & Malone, Beyond Smoke and Mirrors, supra note 34, at 41–47; Arthur
    F. Corwin & Johnny M. McCain, Wetbackism since 1964: A Catalogue of Factors,
    in Immigrants—and Immigrants: Perspectives on Mexican Labor Migration to
    the United States, 67, 68 (Arthur F. Corwin ed., Greenwood Press 1978).

43. See 2011 Yearbook of Immigration Statistics, supra note 35, at 8, table 2; Randall
    Monger & James Yankay, U.S. Legal Permanent Residents: 2012, at 4 & table 3
    (Dept. of Homeland Sec. 2013); Campbell J. Gibson & Kay Jung, Historical
    Census Statistics on the Foreign-born Population of the United States: 1850–
    2000, at 1 (US Census Bureau 2006); Elizabeth M. Grieco, et al., The Foreign-Born
    Population in the United States: 2010, at 2 & table 2 (US Census Bureau 2012).

44. See Motomura, Americans in Waiting, supra note 1, at 51–57, 80–87, 139–142,
    155–157.

45. See, e.g., Mark Krikorian, The New Case Against Immigration: Both Legal and
    Illegal, 21–23 (Sentinel 2008).

46. See Peter Brimelow, Alien Nation: Common Sense about America's Immigration
    Disaster, 9–11, 58–73, 264–265 (Random House 1995); Samuel P. Huntington,
    Who Are We? The Challenges to America's National Identity, 171–177 (Simon
    & Schuster 2004). See also Patrick J. Buchanan, The Death of the West: How
    Dying Populations and Immigrant Invasions Imperil Our Country and
    Civilization, 125 (Thomas Dunne Books 2002). On this phenomenon, see T.
    Alexander Aleinikoff, Semblances of Sovereignty: The Constitution, the State,
    and American Citizenship, 54 (Harvard Univ. Press 2002); Hiroshi Motomura,
    Whose Alien Nation? Two Models of Constitutional Immigration Law, 94
    Mich. L. Rev. 1927 (1996).

47. See John D. Skrentny, The Minority Rights Revolution, 2, 21, 52–57, 61–62
    (Harvard Univ. Press 2002). On official English and English-only laws, see, e.g.,

Ariz. Rev. Stat. § 15–752; Mass. Ann. Laws ch. 71A, § 4; Josh Hill, Devin Ross, & Brad Serafine, Watch Your Language! The Kansas Law Review Survey of Official-English and English-Only Laws and Policies, 57 U. Kan. L. Rev. 669, 673–674 (2009). On bilingual education, see Samuel J. Freedman, It's Latino Parents Speaking Out on Bilingual Education Failures, N.Y. Times, Jul. 14, 2004, at B9; H. G. Reza & Claire Luna, Voters Drawn to Take a Stand on Bilingual Ed, L.A. Times, Feb. 5, 2003, at 1; Ruben Navarrette Jr., It's Time to Dismantle Bilingual Education, Chicago Trib., Jul. 11, 2001, at 17. On ethnic studies, see Fernanda Santos, Arizona: Most of Law on Ethnic Studies Is Upheld, N.Y. Times, Mar. 12, 2013, at A15; Marc Lacey, Rift in Arizona as Latino Class Is Found Illegal, N.Y. Times, Jan. 8, 2011, at A1; Michael Winerip, Racial Lens Used to Cull Curriculum in Arizona, N.Y. Times, Mar. 19, 2012, at A8; Robert Mackey, Arizona Law Curbs Ethnic Studies Classes, N.Y. Times, May 13, 2010. See generally Roger Daniels, Coming to America: A History of Immigration and Ethnicity in American Life, 159–161 (2d ed. Perennial 2002); Higham, Strangers in the Land, supra note 29, at 195 99, 204 212, 235 236; King, Making Americans, supra note 31, at 88 90, 110 113; Juan F. Perea, Demography and Distrust: An Essay on American Languages, Cultural Pluralism, and Official English, 77 Minn. L. Rev. 269, 329–332 (1992); Irene Scharf, Tired of Your Masses: A History of and Judicial Responses to Early 20th Century Anti-Immigrant Legislation, 21 U. Haw. L. Rev. 131, 140–142, 155–161 (1999).

48. See Motomura, Americans in Waiting, supra note 1, at 173.

49. On the attractiveness of workers who would not assimilate, see Motomura, Immigration Outside the Law, supra note 34, at 2049–2051 & nn. 64–65.

50. See Plyler v. Doe, 457 U.S. 202, 219, 220, 222 (1982); Chapter 1 in this volume; Linda S. Bosniak, Membership, Equality, and the Difference That Alienage Makes, 69 N.Y.U. L. Rev. 1047, 1121 1123 (1994).

51. See Chapter 1 in this volume.

52. See Motomura, Americans in Waiting, supra note 1, at 15–62. Compare Adam B. Cox & Eric A. Posner, The Rights of Migrants: An Optimal Contract Framework, 84 N.Y.U. L. Rev. 1403, 1407–1410, 1418–1433 (2009).

53. See 149 U.S. 698, 730 (1893).

54. See INS v. St. Cyr, 533 U.S. 289, 323 (2001).

55. Joseph H. Carens, The Case for Amnesty: Time Erodes the State's Right to Deport, 34 Boston Rev. 7, 8, 10 (2009). Courts have considered the responsibility of government in the different context of constitutional right to protection from harm. DeShaney v. Winnebago County Dep't of Social Services, 489 U.S. 189 (1989), may stand for the proposition that governments have no or limited "responsibility" just because they play some role in creating the situation that caused the harm. The Supreme Court rejected a claim that failure to protect was a violation of an abused child's constitutional rights, but later lower court cases have created a limited exception for a "state-created danger" if a state official acted affirmatively to create the

situation. See, e.g., Bright v. Westmoreland County 443 F.3d 276 (3d Cir. 2006); Jones v. Reynolds 438 F.3d 685 (6th Cir. 2006). See generally Laura Oren, Some Thoughts On the State-Created Danger Doctrine: *Deshaney* Is Still Wrong and *Castle Rock* Is More of the Same, 16 Temp. Pol. & Civ. Rts. L. Rev. 47 (2006–2007).

56. See Peter Andreas, Border Games: Policing the U.S.-Mexico Divide, 7 (2d ed. Cornell Univ. Press 2009). See also Hiroshi Motomura, The Rule of Law in Immigration Law, 15 Tulsa J. Comp. & Int'l L. 139 (2008); see Motomura, Immigration Outside the Law, supra note 34, at 2089–2091.

57. See Motomura, Immigration Outside the Law, supra note 34, at 2049–2051. See also Chapter 6 in this volume. For the view that the United States has effectively had open immigration for persons crossing the Mexican border, see Richard B. Freeman, People Flows in Globalization, 20 J. Econ. Perspectives, 145, 164 (2006).

58. On immigration as affiliation, see Motomura, Americans in Waiting, supra note 1, at 80–114. See also Chapter 1 in this volume; Leo R. Chavez, Outside the Imagined Community: Undocumented Settlers and Experiences of Incorporation, 18 Am. Ethnologist 257, 269 (1991). On property law as the basis for immigration as affiliation, see Ayelet Shachar, The Birthright Lottery: Citizenship and Global Inequality, 27–33 (Harvard Univ. Press 2009).

59. See Linda Bosniak, Amnesty In Immigration: Forgetting, Forgiving, Freedom, 16 Crit. Rev. Int'l Soc. & Pol. Philosophy, 344, 354 (2013); see also Linda Bosniak, Arguing for Amnesty, J. L., Culture & Hum. (Jan. 19, 2012); Bosniak, Amnesty in Immigration, supra, at 352.

60. 457 U.S. at 218–219, 221–223.

CHAPTER 4

Deciding Who Enforces

1. Arizona v. United States, 132 S. Ct. 2492 (2012), oral argument, 2012 WL 1425227, at 33.

2. *Arizona*, oral argument, 2012 WL 1425227, at 46.

3. See Chapter 2 in this volume.

4. See Miranda v. Arizona, 384 U.S. 436, 457, 463 (1966). See also Frederick Schauer, The *Miranda* Warning, 88 Wash. L. Rev. 155 (2013); Yale Kamisar, The Rise, Decline, and Fall (?) of *Miranda*, 8 Wash. L. Rev. 965 (2012); Richard A. Leo, The Impact of *Miranda* Revisited, 86 J. Crim. L. & Criminology 621, 678 (1996). I am grateful to Abner Greene for noting this similarity. For a similar analysis in a different context and a thorough examination of prophylactic rules, see Abner S. Greene, Is There a First Amendment Defense for *Bush v. Gore*?, 80 Notre Dame L. Rev. 1643, 1665–1696 (2005). See also Daryl J. Levinson, Rights Essentialism and Remedial Equilibration, 99 Colum. L. Rev. 857, 899–904 (1999); David A. Strauss, The Ubiquity of Prophylactic Rules, 55 U. Chi. L. Rev. 190, 207 (1988).

5. See Anthony Amsterdam, Note, The Void-for-Vagueness Doctrine in the Supreme Court, 109 U. Pa. L. Rev. 67, 76 80 (1960); Tammy W. Sun, Equality by Other Means: The Substantive Foundations of the Vagueness Doctrine, 46 Harv. C.R.-C.L. L. Rev. 149, 150–151 (2011).

6. See Plyler v. Doe, 457 U.S. 202, 210 n.8 (1982); Chapter 2 in this volume.

7. See Introduction in this volume.

8. 424 U.S. 351, 352 n.1 (1976) (quoting Cal. Lab. Code § 2805(a)); see also Toll v. Moreno, 458 U.S. 1, 12–13 & n.18 (1982); Stephen Lee, Private Immigration Screening in the Workplace, 61 Stan. L. Rev. 1103, 1111 & n.18 (2009).

9. See De Canas v. Bica, 40 Cal. App. 3d 976, 978, 115 Cal. Rptr. 444 (1974).

10. See *De Canas*, 424 U.S. at 357 & n.5. A helpful overview is Ernest A. Young, "The Ordinary Diet of the Law": The Presumption Against Preemption in the Roberts Court, 2011 Sup. Ct. Rev. 253, 270–278. The rich literature on immigration federalism includes (but is not limited to) Margaret Hu, Reverse-Commandeering, 46 U.C. Davis L. Rev. 535 (2012); Marisa S. Cianciarulo, The "Arizonification" of Immigration Law: Implications of *Chamber of Commerce v. Whiting* for State and Local Immigration Legislation, 15 Harv. Latino L. Rev. 85 (2012); Kevin R. Johnson, Immigration and Civil Rights: Is the "New" Birmingham the Same as the "Old" Birmingham, 21 Wm. & Mary Bill Rts. J. 367 (2012); Kevin R. Johnson, Immigration and Civil Rights: State and Local Efforts to Regulate Immigration, 46 Ga. L. Rev. 609 (2012); Keith Cunningham-Parmeter, Forced Federalism: States as Laboratories of Immigration Reform, 62 Hast. L.J. 1673 (2011); Lauren Gilbert, Immigrant Laws, Obstacle Preemption and the Lost Legacy of *McCulloch*, 33 Berkeley J. Emp. & Lab. L. 153 (2012); Clare Huntington, The Constitutional Dimension of Immigration Federalism, 61 Vand. L. Rev. 787, 807–826 (2008); Hiroshi Motomura, Federalism, International Human Rights, and Immigration Exceptionalism, 70 U. Colo. L. Rev. 1361, 1369–1375 (1999); Peter J. Spiro, Learning to Live with Immigration Federalism, 29 Conn. L. Rev. 1627 (1997); Peter J. Spiro, The States and Immigration in an Era of Demi-Sovereignties, 35 Va. J. Int'l L. 121 (1994); Peter H. Schuck, Taking Immigration Federalism Seriously, 2007 U. Chi. Legal F. 57; Hiroshi Motomura, Whose Immigration Law?: Citizens, Aliens, and the Constitution, 97 Colum. L. Rev. 1567, 1587–1601 (1997); Hiroshi Motomura, Whose Alien Nation? Two Models of Constitutional Immigration Law, 94 Mich. L. Rev. 1927, 1945–1946 (1996).

11. See *De Canas*, 424 U.S. at 354–365; *Plyler*, 457 U.S. at 225; Hines v. Davidowitz, 312 U.S. 52, 67 (1941); Crosby v. Nat'l Foreign Trade Council, 530 U.S. 363, 372 (2000). The case was dropped on remand, see Bevles Co. v. Teamsters Local 986, 791 F.2d 1391, 1393–1394 (9th Cir. 1986).

12. See Farmers Branch, Tex., Ordinance 2903 (Jan. 22, 2007); Villas at Parkside Partners v. City of Farmers Branch, 577 F. Supp. 2d 858, 866–874 (N.D. Tex. 2008). See also Villas at Parkside Partners v. City of Farmers Branch, 496 F. Supp. 2d 757, 762 (N.D. Tex. 2007); Equal Access Educ. v. Merten, 305 F. Supp. 2d 585, 608

(E.D. Va. 2004); Nathan G. Cortez, The Local Dilemma: Preemption and the Role of Federal Standards in State and Local Immigration Laws, 61 SMU L. Rev. 47, 53–54 (2008). On later developments, see Villas at Parkside Partners v. City of Farmers Branch, 701 F. Supp. 2d 835 (N.D. Tex. 2010), aff'd, 726 F.3d 524 (5th Cir. 2013) (en banc), cert. denied, 2014 WL 801104 (March 3, 2014). See also Chapter 2 in this volume.

13. 239 U.S. 33, 41 (1915). See also Takahashi v. Fish & Game Comm'n, 334 U.S. 410, 419 (1948). On noncitizen voting, see Chapters 1 and 3 in this volume.

14. See *Plyler,* 457 U.S. at 208 n.5. On LAWA, see Chapter 2 in this volume.

15. See Chamber of Commerce v. Whiting, 131 S. Ct. 1968 (2011); Brief for the Petitioners, 2010 WL 3483324, at *20, *39, *51, Chamber of Commerce v. Whiting, 131 S. Ct. 1968 (2011); Brief for the Respondents, 2010 WL 4216271, at *30–37, *45, *58, Chamber of Commerce v. Whiting, 131 S. Ct. 1968 (2011). See also INA § 274A(h)(2), 8 U.S.C. § 1324a(h)(2).

16. Chamber of Commerce v. Whiting, 131 S. Ct. at 1977–1981.

17. 131 S. Ct. at 1981. For comments on this aspect of *Whiting,* see Villas at Parkside Partners v. City of Farmers Branch, 675 F.3d 802, 810 n.35 (5th Cir. 2012), on rehearing, 726 F.3d 524 (5th Cir. 2013) (en banc), cert. denied, 2014 WL 801104 (March 3, 2014); David A. Martin, Reading *Arizona,* 98 Va. L. Rev. In Brief 41, 43 (2012); Young, Ordinary Diet, supra note 10, at 298.

18. Lozano v. City of Hazleton, 496 F. Supp. 2d 477, 484–485 (M.D. Pa. 2007), aff'd, 620 F.3d 170 (3d Cir. 2010), vacated, 131 S. Ct. 2958 (2011), on remand, 724 F.3d 297 (3d Cir. 2013). See also Chapter 2 in this volume.

19. See 620 F.3d at 213, 221, 222. Compare Cortez, The Local Dilemma, supra note 12, at 64, with Cristina M. Rodríguez, The Significance of the Local in Immigration Regulation, 106 Mich. L. Rev. 567, 620–628 (2008). See also Garrett v. City of Escondido, 465 F. Supp. 2d 1043, 1047–1048, 1057 (S.D. Cal. 2006) (finding that because enforcing local law would burden federal agencies and resources, it was inconsistent with federal law).

20. 304 U.S. 64 (1938).

21. For preemption based on federal agency regulations, see, e.g., PLIVA, Inc. v. Mensing, 131 S. Ct. 2567, 2577–2582 (2011); Geier v. Am. Honda Motor Co., 529 U.S. 861, 874–886 (2000); City of New York v. FCC, 486 U.S. 57, 64–70 (1988); Fidelity Fed. Sav. & Loan Ass'n v. de la Cuesta, 458 U.S. 141, 153–154 (1982). For a contrary view, see, e.g., Arizona v. United States, 132 S. Ct. 2492, 2522 (2012) (Thomas, J., dissenting); Wyeth v. Levine, 555 U.S. 555, 588 (2009) (Thomas, J., concurring in judgment). See generally Young, Ordinary Diet, supra note 10, at 281, 325–328; David S. Rubenstein, Delegating Supremacy?, 65 Vand. L. Rev. 1125 (2012); Ernest A. Young, Executive Preemption, 102 Nw. U.L. Rev. 869 (2008). On recognizing the importance of discretion by looking beyond statutes, see Kerry Abrams, Plenary Power Preemption, 99 Va. L. Rev. 601, 637 (2013). I am grateful to David Rubenstein for raising this important set of issues.

22. For concerns about preemption based on informal executive branch decisions, see, e.g., Rubenstein, Delegating Supremacy?, supra note 21, at 1127; Young, Ordinary Diet, supra note 10, at 255.

23. On the states' role in curbing federal executive power, see Jessica Bulman-Pozen, Federalism as a Safeguard of the Separation of Powers, 112 Colum. L. Rev. 459, 462 (2012). See also Adam B. Cox, Enforcement Redundancy and the Future of Immigration Law, 2012 Sup. Ct. Rev. 31.

24. On concurrent or redundant enforcement, see, e.g., Adam B. Cox, Enforcement Redundancy, supra note 23; Young, Ordinary Diet, supra note 10, at 254, 257–261.

25. See SB 1070 §§ 2(B), 3, 5(A), 5(C) 6, Ariz. Rev. Stat. Ann. §§ 11–1051(B), 13–1509(A), 13–2928(C), 13–2929(A), 13–3883(A)(5). See David Sherfinski, N. Va. Enforces Immigration Laws as Ariz. Rages, Wash. Examiner, Apr. 29, 2010; Nick Miroff, Citing Cost, Prince William Delays Immigrant Measures Support of Crackdown Affirmed Amid New Caution, Wash. Post, Oct. 3, 2007 at A1; Cristina Rodríguez, Muzaffar Chishti, & Kimberly Nortman, Testing the Limits: A Framework for Assessing the Legality of State and Local Immigration Measures, 30 (Migration Policy Inst. 2007).

26. See 703 F. Supp. 2d 980, 1008 (D. Ariz. 2010), aff'd 641 F.3d 339, 366 (9th Cir. 2011). On these state laws, see also Chapter 2 in this volume.

27. 132 S. Ct. 2492, 2501–07 (2012). See also Hines v. Davidowitz, 312 U.S. 52, 60–74 (1941).

28. See 132 S. Ct. at 2501–2502, citing Buckman Co. v. Plaintiffs' Legal Comm., 531 U.S. 341, 347–348 (2001); Wisconsin Dept. of Industry v. Gould Inc., 475 U.S. 282, 288–289 (1986). See also Martin, Reading *Arizona*, supra note 17, at 42; Lucas Guttentag, Immigration Preemption and the Limits on State Power: Reflections on *Arizona v. United States*, 9 Stan. J. Civ. Rts. & Civ. Lib. 1, 42 (2013).

29. On the idea that exclusive federal authority over immigration includes not only the standards but also their application and enforcement, see Gabriel J. Chin & Marc L. Miller, The Unconstitutionality of State Regulation of Immigration Through Criminal Law, 61 Duke L.J. 251 (2011). On the significance of prosecutorial discretion in immigration enforcement, see 132 S. Ct. at 2505 (citing Motor Coach Employees v. Lockridge, 403 U.S. 274, 287 (1971); Martin, Reading *Arizona*, supra note 17, at 45. For post-*Arizona* decisions, see United States v. Alabama, 691 F.3d 1269, 1282–1283, 1285–1288, 1292–1297 (11th Cir. 2012); Hispanic Interest Coalition of Alabama v. Governor of Alabama, 691 F.3d 1236, 1244–1249 (11th Cir. 2012); Georgia Latino Alliance of Human Rights v. Governor of Georgia, 691 F.3d 1250, 1265 (11th Cir. 2012); United States v. South Carolina, 906 F. Supp. 2d 463, 467–469 (D.S.C. 2012); Utah Coalition of La Raza v. Herbert (Case No. 2:11-CV-401) (D. Utah Feb. 15, 2013); Buquer v. City of Indianapolis, 2013 WL 1332158, 7–12 (S.D. Ind. 2013); State v. Sarrabea, 2013 WL 1810228, *4–*12 (La. App. 3d Cir. May 1, 2013). On the Louisiana law, see also Chapter 2 in this volume.

30. Several federal appeals courts later applied this reasoning to allow similar state law provisions to take effect. See United States v. Alabama, 691 F.3d at 1283–1285; *Georgia Latino Alliance of Human Rights*, 691 F.3d at 1267–1268.

31. See 8 U.S.C. § 1373(c).

32. See 132 S. Ct. at 2508; 132 S. Ct. at 2526 (Alito, J., dissenting). See also United States v. Arizona, 641 F.3d 339, 379 (9th Cir. 2011) (Bea, J., dissenting) (emphasizing federal discretion not to take action).

33. See Chapter 1 in this volume.

34. See, e.g., INA §§ 275, 276, 8 U.S.C. §§ 1325, 1326.

35. See Chapter 1 in this volume.

36. See Abrams, Plenary Power Preemption, supra note 21, at 628–629.

37. 403 U.S. 365, 371–380 (1971). But see Dennis J. Hutchinson, More Substantive Equal Protection? A Note on *Plyler v. Doe*, 1982 Sup. Ct. Rev. 167, 186.

38. On nonimmigrants, compare Van Staden v. St. Martin, 664 F.3d 56, 58–62 (5th Cir. 2011); League of United Latin American Citizens (LULAC) v. Bredesen, 500 F.3d 523, 533 (6th Cir. 2007); LeClerc v. Webb, 419 F.3d 405, 415–19 (5th Cir. 2005), cert. denied, 551 U.S. 1158 (2007); with Dandamudi v. Tisch, 686 F.3d 66, 72–79 (2d Cir. 2012); Adusumelli v. Steiner, 740 F. Supp. 2d 582, 587–99 (S.D.N.Y. 2010); Kirk v. New York State Dept. of Educ., 562 F. Supp. 2d 405, 409–12 (W.D.N.Y. 2008). Cf. Toll v. Moreno, 458 U.S. 1, 9–10 (1982) (not reaching lawful nonimmigrants' equal protection claims).

39. For criticism of current equal protection doctrine, see, e.g., Gerald L. Neuman, Aliens as Outlaws: Government Services, Proposition 187, and the Structure of Equal Protection Doctrine, 42 UCLA L. Rev. 1425, 1440–1452 (1995); Jason H. Lee, Unlawful Status as a "Constitutional Irrelevancy"?: The Equal Protection Rights of Illegal Immigrants, 39 Golden Gate U. L. Rev. 1, 19–40 (2008). For preemption challenges, see, e.g., Villas at Parkside Partners v. City of Farmers Branch, 496 F. Supp. 2d 757, 764–772 (N.D. Tex. 2007); Garrett v. City of Escondido, 465 F. Supp. 2d 1043, 1054–1057 (S.D. Cal. 2006); Equal Access Education v. Merten, 305 F. Supp. 2d 585, 601–608 (E.D. Va. 2004).

40. Lozano v. City of Hazleton, 620 F.3d 170, 176, 195 & n.19 (3d Cir. 2010), vacated, 131 S. Ct. 2958 (2011), on remand, 724 F.3d 297 (3d Cir. 2013); Lozano v. City of Hazleton, 496 F. Supp. 2d 477, 484–485, 508–510, 538–542, 556–562 (M.D. Pa. 2007), affirmed, 620 F.3d 170 (3d Cir. 2010), vacated, 131 S. Ct. 2958 (2011), on remand, 724 F.3d 297 (3d Cir. 2013). On state or local enforcement increasing the risk of racial discrimination, see Michael A. Olivas, Immigration-Related State and Local Ordinances: Preemption, Prejudice, and the Proper Role for Enforcement, 2007 U. Chi. Legal F. 27, 35; Bill Ong Hing, Institutional Racism, ICE Raids, and Immigration Reform, 44 U.S.F. L. Rev. 307, 318–320 (2009); Huyen Pham, The Private Enforcement of Immigration Laws, 96 Geo. L.J. 777, 781 (2008); Michael J. Wishnie, State and Local Police Enforcement of Immigration Laws, 6 U. Pa. J. Const. L. 1084, 1104 (2004); Michael J. Wishnie, Laboratories of Bigotry?

Devolution of the Immigration Power, Equal Protection, and Federalism, 76 N.Y.U. L. Rev. 493, 497–498 (2001). On race as an element in support for Proposition 187, see, e.g., Neuman, Equal Protection, supra note 39, at 1451–1452; Ruben J. Garcia, Critical Race Theory and Proposition 187: The Racial Politics of Immigration Law, 17 Chicano-Latino L. Rev. 118, 132–142 (1995).

41. See *City of Hazleton*, 496 F. Supp. 2d at 546–48; Lucas Guttentag, The Forgotten Equality Norm in Immigration Preemption and the Civil Rights Act of 1870, 8 Duke J. Con. L. & Pol'y 1 (2013); Lucas Guttentag, Discrimination, Preemption, and Arizona's Immigration Law: A Broader View, 65 Stan. L. Rev. Online 1 (June 18, 2012).

42. On race-related enforcement, see Trevor Gardner II & Aarti Kohli, The C.A.P. Effect: Racial Profiling in the ICE Criminal Alien Program (Warren Inst. 2009). On the stakes in a discrimination claim, see Sun, Equality by Other Means, supra note 5, at 184–187. Thanks to Margo Schlanger from prompting this line of thought. On the neutrality of the statutes as written, see *City of Hazleton*, 496 F. Supp. 2d at 542.

43. See Olivas, State and Local Ordinances, supra note 40, at 55 (analogizing Hazleton ordinance to "our inglorious immigration history of racial exclusion").

44. On the federal government's termination of its 287(g) agreement with the Maricopa County Sheriff's Office, see Statement by Secretary Napolitano on DOJ's Findings of Discriminatory Policing in Maricopa County, Department of Homeland Security Press Release, Dec. 15, 2011. For earlier versions of my analysis of state and local authority, see Hiroshi Motomura, Immigration Outside the Law, 108 Colum. L. Rev. 2037, 2063–2065 (2008); Hiroshi Motomura, The Rights of Others: Legal Claims and Immigration Outside the Law, 59 Duke L.J. 1723, 1743–1745 (2010). For views consistent with some parts of this analysis, see Guttentag, Discrimination, Preemption, and Arizona's Immigration Law, supra note 41; Guttentag, Immigration Preemption, supra note 28, at 35–42; Abrams, Plenary Power Preemption, supra note 21, at 638; Jennifer M. Chacón, The Transformation of Immigration Federalism, 21 Wm. & Mary Bill Rts. J. 577 (2012); Peter Margulies, Taking Care of Immigration Law: Presidential Stewardship, Prosecutorial Discretion, and the Separation of Powers, 94 B.U. L. Rev. 105, 169–171, (2014); Angela M. Banks, The Curious Relationship Between "Self-Deportation" Policies and Naturalization Rates, 16 Lewis & Clark L. Rev. 1149, 1149 (2012); Sun, Equality by Other Means, supra note 5, at 178–194; Adam Winkler, Free Speech Federalism, 108 Mich. L. Rev. 153, 160–163 (2009).

45. Dred Scott v. Sandford, 60 U.S. 393 (1857).

46. 132 S. Ct. at 2511 (Scalia, J., dissenting).

47. See 403 U.S. 365, 371–80 (1971); 426 U.S. 67, 77–87 (1976). See also Bernal v. Fainter, 467 U.S. 216, 219 (1984). See generally Gerald M. Rosberg, The Protection of Aliens from Discriminatory Treatment by the National Government, 1977 Sup. Ct. Rev. 275, 283–293; Harold Hongju Koh, Equality with a Human

Face: Justice Blackmun and the Equal Protection of Aliens, 8 Hamline L. Rev. 51, 98–102 (1985); Hiroshi Motomura, Immigration and Alienage, Federalism and Proposition 187, 35 Va. J. Int'l L. 201, 205–206 (1994); Neuman, Equal Protection, supra note 39, at 1430–1440. On commentary viewing *Diaz* as a preemption decision, see David F. Levi, Note, The Equal Treatment of Aliens: Preemption or Equal Protection?, 31 Stan. L. Rev. 1069, 1085–1086, 1088 (1979); Michael J. Perry, Modern Equal Protection: A Conceptualization and Appraisal, 79 Colum. L. Rev. 1023, 1060–1065 (1979).

48. See Koh, Equality with a Human Face, supra note 47, at 98–99.

49. See Hiroshi Motomura, Americans in Waiting: The Lost Story of Immigration and Citizenship in the United States, 16–17, 23–24 (Oxford Univ. Press 2006) (tracing developments that led to the Chinese exclusion laws); see also Chapter 2 in this volume. See also Spiro, Learning to Live with Immigration Federalism, supra note 10, at 1635.

50. See Wishnie, Laboratories of Bigotry?, supra note 40, at 511 n.96; Lee, Unlawful Status, supra note 39, at 28–29. See also Neuman, Equal Protection, supra note 39, at 1436–1440; Motomura, Immigration and Alienage, supra note 47, at 206–207; Rosberg, Protection of Aliens, supra note 47, at 284. On varying approaches among local police departments, see Ingrid V. Eagly, Criminal Justice for Noncitizens: An Analysis of Variation in Local Enforcement, 88 N.Y.U. L. Rev. 1126 (2013). On Secure Communities, see Eagly, Criminal Justice for Noncitizens supra, at 1148–1149, 1212–1218; Adam B. Cox & Thomas J. Miles, Policing Immigration, 80 U. Chi. L. Rev. 87 (2013); Chapter 2 in this volume.

51. See Schuck, Taking Immigration Federalism Seriously, supra note 10, at 60–64.

52. On the value of transparency and deliberation in national security cases, see Joseph Landau, Muscular Procedure: Conditional Deference in the Executive Detention Cases, 84 Wash. L. Rev. 661 (2009). On the Gallegly amendment, see Michael A. Olivas, No Undocumented Child Left Behind: *Plyler v. Doe* and the Education of Undocumented Schoolchildren, 42–43 (N.Y.U. Press 2012); Thomas Alexander Aleinikoff, David A. Martin, Hiroshi Motomura, & Maryellen Fullerton, Immigration and Citizenship: Process and Policy, 1052 (7th ed. West 2012).

53. On the difficulties that anti-foreign movements may have in enlisting national government support, see Neuman, Equal Protection, supra note 39, at 1436.

54. This role for state and local government may not only yield the benefits of deliberation in the national arena, but also allow states and localities to exert more influence by working within the federal enforcement. See Jessica Bulman-Pozen & Heather K. Gerken, Uncooperative Federalism, 118 Yale L.J. 1256, 1265–1284 (2009). For the view that the shift toward Secure Communities reflects federal efforts to exercise greater control over state and local involvement in immigration enforcement, see Stephen Lee, Workplace Enforcement Workarounds, 21 Wm. &

Mary Bill of Rts J. 549 (2012); Stephen Lee, De Facto Immigration Courts, 101 Cal. L. Rev. 553 (2013).

55. See Kristin Collins, Sheriffs Help Feds Deport Illegal Aliens, News & Observer (Raleigh), Apr. 22, 2007, at 1A; S. Karthick Ramakrishnan & Pratheepan Gulasekaram, The Importance of the Political in Immigration Federalism, 44 Ariz. St. L.J. 1431, 1448–1483 (2013); Chapter 2 in this volume.

56. Cf. Young, Ordinary Diet, supra note 10, at 255 ("Congress's preemptive intent, in other words, varies by context, and courts faithful to interpreting that intent will thus produce varying results from one context to another.").

57. See Chapter 1 in this volume.

58. See Abrams, Plenary Power Preemption, supra note 21, at 640.

59. See INA § 274A, 8 U.S.C. § 1324a; Collins Foods Int'l, Inc. v. INS, 948 F.2d 549, 553–55 (9th Cir. 1991). See also Kitty Calavita, Employer Sanctions Violations: Toward a Dialectical Model of White-Collar Crime, 24 L. & Soc'y Rev. 1041, 1046–1055, 1057, 1060 (1990); Chapter 1 in this volume. On the private enforcement role generally, see Lee, Private Immigration Screening, supra note 8; Pham, Private Enforcement, supra note 40.

60. See F. Ray Marshall, Economic Factors Influencing the International Migration of Workers, in Views across the Border 163, 169 (Stanley R. Ross ed., 1978). See also Jennifer Gordon, Suburban Sweatshops: The Fight for Immigrant Rights, 49–50 (Harvard Univ. Press 2005); David Bacon, Illegal People: How Globalization Creates Migration and Criminalizes Immigrants, 3–21, 131, 142–145 (Beacon Press 2008). On recent developments, see Aleinikoff, Martin, Motomura, & Fullerton, Immigration and Citizenship, supra note 52, at 962–972 (7th ed. West 2012). On workplace rights, see also Chapter 5 in this volume. See also S. 744, § 3101, 113th Cong., 1st Sess. (2013) (making E-Verify mandatory for all employers after a phase-in period and limiting employer discretion to use E-Verify to check employees' work authorization).

61. See Discharge, Deportation, and Dangerous Journeys (Seton Hall Law School & New York Lawyers for the Public Interest 2012); David Pitt, US Hospitals Send Hundreds of Immigrant Patients Back to Home Countries to Curb Cost of Care, Assoc. Press, Apr. 23, 2013; David Pitt, A Look at Immigrant Patients Deported by US Hospitals, Assoc. Press, Apr. 23, 2013; Caitlin O'Connell, Return to Sender: Evaluating Medical Repatriations of Uninsured Immigrants, 87 Wash. U. L. Rev. 1429, 1447–1450 (2010); Deborah Sontag, Immigrants Facing Deportation by U.S. Hospitals, N.Y. Times, Aug. 3, 2008, at A1.

62. See Francisco E. Balderrama & Raymond Rodríguez, Decade of Betrayal: Mexican Repatriation in the 1930s (rev. ed. Univ. of New Mexico Press 2006); Joseph Nevins, Operation Gatekeeper and Beyond: The War on "Illegals" and the Remaking of the US-Mexico Boundary, 136–138 (Routledge 2010).

63. See More Than a Minute, Ariz. Republic, May 8, 2005, at 4V; Kristina Davis, Keeping the Peace, San Diego Union–Trib., Jul. 1, 2007, at N1; Michael Leahy,

Crossing the Line, Wash. Post, Mar. 19, 2006, at W12; Carla Marinucci, Governor Defends Border Watchers, S.F. Chron., Sept. 22, 2005, at B1; Timothy Egan, Wanted: Border Hoppers. And Some Excitement, Too, N.Y. Times, Apr. 1, 2005, at A14. See also Harel Shapira, Waiting of José: The Minutemen's Pursuit of America (Princeton Univ. Press 2013); Roxanne Lynn Doty, The Law into Their Own Hands: Immigration and the Politics of Exceptionalism (Univ. of Arizona Press 2009); Roxanne Lynn Doty, States of Exception on the Mexico-U.S. Border: Security, "Decisions," and Civilian Border Patrols, 1 Int'l Pol. Soc. 113 (2007). On border webcams, see Arthur H. Rotstein, Groups Use Cameras to Keep Watchful Eye on Border, Oakland Trib., Apr. 19, 2008; Alicia A. Caldwell, Texas Governor Proposes Webcams along Border, S. Fla. Sun-Sentinel, June 9, 2006, at 2A; Assoc. Press, Texas Border Cam Test Catches 10 Illegal Immigrants, Chicago Sun-Times, Jan. 8, 2007; Editorial, Good Money after Bad: Border Cameras Provide Little More Than Costly Photo Ops, Houston Chron., Apr. 27, 2010.

CHAPTER 5

Building Communities

1. See Lorelei Laird, The Dream Bar, Am. Bar Ass'n J. 50, 51 (Jan. 2013); Florida Board of Bar Examiners Re: Question as to Whether Undocumented Immigrants Are Eligible for Admission to the Florida Bar, No. SC11-2568 (Fla. Apr. 4, 2013).
2. See generally Peter J. Spiro, Formalizing Local Citizenship, 37 Fordham Urb. L.J. 559, 560 (2010); Rose Cuison Villazor, "Sanctuary Cities" and Local Citizenship, 37 Fordham Urb. L.J. 573 (2010); Pratheepan Gulasekaram, Sub-National Immigration Regulation and the Pursuit of Cultural Cohesion, 77 U. Cin. L. Rev. 1441 (2009); Cristina Rodríguez, The Significance of the Local in Immigration Regulation, 106 Mich. L. Rev. 567, 581–609 (2008); Noah Pickus & Peter Skerry, Good Neighbors and Good Citizens: Beyond the Legal-Illegal Immigration Debate, in Debating Immigration, 95, 111–113 (Carol Swain ed., Cambridge Univ. Press 2007). On "alien citizenship," see Linda Bosniak, Universal Citizenship and the Problem of Alienage, 94 Nw. U.L. Rev. 963, 978 (2000). On the relationship between local citizenship and sanctuary laws, see Spiro, Formalizing Local Citizenship, supra note 2, at 566–567. On local political participation, see Rick Su, Urban Politics and the Assimilation of Immigrant Voters, 21 Wm. & Mary Bill Rts. J. 653 (2012).
3. See Nina Rabin, Mary Carol Combs, & Norma González, Understanding *Plyler's* Legacy: Voices from Border Schools, 37 J.L. & Educ. 15, 58 (2008).
4. See Michael A. Olivas, No Undocumented Child Left Behind: *Plyler v. Doe* and the Education of Undocumented Schoolchildren, 35–61 (N.Y.U. Press 2012); Rabin, Combs, & González, Understanding *Plyler's* Legacy, supra note 3, at 50–61; Chapter 2 in this volume.

5. See Beason-Hammon Alabama Taxpayer and Citizen Protection Act, Pub. Act No. 535, 2011 Al. ALS 535 (Ala. 2011); Letter from Thomas E. Perez, Asst. Atty. Gen., to Dr. Thomas R. Bice, State Supt. of Education, 2 (May 1, 2012); Mary Orndorff, DOJ Looks at State School Records, Birmingham News, Nov. 5, 2011, at A1; Hispanic Interest Coalition of Alabama v. Governor of Alabama, 691 F.3d 1236, 1244–49 (11th Cir. 2012); Olivas, No Undocumented Child, supra note 4, at 45; Chapter 2 in this volume.

6. For a version of the DREAM Act, see S. 744, § 2103, 113th Cong., 1st Sess. (2013). For prior versions, see Development, Relief, and Education for Alien Minors (DREAM) Act of 2011, S. 952, 112th Cong. (2011); H.R. 1842, 112th Cong. (2011). See also Chapter 6 in this volume. On DACA, see Memorandum from Janet Napolitano, Secretary of Homeland Sec., to David V. Aguilar, Acting Commissioner, U.S. Customs & Border Prot., Alejandro Mayorkas, Director, U.S. Citizenship & Immigration Servs., & John Morton, Director, U.S. Immigration & Customs Enforcement, on Exercising Prosecutorial Discretion with Respect to Individuals Who Came to the United States as Children, June 15, 2012; Chapter 1 in this volume. On federal health care eligibility, see 77 Fed. Reg. 52614, 52616 (Aug. 30, 2012) (adding 45 C.F.R. § 152.2(8)). On driver's license restrictions, see Ariz. Exec. Order 2012–06; Paul Hammel, Second Lawsuit to Challenge Driver's License Denial, Omaha World-Herald, June 11, 2013, at 1B; Fernanda Santos, State Defends Immigrant License Limits, N.Y. Times, Mar. 23, 2013, at A13; Kim Severson, North Carolina to Give Some Immigrants Driver's Licenses, With a Pink Stripe, N.Y. Times, Mar. 6, 2013, at A14.

7. See Calif. Stats. 2001, c. 814 (A.B. 540), codified at Calif. Educ. Code § 68130.5; Chapter 2 in this volume.

8. See Calif. Educ. Code §§ 66021.6, 66021.7, 69508.5, 68130.7, 76300.5.

9. See Leisy Abrego, Legitimacy, Social Identity, and the Mobilization of Law: The Effects of Assembly Bill 540 on Undocumented Students in California, 33 Law & Soc. Inquiry 709, 723–729 (2008); Rodríguez, Significance of the Local, supra note 2, at 605–608.

10. For an overview of challenges to resident tuition for unauthorized migrants, see Michael A. Olivas, Dreams Deferred: Deferred Action, Prosecutorial Discretion, and the Vexing Case(s) of DREAM Act Students, 21 Wm. & Mary Bill Rts. J. 463, 464–469 (2012).

11. See Pub. L. No. 104–208, 110 Stat. 3009–546. On 8 U.S.C. §§ 1621 and 1623, see Michael A. Olivas, IIRIRA, The DREAM Act, and Undocumented College Student Residency, 30 J.C. & U.L. 435, 449–455 (2004); Victor C. Romero, Noncitizen Students and Immigration Policy Post-9/11, 17 Geo. Immigr. L.J. 357 (2003); Victor C. Romero, Postsecondary School Education Benefits for Undocumented Immigrants: Promises and Pitfalls, 27 N.C. J. Int'l L. & Com. Reg. 393, 398–407 (2002); Jessica Salsbury, Comment, Evading "Residence": Undocumented Students, Higher Education, and the States, 53 Am.

U. L. Rev. 459, 476–480 (2003). Legislation passed by the U.S. Senate in 2013 would repeal section 1623, see S. 744, § 2103(d), 113th Cong., 1st Sess. (2013).

12. Martinez v. The Regents of the University of California, 50 Cal. 4th 1277, 241 P.3d 855, 117 Cal. Rptr. 359 (2010), cert. denied, 131 S. Ct. 2961 (2011). For lawsuits dismissed for lack of standing, see, e.g., Day v. Bond, 500 F.3d 1127, 1132–1139 (10th Cir. 2007); Immigration Reform Coal. of Tex. v. Texas, 706 F. Supp. 2d 760, 764–765 (S.D. Tex. 2010); Mannschreck v. Clare, Ci:10–8 (Neb. Dist. Ct. Aug. 19, 2010). See also Kevin Abourezk, Judge Tosses Suit on Tuition to Illegal Immigrants; Plaintiffs Likely to Refile Suit, Lincoln J. Star, Dec. 18, 2010, at A1. From the opposite political direction, several lawsuits challenged state laws in New Jersey and Florida that denied resident tuition to US citizen students if their parents lacked lawful immigration status. On both types of cases, see Olivas, Dreams Deferred, supra note 10, at 465–468. For criticism of resident tuition eligibility, see Brief of U.S. Representative Lamar Smith, Steve King, et al., Martinez v. Regents of the University of California, 50 Cal. 4th 1277 (Cal. 2010) (No. S167791); Kris W. Kobach, Immigration Nullification: In-State Tuition and Lawmakers Who Disregard the Law, 10 N.Y.U. J. Legis. & Pub. Pol'y 473, 498–507 (2006–2007).

13. See 50 Cal. 4th at 1288–1298. See 50 Cal. 4th at 1296–1298.

14. See Laird, The Dream Bar, supra note 1, at 51; Claudia Torrens, Mexican Immigrant with NYC Law Degree Is in Limbo, Assoc. Press, Mar. 6, 2012; Olivas, Dreams Deferred, supra note 10, at 537.

15. See Garcia on Admission, Case No. S202512, California Supreme Court, Order to Show Cause, May 16, 2012. See also Laird, The Dream Bar, supra note 1, at 51; Paloma Esquivel, Can Illegal Immigrant Practice Law?, L.A. Times, June 11, 2012, at A1; Olivas, Dreams Deferred, supra note 10, at 535–536.

16. See 8 U.S.C. §1621(d).

17. See Brief of Nicholas Kierniesky as Amicus Curiae, In Re: Sergio Garcia (No. S202512) (California Supreme Court); Brief of Larry Desha as Amicus Curiae, In Re: Sergio Garcia (No. S202512) (California Supreme Court); Brief of United States of America as Amicus Curiae 5–12, In Re: Sergio Garcia (No. S202512) (California Supreme Court).

18. See In re Sergio C. Garcia on Admission, S202512 (Cal. Jan. 2, 2014).

19. See Chapter 4 in this volume.

20. To apply some of the framework in Heather Gerken, Foreword: Federalism All the Way Down, 124 Harv. L. Rev. 4 (2010), local integration is a matter of voice, whereas allowing possibly discriminatory measures to exclude unauthorized migrants confers too much power on states and localities as sovereigns.

21. See Linda S. Bosniak, Exclusion and Membership: The Dual Identity of the Undocumented Worker under United States Law, 1988 Wis. L. Rev. 955, 978–979; Conn. G.S.A. Const. Art. 1 § 10. See also Jason H. Lee, Unlawful Status as a "Constitutional Irrelevancy"?: The Equal Protection Rights of Illegal Immigrants, 39 Golden Gate U. L. Rev. 1, 12 (2008); Developments in the Law—Immigration

Policy and the Rights of Aliens: The Rights of Undocumented Aliens, 96 Harv. L. Rev. 1433, 1454–1455 (1983). On the oral argument in *Plyler*, see Chapter 1 in this volume.

22. See Christopher D. Nelson, Protecting the Immigrant Family: The Misguided Policies, Practices and Proposed Legislation Regarding Marriage License Issuance, 4 U. St. Thomas L.J. 643, 647–656 (2006–07); Ariz. Const. Art. 2, § 35; Ariz. Const. Art. 2, § 22 (constitutionality upheld in Lopez-Valenzuela et al v. Maricopa County, 2013 WL 2995220 (9th Cir. June 18, 2013)); Kristina M. Campbell, The Road to S.B. 1070: How Arizona Became Ground Zero for the Immigrants' Rights Movement and the Continuing Struggle for Latino Civil Rights in America, 14 Harv. Latino L. Rev. 1, 6–7 (2011); Beason–Hammon Alabama Taxpayer and Citizen Protection Act, Pub. Act No. 535, § 27, 2011 Al. ALS 535 (Ala. 2011); United States v. Alabama, 691 F.3d 1269, 1292–1295 (11th Cir. 2012).

23. See INA § 274A, 8 U.S.C. § 1324a; Bosniak, Exclusion and Membership, supra note 21, at 1007.

24. Hoffman Plastic Compounds, Inc. v. NLRB, 535 U.S. 137, 140, 142, 151, 152 (2002).

25. See National Labor Relations Act, 29 U.S.C. §§ 151–169; Title VII of the Civil Rights Act of 1964, 42 U.S.C. §§ 2000e to 2000e–17; Rivera v. NIBCO, Inc., 364 F.3d 1057, 1061 (9th Cir. 2004); Escobar v. Spartan Sec. Serv., 281 F. Supp. 2d 895, 896 (S.D. Tex. 2003); Fair Labor Standards Act, 29 U.S.C. §§ 201–219; Zavala v. Wal-Mart Stores, Inc., 393 F. Supp. 2d 295, 323 (D.N.J. 2005); Singh v. Jutla, 214 F. Supp. 2d 1056, 1056 (N.D. Cal. 2002). See generally David Bacon, Illegal People: How Globalization Creates Migration and Criminalizes Immigrants, 135 (Beacon Press 2008).

26. See 535 U.S. at 153–156 (Breyer, J., dissenting). The majority was concerned with a different systemic effect—the incentives that granting full remedies would give future unauthorized workers to come to the United States. See 535 U.S. at 151. See also Michele Wucker, Lockout: Why America Keeps Getting Immigration Wrong When Our Prosperity Depends on Getting It Right, 113 (Public Affairs 2006).

27. On the practical obstacles to assertion of workplace rights, see Bosniak, Exclusion and Membership, supra note 21, at 993–994. See generally Keith Cunningham-Parmeter, Redefining the Rights of Undocumented Workers, 58 Am. U. L. Rev. 1361, 1389 (2009); Lori Nessel, Undocumented Immigrants in the Workplace: The Fallacy of Labor Protection and the Need for Reform, 36 Harv. C.R.-C.L. L. Rev. 345, 347 (2001). Cf. Derrick A. Bell, Jr., Comment, *Brown v. Board of Education* and the Interest-Convergence Dilemma, 93 Harv. L. Rev. 518 (1980) ("The interest of blacks in achieving racial equality will be accommodated only when it converges with the interests of whites").

28. See Nathaniel Popper, In Rubashkins' Backyard, Another Tale of Labor Strife, The Forward, Aug. 22, 2008, at 1. On the Postville raid, see Chapter 1 in this volume. On later developments at Agri Processors, see Maggie Jones, Postville, Iowa, Is

Up for Grabs, N.Y. Times Mag., July 11, 2012, at MM34; Julia Preston, Large Iowa Meatpacker in Illegal Immigrant Raid Files for Bankruptcy, N.Y. Times, Nov. 6, 2008, at A21; Julia Preston, 27-Year Sentence for Plant Manager, N.Y. Times, June 22, 2008, at A18.

29. See Agri Processor Co. v. NLRB, 514 F.3d 1, 2, 7–9 (D.C. Cir. 2008). See also Sure-Tan, Inc. v. NLRB, 467 U.S. 883 (1984).

30. On work as a place where personal ties form, see Cynthia Estlund, Working Together: How Workplace Bonds Strengthen a Diverse Democracy, 117 (Oxford Univ. Press 2003).

31. *Hoffman*, 535 U.S. at 148–150, 153, 155–156 (Breyer, J., dissenting); see also Cunningham-Parmeter, Rights of Undocumented Workers, supra note 27, at 1393–95.

32. See Balbuena v. IDR Realty LLC, 845 N.E. 2d 1246, 1249–1251 (N.Y. 2006); Mark Johnson, Court Backs Illegal Immigrants on Lost Wages, Albany Times Union, Feb. 22, 2006, at E1; Majlinger v. Cassino Constr. Corp., 1 Misc. 3d 659, 660, 766 N.Y.S.2d 332, 333 (Sup. Ct. Richmond Cnty. 2003); Madeira v. Affordable Housing Found., Inc., 469 F.3d 219, 223–224 (2d Cir. 2006); Ambrosi v. 1085 Park Ave. LLC, 2008 WL 4386751 (S.D.N.Y. Sept. 25, 2008).

33. See *Balbuena*, 845 N.E. 2d at 1258; *Madeira*, 469 F.3d at 223–224, 228; *Ambrosi*, 2008 WL 4386751, at *13. For cases granting remedies under the Fair Labor Standards Act to unauthorized workers because of the seriousness of not paying for work performed, see, e.g., Chellen v. John Pickle Co., 446 F. Supp. 2d 1247, 1276–1277, 1279–1281 (N.D. Okla. 2006); Zavala v. Wal-Mart Stores, Inc., 393 F. Supp. 2d 295, 322–325 (D.N.J. 2005); Galaviz-Zamora v. Brady Farms, Inc., 230 F.R.D. 499, 501–503 (W.D. Mich. 2005); Flores v. Amigon, 233 F. Supp. 2d 462, 463–464 (E.D.N.Y. 2002). Singh v. Jutla, 214 F. Supp. 2d 1056, 1058–1059 (N.D. Cal. 2002). See generally Cunningham-Parmeter, Rights of Undocumented Workers, supra note 27, at 1370 & n.55.

34. See In re Perez-Cruz, No. A95 748 837, slip op. (Immigration Ct. L.A., Cal. Feb. 9, 2009), appeal filed.

35. See INS v. Lopez-Mendoza, 468 U.S. 1032, 1050 (1984) (holding that the exclusionary rule does not apply in civil deportation hearings held by the INS).

36. 468 U.S. 1032, 1041, 1043–1046, 1048–1050 (1984).

37. See 468 U.S. at 1050–1051. On the egregious violation exception, see Oliva-Ramos v. Attorney General, 694 F.3d 259, 272, 275 (3d Cir. 2012); Puc-Ruiz v. Holder, 629 F.3d 771 (8th Cir. 2010); Pinto-Montoya, v. Mukasey, 540 F.3d 126, 131 (2d Cir. 2008); Almeida-Amaral v. Gonzales, 461 F.3d 231, 237 (2d Cir. 2006); Orhorhaghe v. INS, 38 F.3d 488, 501 (9th Cir. 1994); Gonzalez-Rivera v. INS, 22 F.3d 1441, 1450–1449 (9th Cir. 1994). For immigration judge rulings relying on the egregious violation exception to suppress unlawfully obtained evidence, see, e.g., In re Reyes-Basurto, slip op. at 7–9 (Immigration Ct. N.Y., N.Y. May 28, 2009), Legal Action Ctr., American Immigration Council, Enforcement, Motions to

Suppress: A General Overview (2013). See generally Elizabeth Rossi, Revisiting *INS v. Lopez-Mendoza*: Why the Fourth Amendment Exclusionary Rule Should Apply in Deportation Proceedings, 44 Colum. Hum. Rts. L. Rev 477 (2013); Hiroshi Motomura, The Rights of Others: Legal Claims and Immigration Outside the Law, 59 Duke L.J. 1723, 1762–1773 (2010); Jennifer Chacón, A Diversion of Attention? Immigration Courts and the Adjudication of Fourth and Fifth Amendment Rights, 59 Duke L.J. 1563 (2010); Kevin R. Johnson, The Case Against Race Profiling in Immigration Enforcement, 78 Wash. U. L.Q. 675, 693–711 (2000); United States v. Brignoni-Ponce, 422 U.S. 873, 885–886 (1975).

38. See In re Perez-Cruz, No. A95 748 837, slip op. (Immigration Ct. L.A., Cal. Feb. 9, 2009), appeal filed.

39. This pragmatic approach is consistent with Justice O'Connor's observation in *Lopez–Mendoza* that it might be appropriate to revisit Fourth Amendment remedies if the government did not adequately control and supervise immigration enforcement and constitutional violations become widespread. See Stella Burch Elias, "Good Reason to Believe": Widespread Constitutional Violations in the Course of Immigration Enforcement and the Case for Revisiting *Lopez-Mendoza*, 2008 Wis. L. Rev. 1109.

40. See INA § 212(h), 8 U.S.C. § 1182(h) (waiver of inadmissibility for crimes); INA § 212(i), 8 U.S.C. § 1182(i) (waiver of inadmissibility for fraud or willful misrepresentation); INA § 237 (a)(1)(H), 8 U.S.C. § 1227(a)(1)(H) (waiver of deportability for misrepresentation); INA § 240A(b), 8 U.S.C. § 1229b(b); T. Alexander Aleinikoff, David A. Martin, Hiroshi Motomura, & Maryellen Fullerton, Immigration and Citizenship: Process and Policy, 756–757 (7th ed. West 2012); Chapter 1 in this volume.

41. On the constitutional relevance of the effects that government immigration decisions have on citizens, see Adam B. Cox, Citizenship, Standing, and Immigration Law, 92 Cal. L. Rev. 373, 374 (2004); Hiroshi Motomura, Whose Immigration Law?: Citizens, Aliens, and the Constitution, 97 Colum. L. Rev. 1567, 1584–1586, 1601–1602 (1997); Hiroshi Motomura, Whose Alien Nation?: Two Models of Constitutional Immigration Law, 94 Mich. L. Rev. 1927, 1946–1952 (1996). On the arguments against Proposition 187, see Linda S. Bosniak, Opposing Prop. 187: Undocumented Immigrants and the National Imagination, 28 Conn. L. Rev. 555, 558, 566 (1996). See also Joseph Nevins, Operation Gatekeeper and Beyond: The War on "Illegals" and the Remaking of the US-Mexico Boundary, 141 (Routledge 2010). On Proposition 187, see Chapter 2 in this volume.

42. See Gerald L. Neuman, Aliens as Outlaws: Government Services, Proposition 187, and the Structure of Equal Protection Doctrine, 42 UCLA L. Rev. 1425, 1441 (1995); see also Nevins, Operation Gatekeeper, supra note 41, at 140; Bosniak, Exclusion and Membership, supra note 21, at 956; Pub. L. No. 99–603, 100 Stat. 3359.

43. See In re Perez-Cruz, No. A95 748 837, slip op. (Immigration Ct. L.A., Cal. Feb. 9, 2009), appeal filed; In re Herrera–Priego, No. [redacted], slip op. at 20–25 (Immigration Ct. N.Y., N.Y. July 10, 2003). See also Motomura, The Rights of Others, supra note 37, at 1762–1770; Michael J. Wishnie, Introduction: The Border Crossed Us: Current Issues in Immigrant Labor, 28 N.Y.U. Rev. L. & Soc. Change 389, 389–393 (2004); Hiroshi Motomura, Immigration Law after a Century of Plenary Power: Phantom Constitutional Norms and Statutory Interpretation, 100 Yale L.J. 545 (1990).

44. See Chapter 6 in this volume.

45. On integration and access to equality, see Chapter 3 in this volume.

46. See generally Annie Decker, Preemption Conflation: Dividing the Local from the State in Congressional Decision Making, 30 Yale L. & Pol'y Rev. 321, 358 (2012); Spiro, Formalizing Local Citizenship, supra note 2, at 560.

47. On the overall economic impact of immigration, see, e.g., Giovanni Peri, The Impact of Immigrants in Recession and Economic Expansion, 6 (Migration Policy Inst. 2010); Heidi Shierholz, Immigration and Wages: Methodological Advancements Confirm Modest Gains for Native Workers, 1, 3–4 (Economic Policy Inst. 2010); Rakesh Kochhar, Growth in the Foreign-Born Workforce and Employment of the Native Born, 27 (Pew Hispanic Ctr. 2006); Gianmarco I. P. Ottaviano & Giovanni Peri, Rethinking the Gains from Immigration: Theory and Evidence from the U.S., NBER Working Paper No. 11672 (National Bureau of Economic Research 2005); David Card, Is the New Immigration Really So Bad?, NBER Working Paper No. 11547 (National Bureau of Economic Research 2005). For an overview, see Adam Davidson, Do Illegal Immigrants Actually Hurt the U.S. Economy, N.Y. Times Mag., Feb. 12, 2013, at MM17. On the related but distinct question of the economic impact of conferring lawful immigration status on unauthorized migrants, see, e.g., Giovanni Peri, The Economic Windfall of Immigration Reform, Wall St. J., Feb. 13, 2013, at A15. For further discussion, see Chapter 7 in this volume.

48. For the related call for local voting rights for noncitizens—including unauthorized migrants—because local voting affects their daily lives more directly through school, housing, roads, and the like, see Adam B. Cox & Eric A. Posner, The Rights of Migrants: An Optimal Contract Framework, 84 N.Y.U. L. Rev. 1403, 1452 (2009).

49. See Illegal Immigration Reform and Immigrant Responsibility Act of 1996, Pub. L. No. 104–208, 110 Stat. 3009–546; INA § 235(b)(1), 8 U.S.C. § 1225(b)(1); INA § 236(c), 8 U.S.C. § 1226(c); INA § 238(b), 8 U.S.C. § 1228(b); INA § 240A, 8 U.S.C. § 1229b; INA § 241(a)(5), 8 U.S.C. § 1231(a)(5); INA § 242(a)(2), 8 U.S.C. § 1252(a)(2). See Chapter 2 in this volume. On McCollum's efforts, see H.R. 321, 106th Cong. (1st Sess. 1999); H.R. 4730, 105th Cong. (2d Sess. 1998); Anthony Lewis, The Quality of Mercy, N.Y. Times, Feb. 27, 1999, at A15. On private bills, see Chapter 6 in this volume.

50. On local perspectives making harms real, see Antje Ellermann, States Against Migrants: Deportation in Germany and the United States, 16–17, 121–146 (Cambridge Univ. Press 2009); Rainer Bauböck, There is a Mismatch Between Citizens' Moral Intuitions and Their Political Views, Boston Review, May/June 2009; Stephen H. Legomsky, Portraits of the Undocumented Immigrant: A Dialectic, 44 Ga. L. Rev. 65, 70 (2009); Ken Belson & Jill P. Capuzzo, Towns Rethink Laws Against Illegal Immigrants, N.Y. Times, Sept. 26, 2007, at A1.

51. Michael Walzer, Spheres of Justice: A Defense of Pluralism and Equality, 39 (Basic Books 1983) (citing Henry Sidgwick, The Elements of Politics, 295–296 (Macmillan 1891)). See Chapter 3 in this volume.

52. See Chapter 3 in this volume.

53. See, e.g., Jennifer Gordon, Tensions in Rhetoric and Reality at the Intersection of Work and Immigration, 2 U.C. Irvine L. Rev. 125, 136–145 (2012); Ethan Bronner, U.S. Workers Sue as Big Farms Rely on Immigrants, N.Y. Times, May 7, 2013, at A1.

54. See Elizabeth Fussell, Hurricane Chasers in New Orleans: Latino Immigrants as a Source of a Rapid Response Labor Force, Hispanic J. of Behavioral Sciences OnlineFirst (July 15, 2009); Kevin R. Johnson, Hurricane Katrina: Lessons about Immigrants in the Administrative State, 45 Hous. L. Rev. 11, 58 64 (2008); Broken Levees, Broken Promises: New Orleans' Migrant Workers in Their Own Words (Southern Poverty Law Center 2006); Haley E. Olam & Erin S. Stamper, The Suspension of the Davis Bacon Act and the Exploitation of Migrant Workers in the Wake of Hurricane Katrina, 24 Hofstra Lab. & Emp. L.J. 145 (2006); Sam Quinones, Migrants Find a Gold Rush in New Orleans, L.A. Times, Apr. 4, 2006, at A10. On the effects of in-migration of immigrants on out-migration of natives, see Emilio A. Parrado & William Kandel, Industrial Change, Hispanic Immigration, and the Internal Migration of Low-Skilled Native Male Workers in the United States, 1995–2000, 40 Soc. Sci. Research 626 (2011).

55. See Jack Miles, Blacks v. Browns, The Atlantic Monthly 41 (Oct. 1992). On the effects of immigration on African American communities, see Frank D. Bean, Cynthia Feliciano, Jennifer Lee, & Jennifer Van Hook, The New U.S. Immigrants: How Do They Affect Our Understanding of the African American Experience?, 621 Annals Amn. Acad. of Pol. & Soc. Sci. 202 (2009); David C. Koelsch, Panic in Detroit: The Impact of Immigration Reforms on Urban African Americans, 5 Geo. J.L. & Pub. Pol'y 447 (2007); Jennifer Gordon & R. A. Lenhardt, Citizenship Talk: Bridging the Gap Between Immigration and Race Perspectives, 75 Fordham L. Rev. 2493 (2007); Kevin Johnson & Bill Ong Hing, The Immigrant Rights Marches of 2006 and the Prospects for a New Civil Rights Movement, 42 Harv. C.R.-C.L. L. Rev. 99 (2007).

For expressions of concern regarding the effects of immigration, especially unauthorized migration, on poor African Americans, see, e.g., Roy L. Brooks & Kirsten Widner, In Defense of the Black/White Binary: Reclaiming a Tradition of Civil Rights Scholarship, 12 Berkeley J. Afr.-Am. L. & Pol'y 107, 127–128 (2010). Toni Morrison, On the Backs of Blacks, in Arguing Immigration: The Debate over the Changing Face of America, 97 (Nicolaus Mills ed., Touchstone 1994); Carol M. Swain, The Congressional Black Caucus and the Impact of Immigration on African American Unemployment, in Debating Immigration, 175 (Carol M. Swain, ed., Cambridge Univ. Press 2007).

CHAPTER 6

Legalization and the Rule of Law

1. On political developments in the period from 2000 to 2011, see Marc R. Rosenblum, U.S. Immigration Policy since 9/11: Understanding the Stalemate over Comprehensive Immigration Reform (Migration Policy Inst. 2011). On bipartisan support for major immigration legislation in 1986 and 1996, see S. Karthick Ramakrishnan & Pratheepan Gulasekaram, The Importance of the Political in Immigration Federalism, 44 Ariz. St. L.J. 1431, 1464 (2013).

2. On John McCain, see Ryan Lizza, Getting to Maybe: Inside the Gang of Eight's Immigration Deal, The New Yorker (July 24, 2013). On immigration issues in Republican primaries, see Paul Davenport, Immigration a Focus of GOP Debate in Senate Race, Ariz. Capitol Times, Aug. 16, 2012; Ted Cruz, David Dewhurst Texas Senate Primary Race Gets Ugly over Immigration, Guest Worker Policy, Huffington Post, June 28, 2012; Michael Cooper & Paul Vitello, Immigration Moves to Front and Center of G.O.P. Race, N.Y. Times, Dec. 12, 2007, at A30. On George W. Bush, see The White House, Fact Sheet: Fair and Secure Immigration Reform, Jan. 7, 2004; Mike Allen, Bush Proposes Legal Status for Immigrant Labor, Washington Post, Jan. 8, 2004, at A01; Eric Schmitt, Bush Aides Weigh Legalizing Status of Mexicans in U.S., N.Y. Times, July 15, 2001, at A11.

3. On the Latino vote in the 2012 presidential election, see Mark Hugo Lopez & Paul Taylor, Latino Voters in the 2012 Election, 4–10 (Pew Hispanic Ctr. 2012). For the Republican Party platform, see We Believe in America: Republican Party Platform (2012).

4. On enforcement during this period, see Doris Meissner, Donald M. Kerwin, Muzaffar Chishti, & Claire Bergeron, Immigration Enforcement in the United States: The Rise of a Formidable Machinery, 118–119 (Migration Policy Inst. 2013). On skepticism of the administration's immigration-related policies among Latino voters who otherwise were likely Obama supporters, see Julia Preston, While Seeking Support, Obama Faces a Frustrated Hispanic Electorate, N.Y. Times, June 11, 2012, at A10. On the political background of DACA, see Miriam Jordan, Anatomy of a Deferred-Action Dream, Wall St. J., Oct. 15, 2012, at A2 Julia Preston, Young Immigrants Say It's Obama's Time to Act, N.Y. Times, Dec. 1, 2012, at A1; Michael A. Olivas, Dreams Deferred: Deferred Action, Prosecutorial Discretion, and the Vexing Case(s) of DREAM Act Students, 21 Wm. & Mary Bill

of Rts. J. 463, 464–465, 472–475 (2012). On DACA generally, see also Chapters 1 and 5 in this volume; later in this chapter.

5. On Kris Kobach's role in the Romney campaign, see Immigration and the Campaign, N.Y. Times, Feb. 21, 2012, at A24; Ed Pilkington, Mitt Romney in Talks over Nationwide Version of Tough State Immigration Laws, The Guardian, Feb. 24, 2012; Alan Greenblatt, Will Backing of Anti-Immigration Movement's "Dark Lord" Haunt Romney?, NPR, Jan. 25, 2012. For the presidential debate exchange, see Commission on Presidential Debates, President Barack Obama and Former Gov. Mitt Romney Participate in Candidates Debate, Oct. 16, 2012.

6. On the drafting of proposals by legislators in Congress (including John McCain) and the White House, see Emmarie Huettman & Ashley Parker, House Panel Set to Offer Several Immigration Bills, N.Y. Times, Apr. 26, 2013, at A11; Michael D. Shear & Julia Preston, Obama's Plan Sets Long Line for Citizenship, N.Y. Times, Feb. 18, 2013, at A1.

7. See S. 744, § 2103, 113th Cong., 1st Sess. (2013).

8. For supporters adopting the term, see, e.g., Linda Bosniak, Amnesty in Immigration: Forgetting, Forgiving, Freedom, 16 Crit. Rev. Int'l Soc. & Pol. Philosophy 344 (2013); Bill Ong Hing, The Case for Amnesty, 3 Stan. J. C.R. & C.L. 233 (2007). On the amnesty concept, see Craig Kyle Hemphill, Am I My Brother's Keeper?: Immigration Law Reform and the Liberty That Is America: A Legal, Theological and Ethical Observation on the Debate of Allowing Immigrant Amnesty, 15 Tex. Hisp. J. L. & Pol'y 51 (2009); Bryn Siegel, The Political Discourse of Amnesty in Immigration Policy, 41 Akron L. Rev. 291 (2008). For other terms, see Marc Rosenblum, Randy Capps, Serena Yi-Ying Lin, Earned Legalization: Effects of Proposed Requirements on Unauthorized Men, Women, and Children (Migration Policy Inst. 2011); S. 2381, 108th Cong., 1st Sess. (2004) ("earned adjustment").

9. See S. 744, § 2103, 113th Cong., 1st Sess. (2013); Development, Relief, and Education for Alien Minors (DREAM) Act of 2011, S. 952, H.R. 1842, 112th Cong., 2d Sess. (2011); Comprehensive Immigration Reform Act of 2006, S. 2611, §§ 621–632, 109th Cong., 2d Sess. (2006). See generally T. Alexander Aleinikoff, David A. Martin, Hiroshi Motomura, & Maryellen Fullerton, Immigration and Citizenship: Process and Policy, 1144–1145 (7th ed. West 2012); House Passes DREAM Act; Senate Tables Bill, 87 Interpreter Releases 2334, 2419 (2010); Lauren Gilbert, Obama's Ruby Slippers: Enforcement Discretion in the Absence of Immigration Reform, 116 W. Va. L. Rev. 255, 267–270 (2013). On this group of unauthorized migrants, see Alejandro Portes & Ruben G. Rumbaut, Legacies: The Story of the Immigrant Second Generation, 24 (Univ. of California Press 2001); Ruben G. Rumbaut, Ages, Life Stages, and Generational Cohorts: Decomposing the Immigrant First and Second Generations in the United States, 38 Int'l Migr. Rev. 1160 (2004).

10. Development, Relief, and Education for Alien Minors (DREAM) Act of 2011, S. 952, 112th Cong. §§ 3(a), 3(b), 5(a) (2011).

11. See Memorandum from Janet Napolitano, Secretary of Homeland Sec., to David V. Aguilar, Acting Commissioner, U.S. Customs & Border Prot., Alejandro Mayorkas, Director, U.S. Citizenship & Immigration Servs., & John Morton, Director, U.S. Immigration & Customs Enforcement, on Exercising Prosecutorial Discretion with Respect to Individuals Who Came to the United States as Children, June 15, 2012. On the potential beneficiaries, see Jeanne Batalova & Michelle Mittelstadt, Relief from Deportation: Demographic Profile of the DREAMers Potentially Eligible under the Deferred Action Policy (Migration Policy Inst. 2012).

12. See S. 744, §§ 2101, 2103, 113th Cong., 1st Sess. (2013).

13. See Chapters 1 and 3 in this volume; Hiroshi Motomura, Americans in Waiting: The Lost Story of Immigration and Citizenship in the United States, 42–62, 80–114 (Oxford Univ. Press 2006).

14. See Roberto G. Gonzales & Leo R. Chavez, "Awakening to a Nightmare": Abjectivity and Illegality in the Lives of Undocumented 1.5-Generation Latino Immigrants in the United States, 53 Current Anthropology 255, 265–266 (2012). See also Ariana Mangual Figueroa, "I Have Papers So I Can Go Anywhere": Everyday Talk about Citizenship in a Mixed-Status Mexican Family, 11 J. Language, Identity & Educ. 291 (2012); Carola Suárez-Orozco, Hirokazu Yoshikawa, Robert T. Teranishi, & Marcelo M. Suárez-Orozco, Growing Up in the Shadows: The Developmental Implications of Unauthorized Status, 81 Harv. Educ. Rev. 438 (2011); Sarah S. Willen, Toward a Critical Phenomenology of "Illegality": State Power, Criminalization, and Abjectivity among Undocumented Migrant Workers in Tel Aviv, Israel, 45 Int'l Migration 8 (2007); Cecilia Menjívar, Liminal Legality: Salvadoran and Guatemalan Immigrants' Lives in the United States, 111 Am. J. Soc. 999 (2006).

15. Plyler v. Doe, 457 U.S. 202, 218 n.17 (1982).

16. See Office of the Under Sec'y of Def. for Pers. & Readiness, Strategic Plan for Fiscal Years 2010–2012, at 8 (Dept. of Defense 2009).

17. See U.S. Const. amend. XIV, § 1; United States v. Wong Kim Ark, 169 U.S. 649, 693 (1898); Garrett Epps, The Citizenship Clause: A "Legislative History," 60 Am. U. L. Rev. 331, 332–34 (2010); Chapter 3 in this volume; Aleinikoff, Martin, Motomura, & Fullerton, Immigration and Citizenship, supra note 9, at 50–80. For skepticism of the prevailing interpretation, see Peter H. Schuck & Rogers M. Smith, Citizenship Without Consent: Illegal Aliens in the American Polity, 118 (Yale Univ. Press 1985). For counterarguments, see Societal and Legal Issues Surrounding Children Born in the United States to Illegal Alien Parents: J. Hearing Before the Subcomm. on Immigration and Claims and the Subcomm. on the Constitution of the H. Comm. on the Judiciary, 104th Cong., 103–109 (1995) (statement of Gerald L. Neuman, Professor, Columbia University Law School); Gerald L. Neuman, Back to *Dred Scott*?, 24 San Diego L. Rev. 485, 489 (1987).

For more recent arguments for reading the citizenship clause narrowly, see Dual Citizenship, Birthright Citizenship, & the Meaning of Sovereignty: Hearing Before the Subcomm. on Immigration, Border Sec., & Claims of the H. Comm. on the Judiciary, 109th Cong., 59 (2005) (prepared statement of John C. Eastman, Professor, Chapman University School of Law); William Ty Mayton, Birthright Citizenship and the Civic Minimum, 22 Geo. Immigr. L.J. 221, 224 (2008); Charles Wood, Losing Control of America's Future—The Census, Birthright Citizenship, and Illegal Aliens, 22 Harv. J.L. & Pub. Pol'y 465, 466–468 (1999). On several state legislative bills to issue special birth certificates to children with unauthorized migrant parents, see Julia Preston, State Lawmakers Outline Plans to End Birthright Citizenship, Drawing Outcry, N.Y. Times, Jan. 6, 2011, at A16. For proposed constitutional amendments, see, e.g., H.R.J. Res. 357, 102d Cong. (1991); H.R.J. Res. 46, 109th Cong. (2005); H.R.J. Res. 42, 108th Cong. (2003); Birthright Citizenship Act of 2011, § 2(a), H.R. 140, 112th Cong. (2011).

18. See Child Citizenship Act of 2000, Pub. L. 106–395, 114 Stat. 1631 (amending INA § 320, 8 U.S.C. § 1431).

19. On the use of the term "anchor baby," see Julia Preston, Anchor Baby: A Term Redefined as a Slur, N.Y. Times, Dec. 9, 2011, at A21; Nathaniel O'Neal, Anchor Baby Phrase Has Controversial History, abcnews.go.com, July 3, 2010. On the ability of children to petition for parents, see INA § 201(a), (b)(2)(A)(i), 8 U.S.C. § 1151(a), (b)(2)(A)(i). On consent as the basis for granting citizenship, see Schuck & Smith, Citizenship Without Consent, supra note 17, at 94. On the erosion of citizenship based on the place of birth, see Catherine Dauvergne, Making People Illegal: What Globalization Means for Migration and Law, 132, 135 (Cambridge Univ. Press 2008).

20. On the reasons for citizenship based on birth on U.S. soil, see Peter J. Spiro, Beyond Citizenship: American Identity after Globalization, 18–19 (Oxford Univ. Press 2008); Christopher L. Eisgruber, Birthright Citizenship and the Constitution, 72 N.Y.U. L. Rev. 54, 65–85 (1997); David A. Martin, Membership and Consent: Abstract or Organic?, 11 Yale J. Int'l L. 278, 282–284, 291–294 (1985). On the interests of migrants, sending countries, and receiving countries in granting citizenship based on birthplace or parentage, see Adam B. Cox & Eric A. Posner, The Rights of Migrants: An Optimal Contract Framework, 84 N.Y.U. L. Rev. 1403, 1438–1441 (2009).

21. *Plyler*, 457 U.S. at 230.

22. See Hiroshi Motomura, We Asked for Workers, But Families Came: Time, Law, and the Family in Immigration and Citizenship, 14 Va. J. Soc. Pol'y & L. 103, 112–118 (2006). Similar reasons may justify the settled rule that redistricting of congressional seats is based on the entire population, not just the voting population. See Chen v. City of Houston, 206 F.3d 502, 523 (5th Cir. 2000); Daly v. Hunt, 93 F.3d 1212, 1227–1228 (4th Cir. 1996); Garza v. County of Los Angeles, 918 F.2d 763, 774–775 (9th Cir. 1990), cert. denied, 498 U.S. 1028

(1991). See also Adam Liptak, One Person One Vote (or Was That One Voter One Vote?), N.Y. Times, Mar. 19, 2013, at A14; Joseph Fishkin, Weightless Votes, 121 Yale L.J. 1888, 1890–1891 (2012); Nathaniel Persily, The Law of the Census: How to Count, What to Count, Whom to Count, and Where to Count Them, 32 Cardozo L. Rev. 755, 774–777 (2011). See generally Marta Tienda, Demography and the Social Contract, 39 Demography 587, 603–605 (2002). For criticism of the current practice, see *Garza*, 918 F.2d at 782–784 (Kozinski, J., dissenting); Wood, Losing Control of America's Future, supra note 17, at 468–474; Stacy Robyn Harold, Note, The Right to Representation and the Census: Is It Permissible for Congress to Exclude Illegal Immigrants from the Apportionment Base?, 53 Wayne L. Rev. 921, 933 (2007). For a proposed constitutional amendment to limit reapportionment to citizens, see H.R.J. Res. 53, 109th Cong. (2005).

23. See Paul Taylor, Mark Hugo Lopez, Jeffrey S. Passel, & Seth Motel, Unauthorized Immigrants: Length of Residency, Patterns of Parenthood, 6 (Pew Hispanic Ctr. 2011); Jeffrey S. Passel & D'Vera Cohn, Unauthorized Immigrant Population: National and State Trends, 2010, at 12–13 (Pew Hispanic Ctr. 2011); MPI Updates National and State-Level Estimates of Potential DREAM Act Beneficiaries (Migration Policy Inst. 2010); Jeanne Batalova & Margie McHugh, DREAM vs. Reality: An Analysis of Potential DREAM Act Beneficiaries (Migration Policy Inst. 2010).

24. On U.S. citizen children and removal, see, e.g., Acosta v. Gaffney, 558 F.2d 1153, 1157–1158 (3d Cir. 1977); Oforji v. Ashcroft, 354 F.3d 609, 617 (7th Cir. 2003). For decisions finding that noncitizens did not establish eligibility for cancellation of removal because they did not show that deportation would cause exceptional and extremely unusual hardship to qualifying relatives, see, e.g., In re Andazola-Rivas, 23 I. & N. Dec. 319, 322 (BIA 2002); In re Monreal-Aguinaga, 23 I. & N. Dec. 56, 65 (BIA 2001). See also Seth Freed Wessler, Nearly 205K Deportations of Parents of U.S. Citizens in Just over Two Years, Colorlines, Dec. 17, 2012. On the effects of a parent's unauthorized status on the development of children and youth, see Hirokazu Yoshikawa & Jenya Kholoptseva, Unauthorized Immigrant Parents and Their Children's Development: A Summary of the Evidence (Migration Policy Inst. 2013). On the effects of the deportation of parents on their children, see Randy Capps, Rosa Maria Castañeda, Ajay Chaudry, & Robert Santos. Paying the Price: The Impact of Immigration Raids on America's Children (National Council of La Raza and Urban Inst. 2007); Memije v. Gonzales, 481 F.3d 1163, 1164–1169 (9th Cir. 2007) (Pregerson, J., dissenting).

On the role of children in immigrant families, see Vikki S. Katz, How Children of Immigrants Use Media to Connect Their Families to the Community, 4 J. Children & Media 298 (2010); Jennifer Reynolds & Marjorie Faulstich Orellana, New Immigrant Youth Interpreting in White Public Space, 111 American Anthropologist 211 (2009); Marjorie Faulstich Orellana, Lisa Dorner, & Lucila Pulido, Accessing

Assets: Immigrant Youth's Work as Family Translators or "Para-phrasers," 50 Soc. Probs. 505 (2003). See also Carola Suárez Orozco, Marcelo Suárez-Orozco, & Irina Todorova, Learning a New Land (Harvard Univ. Press 2008).

25. See Immigration Reform and Control Act of 1986, Pub. L. No. 99–603, 100 Stat. 3359; INA §§ 210(a)(2)(A), 245A(a), (b), 8 U.S.C. §§ 1160(a)(2)(A), 1255a(a), (b). For the numbers, see Ruth Ellen Wasem, Alien Legalization and Adjustment of Status: A Primer, 5 (Cong. Research Serv. 2010); see also Ruth Ellen Wasem, Unauthorized Aliens Residing in the United States: Estimate since 1986, at 1–2 (Cong. Research Serv. 2012); U.S. Dept. of Justice, 1993 Statistical Yearbook of the Immigration and Naturalization Service, 183 (1994); U.S. Immigr. & Naturalization Serv., Immigration Reform and Control Act: Report on the Legalized Alien Population (1992). See also Chapter 1 in this volume.

26. See Immigration Reform and Control Act of 1986 (IRCA) §§ 101–117, 301–305, Pub. L. No. 99–603, 100 Stat 3359, 3360–3384, 3411–3434. Chapter 7 will discuss IRCA's temporary worker programs. On fraudulent claims, see David North, Before Considering Another Amnesty, Look at IRCA's Lessons, 7 8 (Center for Immigr. Studies 2013). For objections to IRCA, compare Kris W. Kobach, Immigration, Amnesty, and the Rule of Law, 36 Hofstra L. Rev, 1323, 1330 (2012) (IRCA invited fraudulent claims) with Cecilia Muñoz, Unfinished Business: The Immigration Reform and Control Act of 1986 (National Council of La Raza 1990) (arguing against employer sanctions, among other policy suggestions). On family members, see U.S. Immigr. & Naturalization Serv., Immigration Reform and Control Act, supra note 25, at 7; Immigration Act of 1990, § 301, Pub. L. No. 101–649, 104 Stat. 4978, 5029–5030.

27. See Comprehensive Immigration Reform Act of 2007, S. 1639, §§ 601, 602, 110th Cong., 1st Sess. (2007). See generally Wasem, Unauthorized Aliens, supra note 25, at 4. On the residence period for naturalization, see INA § 316(a), 8 U.S.C. § 1427(a). For other proposals, see, e.g., Comprehensive Immigration Reform for America's Security and Prosperity Act (CIR ASAP) Act of 2009, H.R. 4321, 111th Cong. (2009); Agricultural Job Opportunities, Benefits, and Security (AgJOBS) Acts of 2009 (S. 1038, H.R. 2414), 111th Cong. (2009).

28. See *Plyler*, 457 U.S. at 219–220, 226; see also Linda S. Bosniak, Membership, Equality, and the Difference That Alienage Makes, 69 N.Y.U. L. Rev. 1047, 1121–1123 (1994).

29. See Chapters 1 and 3 in this volume. On the persistence of the opposing view, see Joseph Nevins, Operation Gatekeeper and Beyond: The War on "Illegals" and the Remaking of the US-Mexico Boundary, 175–181 (Routledge 2010); Michele Wucker, Lockout: Why America Keeps Getting Immigration Wrong When Our Prosperity Depends on Getting It Right, 224 (Public Affairs 2006).

30. See *Plyler*, 457 U.S. at 230. I am grateful to Noah Zatz for suggesting this line of thought. See also 457 U.S. at 218 n.17 (quoting Administration's Proposals on Immigration and Refugee Policy: J. Hearing before the Subcomm. on Immigration,

Refugees, & Int'l Law of the H. Comm. on the Judiciary and the Subcomm. on Immigration & Refugee Policy of the S. Comm. on the Judiciary, 97th Cong., 1st Sess. 9 (1981) (testimony of William French Smith, Atty. Gen. of the United States)).

31. I am indebted to Deep Gulasekaram for discussing this point with me.

32. On advocacy by United We Dream, see Julia Preston, Young Immigrant Activists Cast a Wider Net, N.Y. Times, Dec. 3, 2012, at A12; Ted Hesson, United We Dream Releases Its Immigration Reform Platform, ABC News/Univision (Dec. 3, 2012).

33. For views along these lines, see, e.g., Aaron Blake, No Path to Citizenship for Illegal Immigrants, washingtonpost.com, Mar. 3, 2012; Patrick Buchanan, Upholding Law Requires Courage, Mr. Holder, Tulsa World, Feb. 25, 2009, at A18.

34. On developments since the 1990s, see Chapters 1 and 2 in this volume. On legalizations generating expectations of further legalizations, see Cox & Posner, The Rights of Migrants, supra note 20, at 1431. For the cutoff date in the 2013 Senate bill, see S. 744, § 2101(a), 113th Cong., 1st Sess. (2013).

35. On reasons for unauthorized migration to the United States, see Wasem, Unauthorized Aliens, supra note 25, at 13–15; Ruth Ellen Wasem, Immigration Issues in Trade Agreements, 13–17 (Cong. Research Serv. 2005); Joseph H. Carens, The Case For Amnesty: Time Erodes the State's Right to Deport, 34 Boston Rev. 7, 10 (2009).

36. See, e.g., Kris R. Kobach, Reinforcing the Rule of Law: What States Can and Should Do to Reduce Illegal Immigration, 22 Geo. Immigr. L.J. 459, 482 (2008).

37. See generally Katie R. Eyer, Administrative Adjudication and the Rule of Law, 60 Admin. L. Rev. 647, 653–657 (2008); Richard Fallon, "The Rule of Law" as a Concept in Constitutional Discourse, 97 Colum. L. Rev. 1, 8–9 (1997); Hiroshi Motomura, Immigration Outside the Law, 108 Colum. L. Rev. 2037, 2085–2092 (2012); Hiroshi Motomura, The Rule of Law in Immigration Law, 15 Tulsa J. Comp. & Int'l L. 139, 144–151 (2008).

38. Fernandez–Vargas v. Gonzales, 548 U.S. 30, 35–36 (2006).

39. See Illegal Immigration Reform and Immigrant Responsibility Act of 1996, Pub. L. No. 104–208, sec. 305(a)(3), 110 Stat. 3009–3546, 3599; INA § 241(a)(5), 8 U.S.C. § 1231(a)(5); Aleinikoff, Martin, Motomura, & Fullerton, Immigration and Citizenship, supra note 9, at 1212–1216. On retroactivity, see INS v. St. Cyr, 533 U.S. 289, 316 (2001) (citing Landgraf v. USI Film Products, 511 U.S. 244, 265–266 (1994)).

40. *Fernandez-Vargas*, 548 U.S. at 33, 42–46 (2006). See also Morales-Izquierdo v. Gonzales, 486 F.3d 484, 498 (9th Cir. 2007) (en banc).

41. *Fernandez-Vargas*, 548 U.S. at 47, 51–52 (Stevens, J., dissenting).

42. On cancellation, see Chapter 1 in this volume; Illegal Immigration Reform and Immigrant Responsibility Act of 1996, Pub. L. No. 104–208, § 304, 110 Stat. 3009–3546, 3009–3587, 3597; INA § 240A, 8 U.S.C. § 1229b; Aleinikoff, Martin, Motomura, & Fullerton, Immigration and Citizenship, supra note 9, at 755–773;

Motomura, Americans in Waiting, supra note 13, at 54–57, 98–99. See generally Gerald L. Neuman, Discretionary Deportation, 20 Geo. Immigr. L.J. 611, 618–624 (2006) (explaining that uncompromising statutory rules can impose hardship that discretionary mechanisms can ameliorate). For the act of grace notion, see, e.g., INS v. Yueh-Shaio Yang, 519 U.S. 26, 30 (1996); *St. Cyr*, 533 U.S. at 345 (Scalia, J., dissenting).

43. See, e.g., INA § 242(a), (b)(9), 8 U.S.C. § 1252(a), (b)(9).

44. On class actions, see Aleinikoff, Martin, Motomura, & Fullerton, Immigration and Citizenship, supra note 9, at 1307–1312; Jill E. Family, Threats to the Future of the Immigration Class Action, 27 Wash. U. J.L. & Pol'y 71 (2008); David A. Martin, Behind the Scenes on a Different Set: What Congress Needs to Do in the Aftermath of *St. Cyr* and *Nguyen*, 16 Geo. Immigr. L.J. 313, 321, 327 (2002); Hiroshi Motomura, Judicial Review in Immigration Cases After *AADC*: Lessons From Civil Procedure, 14 Geo. Immigr. L.J. 385 (2000). On individual versus systemic review, see INA § 242(b)(9), 8 U.S.C. § 1252(b)(9); McNary v. Haitian Refugee Ctr., Inc., 498 U.S. 479, 489–494 (1991).

45. See In re Compean (*Compean II*), 25 I. & N. Dec. 1, 2–3 (Att'y Gen. 2009); In re Compean (*Compean I*), 24 I. & N. Dec. 710 (Att'y Gen. 2009). On the absence of a right to appointed counsel, see Aguilera-Enriquez v. INS, 516 F.2d 565, 569 (6th Cir. 1975), cert. denied, 423 U.S. 1050 (1976); INA § 240(b)(4)(A), 8 U.S.C. § 1229a(b)(4)(A). For criticism, see Daniel Kanstroom, Deportation Nation: Outsiders in American History, 4 (Harvard Univ. Press 2007); LaJuana Davis, Reconsidering Remedies for Ensuring Competent Representation in Removal Proceedings, 58 Drake L. Rev. 123, 150–168 (2009). See also The Debates in the Several State Conventions on the Adoption of the Federal Constitution, 555 (Jonathan Elliot ed., 2d ed. 1836) (remarks of James Madison). On the civil characterization, see INS v. Lopez-Mendoza, 468 U.S. 1032, 1038 (1984); Galvan v. Press, 347 U.S. 522, 530–531 (1954); Harisiades v. Shaughnessy, 342 U.S. 580, 594 (1952); Fong Yue Ting v. United States, 149 U.S. 698, 709 (1893). On the practical value of counsel, see Michael Kaufman, Detention, Due Process, and the Right to Counsel in Deportation Proceedings, 4 Stan. J. C.R.-C.L. 113, 144 (2008); Donald Kerwin, Revisiting the Need for Appointed Counsel (Migration Policy Inst. 2005).

46. Under the regulations governing the Board of Immigration Appeals within the Department of Justice, the Attorney General may choose to review a BIA decision. See 8 C.F.R. § 1003.1(h)(1)(i). See *Compean I*, 24 I. & N. Dec. at 714–716; *Compean II*, 25 I. & N. Dec. at 2–3.

47. For an enforcement perspective that relies on the rule of law, see, e.g., 153 Cong. Rec. 15046–15047 (2007) (statement of Sen. Coburn). On the nineteenth-century links between criminal and immigration law, see Chapter 1 in this volume. On the emphasis on migrants' compliance with legal requirements, see Nevins, Operation Gatekeeper, supra note 29, at 139–141. For immigration-related crimes,

see Chapter 4 in this volume. On the connections between immigration control, crime control, and national security, see Jennifer M. Chacón, Unsecured Borders: Immigration Restrictions, Crime Control and National Security, 39 Conn. L. Rev. 1827, 1853 (2007); Pratheepan Gulasekaram, Why a Wall?, 2 U.C. Irvine L. Rev. 147, 173–176 (2012). On the criminal prosecution of immigration-related offenses, see Ingrid V. Eagly, Prosecuting Immigration, 104 Nw. U. L. Rev. 1281 (2010); Jennifer M. Chacón, Managing Migration Through Crime, 109 Colum. L. Rev. Sidebar 135 (2009). On the expansion of crime-based removal from the United States, see Juliet Stumpf, The Crimmigration Crisis: Immigrants, Crime, and Sovereign Power, 56 Am. U. L. Rev. 367, 379–392 (2006); Daniel Kanstroom, Deportation Nation, supra note 45; Stephen H. Legomsky, The New Path of Immigration Law: Asymmetric Incorporation of Criminal Justice Norms, 64 Wash. & Lee L. Rev. 469 (2007); Teresa A. Miller, Blurring the Boundaries Between Immigration and Crime Control after September 11th, 25 B.C. Third World L.J. 81 (2005); Catherine Dauvergne, Making People Illegal, supra note 19, at 16.

48. On moral comfort from the legal/illegal line, see Kathleen Arnold, Enemy Invaders: Mexican Immigrants and US Wars Against Them, 6 Borderlands 3 (2007); Dauvergne, Making People Illegal, supra note 19, at 164. See also Chapters 1 and 3 in this volume.

49. See Shortfalls of the 1996 Immigration Reform Legislation: Hearing before the Subcomm. on Immigration, Citizenship, Refugees, Border Security and International Law of the H. Comm. on the Judiciary, 110th Cong. 42 (2007) (statement of Hiroshi Motomura, Kenan Distinguished Professor of Law, University of North Carolina-Chapel Hill). See Austin Sarat, At the Boundaries of Law: Executive Clemency, Sovereign Prerogative, and the Dilemma of American Legality, in Legal Borderlands: Law and the Construction of American Borders, 19 (Mary L. Dudziak & Leti Volpp eds., Johns Hopkins Univ. Press 2006).

50. Pub. L. No. 99–603, 100 Stat. 3359. See also Hiroshi Motomura, What Is "Comprehensive Immigration Reform?" Taking the Long View, 63 Ark. L. Rev. 225, 235–238 (2010).

51. See INA § 240A(b)(1)(D), 8 U.S.C. § 1229b(b)(1)(D); Alien Registration Act of 1940, ch. 439, § 20, 54 Stat. 671, 672; INS v. Chadha, 462 U.S. 919, 933 (1983); Matter of C–V–T–, 22 I & N Dec. 7, 11–12 (1998). See generally Richard A. Boswell, Crafting an Amnesty with Traditional Tools: Registration and Cancellation, 47 Harv. J. on Legis. 175, 190–95 (2010). For the precursor of a related provision for permanent residents, see Immigration Act of 1917, ch. 29, § 3, 39 Stat. 874, 878. See generally Chapter 1 in this volume; Aleinikoff, Martin, Motomura, & Fullerton, Immigration and Citizenship, supra note 9, at 750–778.

52. See INA § 249, 8 U.S.C. § 1259; Aleinikoff, Martin, Motomura, & Fullerton, Immigration and Citizenship, supra note 9, at 672–673. For statutory precursors, see Act of Oct. 3, 1965, Pub. L. No. 89–236, § 19, 79 Stat. 911, 920; Act of Aug. 8, 1958, Pub. L. No. 85–616, 72 Stat. 546; Nationality Act of 1940, ch. 876, § 328, 54

Stat. 1137, 1151–1152; Registry Act of 1929, ch. 536, § 1(a)(1), 45 Stat. 1512, 1512–1513. See generally Boswell, Crafting an Amnesty, supra note 51, at 180–189; Andorra Bruno, Immigration: Registry as Means of Obtaining Lawful Permanent Residence (Cong. Research Serv. 2001); Monica Gomez, Note, Immigration by Adverse Possession: Common Law Amnesty for Long-Residing Illegal Immigrants in the United States, 22 Geo. Immigr. L.J. 105, 119 (2007). For the prior statute of limitations, see Act of Mar. 3, 1903, ch. 1012, § 20, 32 Stat. 1213, 1218; Act of Feb. 20, 1907, ch. 1134, § 20, 34 Stat. 898, 904–905; Immigration Act of 1917, ch. 29, § 19, 39 Stat. 874, 889. For repeal of the prior statute of limitations, see Act of May 26, 1924, ch. 190, § 14, 43 Stat. 153, 162. For the numbers, see 2012 Yearbook of Immigration Statistics, table 7 (Dept. of Homeland Sec. 2013).

53. See David A. Martin, Thomas Alexander Aleinikoff, Hiroshi Motomura, & Maryellen Fullerton, Forced Migration: Law and Policy, 93–95 (2d ed. West 2013).

54. See Estelle T. Lau, Paper Families: Identity, Immigration Administration, and Chinese Exclusion, 116–120 (Duke Univ. Press 2006); Mae M. Ngai, Impossible Subjects: Illegal Aliens and the Making of Modern America, 204, 218–224 (Princeton Univ. Press 2004); Bill Ong Hing, Making and Remaking Asian America Through Immigration Policy 1850–1990, at 75 (Stanford Univ. Press 1993); Roger Daniels, Guarding the Golden Door: American Immigration Policy and Immigrants since 1882, at 156–158 (Hill & Wang 2004).

55. See Cuban Adjustment Act, Pub. L. No. 89-732, 80 Stat. 1161 (1966). See generally Joyce A. Hughes & Alexander L. Alum, Rethinking the Cuban Adjustment Act and the U.S. National Interest, 23 St. Thomas L. Rev. 187, 194–199 (2011); Deborah M. Weissman, The Legal Production of the Transgressive Family: Binational Family Relationships Between Cuba and the United States, 88 N.C. L. Rev. 1881, 1892–1901 (2010); Ruth Ellen Wasem, Cuban Migration to the United States: Policy and Trends (Cong. Research Serv. 2009); Maryellen Fullerton, Cuban Exceptionalism: Migration and Asylum in Spain and the United States, U. Miami Inter-Am. L. Rev. 527, 552–554 (2004); Note, The Cuban Adjustment Act of 1966: ¿Mirando por los Ojas de Don Quijote o Sancho Panza?, 114 Harv. L. Rev. 902, 903–908 (2001).

56. See Nicaraguan Adjustment and Central American Relief Act NACARA, Pub. L. No. 105-100, §§ 201–204, 111 Stat. 2160, 2193–2201 (1997); Haitian Refugee Immigration Fairness Act of 1998, Pub. L. No. 105-277, §§ 901–904, 112 Stat. 2681–538, 542 (1998). On NACARA, see Susan Bibler Coutin, Nations of Emigrants: Shifting Boundaries of Citizenship in El Salvador and the United States, 46–72 (Cornell Univ. Press 2007). On the disparity in treatment, see Hiroshi Motomura, Whose Alien Nation? Two Models of Constitutional Immigration Law, 94 Mich. L. Rev. 1927, 1940–1941 (1996).

57. See INA § 208, 8 U.S.C. § 1158; Aleinikoff, Martin, Motomura, & Fullerton, Immigration and Citizenship, supra note 9, at 797–919; Martin, Aleinikoff, Motomura, & Fullerton, Forced Migration, supra note 53, at 4. For examples of

government efforts to move asylum seekers to a conceptual category more like unauthorized migrants, see Martin, Aleinikoff, Motomura, & Fullerton, Forced Migration, supra note 53, at 799–800; Dauvergne, Making People Illegal, supra note 19, at 50–68; Sale v. Haitian Centers Council, Inc., 509 U.S. 155 (1993). I am grateful to Stephen Lee for suggesting the relevance of refugees, asylees, and victims of trafficking and crimes.

58. See Convention Relating to the Status of Refugees, arts. 31, 33, July 28, 1951, 19 U.S.T. 6259, 189 U.N.T.S. 137; Protocol Relating to the Status of Refugees, Jan. 31, 1967, 19 U.S.T. 6223, 606 U.N.T.S. 267. See also Convention Against Torture and Other Cruel, Inhuman, or Degrading Treatment or Punishment (CAT), art. 3, adopted Dec. 10, 1984, G.A. Res. 39/46, U.N. GAOR, 39th Sess., Supp. No. 51, U.N. Doc. A/39/51 (1985), entered into force June 26, 1987. On the absence of a Convention duty to admit and grant significant protection to refugees who appear on their territory without legal authorization, see Martin, Aleinikoff, Motomura, & Fullerton, Forced Migration, supra note 53, at 89.

59. On trafficking and crime victims, see INA §§ 101(a)(15)(T)–(U), 101(a)(51), 8 U.S.C. §§ 1101(a)(15)(T)–(U), 1101(a)(51); Aleinikoff, Martin, Motomura, & Fullerton, Immigration and Citizenship, supra note 9, at 421–428. On SIJS, see INA § 101(a)(27)(J), § 203(b)(4), 8 U.S.C. § 1101(a)(27)(J), § 1153(b)(4) (allocating immigrant visas to "special immigrants"). On private bills, see Anna M. Gallagher, Private Bills and Pardons in Immigration (Am. Immigr. Lawyers Ass'n 2008); Margaret Mikyung Lee, Private Immigration Legislation (Cong. Research Serv. 2007); Kati L. Griffith, Perfecting Public Immigration Legislation: Private Immigration Bills and Deportable Lawful Permanent Residents, 18 Geo. Immigr. L.J. 273 (2004); Aleinikoff, Martin, Motomura, & Fullerton, Immigration and Citizenship, supra note 9, at 774.

60. On defining eligibility, see Kathleen Kim, The Coercion of Trafficked Workers, 96 Iowa L. Rev. 409, 436–472 (2011); Dina Francesca Haynes, (Not) Found Chained to a Bed in a Brothel: Conceptual, Legal, and Procedural Failures to Fulfill the Promise of the Trafficking Victims Protection Act, 21 Geo. Immigr. L.J. 337, 349–352 (2007). See also Dauvergne, Making People Illegal, supra note 19, at 69; Donald M. Kerwin, More Than IRCA: US Legalization Programs and the Current Debate (Migration Policy Inst. 2010).

61. On the emergence of expectations and equities, see Dauvergne, Making People Illegal, supra note 19, at 140.

62. On the complexities of allocating enforcement resources, see Chapter 1 in this volume; Motomura, Immigration Outside the Law, supra note 37, at 2054; Motomura, Americans in Waiting, supra note 13, at 176–180. On the reasons to select immigrants at later points in time, see Adam B. Cox & Eric A. Posner, The Second-Order Structure of Immigration Law, 59 Stan. L. Rev. 809, 844–849 (2007); Nancy Chau, Strategic Amnesty and Credible Immigration Reform, 19 J. Labor Econ. 604, 607 (2001).

63. See John Sprankling & Raymond Coletta, Property: A Contemporary Approach, 98 (Thomson Reuters 2012); Jeffrey Evans Stake, The Uneasy Case for Adverse Possession, 89 Geo. L.J. 2419, 2423–2432 (2001).

64. See Mathias Risse, On the Morality of Immigration, 22 Ethics & Int'l Aff. 25, 31–32 (2008); Timothy J. Lukes & Minh T. Hoang, Open and Notorious: Adverse Possession and Immigration Reform, 27 Wash. U. J. L. & Pol'y 123, 129–135 (2008); Gomez, Immigration by Adverse Possession, supra note 52, at 110–117.

65. For statute of limitations proposals, see Mae Ngai, We Need a Deportation Deadline, Washington Post, June 14, 2005, at A21; T. Alexander Aleinikoff, Illegal Employers, 11 Am. Prospect 15, 17 (2000).

66. On past enforcement patterns, see Chapter 1 in this volume.

67. See Chapters 1 and 3 in this volume; Motomura, Immigration Outside the Law, supra note 37, at 2049–2051; Ngai, Impossible Subjects, supra note 54, at 56–90; Aleinikoff, Martin, Motomura, & Fullerton, Immigration and Citizenship, supra note 9, at 511–512.

68. On the construction of the legal/illegal line, including illegality as a proxy for race or ethnicity, see Michael A. Olivas, No Undocumented Child Left Behind: *Plyler v. Doe* and the Education of Undocumented Schoolchildren, 23 (N.Y.U. Press 2012); Daniel Ibsen Morales, In Democracy's Shadow, Fences, Raids, and the Production of Migrant "Illegality," 5 Stan. J. C.R.-C.L. 23 (2009); Leo Chavez, The Condition of Illegality, 45 Int'l Migr. 192 (2007); Nicholas de Genova, The Legal Production of Mexican/Migrant "Illegality," 2 Latino Studies 160 (2004); Susan Bibler Coutin, Questionable Transactions as Grounds for Legalization: Immigration, Illegality and the Law, 37 Crime, Law & Social Change 19 (2002). See also Nevins, Operation Gatekeeper, supra note 29, at 119; Dauvergne, Making People Illegal, supra note 19, at 18; Motomura, Americans in Waiting, supra note 13, at 48–49, 70–71, 128–130, 178–179.

69. On the desire not to let unauthorized migrants gain an advantage over those who have "followed the rules," see Coutin, Nations of Emigrants, supra note 56, at 199.

70. On IRCA as reinforcing and expanding already well-established cross-border migration networks, see Nevins, Operation Gatekeeper, supra note 29, at 169; Peter Andreas, Border Games: Policing the U.S.-Mexico Divide, 86, 140 (2d ed. Cornell Univ. Press 2009).

71. See INA §§ 212(a)(9)(B), 245(a), 8 U.S.C. §§ 1255(a), 8 U.S.C. § 1182(a)(9)(B); Aleinikoff, Martin, Motomura, & Fullerton, Immigration and Citizenship, supra note 9, at 511–518, 595–601; Chapter 1 in this volume. For criticism of the three- and ten-year bars, see David A. Martin, Waiting for Solutions: Extending the Period of Time for Migrants to Apply for Green Cards Doesn't Get at the Real Problem, Legal Times, May 28, 2001, at 66.

72. On the revised waiver process, see 78 Fed. Reg. 535 (2013); Press Release, Secretary Napolitano Announces Final Rule to Support Family Unity during Waiver

Process, Jan. 2, 2013 (U.S. Citizenship & Immigr. Servs.). On the proposed waiver amendment, see S. 744, § 2315(b), 113th Cong., 1st Sess. (2013).

73. See INA § 240A(b), 8 U.S.C. § 1229b(b); Aleinikoff, Martin, Motomura, & Fullerton, Immigration and Citizenship, supra note 9, at 755–63; Chapter 1 in this volume.

74. See INA §§ 207, 244, 8 U.S.C. §§ 1157, 1254a. On temporary protected status, see generally Chapter 1 in this volume.

75. Joseph Carens, The Case For Amnesty, supra note 35.

76. On this series of prosecutorial discretion memos, see Chapter 1 in this volume. On the ICE officers' response to the prosecutorial discretion memos, see Julia Preston, Agents' Union Delays Training on New Policy on Deportation, N.Y. Times, Jan. 8, 2012, at A15; Julia Preston, Obama Policy on Deporting Used Unevenly, Nov. 13, 2011, at A16; Am. Fed. Gov't Emp. Nat'l Council, Vote of No Confidence in ICE Director John Morton and ICE ODPP Assistant Director Phyllis Coven (2010), available at http://www.iceunion.org/download/259-259-vote-no-confidence.pdf; Olivas, Dreams Deferred, supra note 4, at 506. On the ICE officer union's court challenge to DACA, see Crane v. Napolitano, 2013 WL 1744422 (N.D. Tex. Apr. 23, 2013). See also Julia Preston, Agents Sue over Deportation Suspensions, N.Y. Times, Aug. 24, 2012, at A17; Gilbert, Obama's Ruby Slippers, supra note 9, at 275–276; David A. Martin, A Defense of Immigration-Enforcement Discretion: The Legal and Policy Flaws in Kris Kobach's Latest Crusade, 122 Yale L.J. Online 167 (2012); Robert Delahunty & John Yoo, Dream On: The Obama Administration's Nonenforcement of Immigration Laws, The DREAM Act, and the Take Care Clause, 91 Tex. L. Rev. 781 (2013); Shoba Sivaprasad Wadhia, Response: In Defense of DACA, Deferred Action, and the DREAM Act, 91 Tex. L. Rev. See Also 59 (2013); Peter Margulies, Taking Care of Immigration Law: Presidential Stewardship, Prosecutorial Discretion, and the Separation of Powers, 94 B.U. L. Rev. 105 (2014).

77. See S. 744, § 2101(b), 113th Cong., 1st Sess. (2013). See also David Bacon, Illegal People: How Globalization Creates Migration and Criminalizes Immigrants, 56 (Beacon Press 2008).

78. On arguments that the history of US immigration enforcement has given rise to legitimate claims to integration as opposed to immigration or citizenship status, see Chapter 3 in this volume.

CHAPTER 7

Finding Answers

1. On temporary workers, see generally Andorra Bruno, Immigration: Policy Considerations Related to Guest Worker Programs (Cong. Research Serv. 2010); Arin Greenwood, The Case for Reforming U.S. Guest Worker Programs

(Competitive Enterprise Inst. 2008); Ruth Ellen Wasem & Geoffrey K. Collver, Immigration of Agricultural Guest Workers: Policy, Trends, and Legislative Issues (Cong. Research Serv. 2003); Edwin Meese III & Matthew Spalding, Permanent Principles and Temporary Workers (Heritage Found. 2006); Robert E. B. Lucas, International Labor Migration in a Globalizing Economy (Carnegie Endowment 2008); Timothy Charles Brown, A Business Model for Foreign Labor (Hoover Inst. 2007); Tim Kane, Sponsorship: The Key to a Temporary Worker Program (Heritage Found. 2007); Bill Ong Hing, Guest Workers Program with a Path to Legalization (American Immigr. Council 2006); Future Flow: Repairing Our Broken Immigration System (American Immigr. Council 2010).

2. See INA §§ 101(a)(15)(H), 214(g)(1)(B), 8 U.S.C. §§ 1101(a)(15)(H), 1184(g)(1) (B); Kati L. Griffith, U.S. Migrant Worker Law: The Interstices of Immigration Law and Labor and Employment Law, 31 Comp Labor L. & Pol. J. 125 (2009); T. Alexander Aleinikoff, David A. Martin, Hiroshi Motomura, & Maryellen Fullerton, Immigration and Citizenship: Process and Policy, 382–451 (7th ed. West 2012).

3. See INA §§ 101(a)(15)(F), 101(a)(15)(H)(i)(b), 101(a)(15)(L), 8 U.S.C. §§ 1101(a) (15)(E), 1101(a)(15)(H)(i)(b), 1101(a)(15)(L); INA § 214(g)(1)(A), 8 U.S.C. § 1184(g)(1)(A), INA § 214(i), 8 U.S.C. § 1184(i). See generally Aleinikoff, Martin, Motomura, & Fullerton, Immigration and Citizenship, supra note 2, at 402–405, 428–429.

4. See S. 2611, 109th Cong., 2d Sess. (2006), S. 1639, 110th Cong., 1st Sess. (2007); S.1038, 111th Cong., 1st Sess. (2009); S. 744, §§ 2211–2215, 4101–4605, 4701–4703, 113th Cong., 1st Sess. (2013). See also Andorra Bruno, Immigration of Temporary Lower-Skilled Workers: Current Policy and Related Issues, 5–6 (Cong. Research Serv. 2012); Aleinikoff, Martin, Motomura, & Fullerton, Immigration and Citizenship, supra note 2, at 436.

5. See Daniel T. Griswold, Willing Workers: Fixing the Problem of Illegal Mexican Migration to the United States, 11, 19–21 (Cato Inst. 2009); Bill Gates, How to Keep America Competitive, Wash. Post, Feb. 25, 2007, at B7; Edward Alden, America's "National Suicide," Newsweek, Apr. 10, 2011. On temporary workers as more politically palatable than immigrants, see Cindy Hahamovitch, No Man's Land: Jamaican Guestworkers in America and the Global History of Deportable Labor, 110–134 (Princeton Univ. Press 2011); Cristina M. Rodríguez, The Citizenship Paradox in a Transnational Age, 106 Mich. L. Rev. 1111, 1122–1123 (2008); Cindy Hahamovitch, Creating Perfect Immigrants: Guestworkers of the World in Historical Perspective 1, 44 Labor Hist. 69, 72–73 (2003). On migrants' expectations of a temporary sojourn, see, e.g., Jorge Durand & Douglas S. Massey, Borderline Sanity, 12 The American Prospect, at 28, 30 (Sept. 24–Oct. 8, 2001).

6. On exploitation, see, e.g., Mary Bauer, Close to Slavery: Guestworker Programs in the United States, 9–27 (2d ed. Southern Poverty Law Center 2013); Christopher Fulmer, Comment, A Critical Look at the H-1B Program and Its Effects on U.S. and

Foreign Workers—A Controversial Program Unhinged from Its Original Intent, 13 Lewis & Clark L. Rev. 823, 855–856 (2009). On the borders/equality tension, see Chapter 3 in this volume; Hiroshi Motomura, Who Belongs?: Immigration Outside the Law and the Idea of Americans in Waiting, 2 UC Irvine L. Rev. 359, 363–367 (2012). On the harm to equality, see Michael Walzer, Spheres of Justice: A Defense of Pluralism and Equality, 52 (Basic Books 1983); Linda S. Bosniak, Membership, Equality, and the Difference That Alienage Makes, 69 N.Y.U. L. Rev. 1047, 1068–1087 (1994); Cristina M. Rodríguez, Guest Workers and Integration: Toward a Theory of What Immigrants and Americans Owe One Another, 2007 U. Chi. Legal F. 219, 222; U.S. Commission on Immigration Reform, Legal Immigration: Setting Priorities 173 (1995). On a path to citizenship, see Sarah Lueck, Bush Touts His Immigration View as House Republicans Push Theirs, Wall St. J., July 6, 2006, at A4; Jim Rutenberg, G.O.P. Draws Line in Border, N.Y. Times, May 26, 2006, at A1; President George W. Bush, Address to the Nation on Immigration Reform (May 15, 2006); Press Release, Sen. Barack Obama, Obama Statement on President Bush's Speech on Immigration Reform (May 15, 2006).

7. See, e.g., Ron Hira, The H-1B and L-1 Visa Programs: Out of Control, 7–14 (Economic Policy Inst. 2010).

8. See Jeffrey S. Passel & D'Vera Cohn, A Portrait of Unauthorized Immigrants in the United States, 10–11, 16 (Pew Hispanic Ctr. 2009); Daniel Carroll et al., Findings from the National Agricultural Workers Survey (NAWS) 2001–2002: A Demographic and Employment Profile of United States Farm Workers, 18 (Dept. of Labor 2005); S. 744, §§ 2211–2215, 4701–4703, 113th Cong., 1st Sess. (2013).

9. On the emergence of the immigration law system as it relates to unauthorized migration, see Chapter 1 in this volume; Hiroshi Motomura, Immigration Outside the Law, 108 Colum. L. Rev. 2037, 2047–2055 (2008). On the relationship between temporary worker programs and unauthorized migration, see Hahamovitch, No Man's Land, supra note 5, at 110–134; Griswold, Willing Workers, supra note 5, at 19; Mohammad Amin & Aaditya Mattoo, Can Guest Worker Schemes Reduce Illegal Migration?, 3–5 (World Bank 2006); Hiroshi Motomura, Americans in Waiting: The Lost Story of Immigration and Citizenship in the United States, 134 (Oxford Univ. Press 2006); Kitty Calavita, Inside the State, The Bracero Program, Immigration, and the I.N.S., 68 (Routledge 1992).

10. See Chapter 1 in this volume; Motomura, Americans in Waiting, supra note 9, at 134–135; Bruno, Temporary Lower–Skilled Workers, supra note 4, at 5–6 & n.15, 30.

11. See Hoffman Plastic Compounds, Inc. v. NLRB, 535 U.S. 137, 151–52 (2002); Chapters 1 and 5 in this volume; Hiroshi Motomura, The Rights of Others: Legal Claims and Immigration Outside the Law, 59 Duke L.J. 1723, 1746–1762 (2010); *Hoffman Plastic Compounds*, 535 U.S. at 153–155 (Breyer, J., dissenting). The 2013 U.S. Senate bill would have reversed *Hoffman*, see S. 744, § 3101, 113th Cong., 1st Sess. (2013).

12. See generally Aleinikoff, Martin, Motomura, & Fullerton, Immigration and Citizenship, supra note 2, at 952–954.

13. See Bauer, Close to Slavery, supra note 6, at 9–27; Michael Holley, Disadvantaged by Design: How the Law Inhibits Agricultural Guest Workers from Enforcing Their Rights, 18 Hofstra Lab. & Emp. L.J. 575, 593–597 (2001).

14. For arguments for labor mobility, see Howard F. Chang, Guest Workers and Justice in a Second-Best World, 34 U. Dayton L. Rev. 3, 7 (2008); Andrew J. Elmore, Egalitarianism and Exclusion: U.S. Guest Worker Programs and a Non-Subordination Approach to the Labor-Based Admission of Nonprofessional Foreign Nationals, 21 Geo. Immigr. L.J. 521, 561–564 (2007); Bauer, Close to Slavery, supra note 6, at 13, 259; Durand & Massey, Borderline Sanity, supra note 5, at 30; Griswold, Willing Workers, supra note 5, at 19.

15. On the permanence of temporary migration, see Philip L. Martin & Michael S. Teitelbaum, The Mirage of Mexican Guest Workers, 80 Foreign Affairs 117, 119–121 (2001).

16. See Adam B. Cox & Eric Posner, The Second-Order Structure of Immigration Law, 59 Stan. L. Rev. 809, 812, 847 (2007).

17. See S. 744, §§ 2101–2111, 113th Cong., 1st Sess. (2013). On legalization as selection, see Gordon H. Hanson, The Governance of Migration Policy, 11 J. Human Dev. & Capabilities 185, 188 (2010); Cox & Posner, Second-Order Structure, supra note 16, at 847.

18. See S. 744, § 4701, 113th Cong., 1st Sess. (2013). For a similar point in the context of assessing the will to enforce immigration laws, see Chapter 1 in this volume.

19. On immigration's theoretical effects on labor markets, see Natl. Res. Council, The New Americans: Economic, Demographic, and Fiscal Effects of Immigration, 135–165 (James P. Smith & Barry Edmonston eds., 1997); Philip Martin & Elizabeth Midgley, Immigration: Shaping and Reshaping America, 61 Population Bull. 1, 20 (2006).

20. See INA § 212(n)(1), 8 U.S.C. § 1182(n)(1); INA § 218(a), 8 U.S.C. § 1188(a) (H–2A); INA § 101(a)(15)(H)(ii)(b), 8 U.S.C. § 1101(a)(15)(H)(ii)(b) (H–2B); 77 Fed. Reg. 10038, 10169 (2012), amending 20 C.F.R. §§ 503, 655. Additional requirements try to focus the L-1 category on fostering international commerce more than simply providing temporary workers. See Aleinikoff, Martin, Motomura, & Fullerton, Immigration, and Citizenship, supra note 2, at 407. For the 2013 Senate bill, see S. 744, §§ 4101–4105, 4211–4214, 4221–4225, 4231–4237, 113th Cong., 1st Sess. (2013).

21. On the new proposed W visa program, see S. 744, §§ 4702–4703, 113th Cong., 1st Sess. (2013).

22. On fees, see INA § 214(c)(9), 8 U.S.C. § 1184(c)(9); Aleinikoff, Martin, Motomura, & Fullerton, Immigration and Citizenship, supra note 2, at 402–405. For the Senate provision, see S. 744, § 4233(a), 113th Cong., 1st Sess. (2013). On screening and selecting employers, see Pia M. Orrenius, Giovanni Peri, & Madeline

Zavodny, Overhauling the Temporary Work Visa System, 3–5 (Hamilton Project & Brookings Inst. 2013); Giovanni Peri, Rationalizing U.S. Immigration Policy: Reforms for Simplicity, Fairness, and Economic Growth, 15–18 (Hamilton Project & Brookings Inst. 2012); Peter H. Schuck & John E. Tyler, Making the Case for Changing U.S. Policy Regarding Highly Skilled Immigrants, 38 Fordham Urb. L.J. 327, 354–355 (2010); Griswold, Willing Workers, supra note 5, at 20.

23. See INA §§ 214(c)(9)(C), 286(s), 8 U.S.C. §§ 1184(c)(9)(C), 1356(s).

24. See Howard F. Chang, The Disadvantages of Immigration Restriction as a Policy to Improve Income Distribution, 61 SMU L. Rev. 23, 25 (2008); Motomura, Immigration Outside the Law, supra note 9, at 2079–2082.

25. See Save America Comprehensive Immigration Act of 2005, §§ 201, 403, H.R. 2092, 109th Cong., 1st Sess. (2005). According to Representative Jackson Lee, the purpose of the fee was "to establish employment-training programs for Americans in lines of work especially affected by undocumented worker growth"). Sheila Jackson Lee, Why Immigration Reform Requires a Comprehensive Approach that Includes Both Legalization Programs and Provisions to Secure the Border, Harv. J. Legis. 267, 281 (2006).

26. On unauthorized migration within the developing world, see Kamal Sadiq, Paper Citizens: How Illegal Immigrants Acquire Citizenship in Developing Countries, 33 (Oxford Univ. Press 2009). On remittances, see M. Angeles Villarreal, U.S.-Mexico Economic Relations: Trends, Issues, and Implications, 9–10 (Cong. Research Serv. 2012); Global Remittances: Formal Remittances as a Share of Gross Domestic Product (GDP) by Migrants' Origin Countries (Migration Policy Inst. 2011); Migrants' Remittances and Related Economic Flows (Cong. Budget Office 2011); Ezra Rosser, Immigrant Remittances, 41 Conn. L. Rev. 1 (2008); Natalie Kitroeff, Immigrants Pay Lower Fees to Send Money Home, Helping to Ease Poverty, N.Y. Times, Apr. 28, 2013, at A23; Julia Preston, Fewer Latinos in U.S. Sending Money Home, N.Y. Times, May 1, 2008, at A1. See also Chapter 1 in this volume.

On the return of skills to sending countries, see Jesús Alquézar Sabadie et al., Migration and Skills: the Experience of Migrant Workers from Albania, Egypt, Moldova, and Tunisia, 44 (World Bank 2010); Michele Wucker, Lockout: Why America Keeps Getting Immigration Wrong When Our Prosperity Depends on Getting It Right, 237 (Public Affairs 2006). For a more skeptical view, see Xinying Chi, Note, Challenging Managed Temporary Labor Migration as a Model for Rights and Development for Labor-Sending Countries, 40 N.Y.U. Int'l L. & Pol. 497, 523–536 (2008). On the safety valve idea, see Joseph Nevins, Operation Gatekeeper and Beyond: The War on "Illegals" and the Remaking of the US-Mexico Boundary, 132 (Routledge 2002).

27. On Philippine government policy, see Chi, Challenging Managed Temporary Labor Migration, supra note 26, at 507–510; Jason DeParle, Downturn Does Little to Slow Migration, N.Y. Times, May 28, 2010, at A4; Jason DeParle,

A Good Provider Is One Who Leaves, N.Y. Times Magazine, Apr. 22, 2007, at F50; Philip Martin, Manolo Abella, & Elizabeth Midgley, Best Practices to Manage Migration: The Philippines, 38 Int'l Migr. Rev. 1544, 1551–1554 (2004). On managing emigration, see generally Taxonomy of the Diaspora-Engaging Institutions in 30 Developing Countries (Migration Policy Inst. 2010); Chi, Challenging Managed Temporary Labor Migration, supra note 26, at 502–511; David Fitzgerald, A Nation of Emigrants: How Mexico Manages Its Migration (Univ. of California Press 2009). On constraints on sending country protections for its emigrants, see Hahamovitch, Creating Perfect Immigrants, supra note 5, at 83.

28. See Michael Hoefer, Nancy Rytina, & Bryan Baker, Estimates of the Unauthorized Population Residing in the United States: January 2011, at 4–5 & table 3 (Dept. of Homeland Sec. 2012); Jeffrey S. Passel & D'Vera Cohn, Unauthorized Immigrant Population: National and State Trends, 2010, at 11 (Pew Hispanic Ctr. 2011).

29. See Chapter 3 in this volume; Motomura, Who Belongs?, supra note 6, at 366.

30. See Chapters 1 and 3 in this volume; Motomura, Americans in Waiting, supra note 9, at 126–132.

31. See Immigration and Nationality Act of 1965 (Hart–Celler Act), Pub. L. No. 89–236, 79 Stat. 911; Pub. L. No. 88–352, 78 Stat. 241; Pub. L. No. 89–110, 79 Stat. 437; Chapter 1 in this volume; Motomura, Americans in Waiting, supra note 9, at 130–132; Hahamovitch, Creating Perfect Immigrants, supra note 5, at 87.

32. See Motomura, Americans in Waiting, supra note 9, at 134; Act of Oct. 3, 1965, Pub. L. No. 89–236, §§ 8, 21(e), 79 Stat. 911, 916, 921; Act of Oct. 20, 1976, Pub. L. 94–571, § 3, 90 Stat. 2703 (1976); Pub. L. No. 95–412, 92 Stat. 907 (1978); Pub. L. No. 96–212, 94 Stat. 102 (1980); Chapter 1 in this volume. For the definition of "immediate relatives," see INA § 201(b)(2)(A)(i), 8 U.S.C. § 1151(b)(2)(A)(i).

33. On the rise in unauthorized migration, see Motomura, Americans in Waiting, supra note 9, at 134. On waiting periods, see Department of State, Visa Bulletin for March 2013; Ruth Ellen Wasem, U.S. Immigration Policy on Permanent Admissions, 12–15 (Cong. Research Serv. 2010); Chapter 1 in this volume. For criticism of applying the standard cap to Mexico, see Douglas S. Massey, Only by Addressing the Realities of North American Economic Integration Can We Solve the Problem, 34 Boston Rev. 16 (May/June 2009).

34. See INA § 101(a)(15)(E), 8 U.S.C. § 1101(a)(15)(E); U.S.-Chile Free Trade Agreement, U.S.-Chile, ch. 14, § 3, June 6, 2003; U.S.-Singapore Free Trade Agreement, U.S.-Sing., ch. 11, § 3, May 6, 2003; North American Free Trade Agreement, U.S.-Can.-Mex., Annex 1603 § C, Dec. 17, 1992, 32 I.L.M. 605, 664–665 (1993). See generally Aleinikoff, Martin, Motomura, & Fullerton, Immigration and Citizenship, supra note 2, at 419–421; Adam B. Cox & Eric A. Posner, The Rights of Migrants: An Optimal Contract Framework, 84 N.Y.U. L. Rev. 1403, 1454 (2009).

35. On the role of workers' home communities, see Eleanor Marie Lawrence Brown, Outsourcing Immigration Compliance, 77 Fordham L. Rev. 2475, 2482,

2493–2496, 2507–2521 (2009). On courts applying the U.S. Constitution to immigration law, see Hiroshi Motomura, Immigration Law after a Century of Plenary Power: Phantom Constitutional Norms and Statutory Interpretation, 100 Yale L.J. 545 (1990).

36. On the relationship between economic integration and Mexico-US migration, see Massey, Only by Addressing the Realities, supra note 33; Douglas S. Massey, Jorge Durand, & Nolan J. Malone, Beyond Smoke and Mirrors: Mexican Immigration in an Era of Economic Integration, 118–121 (Russell Sage Found. 2002); M. Angeles Villarreal & Marisabel Cid, NAFTA and the Mexican Economy, 12–16 (Cong. Research Serv. 2008); Douglas S. Massey & Kristin E. Espinosa, What's Driving Mexico-U.S. Migration?: A Theoretical, Empirical, and Policy Analysis, 102 Am. J. Sociology 939 (1997); Demetrios G. Papademetriou, The Shifting Expectations of Free Trade and Migration, in NAFTA's Promise and Reality: Lessons from Mexico for the Hemisphere, 39 (John J. Audley, Demetrios G. Papademetriou, Sandra Polaski, & Scott Vaughan eds., Carnegie Endowment 2004); Bill Ong Hing, Ethical Borders: NAFTA, Globalization, and Mexican Migration (Temple Univ. Press 2010); Bill Ong Hing, NAFTA, Globalization, and Mexican Migrants, 5 J. L. Econ. & Pol. 87 (2009); David Bacon, Illegal People: How Globalization Creates Migration and Criminalizes Immigrants, 24–25, 33–46, 56–59, 70–77 (Beacon Press 2008).

37. See Douglas Massey, A Better Way to End Unauthorized Immigration, Miller-McCune.com (Jan. 8, 2009).

38. See Motomura, Americans in Waiting, supra note 9, at 173; Chapter 3 in this volume; S. 744, § 2102(c), 113th Cong., 1st Sess. (2013). Compare S. Amdt. 1322 to S.744, § 2215: Immigrant Categories Ineligible for United States Citizenship (June 18, 2013).

39. See Motomura, Americans in Waiting, supra note 9, at 171–173; Chapter 6 in this volume.

40. For the analogous discussion of discussion of unauthorized migrants as Americans in waiting, see Chapter 3 in this volume. On the role of children as adding a time dimension to discussions of the DREAM Act and birthright citizenship, see Chapter 6 in this volume.

41. On workplace protections for temporary workers, see earlier in this chapter. On the same issue for unauthorized migrants, see Chapter 6 in this volume.

42. See S. 744, §§ 2302(c)(3)(B), 4102, 113th Cong., 1st Sess. (2013); INA §§ 101(a)(15)(H)(iii), 214(c)(2), 8 U.S.C. §§ 1101(a)(15)(H)(iii), 1184(c)(2). On T and U nonimmigrant categories, which transition to permanent residence, see Aleinikoff, Martin, Motomura, & Fullerton, Immigration and Citizenship, supra note 2, at 421–428.

43. On measures designed to get migrants to return to their home countries, see Rodríguez, Guest Workers and Integration, supra note 6, at 229 n.24; Hiroko Tabuchi, Japan Pays Foreign Workers to Go Home, N.Y. Times, Apr. 23, 2009, at

B1; Eleanor Marie Lawrence Brown, Visa as Property, Visa as Collateral, 64 Vand. L. Rev. 1047, 1051–1052 (2011).

44. On international economic development initiatives designed to retard emigration, see, e.g., Durand & Massey, Borderline Sanity, supra note 5, at 29–31. On programs intended to entice emigrants to return, see, e.g., Xiang Biao, Emigration from China: A Sending Country Perspective, 41 Int'l Migr. 21, 29 (2003).

45. On how receiving state politics and policies influence the transnational activities of migrants, see Roger Waldinger, Between "Here" and "There": Immigrant Cross–Border Activities and Loyalties, 42 Int'l Migr. Rev. 3, 8 (2008). On the central importance of integration, see Rodríguez, Guest Workers and Integration, supra note 6, at 222–223.

46. On allowing temporary workers the choice to stay or leave, see Janet Murguia, A Change of Heart on Guest Workers, Wash. Post, Feb. 11, 2007, at B7.

47. On guest worker programs as a second-best policy, see Howard Chang, Liberal Ideals and Political Feasibility: Guest-Worker Programs as Second-Best Policies, 27 N.C. J. Int'l L. & Comm. Reg. 465, 468–469 (2002).

48. See Immigration Reform and Control Act of 1986, Pub. L. No. 99–603, 100 Stat. 3359; Chapter 1 in this volume; S. 744, §§ 1101–1123, 113th Cong., 1st Sess. (2013). On the political link between amnesty and enforcement, see Rainer Bauböck, There Is a Mismatch Between Citizens' Moral Intuitions and Their Political Views, 34 Boston Rev. 16 (May/June 2009).

49. Catherine Dauvergne, Making People Illegal: What Globalization Means for Migration and Law, 2 (Cambridge Univ. Press 2008).

50. On the limit current employment-based immigrant admission categories, see Chapter 1 in this volume; INA § 203(b), 8 U.S.C. § 1153(b); Aleinikoff, Martin, Motomura, & Fullerton, Immigration and Citizenship, supra note 2, at 273–293. For provisions that would address both temporary and permanent admissions, see S. 744, §§ 2301(a), 4703(a), 113th Cong., 1st Sess. (2013).

51. On the per-country caps and waiting periods, see INA § 202, 8 U.S.C. § 1152; U.S. Dep't of State, 9 Visa Bulletin No. 18 (2010); Aleinikoff, Martin, Motomura, & Fullerton, Immigration and Citizenship, supra note 2, at 288; Chapters 1 and 3 in this volume. Bernard Trujillo, Immigrant Visa Distribution: The Case of México, 2000 Wis. L. Rev. 713. For the 2013 Senate provisions, see S. 744, § 2306, 113th Cong., 1st Sess. (2013).

52. See Alan Hyde, The Law and Economics of Family Unification, 28 Geo. Immigr. L.J. (forthcoming 2014); Motomura, Americans in Waiting, supra note 9, at 156–159; Hiroshi Motomura, We Asked for Workers, But Families Came: Time, Law, and the Family in Immigration and Citizenship, 14 Va. J. Soc. Pol'y & L. 103, 114–118 (2006); Hiroshi Motomura, The Family and Immigration: A Roadmap for the Ruritanian Lawmaker, 43 Am. J. Comp. L. 511, 542–543 (1995). See Ruben J. Rumbaut, Ties That Bind: Immigration and Immigrant Families in the United States, in Marcelo M. Suárez-Orozco, Carola Suárez-Orozco, & Desirée

Qin-Hilliard, 1 Interdisciplinary Perspectives on the New Immigration, 181–224 (Routledge 2001). See also S. 744, §§ 2301(a)(2), 2305, 113th Cong., 1st Sess. (2013), which would eliminate the category for brothers and sisters of US citizens (but give siblings some advantage in a new point-based system) and would allow permanent residents to petition on the same basis as US citizens for spouses and unmarried minor children.

53. On sending country economies as a factor in emigration and return migration, see Douglas S. Massey et al., Beyond Smoke and Mirrors, supra note 36; Motomura, Immigration Outside the Law, supra note 9, at 2094–2096; Wayne A. Cornelius, Controlling "Unwanted" Immigration: Lessons from the United States, 1993–2004, 31 J. Ethnic & Migr. Stud. 775, 789 (2005); Pam Belluck, Healthy Korean Economy Draws Immigrants Home, N.Y. Times, Aug. 22, 1995, at 1; Kevin Cullen, Going Full Circle: Native Land's New Prosperity Has Many Reversing Their Exodus, Boston Globe, Mar. 19, 2007, at 1A; Kirk Semple, A Land of Opportunity Lures Poles Back Home, N.Y. Times, Sept. 21, 2008, at A37. On the effects of declines in the Irish economy, see Kirk Semple, As Ireland's Boom Ends, Job Seekers Revive a Well-Worn Path to New York, N.Y. Times, July 10, 2009, at A23.

54. See S. 744, §§ 2103(b), 2212(a), 113th Cong., 1st Sess. (2013).

55. See S. 744, §§ 4701–4703, 113th Cong., 1st Sess. (2013).

Index

Page numbers followed by *f* indicate figures. Numbers followed by n indicate notes.